/

NEAL CALLOW

The Empire of Effects

The Empire of Effects

JULIE A.
TURNOCK

Industrial Light & Magic and
the Rendering of Realism

University of Texas Press
Austin

Requests for permission to reproduce material from this work should be
sent to:
    Permissions
    University of Texas Press
    P.O. Box 7819
    Austin, TX 78713-7819
    utpress.utexas.edu/rp-form

♾ The paper used in this book meets the minimum requirements of
ANSI/NISO Z39.48-1992 (R1997) (Permanence of Paper).

Library of Congress Cataloging-in-Publication Data

Names: Turnock, Julie A., author.
Title: The empire of effects : Industrial Light & Magic and the rendering
    of realism / Julie A. Turnock.
Description: First edition. | Austin : University of Texas Press, 2022. |
    Includes bibliographical references and index.
Identifiers: LCCN 2021036678 (print) | LCCN 2021036679 (ebook)
ISBN 978-1-4773-2530-8 (hardcover)
ISBN 978-1-4773-2531-5 (PDF)
ISBN 978-1-4773-2532-2 (epub)
Subjects: LCSH: Industrial Light & Magic (Studio)—History. |
    Cinematography—Special effects—History. | Digital
    cinematography—History. | Computer animation—History. | Realism
    in motion pictures—History. | Motion pictures—Aesthetics—
    History. | Motion picture industry—History.
Classification: LCC TR858 .T87 2022 (print) | LCC TR858 (ebook) |
    DDC 777—dc23
LC record available at https://lccn.loc.gov/2021036678
LC ebook record available at https://lccn.loc.gov/2021036679

doi:10.7560/325308

Contents

Acknowledgments

I would like to thank Senior Editor Jim Burr for making the publication of this book possible. My experience at University of Texas Press has been a pleasure from start to finish. Jim and former Assistant Editor Sarah McGavick, as well as Editing, Design & Production Manager Robert Kimzey and copy editor Jon Howard were highly professional, efficient, and responsive. I am also grateful for the efforts and professionalism of the two peer reviewers, whose detailed, constructive, and highly insightful comments helped me tremendously in the revising stage. I must also express my deep appreciation for the efforts of my research assistant Megan McSwain, who was invaluable in preparing the manuscript, and Susmita Das, for her vital work in the last stages of completion.

The first kernels of the idea for this book came in an article published (in shorter and substantially different form) in *Film History* as "The ILM Version: Recent Digital Effects and the Aesthetics of 1970s Cinematography" (24:2, 2012), and I would like to thank John Belton for including me in that issue. This book has gone through a number of permutations before finding its final form. A great thanks to friends and colleagues who have read or commented on portions of this book in various iterations over the years. Most particular thanks to those who read an early version of the manuscript and provided advice in a deeply productive book conference: Lilya Kaganovsky, Derek Long, Jenny Oyallon-Koloski, Dana Polan, Ariel Rogers, Robert Rushing, and Kristen Whissel; and thank you to Susan Koshy at the Unit for Criticism and Interpretation for organizing. My gratitude also goes to those who read earlier drafts and offered useful critique, including Paul Young and Bob Rehak. Invited talks and conferences provided important feedback. Thanks to Aaron Hunter and Martha Schearer, who invited me to the Women and New Hollywood Conference, Maynooth University, Ireland; Matthew Solomon, who asked me to speak at the

University of Michigan, Charles Acland at Concordia, and Eric Faden at Bucknell. Thanks as well to academic friends who offered support and encouragement and with whom I have talked through ideas: Emily Carman, Allyson Field, Doron Galili, Josh Gleich, Adam Hart, Matt Hauske, Maggie Hennefeld, Laura Horak, Gunnar Iverson, Andrew Johnston, Patrick Keating, Sarah Keller, Seth Kim, Alicia Kozma, Katharina Loew, Paul McEwan, Ross Melnick, Dan Morgan, Christina Petersen, Jennifer Peterson, Scott Richmond, Theresa Scandiffio, Ria Thanouli, Neil Verma, Allison Whitney, Mark Williams, and Josh Yumibe; and a special thanks to Anne Nesbit and Joel Westerdale, who suggested aspects of the title over spritzes at Pordenone. And finally, thanks to my effects subfield colleagues not already mentioned who have proven to be an especially collegial and generous bunch: Tanine Alison, Lisa Bode, Hye Jean Chung, Leon Gurevitch, Kartik Nair, Dan North, Lisa Purse, and Anu Thapa.

I have received a great deal of institutional and collegial support from the University of Illinois at Urbana-Champaign. First of all, I'd like to thank colleagues not already mentioned in the Department of Media and Cinema Studies, most especially Angela Aguayo, Anita Chan, Amanda Ciafone, and CL Cole. The completion of this book would have been significantly delayed without the support of the UIUC Center for Advanced Studies that made a necessary full-year sabbatical possible. The campus Research Board funded vital research trips to archives, as did a fellowship from the Unit for Criticism and Interpretation. I am also proud to have been selected to be a College of Media Scholar. Outside of the University of Illinois, the Harry Ransom Center Thomas G. Smith Research Fellowship in the Humanities yielded a gold mine of important research documents.

This book would truly not have been possible without the existence of research institutions and their dedicated staff, most especially the Margaret Herrick Library, the Harry Ransom Center at the University of Texas at Austin, and the Media History Digital Library. Special thanks to the time, energy, and research leads given by my interview subjects: David Bossert, Michael Eisner, Jean Pierre Flayeux, Peter Kuran, Simon Marinof, and Jeff Okun.

My parents, Ann and Jack Turnock, and my sisters, Jennifer Harding and Amy McMahon, and their families have always been supportive of my academic career and always help me to keep my work in perspective.

And as always, I am most indebted to my husband, Jonathan Knipp, whose insights on and enthusiasm for all kinds of cinema from block-busters to indie horror to international art cinema continue to animate my thinking and spark my imagination. Here's to more decades ahead in front of the IMAX screen. I only wish we could bring Aldo.

9

Introduction

The ILM Version

WITH 450 PEOPLE AND 180 HIGH-POWERED WORKSTATIONS—MORE THAN ANY OTHER ORGANIZATION EXCEPT NASA—[GEORGE LUCAS'S] ILM IS BY FAR THE WORLD'S LARGEST EFFECTS HOUSE, DWARFING RIVALS. . . . THE COMPANY HAS WON 14 OSCARS FOR BEST VISUAL EFFECTS AND 8 FOR TECHNICAL ACHIEVEMENT.

—*LOS ANGELES TIMES*, 1995

ILM DOES MORE BUSINESS THAN ITS FIVE MAJOR COMPETITORS COMBINED.

—*SMITHSONIAN* MAGAZINE, 1990

THE MAGIC CONTINUES TO SPREAD TO MYRIAD EFFECTS HOUSES AROUND THE GLOBE THAT HAVE BEEN FORMED AROUND . . . THE TALENT FORGED IN THE CRUCIBLE OF ILM.

—FILMMAKER JON FAVREAU, 2011

ILM HAS NO PEER, AND THERE'S NO ONE EVEN CLOSE.

—FILMMAKER STEVEN SPIELBERG, 1995

CAN ANYBODY CATCH ILM? NO.

—*HOLLYWOOD REPORTER*, 1998

n the 2019 remake of *The Lion King*, King Mufasa proclaims to his son, Simba: "Everything the light touches is our kingdom." While this line also appears in the original 1994 version, the words carry new valence in this era of Disney's photorealistic reboots of its earlier animated features, when the "light" that touches entirely animated landscapes and characters is digitally generated. Because Disney's market share accounted for nearly 40 percent of the North American box office (as of 2019 before disruptions caused by COVID-19), its decisions—more than any other single studio—control much of the industry as a whole, including how movies look.[1] Movies used to be live-action by definition, and alternatives such as animation were considered exceptions. Since about 2002, when the Academy of Motion Pictures Arts and Sciences introduced a Best Animated Feature category, the industry and its awards categories now define live-action by whether it *looks* like it was captured profilmically, meaning it happened physically in front of the camera.[2] However, with categories seeming to merge in the wake of digital technologies, the industry finds the term "photoreal" useful in creating a distinction between live-action and animation. As the *Los Angeles Times* reported:

> In marketing the film, Disney has carefully avoided defining "The Lion King" as either animated or live-action, instead describing it as "photoreal." For the purposes of the Academy Awards, however, the studio is expected to position the film as live-action rather than animated.[3]

Largely because animation (however sophisticated) is associated with children's fare, live-action is seen to appeal to a wider audience than animation and, perhaps, garner more prestigious awards. For this reason, most productions cling fast to the live-action designation, no matter how intensive the computer-generated imagery (CGI) is in the final film. As the (nearly) entirely CGI *Lion King* remake demonstrates, the term "live-action" is in fact a convenient industrial fiction, and it is a professionally agreed-upon notion of a photoreal aesthetic that makes the discursive fiction possible.[4] As a consequence of this industry self-imagining, the aesthetic of photoreal digitally generated imagery governs nearly all contemporary filmmaking. It is the goal of this book to demonstrate how this nearly universal view of cinematic photorealism has developed.

This aesthetic of cinematic photorealism is realized materially by the effects industry (in the industry, "effects" is often rendered as "FX" or "F/X"). Most theatrically released movies today, whether big budget or low, whether directed by Steven Spielberg, Kathryn Bigelow, Pedro Almodóvar, Zhang Yimou, or Greta Gerwig, employ sizable effects teams. Effects jobs are assigned to companies on a per-shot basis, and the average feature-length film comprises a total of about 3,000 shots. The most expensive blockbusters spend tens of millions of dollars contracting twenty-plus independent effects companies from around the globe to complete about 2,500 effects shots. Films with no visible effects can nevertheless expect 400–1,000 shots to include effects work.[5] Effects artists digitally create everything from vast levitating cities in *Avengers: Age of Ultron* (2015) for live actors to inhabit; to photorealistic, emoting animals in *The Jungle Book* (2016); to safely speeding cars for all the *Fast and Furious* movies. And beyond the highest-budgeted films, effects artists also re-create whole blocks of 1970s Mexico City in *Roma* (2018), add cheering crowds to Wembley Stadium in *Bohemian Rhapsody* (2018), and invisibly erase marks of contemporary Sunset Boulevard from *Once Upon a Time. . . In Hollywood* (2019). While touched by the hands of thousands of artists, all of this work is nevertheless expected to result in a commonly held notion of effects photorealism. The surprisingly consistent international style of effects realism that these companies adhere to—one that impacts the aesthetics of global art cinema and low-budget indies as much as superhero extravaganzas—is not a result of happenstance or coincidence. I contend that the industry-leading effects company Industrial Light & Magic (ILM, originally formed by George Lucas in 1975 as Industrial Light and Magic) has rendered environments such as Mufasa's kingdom, the Death Star in *Star Wars*, and Hogwarts School of Witchcraft and Wizardry believable, no matter which effects company did the actual work.

In fact, I did not expect to write a book focusing on ILM. Initially, I planned to track the development of digital effects aesthetics and the effects industry worldwide over the course of the 1990s to the 2010s. Given ILM's longevity and association with so many blockbuster franchises, I assumed the company would take a privileged position among the many effects houses I was researching. The perception of ILM's greatness, untouchability, and innovation, as suggested in the opening epigraphs attesting to ILM's artistry, influence, technological supremacy, and economic dominance, all appear undisputed—not only in ILM's own public relations rhetoric but also in that of its rivals, industry reporting, and even the moviegoing public at large. If a casual moviegoer can recognize the name of just one effects company, it is Industrial

Light & Magic. Although (as discussed in chapter 1) every report on the effects industry names ILM as the industry leader, there is not much hard financial data to back that up, especially given the famously unstable nature of the effects business. Lucasfilm, as a privately owned company throughout most of its history, was not required to release financial details.[6] Whether or not we can determine ILM's actual economic market dominance, my research has determined that ILM has traded in its perceived dominance to compel other companies to follow its lead. Likewise, academic histories of digital cinema are largely histories of ILM projects, from *Terminator 2: Judgment Day* (1991) to *Jurassic Park* (1993) to the *Harry Potter* franchise to the Marvel Cinematic Universe (MCU) to the latter-day *Star Wars* prequels, sequels, and spinoffs.

The more I researched, the more a few things became clear. First, as the title of chapter 1 suggests, since ILM opened its doors to outside contracts in 1980, the global effects industry has been ILM "versus everybody else." Despite its self-promotion of this theme, ILM has not been a rebel upstart since its earliest days but has indeed earned its title as the "empire of effects." Second, over decades, other prominent companies including Apogee, Boss, Digital Domain (DD), and Weta rose to compete with ILM but could not eclipse it, leading to ILM's outsize influence over all aspects of the effects industry, including business practices, aesthetics, and technology. Third, an aesthetic history of cinematic effects since 1975 is an aesthetic history of ILM. Last, to my own surprise and most unexpectedly, I found that an aesthetic history of ILM was a history of cinematic realism since the 1980s—and not just in effects-heavy mainstream cinema.

What does it mean to place an effects company at the center of inquiry rather than as a postproduction afterthought? What are the industrial implications of being an empire of effects? Industrial histories of cinema have generally aimed for a macro focus (the studio system, media conglomeration) or micro focus (specific players' or entities' intersections within these larger forces). Cinema's so-called below-the-line facilities (that is, postproduction and support industries—beyond sound) have rarely received more than a passing reference in the macro-view academic studies, and effects even less so.[7] This book aims to be a study that finds a middle ground between macro and micro: to widen the scope of significant actors in the industry while contending that entities appearing to be on the margins are in fact exerting pressure on the center. I also assert that media conglomerates control the media discourse about which actors are considered important or impactful to the broader industry. Industry-wise, effects work is simultaneously essential to contemporary filmmaking and peripheral to it. It is to the industry's broader advantage to keep below-the-line entities weak and dependent and to characterize them as outliers. That being said, as I will contend in chapter 3, the media have certainly been effective in furthering ILM's own claims of dominance in the effects sector—but only within its specified realm. To put it another way, being the empire of effects is like installing all the public restrooms and plumbing in a skyscraper: the structure cannot do without such facilities, but the developer does not highlight them in the brochure.

The study of special/visual effects ("VFX" is a common acronym referring to "visual effects") as the intersection of aesthetics and industrial practice not only encourages but also requires a multifaceted methodology.[8] It is a skilled art of aesthetic assumptions about professional standards crossed with expectations about imagery that is both realistic and spectacular. This mandates close formal analysis of sequences from illustrative films. Effects are produced through many ever-evolving interlocking imaging technologies, each with its own configurations and lineages. Within overall film production, the postproduction field is part of what is considered to be global film's postproduction industry, in which it occupies an important and yet marginal position. This activates a "production studies" approach emphasizing economic and industrial factors. The longtime fascination with effects work as illusion is also the center of a series of popular, professional, and academic discourses that explain and characterize this arcane world to interested moviegoers. These communications, from the industry leaders and practitioners as well as entertainment and professional publications, also necessitate careful parsing as well as fact-checking. Above all, these facets have shifting histories to be described. In this way, effects studies' complex web of aesthetic, technological, economic, and discursive analysis helps provide a model to describe moving images as art and technique—and also practice and discourse. I chose to focus on Industrial Light & Magic for several strategic and practical reasons (to be described below), and this book will discuss these facets within the specific example of ILM more or less in turn, chapter by chapter, organized by a loose historical through-line. While this approach works especially well for describing cinematic effects of various eras, it could also be useful for other highly technological arts of moving images, including animation, cinematography, editing, and sound, among others.

Commonsense notions of realism as well as previous scholarship have promoted the aesthetic of realism on display in these effects-heavy films as "perceptual realism," roughly corresponding with a style that mimics "what the eye sees in real life." Unexpectedly, my research found that it was not a reference to human biology that our commonly held notion of effects realism is derived. Instead, it was ILM in the late 1970s that promoted its in-house style so effectively through its nearly half-century of industrial, cultural, and technological dominance that most moviegoers and even most scholars do not even recognize it as a style. The current ILM digital aesthetic is far from "naturally" derived; instead it consists of an idiosyncratic series of codes based on 1970s cinematography cuing materiality, immediacy, and authenticity. When The Walt Disney Company bought ILM in its acquisition of Lucasfilm Ltd. in 2012, ILM's primary value came not in its decades of effects production, or even its impressive (and expensive) R&D, but the associative value that ILM's style of realism had accrued. Consequently, "owning" a style of realism that appears nearly invisible means that entertainment conglomerates yield a culturally powerful rhetorical sway over what viewers accept not only as plausibly real but also as credibly true. Scholars such as Stanley Cavell, David Rodowick, and Laura Mulvey have historically understood cinematic realism primarily in relation to Bazinian philosophical ontology; put another way: What is the relationship of the cinematic image to lived human perception and experience?[9] Instead, I recognize realism as stylized components of an industrial aesthetic with historical contours. This move allows us not only to observe realism as a stylization of camera reality but also to denaturalize it, draining it of much of its power to go by unobserved. Moreover, it helps us reframe debates about cinematic realism to ones that take into account the material conditions of contemporary digital filmmaking that acknowledge its multiplicity (many digitals rather than a singular "digital") and without resorting to either utopian or dystopian rhetoric.

Rather than take ILM's industry standard as a given or its realist aesthetic as inevitable, this book delineates the ILM aesthetic's historically identifiable roots, traceable to complex economic and industrial factors. *The Empire of Effects* tracks ILM from its work on the original *Star Wars* trilogy to its absorption into the Disney empire in 2012, with an emphasis on the digital era of the 1990s to the 2010s. My historical research and visual analysis demonstrate that digital effects' style of realism is far from impoverished, obvious, or juvenile, as Richard Maltby, David Cook, and Justin Wyatt have stated or implied.[10] Neither, as Stephen Prince and Lev Manovich have claimed, is it a natural or inevitable reflection of human vision or technological progress.[11] Far from simple mimicry of the natural world or camera reality, effects realism is a complex, historically specific style that has emerged largely from strategies ILM has deployed to maintain dominance in the effects industry.

The ILM style over the years is associated most strongly with signature franchises such as the *Star Wars, Jurassic Park, Harry Potter,* and *Transformers* films, among others. While the ILM style has been flexible enough to also accommodate the striking but more eccentric effects for films such as *Willow* (1988), *Death Becomes Her* (1992), *Forrest Gump* (1994), *Casper* (1995), *The Great Wall* (2016), and *Warcraft* (2016), it is most strongly associated with the style that derived from 1970s photorealism. The various ideological implications of this style will be treated with more detail in later chapters.

ILM's CG effect aesthetic is based in the 1970s cinematographically inflected style associated with the New Hollywood auteurist movement. It highlights techniques that draw attention to the act of filming by impersonating the presence of a human-operated camera. The style features unstabilized camera movement, haphazard framing, and abrupt changes of focus. Equally significant, the ILM aesthetic emphasizes the stylistic markers of that mode of filmmaking through the lighting aesthetic, with strong reliance on lens artifacts such as flares, intense backlighting, and highlighting of atmospherics such as dust and rain. Finally, these techniques are self-consciously edited into spontaneous-looking sequences that show off and conceal the effects object to best advantage. These techniques—mimicking tropes of 1970s cinematographic self-reflexivity—paradoxically establish a discourse of visual integrity that allows the ILM aesthetic to be read as more truthful and more real than more animated-looking digital styles.[12] At the same time, through editing strategies controlling what we see or think we are seeing, the aesthetic has the added benefit (common to traditional studio-era effects) of preventing the eye from scrutinizing the effects object or environment too carefully.

Further, ILM's association with the biggest film franchises of all time means its aesthetic has garnered the most public attention, and Lucasfilm's and ILM's own public relations (PR) have taken advantage of that fact. Of course, it is expected that good PR bends facts to its company's benefit. However, because the sheer amount of rhetoric about ILM is so pervasive, my research has determined that ILM's often PR-driven and misleading discourse consistently erases the innovations and contributions of equally innovative individuals and companies working on less prominent films. ILM's PR campaign has successfully defined its version of effects realism as realism, more broadly bleeding into the aesthetics of non-blockbuster global cinema, television, advertising, and other media.

Previous Scholarship

Historically, we are several decades into the digital transition within the entertainment industries, and it is no longer sufficient to speak of "the digital" as if it is monolithic, interoperable, or untouched by historical change, as many canonical early treatments of cinematic digital technologies have, including those by Manovich, Rodowick, and Henry Jenkins. Rather than speak in ahistorical generalities about digital technology, *The Empire of Effects* uses primary-source research to make broader theoretical arguments about the specific technologies and industries that surround the ILM aesthetic.

The subfield of "effects studies" within cinema and media studies has been underrepresented in the academic scholarship. Similarly, software studies, media industry studies, and even studio histories have largely ignored effects work, despite its prominence in the most expensive and high-profile output of the moving image entertainment industry. Academic publishing on effects has largely been concerned with the thematic reading of digital effects technology as a topos. Previous scholars in the 1990s and early 2000s such as Warren Buckland, Michele Pierson, and Geoff King theorized how spectacular effects sequences disrupt narrative with "non-narrative" spectacle.[13] Their scholarship was answered by a wave of important monographs by Kristen Whissel, Dan North, Lisa Bode, Lisa Purse, Aylish Wood, and Bob Rehak that argue for a need to recognize that effects sequences generate a discourse that can be read as directly related to the narrative thematics, subjected to allegorical readings or broader cultural discourses and anxieties.[14] Certainly, this book takes part in identifying and analyzing effects as discourse. However, similar to my 2015 book, *Plastic Reality: Special Effects, Technology, and the Emergence of 1970s Blockbuster Aesthetics*, this book also examines the extranarrative discourses created by the specific technologies and the structures of the industry that support them. In sum, the 2015 book argued that the contemporary aesthetic for digital effects is derived from a 1970s aesthetic. *The Empire of Effects* moves the argument of *Plastic Reality* into the blockbuster aesthetics of the digital era in order to explore this point thoroughly.

There are excellent studies that fall primarily into "industrial studies" or "aesthetic studies," but little scholarly work is concerned with giving equal weight to both. David Bordwell, Kristen Thompson, and Janet Staiger's canonical *The Classical Hollywood Cinema* (1985) (as well as their individual works) tends to subsume both the industrial and aesthetic factors beneath the overarching goal to narrativize. Richard Maltby, Justin Wyatt, and J. D. Connor discuss Hollywood cinema through an industrial aesthetic, but like *The Classical Hollywood Cinema*, it is industrial factors that tend to explain the resultant aesthetic.[15] Other excellent industrial studies have some issues in common with *The Empire of Effects*, but they have different concerns. Charles Acland's *American Blockbusters* (2020) researches the origins of the term "blockbuster" and the role of what he calls the "technological tentpole" in organizing contemporary production, as well as the role of digital workers in bringing the bigness to these films.[16] J. P. Telotte's *Mouse Machine* (2008) concentrates on the historical role of technology in the Disney conglomerate.[17] In my study, aesthetics and industrial factors play coequal roles.

Scholars of race in science fiction such as LeiLani Nishime, Adilifu Nama, and Tanine Allison; queer Afrofuturism such as Kara Keeling; and trans* studies such as Eliza Steinbock and Cáel Keegan have brilliantly discussed effects allegorically to question the limit and value of realism to depict the field of alterity.[18] In another vein, scholars of simulation and the posthuman (e.g., Lev Manovich, Sean Cubitt, Steven Shaviro, Judith Halberstam, and Shane Denson) have approached effects in terms of cinema's non- (and even anti-) humanistic cyborg eye.[19] While the overall project of these studies varies, I argue that characterization of digital effects as artifacts of the posthuman inadvertently devalues the labor context of the hundreds upon thousands of human workers who are the actual producers of these supposedly posthuman effects; such a characterization likewise overstates the role of the computer hardware and software in determining its aesthetic.

The subfield of effects studies has recently seen brilliant work that brings effects into broader contexts. Ariel Rogers is concerned with examining how screen technologies display their technological innovation; Hye Jean Chung's book approaches the global effects industry via Foucauldian case studies of specific films; and Bob Rehak is concerned with the relation of art design and effects, primarily within the *Star Wars* and *Star Trek* universes in a science fiction context. Essays by Leon Gurevitch and by Michael Curtin and John Vanderhoef address the industry context of global effects labor. The specific qualities of imaging software Autodesk Maya are the subject of Aylish Wood's valuable study.[20] Again, *The Empire of Effects* provides a model for how to speak to the development of the *aesthetics* of digital technology as it pertains to developments in the entertainment industry by particular actors. In that way, it explores the industrial role ILM has had in forming a culturally powerful aesthetic of realism. It is a model that incorporates production history and technical specificity as well as an analysis of historical aesthetics.

When taking digital effects and their aesthetic as the primary subject matter, most scholarly treatments view the effects industry aesthetic as both natural and monolithic. Most influentially, Stephen Prince has coined the phrase "perceptual realism" in relation to effects aesthetics as a style of realism that takes physical reality as its aesthetic model.[21] Moreover, Lev Manovich has identified a dominant visual style to simulated digital images that is consistent with millennia-long approaches to mimesis following Renaissance image-making.[22] In both cases, instead of parsing special/visual effects' constructed, historically based, and stylized aesthetic, Prince and Manovich accept the contemporary style of effects realism as natural, inevitable, or ahistorical, as it imitates "what the eye sees in real life" (or through a camera lens) or is congruent with humans' urge toward mimesis.[23] This naturalized approach to effects realism is the unstated reason that all outputs of special/visual effects as an industry are considered to be more or less the same. It provides a convenient and reductive reason why a varied and globalized industry would produce such consistent work, rather than asking how it materially came to be.

Contrarily, I contend that, rather than a logical extension of either digital technology or human perception, there is nothing natural or inevitable about the digital realist aesthetic dominant across Hollywood blockbusters and others around the world designed for international distribution. Put simply, over its lifetime ILM has developed an international style and standard of effects realism, then ensures that other companies and other filmmaking cultures must adopt it as well; we as viewers become habituated so that anything other than the expected ILM aesthetic seems "fake" or "bad."

Questions about the aesthetics of cinematic realism, especially in relation to digital technologies, are central to this book. As in my previous book, this study approaches visual aesthetics as inseparable from industrial production and historical scrutiny. In *Plastic Reality*, I addressed the history of the pivotal 1970s and 1980s in special effects production, asserting that the intensification of special effects practice in the late 1970s initiated a technological, aesthetic, and narrative upheaval in filmmaking that was as significant as the introduction of sound in the late 1920s, a claim that proposed an alternative periodization for cinema history beyond the classical/postclassical divide. Moreover, I argued then as now that aesthetics should be seen as a driver of change in cinema history, rather than simply its result. In *Plastic Reality*, I shifted the discussion of cinematic realism away from its traditional discussions based on (typically Bazinian) philosophies of cinema's ontology to one instead based on material historical aesthetics. In other words, there is no transhistorical ultimate realism that effects aesthetics or cinema more broadly are evolving toward. Instead, different industrial and cultural historical contexts mold standards of realism at a given time.

As discussed briefly in *Plastic Reality*, the ILM style of photorealism forms the aesthetic for 2020s digital blockbusters. For this reason, my characterization of 1970s photorealism as a style built by artists at a specific historical moment becomes particularly relevant here, especially as ILM disseminates its house style as a kind of open-source software throughout the effects industry and then eventually becomes a unit of value to its Disney corporate owners. The crucial aspect that carries over to this book is the description of what I call "optical animation"—the "plastic reality" of the previous book—a specific style of photorealism developed at ILM in the 1970s to realize George Lucas's goal that the original *Star Wars* (1977) movie, in his words, "be credible and totally fantastic at the same time."[24] His effects team created a composite mise-en-scène that combined the New Hollywood cinematographic aesthetic with the flexibility of animation (often drawing from experimental animation) to create a historically determined style of photorealism that aligned with 1970s cinematographic styles. At ILM, this style of photorealism later became a reference style in the transition to digital technology, most especially under the effects supervision of longtime ILM artist and supervisor Dennis Muren, and then became visual reference for ILM's mature digital technologies.

Also as discussed in *Plastic Reality*, most effects artists ascribe to an Arnheimian concept of realism, encapsulated as "if *x* existed in the world and then was photographed, how would that look?" Effects elements are generally designed to match or complement live-action footage—the key difference from traditional animation—with the "real world" as only a base starting point. In my previous book, rather than consider "photo+realism" overly literally as an aesthetic simulating camera reality (that is, what an actual camera is able to capture), I considered the term "photorealism" much as it was initially conceptualized in art history. Art historical photorealism describes 2D artwork executed to mimic a photographic aesthetic. It is a loose movement that typically describes mid-twentieth-century painters and graphic artists such as Richard Estes, Chuck Close, and Ralph Goings, who created artworks with purposefully banal and quotidian subject matter, such as a diner still life with a napkin holder and ketchup bottle, presented with irregular framing recalling the look of unprofessional snapshot photography. These artworks used the perceptual cues of photography to create a tromp-l'oeil effect of camera reality to comment on medium specificity and artistic significance. In other words, a print made to look like a photograph nevertheless retains aesthetic traces of its print-based medium. It does not "become" a photograph because it looks like one. By contrast, cinematic photorealism in most cases works to suppress the recognition of the medium instability and erase the technique rather than comment on it. Moreover, cinematic photorealism as it pertains to effects photorealism is not a relation with a stable and consistent identity. In effects photorealism, rather than replicating what the eye or camera lens "really" sees, cinematic photorealism likewise builds, often from scratch, a stylized conception of how the camera lens, film stock, light patterns, movement, and so on have translated images into cinema, often taking significant liberties with camera reality to do so. Understanding photorealism in a way similar to the art historical precedent helps maintain a sensitivity to medium specificity while also understanding how the style can travel across media—and from optical technologies to digital ones—without changing its look very significantly.

I agree with Lev Manovich that there has been a long enculturation to make viewers accept the image of photography and film as reality.[25] Moreover, following Manovich's influential claim, perhaps the 2019 remake of *The Lion King* is just a recent assertion that the ontology of cinema more and more hews to animation rather than the profilmic. However, in the mature digital era when the technological line between effects work and animation has become so thin, it is exactly through this specific aesthetic of photorealism that the industry creates the (illusory) distinction between them. This is also the logic by which the producers of *The Lion King* can claim, and *want* to claim, that their movie is a live-action remake of an animated film rather than another kind of animation. Previously, optical animation of the 1970s and 1980s gave live-action the potential to be nearly as flexible as animation while still retaining the look of cinematography. However, in the digital era, to maintain the designation of live-action, the result cannot be *too* evidently animated. As we shall see, directors such as Jon Favreau and effects artists such as Dennis Muren and many others frequently use the term "photorealism" to describe effects aesthetics to differentiate it both from "digital-looking" CGI effects and mainstream animation aesthetics. Previously as well, the model for effects aesthetics was a fairly straightforward goal to match the look of contemporary cinematography. With digital technology, the model is still called "photorealism," but what that is referring to is much more difficult to characterize. It is in part because the rhetoric used to discuss effects photorealism tends to use it interchangeably with related terms such as "credibility," "authenticity," "naturalism," "convincingness," and "seamlessness." All these correspond to specific (though overlapping) aesthetic techniques. Describing in detail the aesthetic potential and limitations of the strategies that artists used to achieve a photoreal effect helps delineate the aesthetic ramifications of each human/technological assemblage of artist and machine.

The ILM Digital Aesthetic

The consistent ILM realist aesthetic is organized around the production of the illusion that we are seeing "footage" of a profilmic event shot by a camera operated by a human cinematographer. However, the contours of that production have changed significantly since the 1970s. Even though digital technology certainly allows for greater plasticity, mutability, density, and dynamism within the individual frame and the composite mise-en-scène, the goal remains the same: appearing as if no postproduction technology was used at all.

What ILM artists are resisting is what they frequently call the "digi-

Fig. 0.01 *The Revenant* (2015): The ILM-produced CGI bear demonstrates the company's house style through backlighting, long-take staging, and the misty atmospherics of a heavy tree cover.

tal curse," or an aesthetic that recalls animation over photography. Lev Manovich characterized 1990s CGI as "computer vision," or the cyborg eye: a futuristic, smoothly executed hyperrealism, more perfect than human vision.[26] I would add to that characterization of computer vision one that is algorithmically regular and smooth, as well as unmoored by gravity and abstractly "cute" in its undetailed form. Perhaps contradictorily, in the mature digital era ILM artists seek to create an optical look that cues human camera vision but by actually using computer vision: an optical cyborg eye. In other words, they want a computer-made version of the long-standing, influential, and powerful version of the aesthetic ILM developed in the 1980s.

While chapter 2 will provide more context and detail, taking a closer look now at a specific example provides an illustrative point of reference for ILM's influential version of digital photorealism based on ILM's 1970s cinematographic aesthetic. ILM's work on the bear attack in *The Revenant* (2015), a much-discussed sequence in a film nominated for an Oscar for its visual effects, demonstrates ILM's notion of photorealism as credibly spectacular—and even better in that it appears in a movie not publicized as especially effects-heavy.[27] *The Revenant* (figure 0.01) is also an appropriate example of the way the movie's themes on the rugged masculinist colonialist project chime with ILM's unreflective embrace of the bias inherent in clinging to the 1970s New Hollywood style, which is still largely associated with white masculinist auteurist values.

The sequence meets nearly all the expectations associated with the seamlessness of effects photorealism—in an almost literal way. About thirty-six minutes into the film and about five and a half minutes long, the lengthy bear attack has only one visible edit, at about the five-minute mark. In the basic sense, all the physical and zoological expectations of "bearness" are met: she moves with the assumed gravity of her extrapolated weight, how we would imagine a fierce bear defending her cub would instinctually act; her fur looks and moves like short, matted bear fur; and she always maintains the correct proportion in the frame. Gravity, logical movement, perspective, and texture are all basic expectations of effects realism. However, the sequence does not stop at the expected zoological naturalism. It is also evidently an effects spectacle. First of all, the sequence is timed, blocked, and staged like a sexual assault for maximum horrific tension. Not only is it presented virtuosically as largely a single take; we as viewers know without a shadow of a doubt that star Leonardo DiCaprio was never in such close proximity to any real attacking bear—and so logically the bear must be digitally generated. We as viewers hold our breath for the character Hugo Glass even as we know that the "real" DiCaprio was fine.

The overall effect is so persuasive that we hardly ask ourselves how this convincing naturalism is achieved. In fact, the sequence is highly instructive in demonstrating the distinctive ILM aesthetic strategies at play through the three main cinematic aspects ILM manipulates to heighten the photorealism of the effects object in the shot: editing, camera movement, and lighting—specifically, strategic length of takes and careful blocking, haphazard-looking movement, and obscuring lighting. First, the editing: although presented as mostly one take, the sequence is built using invisible digital edits and furthermore is organized into stages and rhythms. The sequence begins with a classic, sudden creature reveal: a closeup of Glass as he aims a rifle toward the foreground as the bear emerges from the shadowy underbrush in the background, advancing on him so quickly from behind that he does not have time to spin the gun around. We as viewers also only gradually realize what is happening. While the majority of the attack is presented as a single take, there are frequent invisible edits camouflaged by whip pans, the bear's body, and even the bear fogging the camera lens with her snorting breath. The sequence exploits the visual credibility and spatial integrity associated with the long take in the way the bear is constantly in the frame and frequently very close to the camera, seeming to give us an unbroken look at her to visually test her "realness." The camera distance also varies so the bear alternates being both close to the camera and also in a wider view in the background. The pacing of the sequence allows the chance for the bear to amble off to take care of her cubs while the camera stays on the injured Glass as he readies his gun, but when the bear returns to attack again, she mostly moves very quickly when her whole body is in frame, and when moving slowly she is either out of frame or in extreme close-up. For contrast, we can recall how other films stage human/fierce animal interactions. For example, *Bringing Up Baby* (1938) puts its leopard in close proximity with stars Katharine Hepburn and Cary Grant through elaborate mobile split screens. Other films stage animal attacks similar to that of the tiger face-off in *Gladiator* (2000), where wide shots of the animal are interspersed with extreme close-ups of the animal's biting maw through rapid disorienting cuts, giving the sense of exciting action but not visual authenticity. Most do not dare use the long take, including the bear attack in *Dawn of the Planet of the Apes* (2014), which is very rapidly cut, about twenty seconds long, and with one good look at the full bear that lasts a few seconds. *The Revenant* bear's long-take presentation "proves" her credibility.[28]

As to the camera movement and framing in *The Revenant*, the wobbly frame and the constantly moving and reframing unstabilized camera gives the impression of a human camera operator filming an unpredictable event, rather than a smoothly planned elegant tableaux such as the leopard attack in *2001: A Space Odyssey* (1968). *The Revenant* scene appears as if it was shot by a foolheartedly brave (and coldly heartless) wildlife cameraperson. The movement varies from rapid whip pans when the bear is shaking her prey in her teeth to slowly tilting movements from Glass's wincing face up to the bear as she pauses. However, when the bear is moving quickly, the camera is usually a beat or two behind the bear's actions, suggesting an operator who does not know what the bear is going to do next but who wants to be sure everything gets filmed.

Lastly, but crucially, is the lighting, which conceals as much if not more than it reveals. The heavy tree canopy provides a plausible reason for the overall dim lighting of the sequence, as well as a filter for the harder light shafts coming from between the backlit tree trunks. The drizzly, misty atmosphere puts damp particles in the air to soften the light further and delineate planes of action. The dim ambiance, backlighting, and what effects artists call "atmospherics" together causes viewers to think they are seeing more of the bear than they actually are. The bear is nearly constantly in frame, but what we see is largely backlit in silhouette. At the end of the sequence, after Glass stabs the bear, both she and Glass roll down a ravine away from the camera—the only wide shot in the sequence.

Certainly, it was not wholly ILM's creative decision to present the shot as a long take; neither was ILM entirely in charge of the pace and timing of the shot. Moreover, many of the aesthetic options must align with the look of rest of the film. Nevertheless, ILM was charged with putting across those filmic choices where it appeared that a real bear was mauling a real movie star. Through this visual analysis, we can see how the sequence's photorealism comes not simply from a zoological or otherwise perceptual matching with reality. Instead, its sense of credibility, authenticity, naturalism, and seamlessness are all built up bit by bit through the specific aesthetic stylistic techniques its ILM artists deemed cinematically appropriate to the sequence.

As a contrast to ILM-produced effects sequences as in *The Revenant*, even when requisite time and money are spent on a mainstream would-be blockbuster, narrow expectations of "good" live-action effects can engender poor reception of a film's effects aesthetic. Plenty of films including *Geostorm* (2017), *The Meg* (2018), and *Greenland* (2020) skate by with derivative and uninspired effects that are nevertheless within generally expected aesthetic parameters. We can see these basic parameters in works from filmmaking teams who are less interested in the effects process, do not have much clout over the production, or simply do not have high enough budgets. In those cases, many CGI-heavy effects sequences gesture at an impoverished (or "cheap") version of ILM's style, but they also barely tweak established patterns. Other approaches, even in those produced by ILM, do not go by uncommented but are instead deemed "bad" effects, even though they are simply not in the expected version of the ILM photorealist style. We can see this demonstrated by the North American failure of the ILM-led *Warcraft*, a film that appropriately took its design cues from the popular video game but whose effects were received by critics and audiences as "bad."

Indeed, *Warcraft* was laughed off the screen in North America by critics as "chintzy" and "soulless, incoherent, Renaissance Faire hooey," and it was likewise rejected by audiences at the box office.[29] *Entertainment Weekly* critic Chris Nashawaty said of the effects, "despite

Fig. 0.02 *Warcraft* (2016): The Orcs here appropriately match the *Warcraft* video game characters but do not fulfill the audience's aesthetics for photorealism.

its massive budget, the special effects look cheap and cheesy," which I would suggest is another way of saying not sufficiently photoreal and "too animated." By way of example, in the first sequence of the film in which the orc lead characters are introduced, Durotan (Toby Kebbel) and Draka (Anna Galvin) engage in couples' banter in a cozy fire-lit room about the child in her very pregnant womb. The film's opening shot fulfils audience effects expectations. Here, Durotan is shown in bust-length close-up. He is lightly backlit, but the scrupulous details of his face, hair, skin, tusks, and tribal ornaments make a strikingly photoreal impression of this computer-generated humanoid creature. His skin tone has visible pores, color variety, texture, and warmth. Although he is mostly still during his voiceover, his eyes are alive—even moist-looking—and his face moves with a subtlety that suggests thinking. The backlighting even shows a faint downy texture on his shoulders. This is the style of photorealism expected from ILM. However, it is the only shot of its kind in the film. When the next shot cuts to a close-up of his waking wife, the detail is more amorphously sketched in (figure 0.02). Her eyes and mouth twitch naturalistically, but her untextured skin is only lightly detailed and synthetically smooth (in comparison to Durotan in the close-ups that bookend this one). Her ornaments suggest bone and metal, but only by context. In the medium shot that follows, Draka is supine in the foreground, highlighting her pregnancy, while Durotan sits crouching in the background, reaching out to clasp her belly. While the initial close-up of Durotan (no doubt the "hero shot" meant to impress in the trailer) was very intricately rendered for photorealistic effect ("if orcs existed and were then photographed") this two-shot reveals the more consistent aesthetic of the movie, one of smooth animatedness to match the perceived expectations of the fan audience familiar with the lower-resolution video game. Instead of humanlike textured skin with pores, veins, and color variation, Draka's pregnant belly and Durotan's upper torso have an overly even, Plasticine look. Much of the depiction of the orcs in the remainder of the film largely follows the ILM play-book: backlighting, atmospherics, unstable camera shots, and longish takes. Their movement is thoroughly naturalistic to their considerable bulk and exaggerated proportions in the expected standardized aesthetic parameters. However, the orcs retain their "animated" Plasticine sheen, like animated action figures or 3D-printed objects.

Why is this animated look evidently a problem for viewers? Perhaps the orcs' evident animatedness pushes the live-action object too much, as Sianne Ngai has contended in another context, toward the realm of the "cute." According to Ngai:

> Cuteness is a response to the "unformed" look of infants, to the amorphous and blob-like as opposed to the articulated or well defined. Indeed the more malleable or easily deformable the cute object appears the cuter it will seem.[30]

In this way, cuteness's unformed, animated look can be seen as the opposite of the photoreal aesthetic, because cuteness is, to Ngai, visually "trivializing." Certainly, for *Warcraft*, cuteness is a look that for most is at odds with the warrior culture depicted here, but generally speaking, animatedness and cuteness for effects artists evoke the risk of distancing—the dreaded "pulling the viewer out of the story." It does so by calling attention to the movie-made artificiality of character design when, ideally, characters should appear natural and seamless with their environment.[31] This perceived trivialization likely connects to why effects artists constantly talk about avoiding the "digital curse" (animatedness) and why Disney feels the 2019 *The Lion King* and other "live-action reboots" need to be classified as live-action, not animation.

The orc characters of *Warcraft* were designed and thoroughly rendered with as much defined detail and movement as, say, the Hulk or any character coming out of ILM's workshop. However, the amorphous aesthetics matching the video game expected by the production leaned too far into animated cuteness rather than *Revenant*-style photoreal environments. However, *Warcraft* hit big in China, where a broader effects realism expectation applies, one that is not so resistant to animatedness, as we shall see in chapter 4.[32]

Methodology

Researching a multibillion-dollar corporation such as ILM within Lucasfilm is always a challenge, even more so now that it is owned by an even bigger conglomerate, The Walt Disney Company. It is difficult to separate public relations from reliable history, and academic accounts very rarely depart from the Lucasfilm/ILM company line. There is virtually no academic, unauthorized, primary-source historical research on either Lucasfilm or ILM.[33] The *Star Wars* films have been subject to academic fan studies and some limited industrial attention by academics. However, the majority of academic works considering ILM tend to cite Lucasfilm-produced sources as fact or do not recognize that the information they are encountering is either PR or couched professional public rhetoric, as John Caldwell has described.[34]

There is a practical reason for this. Not surprisingly, there has been little upside for Lucasfilm to allow outside academic researchers into its archives, especially now that it is owned by Disney. Therefore, it is difficult to obtain reliable, non-ILM-authorized information about the company and its activities. Trade publications such as *Variety* and the *Hollywood Reporter* are useful for compiling the kind of material in chapter 1 regarding announcements of industrial and business dealings and partnerships, but they are likewise subject to the press release and publicity department information provided by Lucasfilm. Therefore, if an ILM spokesperson states on the record to *Variety* in 1989 that ILM had thirty-five Silicon Graphics workstations, the publication generally takes it at face value. In most cases, reporters do not go to Marin County to see for themselves.

When researching Hollywood special/visual effects, one inevitably encounters the long-standing, fan-targeted effects journal *Cinefex*, a subscription-based quarterly that celebrated its fortieth anniversary in 2020 and published its final edition in 2021. *Cinefex* has played an important role to those hoping to join the effects industry as well as to scholars who are writing about it. To the scholar, *Cinefex*'s lengthy and highly detailed articles—typically on three to four movies per issue and that interview key personnel, collect "before and after" images, name the effects companies employed on the production, recount the technology in use, and regale the reader with production anecdotes—are valuable sources of basic information that is otherwise difficult to obtain. Since the 1980s, as the frequent tributes by aspiring filmmakers and effects artists within the pages attest, the *Cinefex* discourse has been absorbed into the artist's image of the excitement and glamor of effects production. In this way *Cinefex* has enjoyed significant access to the practitioners who are happy to be part of the effects story of the films. However, as former Visual Effects Society president Jeff Okun has attested, *Cinefex* articles frequently present the effects production in idealized form. Using as an example of Okun's own experience on Roland Emmerich's *Stargate* (1994), he contended that the *Cinefex* article completely left out the details where he was fired and rehired several times over what he characterized as the director's unreasonable demands.[35] In other words, as detailed as these articles are, they are still choosing to leave out the less collegial or unpleasant aspects of the story. In this way, fan-directed effects and science fiction–oriented publications such as *Cinefex* (1980–2021) and others, including *Cinéfantastique* (1967–2006 in its original incarnation) and *Starlog* (1976–2009), and prominent blogs such as ArtofVFX.com and beforesandafters.com, while thoroughly researched and not authored by Lucasfilm employees, are still limited to the information that the Lucasfilm/ILM interview subjects, press releases, and publicity departments provide. Moreover, although it goes largely unspoken, these sources are also constrained by the story the producers want told in exchange for continued access.

That being said, publicly available entertainment journalism and the mainstream press provide more than just access to press releases and accounts of business dealings and industry analysis. They also provide a rich comparative accounting of what has been written about ILM in relation to other effects houses since the 1990s.[36] Moreover, these sources provide a great deal of discourse to analyze, revealing the image that George Lucas, Lucasfilm, and ILM want to present of themselves as well as how the industry characterizes them.

Despite these challenges, there are a few places where the researcher can find cracks in the façade. For example, there is one (and to my knowledge only one) readily available cache of ILM information outside of corporate hands: the former ILM general manager Thomas G. Smith's papers at the Ransom Center at the University of Texas, Austin.[37] Smith's papers include effects storyboards, contracts, and publicity materials. But most relevant for this study are the Lucasfilm yearbooks, which cover 1982–1991 in the Ransom holdings.[38]

These yearbooks served several purposes for Lucasfilm employees, not unlike house organs during the studio era. The first is similar to high-school yearbooks, in that they were designed to forge a kind of corporate version of school spirit. Namely, yearbooks were distributed at the annual Fourth of July picnic: They feature snapshots of the intramural sports teams as well as dances, babies, pets, and candid poses; people even signed them like high-school yearbooks. Also, like yearbooks, they include portrait photos of every Lucasfilm employee. Smith told me they were also used like school facebooks in the old, lowercase sense, so that people in various departments across Lucasfilm could look up colleagues in other divisions.[39] They even frequently included personal information such as people's occupational and educational history, romantic status, and astrological signs. In an interview with the author, Smith said they were only used in-house and were not given to potential partners or investors.[40]

However, the yearbooks are not simply accounts of corporate culture where one can glimpse the Lucasfilm self-image. For the researcher, while the yearbooks are hardly uncut raw data, they are a gold mine of minimally massaged information for internal use. Because every employee, division, and job title are included, one can track the configuration and transmutation of the Lucasfilm departments, job descriptions, and personnel over time. There are reports of what each department had accomplished that year, projects they worked on, and humorous accounts of what went wrong. Also, alongside the good times, one glimpses accounts of turmoil and rancor within the ranks. Finally, we can glean what the company's priorities and emphases were by not only what is included but by what is left out. This material can be compared to press releases in the entertainment press and secondary sources such as the authorized Lucasfilm publications discussed in chapter 3. Perhaps not surprisingly, this information frequently conflicts with the corporate line, especially when one adds in other unpublished sources such as personal interviews and the less-authorized discourses of former employees.[41]

As valuable as the unauthorized materials such as the yearbooks are, they are not the only sources on ILM available to the researcher. In addition, although effects practitioners are frequently limited by what they can discuss due to nondisclosure agreements and their companies' policies, I was able to interview or access unpublished interviews with a great many effects artists, both retired and currently active. Through these various approaches, a less PR-managed picture of ILM emerges.

ILM's dominance of the effects industry has asserted itself across several axes and across several decades. For that reason, concentrating on just one or even two aspects of ILM's activities or a short time span would not sufficiently describe the scope of its control over the industry. My account of ILM's business, aesthetic, cultural, and technological history over the span of the 1980s to the present day aims to create a historical amalgam that helps explain how and why ILM has been able to maintain such a sway over an entire sector of the entertainment industry for so long. For that reason, although there will be some overlap, the chapters alternate ILM's aesthetic and industrial histories in roughly chronological order. Chapters 2, 4, and 5 provide a more interpretive approach: a historically contextualized aesthetic analysis based on a corpus of representative films. Chapters 1 and 3 include aesthetic analyses but are more empirical, concentrating on ILM's industrial and technological history.

Not unlike Tony Stark's AI assistant Jarvis transforming into Vision, the ILM style has left ILM's control and now has an independent life of its own. The ILM aesthetic is more prevalent than ever in the digital age and still represents the most culturally powerful model for effects aesthetics. One might imagine that ILM as an industrial entity would have become more powerful as a result of its partnership with Disney and the MCU. However, rather than presiding over the effects sector by leading its most prominent productions and demonstrating the state of the art with new "wows," ILM, along with many other companies, is reduced to yet another contracted player producing the MCU's version of nondescript grounded realism. Some practitioners have argued that the MCU version of the ILM style not only flattens it out to a featureless series of rules to follow but also guts the creative spark that kept ILM at the top of the effects business for four decades. The question remains: Is there room for the ILM aesthetic to continue to evolve? Or has Disney now fixed it in *Jurassic Park*–style amber (with DNA to be extracted for replication later on)? What is ILM within the Disney conglomeration?

ONE

ILM Versus Everybody Else

Effects Houses in the Digital Age

[SPECIAL EFFECTS] IS NOT A BUSINESS THAT ANYBODY WHO WAS OUT TO
MAKE MONEY WOULD GET INTO.

—ILM FOUNDER GEORGE LUCAS

THE SPECIAL EFFECTS BUSINESS IS AN OXYMORON.

—SCOTT ROSS, COFOUNDER OF DIGITAL DOMAIN AND
LABOR ACTIVIST

Due to special/visual effects' ubiquity in nearly all high-profile filmmaking today, it would be logical to assume that the effects business, under the direct conglomerate control of the studios, is a lucrative and stable one. However, as described in the introduction, this assumption is wrong. As George Lucas and Scott Ross (quoted just above) insist, one thing becomes abundantly clear when studying the recent Hollywood effects business: it is not an efficiently run, profit-making venture. But if the effects business does not make money, how does it stay in business? It primarily sustains itself through an economic logic more in common with accounts of "labor of love" creative economies.[1] More specifically, it does so largely through promoting the fantasy of working for an idolized cinematic visionary such as George Lucas and contributing to a *Star Wars*–size impact on the cultural landscape—the same fantasy that has driven the effects sector since the poststudio era. The effects business has always been difficult to square with recent depictions of "Hollywood in the New Millennium." Tom Schatz has most influentially characterized the economic logic of the recent history of the movie industry around conglomeration, where large businesses become larger by acquiring competitors and working to create synergy across media by appealing to the largest audience possible.[2] Toby Miller and colleagues have described a "global" Hollywood that uses coercive power as a content provider to force all markets to both adopt and adapt to Hollywood's products and practices.[3] However, an account of the effects industry cannot be neatly absorbed into these broader industry forces.

It is exactly this labor-of-love economy that makes the effects industry different from other motion picture creative economies: It is not just that the effects business does not make money; it is minimally concerned with doing so. Much of the contemporary effects business still holds on to the 1970s ideals of creative labor out of which it emerged. Jeff Menne has described the broader Hollywood context for what he calls a "post-Fordist" (a play on both the twentieth-century system of mass production and the Classical Hollywood director John Ford) approach to industrial creative organization. In his formulation, 1970s self-styled auteurs (e.g., Robert Altman and Francis Ford Coppola) charismatically led production teams willing to trade fair compensation and reasonable work hours for the feeling of the personal satisfaction in creating quality work.[4] Menne convincingly contends that in these new poststudio production structures, the Classical Hollywood "genius of the system" is replaced or transmuted into an auteurist "economy of genius."[5]

It is the effects industry version of this post-Fordist creative economy that has made it an oxymoron: the romantic image as an artist's dream job where working for an auteur trumps such trivialities as health insurance, overtime pay, and union membership. The effects business is able to function only because it exploits the 1970s economy of genius. To movie fans who eventually become effects workers, there is no more revered genius figure than George Lucas, the auteur who built his effects empire by cultivating an image of this idealized workplace. The smaller-scale economy of genius, such as at Lucasfilm and Industrial Light & Magic, has long relied on a workforce that sees the work as a passion project.[6] Even more, the image of the effects industry as a desirable, creative, and fulfilling career for film professionals comes largely from a fantasy promoted by Industrial Light & Magic, whose production of documentaries, coffee-table books, and other kinds of publicity still encourage thousands to jump into the effects business each year in the hope they might someday work on a movie such as *Star Wars*.

The promise of artistic fulfilment is also the lifeblood of houses beyond ILM. And surprisingly, this romanticized notion of creative labor holds for those at the top of the sector as well as those entering it. Effects house Rhythm and Hues (R&H) founder John Hughes candidly states the unofficial credo of the effects artist:

> A vfx [visual effects] company is not a big moneymaking company. The margins are very, very, low. But we were never founded to make money. We're not typical entrepreneurs. We're here because this is what we love to do. As long as we're not losing money, we're ok.[7]

This idealization hits hard against the cold economics of media conglomerates that take advantage of this way of doing business. The truth is, most effects houses are losing money, at least most of the time. Nearly all effects artists toil in anonymity, lack union representation, work long hours with few benefits, and live a peripatetic lifestyle, moving from continent to continent to find work. As the quotes above and other professional rhetoric make clear, the consequences of the effects business's labor of love is precarity.[8] This comfort with low profit yield and high risks is the major reason the effects business is largely not owned and run directly by conglomerates.

ILM has sidestepped these industry troubles by enjoying the financial patronage of its founder, Lucas, who long plowed Lucasfilm profits back into ILM. Until 2012, ILM was privately held by Lucasfilm and thus was not required to post earnings statements or satisfy outside investors. By all accounts, ILM is considered the effects company that everyone in the sector aspires to become.[9] This has allowed for a more secure work environment, a more robust research and development program, and greater investment in technology than other companies could sustain. These advantages have meant that the rules of play for the effects sector, since ILM opened for outside business in 1980, can most accurately be described as "ILM versus everybody else." ILM's total dominance of the effects industry from the early 1980s through the 2010s cannot be understood without recognizing the complex economic and industrial context of the effects business. Moreover, one cannot grasp the business model of other rival top-tier effects companies over that time, including

Digital Domain, Weta, and Sony Pictures Imageworks (Sony PI) and, later, Double Negative, Moving Picture Show, and Framestore (as well as a multitude of less prominent players) without a description of what ILM has represented to the industry, even if it has always been a super-team that, due to its built-in advantages, lesser teams could not hope to surpass. Remarkably, as the labor of the effects artist has shifted from camera whizzes and handmade tinkerers to software gurus in front of monitors, the business model itself has not changed very much. However, the effects business's shift into digital technologies throughout the 1990s challenged companies formed on the 1970s economy-of-genius model to adapt to conglomeration.

The Effects Industry Today: A Primer

It is difficult to make money in the effects industry for several reasons, but mostly because of labor costs. Even though many effects workers are underpaid, the seemingly unending scrolls of contributors appearing in the movie credits attest to the huge roster of artists needed to complete a blockbuster film. The production companies they contract with are constantly trying to keep costs down, often insisting on flat-fee structures (the project-bid model) and undercutting per-shot fees by contracting with lower-cost startups. Also, effects companies are largely responsible for in-house R&D and equipment costs. It may seem that the effects industry has much in common with other digital and effects-related industries. However, I will not be discussing related sectors such as physical effects, traditional makeup prostheses, 3D conversion, digital intermediate, and traditional animation—all of which require separate workforces, skill sets, and labor arrangements,[10] though there is some overlap of activity and personnel. For example, although the 2019 *Lion King* remake and the *Frozen* films are both Disney productions, the artists who animate the motion-capture lion (where the lion has to conform to photorealist standards) are nearly always an entirely different workforce (or occasionally a different division within the same company) than those who animate Elsa, Anna, and Olaf. In this book, I will more narrowly consider the impact of special/visual effects labor within traditional parameters. In other words, I will discuss the current iteration of the traditional special effects industry and specific skill sets. Although this has changed over the years, it remains surprisingly consistent with earlier eras: various kinds of composite work in mattes, miniatures, effects animation, motion capture, and cleanup.

The contemporary special/visual effects industry's independently owned and operated houses provide an interesting problematic within models describing independent creative labor, which again has some issues in common with other areas (especially the video game industry) but also a distinct history and configuration.[11] First, the vast majority of effects houses are and have been independently owned and operated since the post-Paramount decree in the 1950s.[12] Thus, with a few exceptions, effects houses are not owned by the conglomerate studios that employ them. Though reductive, I am defining *independence* broadly here as "not conglomerate-owned." And to be clear, independence cannot in this case be characterized positively as a site of resistance to fight the forces of global conglomeration. The effects industry's in-between status—between artist and technician—combined with a failure to define itself is a major factor blocking it from possessing any kind of collectivization (which nearly all other production categories enjoy to some degree or another).

Most contemporary effects workers do not belong to a union or a guild. Longtime effects artist and current labor advocate Scott Squires explained the lay of the land for effects workers circa 2010:

> By and large everyone working on a major motion picture are in a guild. The director, writers, actors, cinematographers, production designer, costume designer, sound recorder, stunts, special [physical] effects, grips, electricians, props, editors, make-up artists, script supervisors, set decorators, scenic artists, hair stylists, their crews, etc. Even the producers have their own guild. Some of the animation companies (Disney, Dreamworks, Sony Animation) are covered by a guild. Visual effects is one of the few groups working in the film industry that are not unionized. These other guilds all get some type of profit sharing or residuals from the films they work on. Directors, writers and actors get checks based on the success of the film. Most of the below the line union workers get secondary sales (DVDs, etc.) residuals with the studios putting in a percentage into their health and welfare fund (MPI) to help offset health care costs.[13]

Although guilds and unions are often discussed interchangeably, a guild, legally speaking, is a collective bargaining organization for independent contractors, whereas a union is a collective bargaining organization for employees. One entity, the Visual Effects Society (VES), appears to be an effects workers guild, but it is not. Founded in 1997, VES is a professional organization with no labor advocacy component. Its stated mission:

> The Visual Effects Society (VES) is a non-profit professional, honorary society, dedicated to advancing the arts, sciences, and applications of visual effects and to improving the welfare of its members by providing professional enrichment and education, fostering community, and promoting industry recognition.[14]

VES's refusal to challenge and adequately address labor conditions has been a sticking point for many effects activists, including Squires and VFX Soldier blogger Daniel Lay. So, VES looks like a guild similar to the American Society of Cinematographers (ASC), which it is modeled on, but is in fact merely an honorary professional society with minimal industry sway.

How did all this come to pass? Why is the special/visual effects industry neither unionized nor under guild protection, thereby making its workers nearly unique as a labor category within Hollywood-based film production? Put simply, the effects industry's relationship with Hollywood has historically been "dependently independent." It is a complicated story, so I will concentrate on what is relevant to the current situation.[15] In the late 1910s and 1920s, patent-holding effects artists such as Frank Williams (of the famed Williams Process, an early color differentiation composite process), for example, contracted their specialized techniques to the newly formed studios. At the same time, former "trickmen," as they were called, joined with other camera talent such as cinematographers, helping form the ASC, and promoted themselves as masters of "special photographic effects" with skills ordinary cinematographers did not have.[16] Many of these artists eventually landed steady work at the studios; many formed their own optical, title, and effects houses, which often did studio-subcontracted optical shots, operating parallel to studios on a shot-by-shot basis, in a modestly profitable fashion.[17] Fast-forward to the 1970s, when the increase of companies inspired by Industrial Light & Magic popped up to compete for work on science-fiction blockbusters. This is the era that intensified the project-bid system for contracting effects work; instead of a few composite shots here and there, companies were now bidding on providing all the effects for an entire film.

The project-bid model is what makes effects different from other independently contracted Hollywood creative labor. Most other Hollywood-based movie professionals are contracted for work on a specific project under a union- or guild-approved contract for a specific amount of time and should be paid when they go over that contracted time (even if lawsuits suggest this does not always happen). Through the long-standing project-bid model, a surplus of independent houses compete for jobs, often underbidding rivals to get them, and maintain razor-thin profit margins. Houses are locked in to that price, no matter what the future holds (e.g., alterations, delays, or whatever else might affect final costs). A company can easily go bankrupt if the project folds or goes significantly over budget, since the effects company has to cover work already completed and/or budget overruns. This is what happened to Digital Domain, which worked on the now-mostly-forgotten *Jack the Giant Slayer* (2013), a film project that played a role in its bankruptcy.

The "Big Five" Effects Houses

ILM did not create the conditions that keep the effects sector on the edge of insolvency. That blame can be placed squarely on the production entities working to keep effects costs down as the number of effects shots rose. ILM, the industry leader since the 1970s, even today is impacted by these historical industrial factors.

However, ILM's overwhelming economic and industrial advantages have contributed to the problems. ILM created an economic/aesthetic/R&D model that the studios began to expect and forced all others to aspire to, but it was impossible to replicate. Moreover, ILM did not force its model on other companies through coercive business practices but instead through soft-power initiatives.

While many effects companies came and went over the decades, the sector's top-tier companies—those considered first for high-profile blockbusters—from the early to mid-1990s to the mid-2010s remained consistent, though not exactly stable. In 2012, a crucial transition era saw an unprecedented amount of bankruptcies, acquisitions, and reformations. The trade rags and even nonspecialist publications such as *Time* identified the "Big Five" and the "Little Three" effects houses, all of which were mostly independently owned, California-based, and Anglophone. The Big Five were, in order of their founding: Industrial Light & Magic (1978),[18] owned by George Lucas's corporate entity Lucasfilm in the Bay Area; Rhythm and Hues, founded by John Hughes and partners in 1987 in Los Angeles; Sony Pictures Imageworks, founded in 1992 by Sony Studios (formerly Columbia-Tristar) in Los Angeles; Digital Domain, founded in 1993 by James Cameron, Stan Winston, and Scott Ross in partnership with IBM in the Los Angeles area; and Weta, founded by the director Peter Jackson and partners in New Zealand as Weta Digital in 1992 (the only one not based in California).[19] For most of their existences, ILM, R&H, DD, and Weta were independent companies. Sony Pictures Imageworks has always been and remains a subsidiary of the global Sony conglomerate. The Little Three—Double Negative (DNeg, 1998), The Moving Picture Company (MPC, 1987), and Framestore (1994)—are all London-based companies, and were founded around the same time as the Big Five, but did not achieve top-tier status until the 2010s.

How we got to this configuration is a story of ambition and overreach. Rather than succumbing to the temptation to describe the effects business with the classic studio rhetoric, I will refer to the "top tier" of the effects industry rather than the "Big Five." The handful of companies dominating the first three decades of digital effects production emerged out of different corporate contexts, all traceable to a template initially patterned after the 1970s and 1980s effects companies that grew out of the intensification of big effects films. Three of them (ILM, DD, and Weta), were formed by prominent filmmakers (George Lucas, James Cameron, and Peter Jackson, respectively) to exert greater control over the unruly effects work on their own projects. R&H arose from a commercial ad production company and was an early pioneer in computer-generated and computer-assisted imagery. Sony Pictures Imageworks was designed by Sony Pictures to handle in-house effects production and function as an R&D wing. This chapter provides an industrial and economic history to show how ILM was able to lord it over its rivals, both in perception and reality, until it was outmatched by an even bigger player.

This chapter will follow ILM and its rivals on a historical trajectory from the early 1990s to 2014:

1991–1995: The Great Digital Expansion
1996–2000: The First Downturn
2001–2006: A Contradictory "Golden Age"
2007–2014: The Industry "on Fire"

Before the widespread adoption of digital effects, *Jaws* (1975) and *Star Wars* (1977) in the 1970s intensified the demand for elaborate effects programs, contributing to the blockbusterization of the movie industry.[20] Then, the 1980–1991 era represented a transition to an auteur-focused effects company different from the studio spinoffs characterizing the "effects/title/optical" companies that operated in Hollywood midcentury. Because I have established this history more thoroughly elsewhere, the discussion here will be brief.[21] Already in the 1980s, the popular and industry press broadly recognized ILM as the effects industry's undisputed leader, asserting that "ILM does more business than its five major competitors combined."[22] And even taking this rhetoric as hyperbole (which one frequently must when considering ILM press statements), until about 1991–1992, my research has established that ILM held the high end of the effects field largely to itself. Moreover, ILM in the 1980s had already begun to resemble less and less the "scrappy outsider" described in its self-produced hagiography of the 1970s; it had already become an industry behemoth.[23] However, that did not stop its PR machine from continuing to repeat and refine that rebel/outsider image for the next several decades.[24]

Inspired by the example of ILM's work on *Star Wars*, the new style of effects house became the one-stop shop, where a single company completed hundreds of effects shots for a film; at least, that was the aspirational model for effects production. The "five major competitors" were largely made up of companies founded by self-styled "effects auteurs" to be much like ILM: Douglas Trumbull's Future General, John Dykstra's Apogee, Richard Edlund's Boss, as well as Rob Blalack's Praxis and the artist collective DreamQuest. Three of those five companies—Apogee, Praxis, and Boss—were founded by former prominent ILM artists, and Trumbull had an independent status as an effects auteur after well-publicized work on *2001: A Space Odyssey* and *Close Encounters of the Third Kind* (1977). DreamQuest's roster included a well-respected group of effects artists that assembled largely on Douglas Trumbull–led effects projects such as *Close Encounters* and *Star Trek: The Motion Picture* (1979).[25] This initial set of rival companies was fairly frank about their lower status, even Dykstra's Apogee, the industry's recognized runner-up. When asked in an interview "What kind of jobs did Apogee get in the 1980s?" former Apogee employee and later studio effects producer John Swallow replied frankly: "We got work that ILM didn't get. . . . When they were full, we got more work."[26] Most worryingly, these companies did not have the *Star Wars*–size profits to sustain them during lean times given the slender profit margins of the project-bid system.[27] Those factors, along with corporate consolidation and the expense of the conversion to digital technology, caused all these early analog rivals to fold by the early to mid-1990s.

1991–1995: The Great Digital Expansion

As elaborate effects programs and mounting effects shot counts became industry standard through the 1980s, the introduction of photoreal CGI sequences in the early 1990s demonstrated the audience attraction for a new "wow" factor. Two hugely successful ILM effects blockbusters were *Terminator 2: Judgment Day* and *Jurassic Park*, featuring showy displays of photoreal computer-generated dinosaurs and cyborgs, and they captured the early 1990s public imagination, even though the films included only a small number of shots with CGI (about fifty to sixty each).[28] After these hits, many productions were keen to include more extensive CGI effects sequences in their films, but the companies equipped with the technology and artists to provide them were very few and very expensive. This meant that, by 1991, a gap in the market had opened up. For the first time, several serious rivals with significant financial backing rose to challenge ILM, and those companies' rhetoric proclaimed that such was their plan.[29] ILM's highly trained personnel were also a target. Many of the new companies, most aggressively Digital Domain and Sony Pictures Imageworks, poached executives and talent directly from ILM.[30]

The huge successes during this period also included *Forrest Gump* and *Toy Story* (1995, albeit in feature animation), films that expanded the industry's notion of what was possible and foreshadowed the potential in different narrative contexts, from summer blockbusters to Oscar hopefuls. The audience attraction as well as the expense of digital conversion led to three important industrial trends in the early to mid-1990s: director/effects house collaborations, studios' move to in-house effects teams, and effects houses' first round of attempts at media diversification.

The first trend saw prominent directors establish their own effects companies to emulate ILM's structural model. James Cameron's Digital Domain, founded in a partnership with physical effects master Stan Winston and former ILM executive Scott Ross (as well as a 50 percent investment from the computing giant IBM), was designed to compete with ILM's Lucasfilm bankroll. Cameron did not like relying on ILM for the CGI effects in *The Abyss* (1989) and *Terminator 2.* Owning the effects company seemed like the best way to control the effects on his productions. Weta Workshop was a New Zealand company that preexisted its partnership with Peter Jackson, but they formally collaborated in 1992 to make Jackson's *Heavenly Creatures* (1994). Weta Workshop expanded to Weta Digital in 1992 and slowly gained prominence through the 1990s, culminating with the epic *Lord of the Rings* trilogy, the first of which was released in 2001.

The second trend in the early 1990s saw the major studio and production facilities Warner Bros., Fox, Paramount, Disney, Sony, and also Dreamworks create or acquire in-house effects teams. Like Cameron, it seemed logical that studios should want to directly own and control this increasingly central sector of the filmmaking process. Late in the period of digital expansion, the *Hollywood Reporter* put it skeptically:

> About [1994–1995], a theory rippled through studio exec suites that the pricey digital work beginning to creep into all aspects of movie production could be managed cost effectively by acquiring an ownership position in an effects vendor or even creating an elaborate on-lot effects unit.[31]

In the mid-1990s, a wave of studio acquisitions suggested a major shift in studio ownership of effects houses along the Sony PI model. Starting in 1993, Warner Brothers created Warner Digital, which grew to a staff of 300.[32] Disney acquired prominent 1980s effects team Dream-Quest Images in 1996.[33] 20th Century Fox combined two smaller effects houses, VIFX and Blue Sky animation, to create an in-house effects team. Others did not buy effects houses outright but increased investment in companies. Dreamworks bought a 40 percent stake in the longtime house Pacific Data Images, and Digital Domain made a deal with MGM.[34] As we shall see in the next period, the *Hollywood Reporter*'s skepticism was well founded. Studio ownership of effects houses proved to be short-lived. Like Cameron, the studios underestimated the financial downside of owning and operating an effects house.

The third trend saw effects companies attempting to diversify into other media and benefit from the belief that they were positioned to take advantage of an upcoming wave of digital convergence. While the dream of the earlier cycle of effects houses was to work only for feature effects blockbusters (again, like ILM), the newly digital sector's tenuous profit margins meant they felt pressure from investors, shareholders, and/or corporate masters to create alternative, more consistent revenue streams. Rhythm and Hues, the smallest of the top tier, emerged from an early pioneer of diversified media content. R&H was an offshoot of the legendary 1970s–80s ad production and effects company Robert Abel and Associates, formed from Abel personnel shortly after the founder sold the company in 1987.[35] R&H moved into digital effects out of TV ads, most prominently the digitally animated Coca-Cola polar bear ads that debuted in 1993. Through this association, Rhythm and Hues created a niche in CGI animal effects that it occupied for decades. Again, the top-tier companies—even ILM to a lesser degree—realized they could not exist on features alone. So once again, under the assumption that digital skills would cross over to other modes of production, they struggled to create revenue streams in other sectors such as TV ads and video games or branch out into the producer side, especially with feature animation.

While it was a stated goal to be a one-stop shop where any production could commission any kind of effects at any scale, the top tier's distinct histories and backgrounds allowed for differentiation and specialization. Put simply, we can characterize the effects houses' brand identities. ILM touted artisanal, handmade integrity and flawless magic from its "technical wizards."[36] Digital Domain promoted a forward-thinking, sleek futurism with military efficiency[37] and proclaimed itself the most digitally advanced of the effects houses. Weta publicized the wonder of its fantasy imagination, physical effects workshop, and outsider status in New Zealand.[38] The Weta brand was ILM circa 1977—the lean, hungry young creative upstarts rooted in physical effects traditions but with a fresher approach. Rhythm & Hues marketed itself as technologically savvy, but with a freewheeling, hippie-style eccentricity. R&H played up its sense of whimsy through its expertise in animal effects and the natural world, with strongly anthro- and zoomorphic characterizations.[39] Sony Pictures Imageworks, with the least specific image profile, is the most difficult to characterize. Sony PI did not have a Cameron or a Jackson as creative figurehead. What it did have above all else was its association with Sony. In other words, it boasted its well-funded ability to do anything.[40]

All these companies wanted to be ILM.

Sony PI emulated ILM in that it was backed by deep corporate pockets who saw the effects division as part of broader R&D interests. As of publication, Sony PI is still the only major effects company that was and is designed to be an in-house effects team for a major studio. Sony bankrolled Sony PI so that it could potentially inform other areas of the electronics giant's divisions. In that way, like ILM, it was under less financial pressure than the other freestanding, independently held companies such as Rhythm & Hues and its smaller rivals, who had to hustle for steady work. This heavy investment from the Sony company should have meant fairly quick competitive parity with ILM.

However, as both Sony PI and newcomer Digital Domain soon discovered, it was going to take more than money. Digital Domain cofounder James Cameron had worked with ILM on *The Abyss* and *Terminator 2* and no doubt saw the advantage of shaping an effects team based on his own interests and aesthetic, rather than borrowing Lucas's. Also, like Lucas, he wanted more intellectual property control over his creations, which applied to licensing and ancillary businesses. Rather than ILM's rather quaint and artisanal adherence to optical approaches (even as it increasingly digitized), Cameron's big promotional splash was to make ILM look outdated by plunging definitively into computer-generated effects. As Cameron put it, in a bit of sloganeering: "It will all be done at a workstation. Your film will now be in the digital domain."[41]

For financial partner IBM, like Sony, the advantage was that "IBM will also use the company as an R&D lab to develop software applications for other industries, ranging from medicine to construction, and even produce material for its long-rumored digital network,"[42] again following ILM, and in line with Sony PI. *Variety* described DD's financial arrangement:

> The deal gives IBM a 50 percent equity stake in Digital Domain, the remainder evenly split among Cameron, Ross, and Winston. The ownership of new products would be decided case by case, with IBM getting first look.[43]

With an optimism that surely would make its founders laugh today, *Variety* reported: "Though Big Blue [IBM] doesn't expect the new company to be profitable in the first year, a 'very good' rate of return is expected within three years."[44]

Although the *Wall Street Journal* proclaimed in 1994 that "Industrial Light . . . is still the industry leader by far,"[45] DD, in signature brash Cameron style, moved quickly and aggressively to take on ILM. The company's quick ascent inspired intense industry resentment. As one anonymous rival put it, "[DD] didn't work up from a small company paying dues, [but] stole everybody's talent."[46] Although its first priority would be effects work for major motion pictures, DD expected to eventually develop "properties for other mediums, ranging from interactive entertainment to videogames." Speaking the corporate language of convergence, Cameron said: "Once digital, films can be turned into a pay-per-view movie, vidgame or interactive story. We intend on entering the interactive visual markets."[47] Digital Domain in its early days had broad-reaching ambition for what it thought an effects house could do. However, these ambitious goals met with resistance from the corporate studios who wanted to keep expensive effects costs down and not share either profits or intellectual property, even in the face of Cameron's considerable clout.

Although geographically an outlier to the other 1990s houses based in California, Weta Digital was founded with many of the same goals as ILM and Digital Domain—that is, a workshop to support a filmmaker's projects, in this case the New Zealand director Peter Jackson. However, while its influence over the industry has been substantial, Weta has existed on a smaller scale than its California-based rivals. In this early stage, Weta was still working exclusively on Jackson projects such as *Heavenly Creatures*. Weta opened to outside (non-Jackson) projects only in 2004, bolstered by a controversial labor and tax rebate agreement with the New Zealand government that allowed it to keep its prices lower than its US-based competitors.[48] In this way, Weta played an important role in what would characterize the next period: the increasing competition for international tax incentives to lure personnel and international productions to far-flung parts of the world. In this earlier digital expansion period, while Weta was not yet as big as others in the top tier, it was making moves to become so.

The last of *Time* magazine's Big 5, Rhythm and Hues took a different trajectory. Although not founded by a powerful filmmaker or a large corporate entity, its roots, like ILM, were in hippie psychedelia and a strong self-image as creative rebels.[49] Several of its original personnel had been involved with the early wave of digital companies in the early 1980s, including the company Information International, Inc. (also known as Triple-I). However, R&H early on built a niche by focusing on animals and creatures, both photorealistic and more whimsically stylized. Founded in 1987, R&H's two big professional breakouts came in the mid-1990s: the aforementioned animated Coca-Cola polar bear ads (1993), and the talking farm animal feature film *Babe* (1995). Although not exclusively, its projects over the next twenty years strongly emphasized animals and digitally generated characters, including *Ace Ventura: Pet Detective* (1994), *Babe: Pig in the City* (1998), *How the Grinch Stole*

Christmas (2000), *Night at the Museum* (2006), *Alvin and the Chipmunks* (2007), and *Life of Pi* (2012). As the least capitalized and diversified of the top tier, Rhythm and Hues also frequently skirted the edge of bankruptcy, leveraging fortuitous sleeper successes such as *Babe* to keep it solvent.

The example of how Rhythm and Hues produced the effects for *Babe* in 1995 under the restrictions of the industry-standard project-bid model is a typical case of how most effects houses had to work in the digital age. It treated the hundred-plus computer-generated images it created for *Babe* (a very large amount for the time) as a loss leader.[50] R&H went into debt to win the bid and then complete the work, which cost far more than projected. After production on *Babe* ended, and even after having won an effects Oscar for its work on the film, R&H was forced to make deep layoffs and was in the red for at least another year.[51] It did not participate in any back-end profits for the film, so any benefit that accrued to the company was solely in the prestige it earned for R&H. Fortunately, that reputation was enough to keep it working and got it back to profit. However, it demonstrates the bid-low, eat-the-cost willingness of many companies that intensified in later years—and would eventually lead to R&H's downfall.

ILM, in large part, counted on this kind of precarity in its rivals' profit margins to stay dominant. As George Lucas put it around 1995:

> ILM is also a company where it has to make enough money to develop the state of the art. So everything has to be done extremely efficiently and they have to generate enough money year after year to be able to buy new equipment. It's a very capital intensive business so that means a huge amount of money is reinvested every year after year after year. And most companies can't do that. In most places someone wants to take money out of a company and put it someplace else or people can't develop enough resources to do that. It's like anything else—you build up an organization with capital and equipment and all that kind of thing to a high level so it can function.[52]

Similarly, in response to the newly launched Digital Domain and Sony Pictures Imageworks, Lucas professed not to be worried by the new competition: "This is not a high-profit business. And the studios are handicapped by their own bureaucratic structures and high costs. . . . The studios will lose interest."[53] ILM had reason to project confidence. As the *Los Angeles Times* put it in 1995 about ILM: "Staff number at 450 count. [It boasts] 180 high powered workstations—more than any other organization except NASA—ILM is by far the world's largest fx house, dwarfing [the others]."[54] The rise of serious rivals nevertheless impacted ILM's public rhetoric and business dealings. Acknowledging the difficult financials of the effects sector, George Lucas in 1991 confessed that ILM did not pay for itself. It is in this context that he admitted "it's not a business that anybody who was out to make money would get into."[55]

ILM began to lean in to luxury branding, promoting itself as "more expensive, but worth it." As Scott Ross (still at ILM at this time, before moving to DD) put it, you get what you pay for: "If ILM charges a premium price, it also provides premium quality."[56] Lucas continued that ILM's was not always the low bid, but it was always on time and on budget. "As we get underbid, we watch very carefully what happens on a picture, and rarely have they come in for under what we had originally bid."[57]

The great digital expansion of 1991–1995 established a field of digital effects companies with many ambitious goals for what a company could do, especially to help make more money for itself. They positioned themselves rhetorically as the most qualified to help lead the industry into the digital future. However, despite what appeared to be a boom time for blockbuster, effects-driven cinema, these new companies were already facing problems. It turned out they were not as well equipped or capitalized enough for the digital turn as they thought.

1996–2000: The First Downturn

To describe this era of digital effects a downturn may seem counterintuitive. After all, the late 1990s saw *Titanic* (1997), the most successful film ever at the time and very much driven by elaborate and impressive—and previously impossible—photoreal digital effects. Also, *Toy Story* (1995) made feature-length digital animation a focus for studios and, briefly, for effects companies. The era saw films made with increasing numbers of effects shots, such as *Independence Day* (1996) and *Twister* (1996). And the end of the period was capped by the hugely anticipated prequel *Star Wars: Episode I—The Phantom Menace* (1999) and surprise hit *The Matrix* (1999). However, the activity of this era demonstrates how and why production companies and studios eventually decided it was not worth it to own effects companies outright. The huge financial success of a few films masked problems the effects sector faced in an overall industry downturn as well as their own too-fast expansion that forced cuts and layoffs. And though the most popular movies were still amazing audiences with digitally generated effects, cheaper films (some completed by ILM) rushed through production started a wave of CGI fatigue and increased criticism of "bad" digital aesthetics, including for films like *Dante's Peak* (1997), *Anaconda* (1997), *Godzilla* (1998), and *The Mummy* (1999).[58] On top of that, effects companies with conglomerate owners or heavy outside investment faced pressure to make a profit. This goal was always difficult, especially in light of the studios' reluctance to pay more for either the "better" effects they demanded or investment in R&D. The effects companies responded with a new round of initiatives to increase revenue streams, for example by diversifying with ad divisions, attempts to get into video-gaming, and venturing into feature live-action and animation production.

While competition from well-funded rivals forced ILM to streamline and prioritize in the early 1990s, by the end of the decade it had reestablished its place at the top of the sector. It was able to do this in part because of strategic technological investments in the lead-up to the *Star Wars* prequels, beginning with *Episode I—The Phantom Menace* in 1999. But ILM actually did not have to do very much. ILM's rivals found staying afloat in the fast-changing digital era much more difficult than they expected, and corporate investors found the business much less attractive than imagined.

Significantly, during the late 1990s downturn, and perhaps at least partly causing the retraction, the studios began to rethink the in-house digital expansion strategy of the early 1990s. The high cost of the effects business proved stubbornly resistant to any business model that made significant profits. Corporate boards expected around a 10 percent return on investment, and instead effects divisions were achieving closer to 1 percent or even a negative return.[59] Warner executives were apparently "surprised" to learn "the operations won't see a profit any time soon."[60] And even companies who regarded effects wings as R&D, such as Sony and IBM's stake in DD, put pressure on effects companies: if they were not going to turn a profit, at least lose less money. Moreover, the other studios realized it would require investing more R&D dollars than expected to compete with ILM and upstart Digital Domain. It therefore became financially advantageous for studios to contract with independent companies—so long as the effects houses stayed weak and took all the financial risks. In this wave of closures, rumors swirled that Sony also planned to close down Sony PI.[61] However, a spate of new deals in

1998 quashed those rumors. Sony instead increased its investment in Sony PI and opened a state-of-the-art digital facility.[62] Soon, Sony PI was the only remaining conglomerate-owned effects house.

One might assume that Digital Domain in this period would be riding high, enjoying the success of *Titanic*, then the highest-grossing domestic box-office smash of all time. But DD faced financial turmoil. In fact, DD could be seen as the paradigm: a digital effects company working every angle possible to overcome the economic challenges yet barely scraping by. Surprisingly, DD's affiliation with Cameron did not mean it would automatically win bids to work on his films. A major difference from DD was that George Lucas owned ILM outright. Cameron was a partner in DD along with other partners. As *Variety* reported:

> Cameron owns one-third of the founders' share of 29.7 percent. Ross said Cameron receives no salary, no fee and no payments through DD on the "Titanic" job, or through any other work on any movie DD has done to date. . . . "The idea, of course," said Ross, "is for the profits to flow through to the shareholders. That hasn't happened so far." Cameron, as an owner, profits from any business that builds the value of his company.[63]

So, when Cameron needed effects for *Titanic*, DD had to put in a bid like anyone else. And once it won the job, Cameron, unlike Lucas at ILM, did not plow the profits from his films back into DD. This was a famously troubled shoot, and it was initially reported that DD lost money on *Titanic* due to reshoots and unexpected extra effects shots and had to contract out many shots.[64] Even before the film came out in December 1997, this shortfall forced DD to cut fifty-four staffers.[65] Prerelease buzz had predicted doom for *Titanic*, making the future seem grim for DD.

In light of the universal assumption that *Titanic* was going to fail, we can understand some of these public statements as PR to reassure investors that expensive effects were not going to contribute to the film's financial problems. In the end, due to *Titanic's* record-breaking box-office success and Oscar for Best Picture, Digital Domain ultimately looked better than feared. In the end, *Titanic* ended up as a mixed bag for DD: It did not secure a long-term future for DD; it simply confirmed the business model according to which effects houses would live and die. At the height of production, along with work on *Dante's Peak* and *The Fifth Element* (1997), DD employed more than a thousand.[66] After delivering the effects shots in the summer for *Titanic's* December release, DD had to let go the additional workers and lay off nearly a hundred regular employees.[67]

Despite the Oscar sheen of *Titanic*, the digital downturn ultimately meant loss of marquee name recognition at DD. In August 1998, Cameron and Stan Winston resigned from DD's board, ending their involvement with the company. What the *Hollywood Reporter* called the "latest evidence of growing dissatisfaction on both ends of the relationship,"[68] Cameron could not keep sufficient control over his effects work, and investors could not make sufficient profits. Despite the ominous departures, the trades reported that notoriety from *Titanic* should help DD rise above its recent business challenges. Recognizing industry-wide stagnation, DD's challenges were uniformly linked to too many shops chasing too few effects dollars, and it was "not a question of quality of [DD's] work."[69] Nevertheless, the exits of Cameron and Winston were hardly a show of confidence.

Like DD, Rhythm & Hues was also reorganizing because of and despite a single prominent success: *Babe*.[70] For R&H, while never making major profits, modest ongoing success allowed it to acquire rival VIFX from Fox in 1999, bringing its staff of 390 in line with other major effects companies and reinforcing R&H's position in the top tier.[71] The expansion also allowed it to diversify beyond its animal animation reputation into traditional effects territory for films such as *Anna and the King* (1999) and *The Green Mile* (1999).[72]

R&H's ambitions led it to spearhead a significant (albeit failed) revenue stream for the industry. Instead of contributing to the losing battle with studios and production entities to maintain intellectual property rights over digital characters, R&H would try to become a film producer, not just a vendor. That meant a push to develop its own slate of films. Therefore, it tried to parlay its experience into becoming a producer of live-action and full-length animation projects. The president of R&H's film division, Richard Hollander, was optimistic at the time:

> We're developing everything we can. Our goal is to produce and own the material. That's the direction for our motion picture, TV, games and Internet work. In my wildest dream, we'd be producing f/x only for our own films.[73]

R&H was not alone in this "wild dream." DD, along with the lower-tier effects houses Manex Visual Effects and Pacific Data Images, announced their own slate of pictures, and more would do so. However, none, according to *Variety*, "had yet to bring a project to fruition."[74]

Meanwhile, during this downturn, ILM had the enviable position of watching from above. As the *Hollywood Reporter* put it in 1997: "ILM is probably the only effects house that isn't desperate for work right now."[75] ILM was defying nearly every downward industry trend. It was staffing up for the *Star Wars* prequels to an unprecedented 950 regular staff members. Moreover, after predictions that ILM would finally feel pressure from rivals, it actually helped bail out other companies that got underwater on high-profile projects, including DD on *Titanic* as well as Sony PI on *Contact* (1997) and *Starship Troopers* (1997). By 2000, ILM remained the largest effects company (not including temporary staff), with a regular staff of about 1,000—a number other companies reached only during temporary ramp-ups.[76] When ILM announced its deal for the first *Harry Potter* movie (*Harry Potter and the Sorcerer's Stone* [2001]), *Variety* put it succinctly: "ILM is continuing its dominance of the SFX biz."[77]

At the beginning of the transition to digital effects, there was ILM and then everyone else. By the turn of the century, the top tier included four companies: ILM, Sony Pictures Imageworks, Digital Domain, and Rhythm & Hues. ILM held firm as the premier effects house, but by the end of this downturn a relatively stable set of players had been established.[78] Weta Digital, quiet on the other side of the world, would soon enough join the others to make up the Big Five. The next era would also add upstart competition from three firms based in the United Kingdom: The Moving Picture Company, Double Negative, and Framestore.

2001–2006: The Contradictory "Golden Age" of the Millennial Blockbuster

The superhero, science-fiction, and fantasy blockbuster boom of the 2000s has often been discussed as a post-9/11 retrenchment into distraction and escapism.[79] Indeed, they soothed audiences' anxieties in an unstable geopolitical era in which the individual seems more powerless than ever and tales of omnipotence, agency, heroism, and fellowship seemed uncommonly attractive. Whether or not this is true, blockbuster movies, in order to present these fantasy conflicts, required ever-more elaborate effects. As *Variety* reported, studios were greenlighting effects-driven films; unlike the late 1990s, there was plenty of work to go around for effects houses.[80]

While the superhero/sci-fi/fantasy blockbuster could be seen as a golden age for the geeks who loved them (not to mention studios' balance sheets), the era was double-edged for the effects sector. On one hand, the top-tier houses no longer needed to scrounge for work and were working to capacity, even expanding with offshore branches. Many medium-size and smaller companies were springing up around the world. This did not mean greater financial stability, however, as effects houses expanded at what would prove to be an unsustainable rate, and newer, more nimble houses undercut them in price.

Another factor impacting effects companies and international expansions was the so-called *Harry Potter* effect. This industry buzzword has been applied in other contexts (especially in the publishing business), but in this context the *Harry Potter* effect signaled the geographical shift in effects work to the United Kingdom, specifically the Soho district in London.[81] Yet this was merely the most visible marker of a cascading series of conditions that moved effects work definitively away from California to all corners of the globe, especially the United Kingdom, Canada, New Zealand, and Asia. While the *Harry Potter* effect is a catchy phrase, it is unlikely that J. K. Rowling's insistence on shooting the series in the United Kingdom with UK actors (despite selling the film rights to the American studio Warner Bros.) was the only factor that shaped the growth of UK-based effects production.[82] Instead, it was the United Kingdom's expansion of subsidies and tax incentives that suddenly made production there much more attractive to American studios.[83] According to the R&H executive Lee Berger: "The tax credit trend in London changed the game and started the [tax credit] trend [of the 2000s]."[84]

Chasing tax credits around the world became a hallmark of this era.[85] However, the United Kingdom was not the first or only one to offer incentives. Tax credits are part of general production incentives, whereby local and national governments attract film and media work through generous tax rebates for effects work—for example, a 17.5 percent rebate in Vancouver, 20–25 percent in the United Kingdom, and up to 43 percent in Montreal.[86] More so than any specific production or series of productions, tax rebates are what turned the United Kingdom into a major destination.[87]

In fact, it was not UK houses but rather the California-based ILM (with an assist from Rhythm & Hues) that became the lead effects companies for *Sorcerer's Stone*; initially, at least, UK effects companies did not participate. The UK effects company buildup began tentatively, with the second *Harry Potter* installment, *Harry Potter and the Chamber of Secrets* (2002), in which Framestore played a supporting role to ILM. ILM did not cede the franchise to the UK companies completely until the seventh film (of eight total) in the series, *Harry Potter and the Deathly Hallows: Part 1* (2010), although UK companies began to dominate by the fourth, *Harry Potter and the Goblet of Fire* (2005). Moreover, the Soho companies credit their collaboration with ILM over the course of the series with "raising their game" to the international level, as will be discussed in chapter 4.[88] The results would not fully flower until the 2010s, when UK companies began to pick up work after bankruptcies in Hollywood and the fruition of tax incentives. MPC and DNeg graduated from regional, lower-budget, lower-profile films such as *Pride and Prejudice* (2005) and *Slumdog Millionaire* (2008) and as a support house for the *Harry Potter* and James Bond franchises to playing a central role in the *Fast and Furious* and *Hunger Games* franchises, as well as US-based blockbusters such as *Godzilla* (2014), *Maleficent* (2014), and the Marvel superhero movies. Framestore's rise was even more precipitous, moving from largely UK TV work such as *The Thick of It* (beginning with season 3) and *Doctor Who* (starting with the season 5 Matt Smith Doctor in 2010) to being the lead house for *Gravity* (2013) and the biggest Marvel blockbusters and Hollywood franchises by the early 2010s.

The *Harry Potter* effect eventually led to the expansion of existing but smaller UK companies, including MPC, DNeg, and Framestore, into major competitors with the top tier. The same tax incentives that benefited the London houses eventually meant that several firms among the top tier, including ILM, opened their own London production facilities. To combat the rising costs of labor, the US-based top tier also began opening international offices in other subsidy-friendly countries such as Canada and Australia. They also opened branches in locations such as China, India, and Singapore to further lower labor costs. The need to compete with these international incentives pressured the New Zealand government to bend over backward to keep Peter Jackson's Tolkien productions in the country, showering Weta with even greater tax incentives and liberal labor policies for international effects workers.[89]

Meanwhile, at ILM, future prospects initially looked great. It was releasing the second of three *Star Wars* prequels, which were making huge returns, even as they divided fans and were panned by critics. Also, ILM had several high-profile tentpoles lined up for work, including *Van*

Helsing (2004), Disney's *Pirates of the Caribbean* (2003), Ang Lee's *Hulk* (2003), *Harry Potter and the Chamber of Secrets*, and *Terminator 3: Rise of the Machines* (2003).[90] However, in 2005 the trade press sensed vulnerability at ILM, in what the technology reporter David S. Cohen described as "an industry-wide trend away from big effects houses."[91] Among ILM's early-2000s projects, only the *Harry Potter* sequel and the first *Pirates of the Caribbean* film were well-received hits. Fans complained especially about the effects in the *Star Wars* prequels, disliking what they considered those films' foregrounded animated digital look in contrast to the analog aesthetic of the original trilogy.[92]

ILM was indeed at a crossroads at the end of the *Star Wars* prequels. In 2005, it had more than a thousand regular employees.[93] ILM issued press releases touting a move of its facilities into the city of San Francisco at the lavish Letterman Digital Arts Center at the Presidio (away from the long-standing home in Marin County, across the Golden Gate Bridge). Also, ILM and Lucasfilm were shifting into offshoring labor to lower-cost locations and diversifying into ads, video-gaming, and animation. The year 2004 saw the creation of Lucas Animation (US) and Lucas Animation Singapore.[94] All this was just the beginning of its overseas expansion.

ILM workers, however, received this news of expansion and offshoring less as an opportunity and more as a threat. In a portent of things to come, in 2004 ILM experienced labor actions, as union members demonstrated outside ILM's San Rafael headquarters regarding "management changes, the longer commute to the Presidio and job security" as well as the potential outsourcing of jobs from California to the new Lucas facility in Singapore."[95] *Variety*'s Cohen also noted that the ILM team was unhappy with the plan to "create synergies by moving its artists from visual effects to games to animation, as the workload demands, which many artists see as a demotion."[96] ILM workers were feeling threatened by globalization, a sign of things to come across the sector. And this was just one of the first signs that worker morale was eroding across the industry due to the evident forces of globalization.

Weta Digital and Weta Workshop in New Zealand, among the top tier, were uniquely positioned to take advantage of the turmoil. Certainly, the golden age of the fantasy epic is closely associated with Peter Jackson's *Lord of the Rings* franchise. As Weta cofounder Richard Taylor put it: "Without a doubt, *The Lord of the Rings* has had the greatest impact on the growth of the special effects business" in New Zealand, signaled by three consecutive Academy Awards for Visual Effects for all three *Lord of the Rings* (2001–2003) films.[97] Weta's work wowed international audiences with motion-captured CGI characters such as Gollum, who convincingly acted alongside live-action actors, as well as the impressive battle sequences generated by Massive, its crowd-simulating proprietary software, which rapidly became the industry benchmark.[98] Weta thus began to challenge ILM, not as the biggest or most prosperous house but as perhaps the most innovative and up-to-date. In other words, it marketed itself as a circa-1978 ILM: small, scrappy, creative, and innovative—and much cheaper. And the increased ability to share large files over networks meant that distances and time zones did not hamper Weta's relationship with clients.

One of the things that distinguished Weta was its emphasis on the Weta Workshop's physical (i.e., nondigital) effects work. Weta Workshop's five divisions—makeup and prosthetics, armor, weapons, creatures, and miniature environments—were promoted as differentiating Weta from other all-digital top-tier companies.[99] And according to the *Hollywood Reporter*, Weta was becoming "even more prominent because of the quality of its work and the fact that its price point is considerably lower than those of US counterparts."[100]

By 2006, Weta had grown from a smallish effects company in far-away New Zealand into, according to *Variety*, "one of the world's most successful visual effects shops, with more than 400 staffers."[101] While filesharing over long distances did not disadvantage Weta, labor issues certainly did. Rather than open overseas branches, Weta opted to bring workers to it, and most of the talent was imported from the United States. This meant that Weta has been entwined, often controversially, with the New Zealand government. Along with the tax incentives and subsidies, strings were pulled for Weta in other aspects. For example, facilities manager Suzanne Labrie claimed that Weta "has a great relationship with immigration authorities."[102] In fact, the New Zealand government has been so generous to Weta and Jackson that many New Zealand residents have protested that generosity.[103]

To the industry, Weta's gain was understood as ILM's loss, especially since Weta's formation was so closely based on the ILM model. By 2004, *Variety* began wondering why ILM was no longer dominating at the awards ceremonies. In 2004, it had been five years since ILM won the Oscar for visual effects. In fact, ILM had conspicuously been losing to Weta's *Lord of the Rings* films.[104] The financially successful but aesthetically criticized *Star Wars* prequels were cracks in ILM's invincible façade. ILM was still considerably larger than Weta, but Weta was starting to garner all of the glowing press and reputation for innovation.

Meanwhile, conditions had not improved for the other top-tier houses, which were even more desperate for revenue streams and cost savings. They were still searching for ways to diversify and chasing low-cost labor and tax subsidies. Rhythm & Hues held steady and even expanded during this time, setting up a shop in Kuala Lumpur to complement existing overseas facilities in Vancouver, Mumbai, and Hyderabad.[105]

Like Rhythm & Hues earlier, all the major houses attempted to expand into what they hoped would be the lucrative area of feature-length animation.[106] However, most of the other companies were equally unsuccessful. In 2002, it was enough of a trend for a lengthy *Variety* article titled "CG Shops Set to Tackle Toon Territory." Citing the box-office successes of Dreamworks' *Shrek* (2001) and Pixar's *Monsters, Inc.* (2001), *Variety* proclaimed that

> f/x facilities are readying to step in and tackle high-profile titles, looking not only to prove their abilities in the toon arena, but to expand their businesses beyond flashy visuals solely for live-action pics.[107]

However, the vast majority of animation projects by effects teams announced in this period never came to fruition, including Sony PI's *Astro Boy* (2009), ILM's *Curious George* (2006), and others.[108]

Following the departures of its founders, Digital Domain was also diversifying production. In 2001–2002, it added a motion graphics department (for ad work), partnered with the long-standing New York graphics company R/Greenberg to produce film title sequences, and attempted to get into software sales and licensing.[109] However, DD's industry shocker came in 2006 when director Michael Bay, along with former NFL star quarterback Dan Marino and others, bought DD for nearly $35 million.[110] The trades speculated that Bay was acquiring DD for use in his upcoming *Transformers* (2007) film.[111] As the *Hollywood Reporter* put it: "George Lucas has ILM, Peter Jackson Weta, and now Michael Bay has Digital Domain. DD has seen its business eclipsed during the past decade by Sony PI, Weta and Rhythm and Hues."[112] This move pushed out CEO (and last remaining original founder) Scott Ross, who turned his focus to advocating for improved labor conditions within the VFX business.[113]

Even in the so-called Golden Age of fantasy blockbusters in the early 2000s, we can see many of the intertwined issues that fueled the next era's crises. The offshoring of work, intense working conditions, narrow profit margins, digital effects technology's resistance to actual convergence, and attempts to be all things to all clients proved to create an unsustainable system for most houses. The industry press blamed much of this crisis—however unfairly—on ILM's dominance.

2007–2014: The Industry "On Fire"

In 2007, a period of upheaval for the effects industry, Tim Sarnoff of Digital Domain said: "[The industry's crises are] not yet an 'on-fire' problem. This is more like a grill getting hotter."[114] By that year, as many commentators remarked, the major studios and large production companies shifted priorities away from midbudget films (traditionally not overly reliant on effects) to effects-heavy blockbuster tentpole productions.[115] Also, the effects wizardry of the previous era had begun to seem less like amazing magic tricks and more like business as usual. The average number of effects shots on a tentpole product increased considerably. Again, most blockbusters feature 2,000–2,500 total shots. As visual effects supervisor and then–VES chair Jeff Okun put it:

> If you go back to 1997, a big show had 300–400 [effects] shots. The standard today [2007] for a show that has no visible visual effects shots is 400 [effects] shots. For a show with visible visual effects shots, it's 800–1,200. A visual effects extravaganza is 1,800–2,000.[116]

Production companies felt pressure to produce a large number of effects-intensive tentpoles per year while keeping effects costs down. This meant that, by around 2007, this brew of factors, combined with financially overextended effects houses and shorter delivery deadlines, finally produced a serious crisis—the effects industry "on fire." The long-standing top tier—ILM, Sony PI, R&H, DD, and Weta—were facing increased competition, especially from the emerging UK houses achieving similar size and impact, as well as smaller international boutique houses that undercut pricing and deadline conventions. While acknowledging these factors, the trades suggested ILM was at the center of the problem, setting unrealistic expectations for the rest of the industry through what was supposed to be the onetime expediated schedule for its work on the 2005 Steven Spielberg film *War of the Worlds*.

A much-discussed 2007 article in *Variety* pointedly labeled the increasingly untenable effects industry situation the "*War of the Worlds* effect":

> Two years ago, ILM delivered eye-popping visual effects for Paramount's "War of the Worlds" only three months after the end of principal photography. That set the bar impossibly high, so that producers now routinely demand "the 'War of the Worlds' schedule."[117]

ILM's unusually shortened *War of the Worlds* effects postproduction schedule was meant to be an exception, not a model for productions to come. As another article pointed out, the fast turnaround was due to careful planning on ILM's part.[118] Director Spielberg and effects supervisor Dennis Muren knew about the time crunch in advance and carefully planned and budgeted for it. But they could not plan for the production's broader negative impact: "One f/x pro says, 'people lost years off their lives working 24/7' on the pic."[119] That ILM pulled it off now meant producers knew it was a possibility, and shorter postproduction time lines theoretically meant less money spent on expensive effects.

This insistence on a *War of the Worlds*–type schedule caused tensions across several productions, including *Pirates of the Caribbean: At World's End* (2007). The film's visual effects supervisor, John Knoll, called it "a freakin' miracle" that the film was done on time.[120] As *Variety* succinctly put it:

> [*At World's End*] is just one tip of an iceberg that's sending a chill through the visual effects industry. Visual effects houses are worried about the increasing demand for more product, at higher quality, in less time. Some effects houses have been losing key workers, and a few are threatening to shutter, because of the shifting economics.[121]

And the fact that no major films missed their opening dates merely reinforced the feasibility of producers' demands.

While ILM's efficiency and bankroll caused trouble for other, less well-funded or staffed houses who struggled to keep up, the *War of the Worlds* production was clearly a scapegoat for larger problems in the industry, caused primarily by the production entities themselves. The studios' position was understandable. This high number of required effects shots also meant a great deal of risk for the production entity. What if the effects company was not going to make its deadline? What if the effects company went bankrupt midproduction (something that had in fact happened)? It became evident that no single top-tier house was equipped to handle the 2,000 effects shots for an entire film, even if all its resources were focused on a single production.[122] This meant more effects companies collaborating on a single movie. Warner executive Chris DeFaria described the logic behind the emerging practice of piecemealing, a new effects production paradigm in which the studio deliberately splits up the effects jobs among a network of effects houses: "Any company would be taxed to do [1,200–2000 shots]. We don't think it's good business to put that much work through a narrow pipeline."[123] Piecemealing had the added advantage of leveling the importance of any one company to the overall production.

This process of divide-and-conquer was abetted by the fact that the cost of digital effects had decreased to a level that did not require a large company; neither did the production require Hollywood-sized resources, making it easier for production entities to lowball effects companies. The more accessible cost of digital effects meant smaller boutique houses, willing to work cheap, were popping up, creating competition and undercutting per-shot prices for the top tier (reportedly to the tune of a 30–40 percent decrease).[124] Basic, uncomplicated effects work such as wire removal or simple compositing could be done by anyone anywhere with a very small crew using desktop computers and off-the-shelf software, whether in California, India, or Kosovo. Studios were able to pit larger companies against smaller companies to lower prices, making the already precarious labor situation for effects teams tilt even more to the production companies' benefit.

This time, however, the situation was to ILM's detriment. Over the next five years, it is fair to say, the industry was engulfed in a dangerous, spreading inferno of dysfunction. Increased demand for more and more effects shots combined with unrealistic expectations, through punishing work schedules and razor-thin profit margins, had other consequences as well. Rather than staff up in California, the houses accelerated outsourced work to lower-cost locations such as India, Malaysia, and Singapore so they could produce around the clock.[125]

Shortly after the 2007 *War of the Worlds* article appeared in *Variety*, debates over what to do about the problems of plummeting per-shot rates and labor instability raged among effects workers. The discussions that began with shortened post schedules were snowballing into various, interrelated beefs the effects workers had: overwork due to long hours at deadline crunch times; lack of union or guild protection, leading to unpaid overtime and lack of benefits; and a peripatetic lifestyle that had sought-after workers on the road from Los Angeles to Wellington to Vancouver to Chennai for months at a time as companies chased tax refunds, with less prominent workers constantly moving as companies folded and reformed in far-flung locations.[126] These difficult conditions meant that many workers were simply abandoning the field, leaving a gap in experience and clout. Smaller but previously robust companies such as Giant Killer Robots, The Orphanage, and many more from the lower tiers were exiting the business, leaving a gaping hole in the middle of the field.[127] "Exploitation" became a constantly repeated term, and workers began to feel that the field needed to organize in order to improve conditions.

While these problems had been percolating for some time on the lower end of the sector, now the top tier was feeling it as well. The very fact that ILM and Sony PI, two houses at the top of the field, felt the need to speak up on the issue in such a public forum as the *War of the Worlds* article in *Variety* underscores the frustrations felt throughout the effects industry. In fact, however, the top-tier companies could be seen to be exacerbating the problem. They had been rapidly expanding into lower-priced labor markets, by building new facilities and acquiring existing companies, and were replacing regular staff with short-term contracts. Sony PI, for example, acquired a branch in Chennai, to be renamed Imageworks India, in a plan to quadruple its workflow.[128]

Sony PI as Sony R&D had always had a different business model than other effects companies. However, by 2009, "one of the grimmest periods in memory for the post-production and visual effects business in Hollywood," as *Variety*'s Cohen put it, rumors swirled again that Sony might shrink or shut down Sony PI.[129] Sony PI denied this and began to position itself as reliable in the face of upstart competition in an unstable business.[130] Notably, in the tumultuous time that would follow, Sony PI, along with Weta, remained one of the only firms in the top tier to experience neither bankruptcy nor buyout[131] Sony PI did, however, move its main headquarters to tax-friendly Vancouver in 2014.[132]

Digital Domain had been limping along after the stunning takeover by Michael Bay and partners in 2006. That partnership did not last long, and Bay and his people were out by 2009.[133] DD was briefly resurgent in 2008–2009 with its high-profile and Oscar-winning work for *The Cu-*

rious Case of Benjamin Button (2008), which prompted an expansion to Vancouver, India, China, and London. However, in the end it was not enough to keep DD solvent.[134]

In September 2012, twenty-year industry stalwart Digital Domain— long considered the industry's second most powerful effects company— declared bankruptcy, signaling that the industry wildfire had reached crisis stage. Initially, DD looked like it might be able to regroup and reorganize quickly. However, problems were deeper than expected. As was normal, DD had gone into debt to finish a few prominent projects, in this case *Ender's Game* (2013) (which DD was doing at cost for an equity stake in the film) and *Jack the Giant Slayer* (for which DD had to absorb costs for new software and last-minute changes from the production), and then make it up with the next prominent project. The double-whammy had instead entirely capsized the company.[135] News emerged that DD's employees had not been paid for many outstanding jobs.[136]

After a few tortuous months of near-misses with finding a new buyer, in an ironic turnabout, DD was bought out of bankruptcy by the Chinese company Beijing Galloping Horse and the India-based Reliance Media-Works.[137] *Variety* uncharitably (and perhaps jingoistically) described the buyer as a "Hong Kong scrap-trading company" in a mysterious and complex deal, leaving DD "well-funded" and still modestly in operation, but its future in Los Angeles was unclear.[138] By 2014, the situation had improved somewhat; DD delivered effects for *Maleficent* and *X-Men: Days of Future Past* that year. *Variety* declared that, as of September 2014, it remained on the "sick list" but was still in business.[139] In fact, since 2014, DD has mounted a tentative reemergence into prominence, mostly with a specialty in digital doubles for movies such as *Deadpool* and *X-Men: Apocalypse* (both 2017).[140]

However, the wildfire continued to spread. In 2013, Rhythm & Hues followed Digital Domain into bankruptcy. While the reasons for DD's bankruptcy had seemed difficult to attribute to industry analysis, R&H's problems had been clear to many for some time. Since 2008, R&H aggressively expanded, opening five international outposts over the course of a few years.[141] In fact, it was "credited" with "pioneering" effects offshoring in the early 2000s, and by 2012, 80 percent of its work was no longer completed in California.[142]

Finally, in February 2013, just before it won the Oscar for VFX on *Life of Pi* (2012), Rhythm & Hues also entered bankruptcy, alongside smaller companies such as US-based Asylum VFX, The Orphanage, CafeFX, and ImageMovers Digital.[143] Other prominent companies, such as Northern California's Tippett Studio and London-based The Mill, severely downsized operations and laid off workers.[144] Eric Roth, executive director of the Visual Effects Society, said he hoped this would alert the entire industry to the crisis: "From all accounts R&H was a company that appeared, from the outside, to be well run, to take care of its employees, to take advantage of worldwide tax incentives and have locations in other countries."[145] R&H, like DD, found itself out of cash due to a few problematic productions, in this case *Snow White and the Huntsman* (2012), for which Universal canceled its contract when production was already under way. Other productions, such as *The Hunger Games: Catching Fire* (2013), pulled their work from R&H.[146] Cohen at *Variety* pulled together the various factors making R&H an emblem of the untenable effects business:

> Because [R&H's] revenues and profits are so unpredictable, visual effects studios like R&H generally lack access to short-term bank financing that lets other kinds of similar-sized business smooth over bumps in cash flow. . . . But the bigger problem for R&H has been its reliance on just a few clients. Some 80 percent of its feature vfx business came from Fox and Universal, so it became very vulnerable to changes in their slates and schedules. Then they sneezed—and Rhythm & Hues got galloping pneumonia.[147]

R&H was not mismanaged or the victim of financial manipulation. It played the game under impossible rules while, by all accounts, providing an ethical and equitable workplace. For this reason, the R&H bankruptcy was more of a wakeup call compared to DD's downfall. As Eric Roth put it:

> If a company like [R&H] can't survive in today's marketplace, is this the moment in time when the industry at large takes notice and says maybe we need to take a fresh look at how we do business?[148]

R&H was bought at auction by the US- and India-based animation company Prana in March 2013.[149] Unlike DD, R&H would not recover from bankruptcy. In 2013, Prana sold R&H's El Segundo campus, and the Malaysian branch was spun off into Tau Films, a company that largely does effects work and animation for East Asian productions, especially in mainland China.[150]

Since the 1970s, while other companies struggled to stay afloat or when the broader industry was in turmoil, ILM stood above the fray. However, ILM underwent its own organizational drama, one that potentially has the widest-reaching consequences for the effects business. ILM began the 2007–2014 period with industry dominance, leading or contributing to four summer 2007 franchises: *Pirates of the Caribbean: At World's End, Evan Almighty, Transformers,* and *Harry Potter and the Order of the Phoenix.*[151] ILM also won its first effects Oscar in years for the second *Pirates of the Caribbean* film. Also, like the other companies, ILM had opened offshore facilities in Singapore and London and was expanding into partnerships in Beijing.[152]

ILM's independence and financial stability came to an end in 2012, when the effects business was dealt the biggest shocker of all. George Lucas sold his Lucasfilm holdings, including ILM, to The Walt Disney Company. The entertainment conglomeration already had substantial holdings in related entertainment properties including Marvel Entertainment, Pixar, Miramax, and ABC Television Group.[153] Without Lucas's sentimental attachment to ILM and in the context of an industry on fire, many speculated that Disney would sell off ILM rather than continue the Lucas-style patronage it had enjoyed for decades.[154] Rumor had it, at least initially, that ILM was the least attractive component of the sale for Disney.[155]

However, in the short term, the sale's impact on ILM appeared to be negligible. With upcoming new installments in the *Star Wars* series quickly announced and continuing into several projected feature films and related ancillary projects, ILM could expect to be well funded for the foreseeable future. And since the sale, ILM has been busy with signature properties, having led effects production on *Transformers: Age of Extinction* (2014) and *Jurassic World* (2018) and its sequel, most of the Marvel superhero movies, and all the *Star Wars* sequels and spinoffs. One thing is clear: ILM is not the in-house effects team for Disney productions. For example, it did not do the effects for other high-profile Disney releases such as the live-action adaptations *Cinderella* (2015), *Beauty and the Beast* (2017), and *The Lion King* (2019).

Adding to the top tier's woes, international tax credits and offshoring had decimated the California-based effects presence. By the end of 2015, ILM remained mostly in California, with outposts in London and Singapore. Digital Domain also remained in California, but in a greatly diminished capacity. Sony Pictures Imageworks moved its main headquarters to Vancouver, and Rhythm & Hues was gone. And despite efforts toward so-called global town halls linking effects workers in Los Angeles, Vancouver, Wellington, and other locales, the dispersal from California across international borders meant the collapse of the labor-organizing initiatives in the wake of the DD and R&H bankruptcies. And labor remained an intractable problem within the industry. R&H executive Lee Berger estimated that "90 percent of the cost in the VFX industry is labor, which means there are few ways to reduce costs in other areas."[156] And the effects industry did not enjoy the same kind of creative clout, assisted by agents, guilds, and unions, to combat the conglomerate forces that kept them all weak.

The industry did in fact stabilize between 2015 and 2018. However, the studios' change in strategy—led by Disney's Marvel Studios—that helped put out the fire did not result in conditions that could be considered more equitable or profitable for effects companies. The Marvel Studios superhero franchise required 2,000-plus effects shots per film, with an unprecedented release rate of roughly three films per year. Marvel Studios intensified piecemealing, employing twenty to thirty effects companies at a time, and made it standard practice. This strategy helps keep the sector fully employed while making sure producers pay a minimum. This massive control over the entire effects sector meant that, by 2018, the effects industry's fires were more or less out. It also meant that the effects industry, ILM included, was reliant on business from Marvel Studios. ILM did indeed lead the effects teams at the beginning of the MCU with *Iron Man* in 2008 and has continued to be involved in nearly every MCU film since. However, I will establish in chapter 5 that a byproduct of Disney's manipulation of the effects business through its Marvel Studios properties was a downgrading of ILM's dominance. Put simply, within the Marvel Studios paradigm ILM is merely one effects company among many. The industry's flattening under Disney and Marvel has led to greater stability in the effects sector—but also to a disheartening aesthetic sameness as effects companies lost the incentive to push R&D in attempting to outdo rivals.

Established out of a 1970s economy of genius and grown out of the artists' labors of love, ILM is now a subsidiary of the largest entertainment conglomerate in the world. Disney's acquisition of ILM is where the forces of conglomeration come in conflict with the economy of genius. If the effects business is indeed an oxymoron, what value does corporate giant Disney find in ILM? In fact, rather than sell off ILM, as many expected, Disney has mined its new acquisition for parts. In line with Disney's business practices, it appears to have come to the realization that ILM's value was not in its direct profitmaking ability but as a perceived (i.e., nonliteral) patent on realist aesthetics. But what exactly is the value of the ILM aesthetic? Chapter 2 will demonstrate how ILM's value derives from its specific ILM aesthetic. Honed over decades and reinforced by economic dominance, technological ingenuity, and the rhetorical power of its public relations, the ILM aesthetic is able to masquerade as simple, unexamined realism. That is what makes ILM valuable to Disney. In other words, through ILM, hyperbolically one could say that Disney owns cinematic realism. Chapter 2 will describe the derivation of the ILM aesthetic, its specific aesthetic building blocks, and the rhetorical value that style has accrued as transparent reality.

Perfect Imperfection

TWO

ILM's Effects Aesthetics

WHAT COUNTS IS HOW THE MOVIE LOOKS, NOT NECESSARILY THE PERFECTION OF THE TECHNIQUE.

—ILM EFFECTS SUPERVISOR DENNIS MUREN

When The Walt Disney Company bought Lucasfilm for just more than $4 billion in 2012, it understood that Lucasfilm's primary value was its *Star Wars*–derived intellectual property rather than the accumulated value of its parts, which included Industrial Light & Magic.[1] Despite its dominance, ILM's value to Disney did not derive from its economic impact on the effects sector over its decades of operations. And ILM's value was not in the literal form of copyrights, meaning intellectual property rights secured through legal means. Instead, its value derives from a less tangible but identifiable industry perception that its realist aesthetic had accrued since the late 1970s. The fact that the ILM realist aesthetic is a naturalized set of formal strategies and not officially copyrightable was the very currency that allowed its aesthetic to be open-sourced—that is, disseminated globally without legal barriers to become the industry standard. (Put simply, no one can copyright something as intangible as an aesthetic.)

One might assume the ILM aesthetic would have changed a great

59

deal since being developed for the initial *Star Wars* films, given the great changes in imaging technology since the 1970s. However, the ILM aesthetic has remained remarkably consistent over the years, despite the industry's wholesale shift to digital technology. The original *Star Wars* trilogy, *Close Encounters*, and a few other films of the era such as *Indiana Jones and the Raiders of the Lost Ark* (1981) are often said, especially by directors of digital blockbusters such as J. J. Abrams and Jon Favreau (as well as some critics), to comply with or "hold up" against contemporary standards of cinematic realism. This is in contrast to other films of the same era such as *Logan's Run* (1976), *Clash of the Titans* (1981), and *Dune* (1984), which are judged not to hold up as well.[2] I contend that what this seemingly subjective judgment affirms is not that *Star Wars* and its peer films especially conformed to "reality" or that the films represent a progressive "step forward" for effects realism, as is usually asserted. Rather, it indicates the extent to which the effects aesthetics developed for the *Star Wars* franchise continue to dominate the aesthetics of digital cinematic production. In other words, these films' effects, produced by ILM artists, hold up to contemporary standards because they set the standards in the late 1970s and early 1980s and continue to do so today. They were deemed the best then, as they are today.

Most viewers are so habituated to ILM's naturalistic aesthetic that they do not even recognize it as a specific, historically contingent style. Specifically, the ILM style comprises techniques derived from 1970s cinematography that enhance and exaggerate marks of the act of filming. The ILM aesthetic influence extends well beyond the science fiction and fantasy blockbusters for which it is best known. ILM's patterns and codes are so deeply embedded in contemporary filmmaking that even films not produced by ILM, and those not associated with heavy effects work (such as comedies, historical dramas, and thrillers), use its codes as associative reference points. If, as asserted in chapter 1, ILM's most valuable intellectual property is the ability to set an unquestioned "natural" style of cinematic realism, then unmasking and describing the ILM aesthetic as a style also drains it of the power to stand in as naturalized perceptual realism. As soon as one begins to see it as a style, it is hard to unsee it. (In other chapters I will discuss alternatives to and adaptations of the ILM aesthetic.)

Where does this commonsense notion of "what looks real" come from? When we viewers watch films such as *Star Wars: The Force Awakens* (2015), *Mad Max: Fury Road* (2015), and *Avengers: Endgame* (2019) (considered on the positive side) or *X-Men Origins: Wolverine* (2009), *Warcraft* (2016), and *Cats* (2019) (considered more negatively), how can we state with confidence whether the effects were good or not? A common notion of realism in effects, even in the rhetoric of effects artists, involves an appeal-to-the-eye test—the sense that the eye just knows when it looks right. This notion of optical reliability as an aesthetic has been underexamined. Stephen Prince influentially suggested that effects realism should be characterized as *perceptual realism*, a transhistorical aesthetic that replicates what the eye sees "in real life" and, moreover, "improves" to be more perfect to the eye as technology advances.[3] As stated in the introduction, these kinds of theories prove the extent to which ILM artists have persuaded viewers into believing their house style *is* perceptual realism.

This chapter asks: How do recent effects-driven films, led by ILM, convey this sense of transparent realism? What makes this specific style so convincing? I'm referring to the recent installments of blockbuster franchises including *Star Wars* (2015, 2017, 2019), *Star Trek* (2009, 2013, 2016), *Transformers* (2007, 2009, 2011, 2014, 2017, 2018), and *Iron Man* (2008, 2010, 2013), plus many, many other films. I contend that ILM's 1970s and 1980s style of cinematographic realism for digital effects aesthetics has economically exploitable value because it heightens the film's truth value—its status as believable reality—especially at moments within the film when meanings are unstable or reality is in question. In other words, the style is most effective when a film needs the viewers to believe what they are seeing, whether that be in an imaginary effects object such as the Death Star or a rhetorically important historical conjecture such as the fictional character Forrest Gump meeting President John F. Kennedy. Finally, I contend that non-effects-heavy films frequently make use of the ILM aesthetic as discourse to render authenticity and grounded reality to their subject matter's interpretation, on one hand, or to spectacularize moments of intensity or fantasy within a realist setting on the other.

One of the reasons that the commonsense notion of what-the-eye-sees realism is so prevalent in academic and popular discourse is due to the often misleading nature—or selective misreading—of practitioner discourse. Artist statements frequently appear to be giving credence to a notion of a perceptual, biologically based model for realism.[4] For example, the matte painter on *The Empire Strikes Back* (1980), Harrison Ellenshaw, states this about effects compositing:

All that matters is if the audience will believe it on the screen. The fact is that people who know nothing about how these things are done can still tell us whether the effect is good or bad. . . . We say, "What do they know?" But they *know*. They've used their eyes all their lives and they know when something doesn't look exactly right.[5]

It seems that Ellenshaw is repeating the same commonsense notion that the audience believes (or not) that an effect in the movie looks real because "they've been using their eyes all their lives." In other words, what looks "real" is validated through biologically determined cues. However, the phrase "on the screen" substantiates that he is talking about using their eyes at the movies. In fact, thinking about effects *as* cinematic aesthetics has been so baked in to ILM's working method since the 1980s that, in statements about the effects "looking right," the qualifier "in the movies" almost goes without saying. Nevertheless, ILM artists in their statements from the analog 1970s to the digital 2010s nearly always reaffirm in some way that they are talking about realism as it appears on movie screens, as opposed to the eye's experience of real-life phenomena.

In the digital age, effects artists make similarly confusing statements about their priorities. In the digital arts, practitioners' rhetoric frequently utilizes scientistic language to highlight the use of computer algorithms to replicate a notion of physical or biological descriptions such as the weight of the body in space, the blood beneath the skin, the texture and movement of hair, or a gleam in the eye.[6] However, what they rarely emphasize, because it is so obvious (to them, at least), is that the gleam in the eye they are replicating is one meant to match cinematographic practices, such as the eye light, which is much more pronounced on the movie screen than in most real-life conditions. Therefore, the artists' reference is in fact the highly artificial cinematic lighting configuration into which the object is being placed.

ILM and other effects artists creating CGI creatures and characters consistently make statements alluding to "anatomy" or "gravity" and other biological or physics-based models for realism. However, even statements that seem to reinforce this we're-just-looking-to-real-life approach return to how artists prioritize the codes and patterns of cinematic realism that disregard or deform experiential reality. For an example of this discursive slippage, we can look to *Cinefex*'s account of the effects production for Ang Lee's 2003 *Hulk* (figure 2.01), a project

Fig. 2.01 *Hulk* (2003): Here, the Hulk's intense greenness makes him look flat against his surroundings. The production experienced a conflict between director Ang Lee's desire to reconcile the CGI Hulk with his comic-book look and ILM's standards for photorealism.

headed by Dennis Muren, visual effects supervisor and primary architect of the ILM aesthetic since the 1970s. At the time, the film challenged its effects team with an unusually high number of complex shots of its acting, fully CGI main character[7]. Discussing building the CGI Hulk, ILM animator and creature supervisor Paul Giacoppo stated:

> Before we rendered Hulk, we'd have "anatomy dailies" on every shot . . . [we] would review muscle performance. . . . We all became students of anatomy and became very astute as [to] how muscles fire, how they relax, and in what order they fire. Based on that knowledge, we artistically sculpted every frame, working with muscle sculptures to get every shot right.[8]

Notice how Giacoppo moves deftly from a discussion of anatomy to one of film form. Certainly, the ILM artists understand that the CGI Hulk character must conform generally to expectations of how human muscles really work. However, as the last sentence suggests, what matters is not that Hulk reads as (super) human but that he reads as an *actor in a movie*. None of the copious research and detail is any good if the Hulk does not read as similarly dense, heavy, and agile as the human actors surrounding him, and that means how they appear when photographed. In line with other ILM artists, *Hulk* compositing supervisor Marshall Krasser insists: "If an image is completely sharp, it screams 'computer graphics.'" To address this, Krasser reports:

[ILM visual effects supervisor Dennis Muren] told us, "Hide the edges." If you look closely at any character in live photography, you'll notice that the outline against a background is really quite indistinct; so we purposefully used our smoke elements to break up Hulk's edges.[9]

In other words, digital muscular armature and gravity algorithms are the initial steps among many in a complex system of making Hulk appear to be a real character with the same visual status as his live-action costars, rather than a patently animated figure.

Attention to how actors' edges appear in photography points to the effects team's other goals to enhance a realist effect in a cinematic context—counterintuitively, through concealing rather than displaying. A few paragraphs later in the same *Cinefex* article, the account of building CGI Hulk goes into great detail about the problem of blending CGI Hulk with his cinematic mise-en-scène, especially in dealing with what Muren called the "neon sign" effect of having a large, cartoonish green CGI object to totally arrest the eye within the cinematic frame.[10] As effects artists have long known, the more and the longer the eye fixes on an effects object, the more chances the viewers have to think about how a Hulk—no matter how accurately rendered—is an impossible, artificially generated object. To avoid this diegetic (rather than aesthetic) break in seamlessness, effects artists use visual distraction of various kinds, including obscuring lighting strategies (backlighting, silhouetting, light flashes, extreme top lighting), the replication of camera artifacts such as flares, and what effects artists call "atmospherics": elements such as the aforementioned smoke as well as rain, snow, fog, and particulates in the environment that catch the light. These elements, which masquerade as naturalistic environmental features (why wouldn't the lighting in an underground lab be patchy?), keep the eye moving so that the viewer does not scrutinize the effect for too long. It also makes viewers believe they are seeing more than they actually are. Although easier to accomplish digitally, atmospherics are replications of previous ILM effects practice, such as fogging the room so that light patterns were more evident (as Dennis Muren did for *Close Encounters of the Third Kind* and *E.T. the Extra-Terrestrial* [1982]), flashing the frame in time with laser blasts in the original *Star Wars* trilogy, or degrading the image to get a snowy atmosphere in the miniature sequences on the ice planet Hoth in *Empire Strikes Back*.[11]

While making Hulk's skin less aggressively green was part of the strategy, several common obscuring strategies to distract the eye were employed to tamp down the character's extra-greenness within the mise-en-scène and along with it that potentially disruptive train of thought. Visual effects art director Wilson Tang described one such strategy to help Hulk merge with his surroundings:

> The trick to placing Hulk into a scene was to give his basic green color a complexity. . . . For example, we painted dirt maps to make it look like sand was sticking to his body, which gave his skin a brownish tint. Anything we could do to add complexity really helped.[12]

Moreover, for most of *Hulk*, the CGI figure appears at nighttime, in a dimly lit lab, or, conversely, in a desert setting with especially hard overhead lighting as well as backlighting against the sun. Effects artists frequently describe consulting with the director of photography (as was the case with *Hulk*) to simulate the lenses used in physical photography, devising mechanisms for capturing on-set data on actor and character movement, and also going to great lengths to simulate the on-set lighting configurations during postproduction.[13]

Negative audience response to Lee's CGI Hulk creature suggests that the ILM team was not as successful as it had hoped to be in merging the very green Hulk with his earthly and mundane environments.[14] It is easy to assume that the problem was that digital technology had not yet caught up with its ambitions. However, it may also have been a conflict between the director's goals and the ILM team's goals. Corresponding to other aesthetic strategies in the film, such as the panel-like split screens, Lee seems to have wanted to render the Hulk in a more graphic, comic book–appropriate way. As makeup artist Kevin Yagher reported: "Ang wanted [the Hulk character] as bright as possible. Full of life and really bright."[15] But Muren and team, as the quotes from the *Cinefex* article suggests, worked to adhere to their professional assumptions around achieving seamless photorealism.[16]

Through detailed accounts of many films, including *Hulk* in *Cinefex*, it becomes obvious that deploying technology to record data corresponding to perceptual realism is only the barest of starting points in striving for the desired ILM style of effects realism. While "photorealism" comes close to describing ILM's aesthetic, it is evident that "straight" filming (or what is often called "camera reality") is not the primary model either. The 1970s architects of the ILM style, most prominently special effects supervisors Dennis Muren and Richard Edlund, believed that to achieve the style of realism they were working for would mean undermining and even defying the camera reality in live-action shooting, often by exaggerating certain elements of it. Instead, the ILM style begins with physical data (references to live humans and creatures, on-set lighting references) and camera reality (the aesthetic qualities of lenses and lighting artifacts) but then manipulates and stylizes that material to build in texture, camouflage, kineticism, and, most important, flaws.

In *Hulk*, we can see artists working under commonly held but largely unspoken aesthetic assumptions to get the results they are working toward.[17] But where did these assumptions at ILM come from? Typically, practitioners are happy to discuss the more easily accessible and understandable aspects of their aesthetic priorities: seamless compositing, naturalistic character movement, and appropriate, recognizable forms found in nature.[18] What ILM artists tend to talk about less often is wanting the marks of live-action cinematography "as if shot by a human camera operator." ILM's initial task for *Star Wars* was a special effects look that conformed to the live-action cinematography favored by director and producer George Lucas's 1970s New Hollywood peer group, including Martin Scorsese, Steven Spielberg, and Francis Ford Coppola, within a cinematographic aesthetic established in the late 1960s and early 1970s. As I have contended more thoroughly elsewhere, the effects teams of the original *Star Wars* trilogy were charged with matching their effects work with the New Hollywood style of live-action photography.[19] Counterintuitively, after trial and error, the effects artists noticed that the style appeared more naturalistic when it did *not* conceal the act of filming but instead called attention to it. In other words, the action in the completed effects sequence should look as if it could have been filmed on location by an actual, live-action camera, with evident camera operator "mistakes" such as camera wobble, incorrect focus, and awkward framing included. Unlike perceptual realism, the effects style should accentuate the look of caught-on-the-fly environmental effects as only camera lenses and filters perceive them, including how lens flares spread across the frame, as well as how light hits fog, mist, dust, and snow in ways that tend to guide the eye toward the layered planes of the visual field. Moreover, the sequence should be edited so that the effects sequence builds up in short bursts, in a way that creates a dynamic, fast-paced mosaic of the action. Even though New Hollywood cinematographic style had lost its broader cinematic currency by the

Fig. 2.02 *Jurassic Park* (1993): Laura Dern's and Sam Neill's speechlessness at first seeing a dinosaur models astonishment for the audience at seeing a CGI dinosaur.

mid-1980s, aspects of it held on through the digital transition as a reference style at ILM in large part because the unpolished, rough look was effective in suggesting immediacy, authenticity, and empathy, especially in artificial digitally generated elements.

Again counterintuitively, a central tenet of the ILM style is that of displaying technological spectacle. To be perfectly seamlessly realistic and pass by unnoticed as perfect illusion would not be enough to establish ILM as a distinct brand. Whether in science fiction or fantasy films such as *Star Wars* or *Harry Potter*, or naturalistic "real world" films such as *Forrest Gump* and *Pearl Harbor* (2001), the job of ILM's effects work was also to show off as the effects industry's and Hollywood's state-of-the-art firm, demonstrating spectacularly what movies can do now—from the *Star Wars* opening flyovers to *Jurassic Park*'s dinosaurs to the kaiju of *Pacific Rim* (2013).[20] The introduction of dinosaurs in *Jurassic Park* (figure 2.02) will serve an almost clichéd ILM "display of technology" sequence.[21] As park owner John Hammond (Richard Attenborough) takes Grant, Sadler, and Malcolm (Sam Neill, Laura Dern, and Jeff Goldblum) to see the brachiosaur—the film's first display of a digital dinosaur—the diegetic characters extravagantly model wonderment for the audience. As their jeep pulls up, the camera tracks in on Doctor Grant's bewildered face. The camera tracks his expression as he fixes his gaze in the distance, removes his hat, and stands as he agitatedly removes his sunglasses. The shot then cuts to Doctor Sadler, who is not looking in the same direction as Grant but is engrossed with a prehistoric leaf. Grant then physically grabs Sadler's head and turns it toward the dinosaur, upon which she intensifies Grant's astonishment. Her mouth drops open, her eyes grow wide, and she likewise removes her sunglasses and stands to gape at the still-unseen dinosaur. Now sufficiently primed, the audience can now also gape at the technological wonderment of a fully digital photoreal dinosaur, as the camera tilts up to reveal it from hindquarters to head. Grant then blurts redundantly with childlike awe: "It's a dinosaur!" The viewers, like the characters, are invited to be amazed at what our skeptical eyes are beholding.

These elements add up to an ILM aesthetic as a complex illusion: a mix of obvious and subtle, of revealed and concealed, of smooth and rough—in sum, the perfect amount of imperfection. Through its dominance of the effects industry across several vectors, the ILM aesthetic has become the industry default, and effects that deviate too far from that style tend to be received as "bad" by audiences.

The Historical ILM Aesthetic

One of the primary reasons the historical ILM style persisted through the digital era is due to the perceived greater integrity of the "analog" photographic image during the 1970s. What elements did Muren, Edlund, and other ILM artists choose to emulate? First, the cinematographic style they homed in on is a materialist docurealism of the sort associated with Hollywood auteurs such as Hal Ashby (*Harold and Maude* [1971]), Bob Rafelson (*Five Easy Pieces* [1970]), Robert Altman (*Nashville* [1975]), Terrence Malick (*Badlands* [1973]), and Monte Hellman (*Cockfighter* [1974]), which was then popularized by Lucas, Coppola, and Spielberg in hugely popular blockbusters during the mid-1970s. While the 1970s style of *The Godfather* (1972) and *Jaws* remained on the level of live-action cinematography, the nascent ILM team on *Star Wars* went further, simulating that style in wholly artificial special effects environments. The particular contours of the 1970s ILM aesthetic are desirable not only because they convey a general sense of naturalism and realism. ILM's digital effects aesthetics allude to a specific period—the look of certain aspects of 1970s cinematography—before the widespread presence of digital technology. They also generate a rhetoric about naturalism and realism that is as much based on emotional nostalgia for the cinema of the 1970s and 1980s as on any transhistorical notion of what the eye sees in real life. Similar to how what is heuristically referred to as "classical Hollywood cinema" became naturalized around the world, constant repetition has conditioned us to accept this specific historical aesthetic as perceptual realism.

What has changed for ILM's historical aesthetic in the later digital era is a conflict between the professional pressure to be "on brand" by parading its technological superiority versus the economic pressure to achieve unobtrusive transparent realism. As the *Star Wars* prequels (1999–2005) and the production of *Hulk* appear to have proven to ILM, audiences do not appreciate the flaunting of the animated digitalness in CGI effects.[22] In response, the director Jon Favreau evokes the original *Star Wars* trilogy and says of his approach to the effects in 2008's *Iron Man* (led by ILM): "I constantly asked myself, 'what would it really be like to photograph this if it was a real event?' . . . [I wanted the] effect of making you feel as if you were witnessing something real, rather than CG." As we saw in the discussion about *Hulk*, Favreau is tapping into the notion that 1970s-style realism is the obvious approach for overcoming the perceived blatant artificiality—what effects artists call the "digital curse"—of digitally generated effects.[23] ILM digital artists (led by Muren) subsequently determined that the best way to "de-digitalize" the look of digital effects was to take a hard turn back to ILM's 1970s origins.

In 1975, in order to simulate a moving camera during composited aerial dogfights and other sequences for *Star Wars*, the nascent ILM team began using computerized motion control, a device that moved a physical effects camera on a computer-controlled and perfectly repeatable track.[24] While ILM adopted this technology in order to realize shots simulating aerial combat, exploitation and refinement of this new technology during the first three *Star Wars* films instigated other aesthetic choices that allowed diverse kinds of effects footage to look more like live-action cinematography. However, what the artists initially gained in increased potential for kineticism and efficiency meant the computer-programmed tracks created a camera movement that was, to the artists' eye, unnaturally clean and smooth. Richard Edlund discussed how ILM "improved" the look of computerized motion control on *The Empire Strikes Back* by adding a joystick mechanism:

> Our basic philosophy of miniature preprogrammed photography [motion control] is based on the concept that in real photographic situations, especially in battle circumstances, your camera movements are bound to have a certain amount of

random motion. Therefore in order to duplicate the feeling of what you're seeing is being photographed on-the-spot by a human and not by a machine, we program most of our camera moves manually with a joystick device. If you were to have an absolutely perfect move, it would have none of the irregularities that are characteristic of human action, and it would really be rather an uninteresting shot.[25]

Here, Edlund articulates how the computerized camera move of an artificially created environment required the look of human intervention, as if shot by a human camera operator, to appear cinematically "real." According to his developing aesthetic, perfectly smooth effects shots were perceived as inhuman and therefore as somehow wrong.

Likewise, on *The Empire Strikes Back*, Dennis Muren was similarly very detailed as to how "what the eye sees" is translated cinematically, when discussing distance effects on the miniature Hoth sets for that episode:

Any time you put something in the background, there is an aerial haze that has to be in there—which you usually can't get in a 15-ft space on a shooting stage. So . . . you've got to diffuse it. . . . And there is a real resistance to that at first, because you don't want to destroy the image too much and everyone's going for the sharpness and all of that sort of thing. But once a composite comes out with that done to it, the realism is strikingly apparent and you say: "Wow! That's the right thing."[26]

Moreover, the effects artist discovers this by gauging what looks right "when the composite comes back," not while shooting. In other words, neither shooting effects sequences such as live-action nor advanced technology made the effects seem more real. To create the version of live-action cinematography that conformed to the emerging ILM style of realism, Edlund and Muren and others had to perform a good deal of manipulation to the effects image, filtered through their aesthetic discernment.[27]

Again, changing technology did not fundamentally alter ILM's approach later when Muren became a primary mover in ILM's transition to digital technology. In 1995, Muren had already honed a coherent discourse for how to describe the necessary adjustments CGI animators needed to make in order to make CGI effects look "real" by ILM photoreal standards, echoing his statements about *Empire Strikes Back*:

The computer people come from a totally different place. They'd come up with scenes that simply can't be shot by a camera, and thus that the eye won't accept.

For example the computer people often wanted to use very bright colors and crisp stark images in their effects. They want to use every bit of that digital information, but that isn't the way the eye sees. . . . What counts is how the movie looks, not necessarily the perfection of the technique.[28]

Again, the ideal effects sequence should look like it has been shot by a camera operator on location, with the appropriate and expected degradation of the image to maintain the look as if photographed by a human—a 1970s New Hollywood cinematographer. Perfection is the enemy of ILM's realism, and what counts is how the movie looks.

New Hollywood as a Reference Style

Rather than simply try to replicate either a notion of what the naked eye experiences in real life or even straight camera reality, ILM's stroke of genius was to continue to play up an extra level of stylization—aesthetics and techniques that call attention to the act of filming. ILM artists developed a working thesis for how to achieve the style of realism they wanted: profilmic event + technology + human intervention = desired realism effect. Not only did this formula result in an effect that "looked right" to the artist's eye by mining associations with verité filmmaking that further conveyed authenticity and immediacy; it nullified any sense of inhuman automation. Lucas wanted the *Star Wars* films to look as if they were a 1970s road film or documentary—but, amazingly, shot in space—and left it to his effects team to make it happen.[29] Long past the New Hollywood[30] period and into the digital era, ILM continued to appropriate aesthetic associations that had accrued to that style, resulting in a strategy that could be subtly detached from its historical context and adapted and updated to current cinematographic styles. It is a style designed to be evocative of that era associated with authenticity and integrity, but not too literally.

Scholar Bradley Schauer describes New Hollywood cinematography this way:

[The 1970s cinematographers] developed a new naturalistic aesthetic, grounded in diffuse and grainy techniques. This new look was not just another way to counter the artificiality of studio-bound filmmaking; its visual softness also broke with previous norms of realism in Hollywood. Second, [1970s cinematographers] foregrounded the presence of the filmmaker, experimenting with bold new techniques like the handheld camera and the split screen.[31]

Similarly, cinematographer Conrad Hall, whose stylized but unobtrusively naturalistic aesthetic may be the most significant New Hollywood precedent for ILM, describes his approach on *Butch Cassidy and the Sundance Kid* (1969):

> There's always atmosphere between color and me in the form of haze, smog, fog, dust. There's a muting of color that goes on in life. . . . I felt film was too sharp; I didn't see life that sharp and I don't like it that sharp, actually. So I always destroy sharpness.[32]

Edlund and Muren, in their previous quotes, are not likely citing Hall or other cinematographers directly. However, compare their language recounting, in Muren's case, how the "de-sharpening" effect of aerial haze is simulated and stylized through trial and error to create the proper cinematic effect. The contradictory goal is to do so in a way that does not call attention to itself as a cinematic flourish but still provides the impossible "wow" effect (e.g., the battle on the ice planet Hoth in *Empire*). Elements in the original *Star Wars* trilogy add up to what Lucas and others frequently described as an imperfect, abraded "used future" aesthetic, an approach that has long informed ILM's conception of photorealism.

In modeling their effects look for the *Star Wars* films, I suggest, ILM artists emulated shooting styles that emphasized the flexibility of lightweight filming equipment and the observational look of filming with handheld cameras as in, for example, a Direct Cinema documentary. The unpolished, rough look of the "mistakes" in the camera work not only allowed them to borrow the associations of immediacy and authenticity but also provided a certain emotional expressivity and artistic flare. While associated and pioneered in independent or lower-budget filmmaking—by Hal Ashby, Barbara Loden, Robert Altman, Monte Hellman, and Bob Rafelson—this approach (stressing particular aesthetic effects of filmmaking) was subsequently popularized by the filmmakers most associated with 1970s blockbusters—Coppola, Lucas, and Spielberg in their early careers.[33] We can see this aesthetic, for example, in Coppola's *The Rain People* (1969), Lucas's *American Graffiti* (1973), and Spielberg's *The Sugarland Express* (1974) and again later in their blockbusters *Jaws*, *Star Wars*, and *The Godfather*. These filmmakers developed a recognizable group style along with their various cinematographers, including Bill Butler, Vilmos Zsigmond, and Haskell Wexler. But the movement also includes influential cinematographers such as Conrad Hall on *Butch Cassidy and the Sundance Kid*

(1969), Laszlo Kovacs on *Easy Rider* (1969) and *Five Easy Pieces*, Owen Roizman on *The French Connection* (1971), John Alonzo on *Harold and Maude*, and Nestor Almendros on *Cockfighter* and *Days of Heaven* (1978). In these films, the camera darts irregularly among moving vehicles in rhythms that capture the protagonists' restlessness, anxiety, and desperation, stressing rough and erratic unstable camera framing, unintentional-looking light artifacts, and unsteadied mobile tracking shots.[34] It imparted a paradoxical effect of feeling artless and spontaneous (and therefore naturalistic compared to studio fare) while reminding viewers of the camera operator behind the lens. This aesthetic was also appropriate thematically to portray in *Star Wars* the restless and reckless young protagonist searching for his identity. ILM's in-house version of photorealism began as a way to blend its effects with 1970s live-action cinematography, solidified as the house style in the 1980s, and finally coalesced into a citational style in the digital 1990s and beyond, smoothly bridging photochemical and digital practices.

When one compares the original *Star Wars* trilogy to New Hollywood cinematography from the late 1960s and early 1970s, the strong likeness is evident. For example, in *Star Wars*, the shot of Luke Skywalker gazing at the double suns on his desert home planet of Tatooine (shot in Tunisia) closely mirrors a shot of Martin Sheen in a dusty dirt field at the golden hour in *Badlands* (1973) in its soft pastel sunset colors, strongly horizontal composition with distant figure placement at the horizon line, and soft, hazy lighting (figures 2.03 and 2.04). Even more markedly, photography of Tatooine closely matches the textures and color palette of Laszlo Kovacs's cinematography of the dry, desolate southeast California desert where Jack Nicholson works in an oil field (figure 2.05) at the beginning of *Five Easy Pieces* (Rafelson, 1970). Similarly, Luke, Obi-Wan Kenobi, and C-3P0 in front of their landspeeder on Tatooine (figure 2.06) recalls scenes from *Easy Rider* with figures in medium shot in a similar sandy beige desert landscape with direct light patterns on the humans and the reflecting glare off of the metallic hardware.

It should not be a surprise that the style of cinematography in films such as *Star Wars*, *Jaws*, and the later *E.T.* would align with the dominant style of their times. However, in ILM effects sequences, artists did not simply haphazardly ape every aspect of New Hollywood cinematography.[35] Rather than the self-conscious marks of the director-auteur that Schauer remarks on (such as the split screen), or even the specific traits of a well-known cinematographer, the strategy of ILM's artists was to

Fig. 2.03 and Fig. 2.04 *Star Wars* (1977) and *Badlands* (1973): Luke Skywalker's contemplation of the two moons of Tatooine in *Star Wars* is strikingly similar in cinematography to a comparable shot in *Badlands*.

downplay the auteur flamboyance and play up the more subtle marks of the anonymous camera operator.

Below, I describe at length the most prominent and enduring aesthetic markers ILM extracted from New Hollywood for effects work: lens flares, the handheld camera, and backlighting.

The use of lens flares is a striking appropriation of the New Hollywood style for effects realism that is by now almost a cliché.[36] A lens flare is a visual artifact that appears when extremely direct or excessive light causes internal reflections and scattering on the surface of the

Fig. 2.05 *Five Easy Pieces* (1970): The dry desert atmosphere of Tatooine in *Star Wars* is shot similarly to the oilfield where Jack Nicholson works at the beginning of the film.

Fig. 2.06 *Star Wars* (1977): The cinematography of *Star Wars* recalls the strong overhead lighting and metallic reflection of the cinematography in *Five Easy Pieces* and *Easy Rider*.

lens, appearing in the image as a spreading or flickering light pattern (often multicolored and circular). Because such a self-reflexive style calling attention to the material camera was undesirable, lens flares were generally prohibited in studio lighting conventions during the classical era.[37] They were initially popularized as a live-action cinematographic technique in the 1960s and 1970s as part of a documentary materialist aesthetic (as in *Gimme Shelter* [1970]), developed in fiction filmmaking most notably by cinematographers such as Laszlo Kovacs, Vilmos Zsigmond, and Nestor Almendros and featured prominently in influential films such as *Easy Rider, Cockfighter*, and *Shampoo* (1975).[38] Occasionally, flares were also used as marks of character interiority or for other expressive means—for example, when Benjamin's parents lecture him while he is floating aimlessly in the pool in *The Graduate* (1967), or the introduction of Cybill Shepherd's character in *The Heartbreak Kid* (1972). While strikingly showy in the late 1960s and early 1970s, lens flares had become less flamboyant marks of virtuosity by the late 1970s and were absorbed into "normal" filmmaking practices, as seen in more traditional studio fare such as *A Star Is Born* (1976), shot by studio-era cinematographer Robert Surtees.

Easy Rider is such a paradigmatic and influential example of lens flares in the New Hollywood aesthetic that it warrants a thorough description. Shot by Laszlo Kovacs, the lens flares enhance the caught-on-the-fly visual freedom the Peter Fonda and Dennis Hopper characters dream of finding on the road. In the sequence set to "I Wasn't Born to Follow" by the Byrds, the pair ride through the wooded and mountainous area of Arizona around Flagstaff. The nondiegetic song's lyrics focus the sequence's mood. The lyrics—"And wander through the forest / where the trees have leaves of prisms / and break the light in colors"— even poetically suggest lens flares. And the flares enliven the mise-en-scène as they flicker and dance along with the music (figure 2.07)

In a film that often depicts the dark side of rural America, the images

Fig. 2.07 *Easy Rider* (1969): Prismatic lens flares radiate a peaceful mood, suggesting the riders are momentarily realizing their dream of freedom.

Fig. 2.08 *Easy Rider* (1969): Lens flares overwhelm the mise-en-scène, bathing the riders in a spirit of contentment.

set to this song in this sequence are contrastingly idyllic—perhaps the most so within the film. The sequence edits together images of natural beauty, alternating between medium long shots of the duo on their motorcycles shot from a camera in a traveling car rig and point-of-view shots. In the former, a medium-long shot (figure 2.08) of the pair on their bikes, an oblong series of soft pastel flares bathes Fonda's character in the glorious, serene atmosphere of peacefulness that radiates onto Hopper. The points of view are shot from below as if the riders are looking up at the trees, where light coming through the leaves creates numerous prismatic multicolored flares. In shots observing from the rider's point of view, the backlit diffusion silhouetting the trees allows viewers to likewise soak in the atmosphere of serene freedom and independence. As Fonda and Hopper gesture at the glorious scenery, the presence of the flares and their juxtaposition to the backlit natural beauty of the pines enhance the feeling of tranquility and aspiration to the American ideal of perfect freedom they went on the road trip to discover. Crucially, the colorful, decorative flares throughout enhance the natural landscape because they are calling attention to the presence of the camera that is witnessing this fugitive instance of purple mountain majesty. The camera verifies the possibility of achieving the ideal state of freedom by recording it. And within the greater context of the film, which darkens as they progress across the country, the flares' beauty is as fleeting as the moment.

The examples of lens flare use in *Easy Rider* cannot be extrapolated directly to every 1960s and 1970s instance. However, here it demonstrates three vital lessons that effects artists learned from this and similar precedents on how lens flares could work for effects: an eye-catching and expressively decorative composition of the mise-en-scène; a strategy to move the eye around the frame; and, perhaps most important, as proof of the presence of an actual camera.

The earliest example of adding lens flares as an effects technique that I am aware of is seen in *2001: A Space Odyssey*, during the pod-repair sequence, which eventually results in HAL sabotaging Frank's spacewalk and Dave taking another pod out to retrieve his body, climaxing in the famous line "Open the pod bay door, HAL."[39] I have described the effect aesthetic of this section of *2001* as "NASA aspirational," that is, as if shot in space by the ideal version of a Super Panavision 65mm camera and film, through the finest ground lenses, and with the illusion of a single bright point light source.[40] As in *Easy Rider*, the purpose of using lens flares here appears to be a combination of decorative, compositional, and narrative motivations. Also similar to *Easy Rider*, flares add the sought-after enhanced sense of camera reality—the sense that a real camera is recording in space. Significantly, the *2001* effects production also adds flares for visual distraction, another major strategy that later productions would adopt. Throughout the sequence, the headlights on the pod provide the brightest light in the mise-en-scène against the dim black starfield, adding visual dimension to scenes that would seem flat and stark without them. The lights also catch the viewers' eye to keep them from thinking about the effects in the sequence (figure 2.09). Ear-

Fig. 2.09 *2001: A Space Odyssey* (1968): The lens flare on the pod works to distract the eye and enliven the potentially flat all-effects shot.

lier sequences of the film, such as the waltz-time spaceship sequence directly following the famous bone/satellite match cut, are meant to have the viewer behold the effects miniatures and think about the effects' relation to human technological endeavor. It simultaneously represents technology and is technology. Here, the emphasis is on narrative action rather than on thematic contemplation. The kinetic flares move the eye around so that we think of the sequence more in terms of suspense— how is Dave going to get back on the ship? The flares are effective in helping distract us from the effects and to focus us on the action. It was a lesson that later ILM artists took to heart.[41]

By the late 1970s and early 1980s, lens flares in New Hollywood cinema had lost their novelty effect and rarely appeared as "actual" flaring of the lens as in *Easy Rider*. Instead, they appear almost exclusively in effects-heavy films. The original *Star Wars* trilogy used lens flares sparingly, mostly appearing in connection to flashes of action in light saber and blaster battles. However, shortly thereafter, ILM artists deployed them consistently, especially on Steven Spielberg–produced ILM effects projects, including *Close Encounters of the Third Kind*,[42] *Raiders of the Lost Ark*, *Poltergeist* (1982), *E.T. the Extra-Terrestrial*, *The Goonies* (1985), *Indiana Jones and the Temple of Doom* (1984), and *Gremlins* (1984), plus other ILM projects such as *Star Trek 2: The Wrath of Khan* (1982), *Starman* (1984), and *Cocoon* (1985). In those later films of the 1980s, taking cues from *Close Encounters*, flares nearly always convey a thematic purpose such as the materialization and even concretization of the light for various expressive purposes. These include visual instantiations of the otherworldly powers of aliens as in *E.T. the Extra-Terrestrial*, ghosts as in *Poltergeist*, and other metaphysical or supernatural beings as in *Raiders of the Lost Ark*. For example, in *Raiders*, during the climax when the Ark of the Covenant is finally opened, what is implied to be divine light pierces the assembled formation of Nazi soldiers through their torsos with a long, narrow, blue flare. We see another golden flare at the base of the Ark when the divine light slams the lid back on. In *E.T.*, flares emanate from E.T.'s glowing finger as evidence of his supernatural alien powers throughout the film. In the "I'll be right here" climax as E.T. hugs Elliott to say goodbye, a strong, white flare from a source behind E.T. glows as a visual instantiation of their love and friendship. The flares from the spaceship reinforce the "positive energy" the extraterrestrials bring with them to Earth. And again, as in *2001*, in all those effects-heavy examples, the flares help provide the "evidence" that a camera witnessed the scene, establishing the credibility of the effects object while at the same time mobilizing the eye around the mise-en-scène so we as viewers notice the movement and action, not the effects elements.

In digital effects sequences since the 1980s, flares have largely lost the thematic association with metaphysics and the supernatural. Flares are now the go-to additive element in the mise-en-scène to cue a photo-realistic aesthetic.[43] Though maintaining associations with the 1970s and 1980s, they have evolved into a stylistic cue more or less exclusively as an artificial evocation to "prove" an event happened because a human camera operator shot it. Flares and other intense light objects in the mise-en-scène have become so ubiquitous in large part because viewers are so habituated they scarcely notice them. When a flare seems to appear spontaneously in the frame, such as in innumerable long shots of digitally generated landscapes, apparently due simply to light scattering on the lens, the viewer generally does not even notice how much effects work the radiance from the flare is hiding. Namely, it is distracting the viewer's eye from scrutinizing the effects object or composite environment too intently. Just as important, flares "naturally" darkening the effects object greatly decrease detail and therefore the time needed for the rendering job. In other words, as a tool for artists, flares have become a mostly inconspicuous and naturalistic-seeming way to enliven artificial environments while tricking viewers into believing they are seeing more than they really are.

Flares are inconspicuous, of course, when used sparingly. The conspicuous habit of overuse has become most closely associated, to the point of parody, with the director J. J. Abrams.[44] Beyond distraction and verification uses, Abrams's copious deployment of lens flares is designed to associatively remind viewers nostalgically of ILM effects in 1970s and 1980s science fiction and fantasy films.[45] We can see this most prominently and flamboyantly in *Star Trek* (2009) (figure 2.10) and *Super 8* (2011), where decorative lens flares (some achieved physically on the set, some added digitally) wash color dynamically and optimistically over the deck of the *Enterprise* as in *Close Encounters*. Flares in *Super 8* subtly take the viewer back to the 1980s Spielberg classics such as *E.T.* that the film is so strenuously referencing.

Abrams's ostentatiousness with flares is rare, however. Most contemporary uses, as in *Death Proof* (2007) and *Mission: Impossible—Fallout* (2018) are much more subtle. In *Death Proof*, the Quentin Tarantino–directed half of the *Grindhouse* (2007) double-feature, lens flares verify

Fig. 2.10 *Star Trek* (2009): Director J. J. Abrams's self-conscious use of lens flares to evoke the 1980s reaches its flamboyant apex.

that the audacious climactic car stunt, in which Zoë Bell is strapped to the car's hood as Kurt Russell's Stuntman Mike tries to run her car off the road at high speeds, is happening profilmically, not in post-production CGI.[46] More typical in blockbuster filmmaking, in *Mission: Impossible—Fallout*'s non–effects heavy opening sequence, multiple long, colored flares accustom the viewer to later sequences in which lighting configurations help obscure when effects are used heavily. However, while the flares in *Fallout* carry little if any thematic resonance or 1970s nostalgia, their presence slyly bolsters the film's marketing rhetoric about Tom Cruise's stunt work, touting the film's profilmic (Tom Cruise did all his own stunts!) realism.[47]

Importantly, lens flares as formulaic markers of immediacy and authenticity demonstrate the extent to which the ILM style of effects realism departs from perceptual realism. A lens flare cannot be considered a feature of perceptual realism because, generally speaking, one needs a camera lens to "see" a lens flare. Therefore, causing them to happen on set or in the CGI addition are a chief indication that digital designers of photorealistic special effects are more often than not exaggerating the *cinematography* of earlier films, not the perceiver's actual visual experience of the world. Flares are now part of the effects artists' generalized obscuring arsenal, derived from 1970s cinematography, that includes backlighting to silhouette effects objects; fog, dust, and other particulates in the air to make the air sparkle and haze over; as well as strobing the frame to break up consistent vision. And again, though perfectly plausible and natural-seeming, they are all effects that are enhanced and made visible through cinematography, not the human eye.

Another prominent way ILM evokes the act of filming is by artificially suggesting 1960s and 1970s handheld and late 1970s Steadicam shots. Haskell Wexler (Lucas's mentor while shooting *American Graffiti*) directed and shot *Medium Cool* (1969), a film that provided another important aesthetic precedent for the ILM team. The famous verité blending of actual and fictional elements in the account of protests turned violent at the 1968 Democratic National Convention in Chicago combines to produce a jarring sense of authenticity and immediacy.

For example, the handheld camera shots track actress Verna Bloom in her bright-yellow dress through protesting crowds as she searches for her son. Beyond the color of her dress, Bloom is not lit to stand out from the throng and therefore appears illuminated through available lighting.[48] The frame bobs a touch unstably as she moves across it, and the camera tracks her steadily as she weaves in and out of protesters and bystanders. Our sight of her is occasionally blocked when she disappears into the crowd as people pass by the camera, and the framing seeks her out until she reemerges (figure 2.11). The unsteadiness of the image suggests the camera operator is being jostled among the crowd—proving he was there—a sense supported by people constantly coming between the view of Bloom and the camera. The viewer's alignment with the camera is so complete that when the shots of the police assembling (where Bloom does not appear) begin to alternate with those tracking Bloom, which are also shot handheld with similar unstable framing, we seamlessly understand that both crosscutting elements are

Fig. 2.11 *Medium Cool* (1969): Verna Bloom appears to be framed haphazardly by what is actually a carefully executed handheld camera shot.

happening at the same time "in real life." And then later, as the camera bears witness along with Bloom to the police violence visited upon the protesters, still handheld, the verité fusing of fictional and actual is complete. Importantly, in the police attacks, we fear for the safety of *both* Bloom and the anonymous camera operator. Despite the fictionalized framing around Bloom (as well as Robert Forster's cameraman, a separate character to the camera operator filming Bloom), the viewers feel little doubt that what they perceive at the 1968 convention did, in fact, happen. The sequence, not incidentally, also features many lens flares, reinforcing the this-is-really-happening-and-it's-all-unstaged effect. While the handheld effect was self-consciously virtuosic in *Medium Cool*, a more subtle version of the effect was used in *Midnight Cowboy* (1969) and subsequently taken up almost immediately in more mainstream Hollywood productions such as *Love Story* in 1970.

For ILM artists, the associations of handheld shooting with immediacy and spontaneity were a perfect aesthetic precedent for creating elaborate effects sequences with motion control for the original *Star Wars* trilogy, and not only to replicate the look of aerial dogfights in 1940s and 1950s World War II–focused Hollywood films. As several *American Cinematographer* articles published in 1980 attest, elaborating on the aesthetic of a handheld camera for multilayered composite effects shots was one of the major tasks for the ILM effects team on *The Empire Strikes Back*. However, creating shots with that aesthetic meant ILM had to run counter to the smooth technology of motion control. As stated earlier, the benefit of motion-control technology is that it attached the camera to a computer-programmable and perfectly repeatable track, allowing for precisely fitted compositing elements. However, it had the potential to look too perfect and therefore unnatural. The handheld look not only gave them the imperfect aesthetic effect the artists wanted; it had the added bonus of humanizing the motion control. As Richard Edlund put it:

> [You] wanted the material you are photographing to have something of the look of a guy out there with a hand-held Arriflex shooting it—then you want a certain suspense. It would be very peripheral; you wouldn't really understand it; you wouldn't know why it was there—but you would know that the shot had not been done by a machine.[49]

Edlund is saying we are habituated to cinema not looking like our everyday perception but like the creative skill of a human using a camera. We do not expect live-action cinema to look like a machine produced it. While effects require an intensive technological intervention, the goal was to erase the evidence of just how much machinery was required. Instead, the goal was to fuse the human and the machine into a kind of Vertovian cinema-eye, but with the added functionality of greater plasticity. Taking the *Medium Cool* approach into effects realism, this approach helped fuse the live-action and effects footage into an illusion of integrated camera reality. As Edlund suggests, since at least the introduction of computer-assisted motion-control technologies in the 1970s, special effects artists at ILM recognized that no computational algorithm alone generates a photorealistic special effect or, later on, a CGI artifact. Slavishly following an algorithm almost always results in the final shot being received as "too perfect" and therefore "uninteresting" and "wrong to the eye."[50] Showing off the effect is also key, so Edlund does not say "so it doesn't look like there was an effect," only that "a certain suspense" in the shot and unpredictability in the movements imply that humans, not machines, made the effects. Through these examples, effects artists may begin with something based on computation or science, but then this starting point is nearly always tweaked, stylized, or transformed in an attempt to suggest how it would look skillfully and inventively produced by human hands.[51]

As a specific example, a prominent optical precedent for all-artificial effects sequences from *The Empire Strikes Back* is the early "helicopter shot" that finds Luke Skywalker riding a Tauntaun on the ice planet Hoth.[52] In this sequence, the effects team reconceives a traditional miniature stop-motion sequence as an unstabilized aerial shot (figure 2.12). Traditionally, a stop-motion sequence would have been shot straight-on

Fig. 2.12 *The Empire Strikes Back* (1980): This miniature shot combined with stop motion is conceived to look like an unstabilized helicopter shot.

and horizontally, like a diorama come to life. Instead, the motion-control camera rig adds irregular motion on the z-axis, or into the depth across the x-y axis into the horizon. ILM artists enhanced this energetic effect by adding camera wobble into the mechanized motion-control program path that swoops down from a virtual aerial shot to the stop-motion figures, making the shot look like the handheld camera in a helicopter from M*A*S*H (1970), Apocalypse Now (1979), or, more conventionally, the opening helicopter shot in Bob & Carol & Ted & Alice (1969).[53] This sequence meets the ILM goal of generating a special effects shot with all the qualities of a live-action shot—in this case, a subjective camera shot with excitement and immediacy suggesting "you are really there on the ice planet Hoth."[54]

In the analog-to-digital transition film Jurassic Park, the handheld aesthetic proved useful for bridging the gap between the digital dinosaurs and the large-scale animatronics. The film's computer graphics supervisor, George Murphey, explained how to avoid a "too digital" look:

When a Dinosaur clumps through a scene we'd add camera bounce as if the photographer were responding to the earth shaking impact of the creature as its foot hit the ground. Even just the slightest move helps give the impression that there's a real person behind the camera.[55]

This technique was elaborated even further on the sequel Jurassic Park: The Lost World (1997). According to Dennis Muren:

I also wanted to be a lot more flexible with the camera so that everything seemed more spontaneous and natural. For example the stegosaurus is walking through the shot and the sun is flaring the lens. You tilt up into these amazing plates on his back. . . . And that tilt up gave the shot a documentary look. . . . In [The Lost World] I felt we could successfully create more spontaneous camera movements and more spontaneous dinosaur behavior. I've always loved the idea of the shots looking like the camera is reacting to an event instead of cutting and seeing it. The camera pans all over the place to follow the action. You don't get a sense that there's an effects person saying, "we can't pan the camera."[56]

The powerful combination of camera tilt, lens flare, and handheld camera provides the model for much of ILM's later digital effects work through the 2000s.

For examples of how later digital artists used this early ILM technique as a reference style, we can look to ILM's work on the Transformers films. In the first film of the series in 2007, for example, the battle sequences in downtown Los Angeles are shot as if from the shoulder of a combat camera operator, spontaneously on the fly—if that combat photographer were also a Transformer. For example, a virtual camera about four stories high bobbles in the air until it "catches" the action of an Autobot and Decepticon grappling and twisting in the air as they hurtle toward the camera position, smashing the corner of the building as they fly by. The camera whips around and finds the Transformers as they continue fighting in the air, crashing through a building (in slow motion) until dropping hard into the frame at street level, seeming to almost land on the camera. In other words, *Transformers* mixes its impossible ideal viewing points with spontaneous combat-style footage for added excitement and credibility. We can see this aesthetic as well in the faux long-take shots in ILM's effects work on *Terminator Salvation* (2009) and also in Weta's helicopter and banshee flying shots on *Avatar* (2009), where the camera work composes effects objects and characters as if they are moving too fast and erratically to frame properly. This helps create, as Edlund put it, "a certain suspense" to the sequences that read more as "shot by an actual camera" and less as computer-generated. Again, the strategic usefulness to these techniques for digital artists is manifold; they help distract the eye by forcing it to move around the frame, suggesting spontaneity and integrity while hearkening back to an earlier, more analog period.

New Hollywood cinematographic styles have several added benefits to effects-heavy films beyond flares and handheld cameras. Most notably, New Hollywood lighting styles provide models for aiding in effects-obscuring techniques. As one prominent New Hollywood lighting exemplar, we can look to Almendros's cinematography for the cockfighting sequences in *Cockfighter* as well as Hall's in *Butch Cassidy and the Sundance Kid*.[57] In these films (figures 2.13, 2.14, and 2.15), the figures in the foreground are dimly lit against directional spot backlighting from on-set practical fluorescents—hot spots—that light the top-left of the frame, creating strong highlighting to the shape of their hats and shoulders. In *The Empire Strikes Back*, in live-action shots taking place in the aircraft hangar on Hoth, Han Solo and C-3PO are similarly dimly lit themselves, with strong on-set fluorescent hot spots coming from the right background, likewise silhouetting them but also creating an outlining gleam on C-3PO's metallic surfaces, with small points of colored lights scattered around the frame. The large swathes of darkness silhouette the figures, outlining their forms with strong

Figs. 2.13, 2.14, and 2.15 *Cockfighter* (1974), *Butch Cassidy and the Sundance Kid* (1969), and *The Empire Strikes Back* (1980): The lighting style of *The Empire Strikes Back* models its cinematography on such films as *Cockfighter* and *Butch Cassidy*, with strongly backlit exteriors, as well as toplighting in dim interiors punctuated with fluorescent hot spots scattered around the frame.

Fig. 2.16 *E.T. the Extra-Terrestrial* (1982): The bokeh halo effect around the characters helps disguise the fact that *E.T.* is a latex puppet and also intensifies the resonance of the emotional goodbye.

edges, creating the suggestion of forms rather than highly detailed ones. The live-action lighting configuration continues and then seems natural in the all-effects space battles. There, dark-figured spacecraft, backlit by the bright planet, flash with strong lighting elements scattered around the inky mise-en-scène. For example, the bluish white lights circling the backsides of the ships, as well as the fast-moving colored laser beams and flamed strikes, make elements of the hardware gleam and reflect. These effects shots are crosscut with the live-action human actors inside the ships enacting the battle, darkly lit in a like manner by the white point lights and colored lights of the control panels to reinforce the consistency of time and space.

The backlighting configuration with hot spots and flares works just as well for physical effects. To return to the example of the farewell sequence in *E.T.*, the stylized lighting scheme is even more exaggerated than in *Empire*. The Elliot and E.T. figures are very strongly backlit, creating a halo effect, with even more powerful lights from the spacecraft dotting the mise-en-scène, flaring and creating a background out-of-focus bokeh effect (figure 2.16).[58] This helps intensify the emotional resonance suggested by the lens flares discussed earlier while at the same time helping to obscure the fact that the human boy is interacting with a foam latex puppet.

This stylized lighting approach, obscuring but visually enlivening, has remained useful in the digital age for much the same reason: it both outlines and defines but also veils the effects object while at the same time generating emotional and energetic associations. In *Iron Man* in 2008, we see an almost identical lighting strategy to that used in *Empire* and *E.T.* in the nighttime climactic fight between Tony Stark (Robert Downey Jr.) and Obadiah Stane (Jeff Bridges). The transition of the lighting strategy from analog to digital requires very little adjustment. Strong backlighting outlines the dimly lit characters, but their figures lack detail (figure 2.17). Fluorescent orbs light the sequence with hot spots from the bottom-right, and similar practical lights acting as car headlights dot the frame. Focus instability and intense colors dotting the mise-en-scène assist with the obscuring composition. However, the strongest lights, playing the role of the primary light source for the two dimly backlit, glinting metallic suits of armor, are through the two antagonists' suits' power sources at the heart and eye. In a complex and lengthy climactic battle, the strategy of the cinematography and camera work is to suggest more than show. Moving the eye around by playing light over the chrome and metal of the hardware and their primary colors keeps the eye busy to avoid looking too closely at the wholly artificial effects objects pounding away at each other. We see this pattern, set by cinematographer Matthew Libatique, repeated throughout nearly all the films of the MCU, from the first *Iron Man* through to T'Challa's first action sequence in *Black Panther* (2018), where his purple outlined figure leaps in and out of flashlights while he fights kidnappers, all the better to obscure his digital double. And this strategy is far from limited to either *Iron Man* or Marvel Cinematic Universe films; it extends to most

Fig. 2.17 *Iron Man* (2008): The nighttime climactic battle with its backlighting and strong hot spots aids in obscuring the effects objects and also subtly recalls lighting techniques of 1970s and 1980s films such as *Cockfighter* and *E.T.*

Fig. 2.18 *Harry Potter* franchise (2001–2011): Hogwarts establishing shots in the *Harry Potter* franchise are highly detailed, but the frequent lack of atmospherics and other distractions means the image takes on the look of a storybook illustration.

effects-heavy films in general. *Bumblebee* (2018), to take one example, makes use of a similar backlighting strategy as *E.T.* when Hailee Steinfeld's character embraces her (CGI) Transformer friend goodbye, one of many subtle aesthetic nods to the human/space creature relationship of the earlier film. An example for contrast comes in digital matte painting establishing shots and landscape imagery. For example, in *Harry Potter and the Sorcerer's Stone*, establishing shots of Hogwarts are highly detailed and lightly backlit, but the lack of flares, atmospherics, and other distractions means the image takes on the look of a storybook illustration rather than a habitable cinematic environment (figure 2.18).[59] Likewise, the first time Quidditch is portrayed, the sweeping virtual camera long shots of the arena are brightly lit and detailed, but the minimal atmospheric obscuring means that we notice how the crowd's observation towers look blocky and the figures on brooms look very much like digital doubles.

The Creature Reveal: Effects Editing Strategies

ILM's effects realist strategies are not limited to elements of a composite mise-en-scène. Another important element of the stylization of effects naturalism is creating patterns for how the shots are edited together into a sequence. As already stated, in the simplest version, shots with evident digital effects sequences, such as those with CGI creatures, imaginary vistas, or ships, are typically very short and include distracting and obscuring elements such as lens flares and backlighting so that the eye does not examine too closely what it is seeing. These tricks are part of long-standing effects practice nearly as old as cinema's narrative integration. Nevertheless, ILM, in collaboration with the prominent directors who deployed them, systematized these editing patterns over time to best display or obscure their effects objects in effects sequences. These patterns were reinforced as the number of effects sequences intensified and were interspersed more thoroughly into a project of cinematic world-building from the late 1970s onward. And similar to the way *Star Wars* emulated the look of the cinematography of its era, editing patterns of the New Hollywood likewise became part of the way ILM constructed its effects sequences for maximum effectiveness. As Benjamin Wright points out in discussing editor Verna Fields's work on *Medium Cool*, her approach to the film was greatly informed by her documentary work, where footage didn't always match and the best angle wasn't always available. Similarly, on *Jaws* she realized early on that continuity was less important to follow than the dramatic feel of the moment.[60] Of course, the effects team does not have control over editing, which, while also accomplished in postproduction, is done by completely different crews in a parallel but different workflow. However, ILM does produce previsualized effects sequences (in collaboration with specialized previsualization houses such as The Third Floor, for example) that are preapproved by the production. Many productions then execute the previsualized sequences largely unchanged.[61] Effects sequences editing may be fine-tuned in the final cut, but the major elements are blocked out ahead of time.

One of the most important moments historically in an effects film, digital or analog, is the initial reveal of a prominent effects object. Powerful examples include the stop-motion King Kong, model spaceships in *Star Wars*, a CGI brachiosaurus in *Jurassic Park*, and the speaking and acting Gollum in *The Lord of the Rings: The Two Towers* (2002). The reveal determines whether or not the viewer will accept the remaining effects in the film as cinematically credible. ILM is adapting editing patterns that have a long history.[62] Reveals of spectacular effects objects follow a few historically consistent patterns. We might call these heuristically the "Dracula pattern" or the "Frankenstein pattern," based on the reveals of the much-fetishized monsters (actors in effects makeup) in the 1930s Universal horror films.[63] In the Dracula pattern, the creature appears all at once and often suddenly in the frame, and then the shot distance contracts to a closer view. In Tod Browning's 1931 *Dracula*, we see Count

Fig. 2.19 *Drácula* (1931; dir. George Melford): The Hollywood Spanish-language version *Drácula* (produced concurrently with the Tod Browning–directed English version *Dracula*) introduces the title character through a particularly dramatic crane up-and-in, making him appear suddenly as if out of nowhere, astonishing both us and Harker.

Dracula for the first time in full figure (in long shot), on the long steps of his castle as he greets Jonathan Harker. The shots gradually cut in closer to a medium shot as he begins to say his lines. Even more dramatically, in the George Melford Spanish-language version (also 1931), Drácula actively surprises Harker and the viewer. The camera begins by framing Harker at the bottom of the steps, then tilts to Drácula and cranes up rapidly toward him, followed by a cut to Harker looking astonished (figure 2.19). In the Frankenstein pattern, the creature is revealed in parts before we see it as a whole. In James Whale's 1931 *Frankenstein*, we first see the creature as a body part. We see a closeup of a wiggling hand while covered in a sheet on the operating table. The entire creature is later fully revealed, initially silhouetted in a doorway, entering backward, the camera moving in to his head and shoulders from behind as he slowly turns around and moves into the light, followed by a rapid pair of shots that move from closeup to extreme closeup of his face. Then we cut to the full figure of the creature from the front (figure 2.20).

In American cinema up to the 1970s, the Dracula pattern of the sud-

Fig. 2.20 *Frankenstein* (1931): Unlike Count Dracula, the monster in *Frankenstein* appears at first in edited parts, building gradually before eventually being revealed in full figure.

den appearance of the full effects figure was generally more common.[64] In *The Lost World* (1925) and *King Kong* (1933), the first appearance of dinosaurs and Kong, respectively, takes place after a great deal of audience buildup and anticipation—in both cases a long journey to a faraway land filled with dangerous natives and exotic animals. In *The Lost World*, the explorers observe a full-figure stop-motion pterodactyl and brontosaurus-like dinosaur at a distance, via binoculars in cutaways. Kong likewise appears for the first time in almost full form. The stop-motion puppet emerges rapidly and suddenly from the trees into a shot composited with Fay Wray's bound form, to a three-quarter framing. The sequence then cuts between Wray's terrified face to a closeup of the large animatronic head of Kong as she screams. This pattern tends to continue throughout the 1950s science fiction and monster movies, from *The Thing from Another World* (1951) to *Godzilla* (1954) to *War of the Worlds* (1953): the movie tends to cut abruptly to the full-frame effects object, startling the characters and the viewers, followed by closer shots of the effects object.

The famously partial and gradual reveal of the shark in *Jaws* helped set the Frankenstein pattern as dominant in the late 1970s. It is not surprising that ILM, having modeled its effects cinematography on the prominent directors and cinematographers of the era, would likewise internalize and adapt these editing patterns. From the beginning, the ILM team nearly always revealed its creatures gradually in parts. The original *Star Wars* films are chock-full of dangerous monster and villain reveals.[65] Costumed series villain Darth Vader is gradually revealed in silhouette emerging out of the smoky haze of the blaster fire from the extreme background, followed by a cut to a defined closeup of his helmet-covered head (figure 2.21). The effects creatures are even more radically fragmented. In the original 1980 release version, the yeti-like Wampa in *Empire Strikes Back* is never revealed in full figure.[66] His head rises suddenly into the frame for a beat before sweeping Luke off his Tauntaun mount. In *Return of the Jedi*, the reptilian Rancor attacks Luke after he is thrown into the dungeon. The scene uses the device of the slow rise of the dungeon door to reveal it in parts: first its clawed hand, and then its beady eyes and shiny teeth emerge out the darkness of its cave as it begins to lunge forward. ILM artists, especially Dennis Muren, consistently remark that it is more powerful if the effects artist makes the viewers think they are seeing more than they really are, rather than

Fig. 2.21 *Star Wars* (1977): Franchise villain Darth Vader emerges gradually as a silhouette out of the smoke in his introduction.

show the object too obviously or for too long.[67] ILM has developed and elaborated on this reveal strategy, which is closer to *Frankenstein* than to *Dracula*, through the digital transition.

During the digital "novelty" period of the early 1990s, films such as *Jurassic Park* also revealed their effects creatures in parts, but in a characters-on-the-screen-gaze-at-the-effects-object pattern. This pattern was most prominently popularized in the 1970s, especially in Spielberg films such as *Jaws* and *Close Encounters of the Third Kind*.[68] Famously, as already mentioned about *Jurassic Park*, characters on screen serve as an astonished proxy for the audience, with editing alternating between point-of-view shots of Sam Neill's and Laura Dern's intense open-mouthed expressions and the CGI dinosaur they are gaping at.[69]

Acknowledging that effects-object reveals are rather less astonishing twenty-plus years after *Jurassic Park*, *Kong: Skull Island* (2017) serves as one of many later iterations of the ILM effects-object reveal pattern melding mise-en-scène and editing patterns, which we can also see prominently in the series kickoffs to *The Lord of the Rings: The Fellowship of the Ring* (2001), *Harry Potter and the Sorcerer's Stone*, *Iron Man*, *Transformers*, *Pacific Rim*, and *Godzilla* (2014). The ILM effects extravaganza *Kong: Skull Island* has a plot-motivated reason for the New Hollywood look in the overall production design: The movie is set adjacent to the Vietnam War; therefore, the movie's constant narrative and aesthetic reference to *Apocalypse Now* is not incongruous. However, in the Kong reveal in *Skull Island*, digital technology helps exaggerate and meld the aesthetic of New Hollywood realism and ILM-style effects mise-en-scène and editing aesthetics into an almost perfect demonstration of the pattern. After a series of human characters witnessing the heretofore unseen presence of Kong (helicopters having been swatted to the ground, for example), Kong himself is introduced for the first time in fully formulaic ILM style. We first see a series of slow-motion closeup shots of parts of Kong, followed by a strongly backlit full-figure silhouette obscured by smoke and atmospherics, and then finally the fully lit, full figure of the effects object, with Kong hulking over the human eye–level camera (figure 2.22). As we will see in chapter 5, the Marvel Cinematic Universe codified this pattern from the very first appearance of an Iron Man suit in *Iron Man*, through every MCU production, whether with or without the participation of ILM artists.

This effects-object reveal pattern is so ingrained in today's mainstream filmmaking that its associative power appears in non-blockbuster

Fig. 2.22 *Kong: Skull Island* (2017): In the digital era, creature reveals have become highly formulaic: after a series of shots isolating him in parts, Kong's full reveal is backlit and silhouetted against the smoky haze.

Fig. 2.23 *Daddy's Home 2* (2017): Even noneffects films use the effects creature reveal, here for comedic effect upon the introduction of Mel Gibson's character. Like Kong, Gibson emerges backlit with a lens flare and in parts until we see him full-figure.

effects films. It serves as a comedic parody of the monster reveal in *Daddy's Home 2* (2017) and for associative expressivity in the musical biopic *Rocketman* (2019). In the sequence in *Daddy's Home 2*, Mel Gibson's character, as the intimidating father of Mark Wahlberg, is introduced much in the same way as CGI monster King Kong in *Skull Island*. Picking him up at the airport for the holidays, Will Ferrell and Wahlberg wait at the bottom of an escalator. As Gibson appears at the top of the stairs, a strong beam of light appears behind him, creating a backlighting effect as the tempo switches to slow motion (figure 2.23). The closer shot scale of Gibson's form makes him appear to be a threat looming from above. Ferrell gapes from below, impressed but terrified, as Gibson approaches.

The editing then provides a swift series of closer shots of Gibson, his intense glare, and his snarling mouth, interspersed with reaction shots from Ferrell and other awestruck onlookers. The slow motion ends as Gibson, revealed in full form, joins Ferrell and Wahlberg at the bottom of the escalator. Through the unconscious absorption of the CGI object reveal, the movie relays perfectly that the Gibson character *is* King Kong: dangerous, threatening, powerful—but also fascinating and maybe misjudged. The sequence relies on the audience's familiarity with the pattern of CGI creature reveals repeated over and over again in ILM's biggest hits. The sequence in *Daddy's Home 2* does not cite any specific effects reference, but nevertheless it requires familiarity with the trope to have comedic impact.

In *Rocketman*, Taron Egerton as Elton John is introduced much like Darth Vader in the first *Star Wars*. In a long, smoke-filled hallway, the double doors burst open and a backlit figure costumed extravagantly head to toe in a cowl, cape, and headpiece (as well as wings, large-framed glasses, and horns) strides backlit in slow motion first in silhouette before emerging out of the vapor toward the camera (figure 2.24). Close-up shots follow of the details of his bejeweled, sequined, and embroidered costume until he enters what is an incongruous and drably designed set featuring a substance abuse support group. Whether or not the Vader association was entirely purposeful, staging the musician's entrance as a creature reveal frames his depiction as a "warts and all" story of a troubled genius who eventually finds redemption.[70]

In the realm of digital effects, ILM's version of New Hollywood aesthetics became a powerful reference style for providing an "authen-

Fig. 2.24 *Rocketman* (2019): Being introduced in the creature reveal pattern adds character implications to the first appearance of Elton John (portrayed by Taron Egerton) in his musical biopic.

tic" cinematographic look to artificially generated material. Moreover, photorealistic lens flares, virtual handheld cameras, and precise lighting configurations placed within recognizable editing patterns are prominent illustrations of our habituation to and acceptance of often blatant stylization as naturally or perceptually realistic.

ILM Photorealism and Truth Value

The ability to make effects that go unnoticed and pass as perceptual realism is the genius of ILM's hallmark style. What may be surprising, however, is that ILM, as the most dominant special/visual effects producer for decades, has not only set the agenda for how digital effects should look in movies through its industrial and economic power; as digital technology pervades all aspects of cinematic production, it dominates the aesthetic of realism in the cinema and moving image-capture more broadly. In other words, a great deal of image-capture cinematography has come to look like special effects cinematography.[71]

For most viewers, ILM's effects style is not processed as a possible style of realism but simply as what "real" looks like. By extension, the style accepted as "real" bears a great deal of authority to convey not only what is credible but also what is truthful. The ILM aesthetic achieves this feat in part by hearkening to a live-action stylistic precedent that still has close, albeit subconscious, associations with historical cinematic truth value. What is striking, then, is the way that the dominance of the ILM effects style in the digital age has had consequences on cinematic photorealism *as* truth value in films that are not marketed or received as effects films—especially those with historically re-created settings and events.

As a way to consider the motivations for and consequences of deploying the specific photoreal ILM aesthetic on broader cinematic production, it is useful to examine a few films that are not marketed for their effects virtuosity. These include *Roma*, a 2018 Alfonso Cuarón film for which the UK firm MPC, not ILM, was the lead house; Bradley Cooper's present-day musical melodrama *A Star Is Born* (2018); and Barry Jenkins's 1970s-set adaptation of James Baldwin's *If Beale Street Could Talk* (2018). I insist that the cinematic truth value in these films does not derive from a simple nostalgia for 1970s realism or a 1970s setting. Instead, I contend that this association remains active because ILM's realism has conditioned viewers through blockbuster aesthetics. These films (as well as many others) strongly rely *both* on historical styles of cinematic realism and the associations with ILM effects realism to establish and, in fact, design a powerful sense that we can believe what we see.

In another work, I discussed the 2005 Steven Spielberg film *Munich* as an example of using the ILM style as way to entwine historical integrity, visual integrity, and rhetorical integrity.[72] In that film, Spielberg and cinematographer Janusz Kaminski create a visual discourse that distracts from the reality and historical liberties taken with what we are seeing and hearing. The ILM digital aesthetic of the 2000s reinforced truth value through associations with 1970s cinematography. That association has only strengthened over time and can be deployed even more programmatically to entwine the real and the true. This approach has become especially shrewd as digital cinematography has become the default in the majority of film production. Rather than *Munich*'s 1970s references, *Roma* most obviously points to the historical realism of canonical midcentury art films including *Umberto D.* (1952), *The Rules of the Game* (1939), *The Battle of Algiers* (1966), and *The Apu Trilogy* (Satyajit Ray, 1955–1958). However, perhaps counterintuitively, these midcentury references accrue additional truth value for the viewer by deploying an aesthetic strongly inflected by the digital effects blockbuster. *Roma* is a film set in 1970s Mexico City that looks at Cuarón's own personal history through the experience of his family's indigenous housemaid Cleo. The black-and-white film features long takes and virtuoso deep space staging that would make Bazin's eyes goggle. Nevertheless, Cuarón (who served as his own cinematographer) likewise uses the language of ILM effects realism, especially recent blockbuster effects realism, as a vital strategy in creating a rhetorical truth value for a film that relies heavily on the director's own hazy memory and perhaps dodgy impulse to embody the feelings and experiences of a working-class Mixtec woman's life that he can only imagine.[73]

On several occasions in *Roma*, the visual style emphasizes the act of filming: lens flares, atmospherics, and handheld (or Steadicam) tracking cameras suggest several visual rhetorical strategies around believing what we see.[74] For a spectacular but prosaic example, we can examine the sequence in the forest fire near the country house, where adults and children of the house help to put out the fire. The sequence uses several effects strategies to convince us that the fire is large and happening in front of us (figure 2.25). For example, the raging fire backlights the

Fig. 2.25 *Roma* (2018): The use of photorealism techniques associated with blockbuster effects work, such as backlighting, a handheld camera, and long takes, adds authenticity and veracity to an effects sequence in *Roma*.

foreground figures, edging their heads and faces against the flames and glinting off of metallic objects. Lens flares flicker subtly throughout the frame. Atmospheric effects, most prominently smoke but also particles in the air, diffuse and catch the light to add dimension to the depth of field. Calling attention to the act of filming is that all of these elements appear in a slowly tracking, lightly bobbing handheld frame over the course of a two-and-a-half-minute take that encompasses the breadth of the blaze and the people running in and out of the frame. Though especially dazzling in its technical achievement, all these techniques are standard effects practices to make a CGI environment appear more authentic. To put it simply, because we see visible evidence of the blaze being filmed, we are meant to accept that the fire incident happened and not think about the elaborate effects work that went in to achieving it.

In the sequence immediately following the fire as members of the household hike through the countryside, the status of the photorealist aesthetic as truth value becomes more complex and perhaps more telling and representative of the film's realist agenda as a whole. In another extended take, the extreme long shot surveys the stippled foothills while the lightly swaying camera scrolls along the burned-out fields where the children are playing with lizards, throwing balls, and skipping along, as Cleo and the other domestics keep an eye on them (figure 2.26). The visibly pregnant Cleo and another nanny climb up to a ridge, and Cleo likens the scenic, sun-dappled countryside to her home village in Oaxaca. "Although it's drier there, but it feels like it. It sounds like this, and smells the same," she muses. As she closes her eyes wistfully and

Fig. 2.26 *Roma* (2018): Paradoxically, the viewer's access to Cleo's subjectivity feels heightened by cinematographic techniques that evoke photorealist techniques associated with blockbuster effects.

the sun hits her face, dust wafts into the air, catching the light, and the camera starts to pan away from Cleo toward the sun, creating a series of thin, dusty lens flares and blown-out light.

Cleo's unexpected pregnancy makes up the majority of her story arc in the film. This moment of her own absorption into sense memory and nostalgia, at about the halfway point of her pregnancy (and of the film), represents one of the few times in the film when Cleo talks unguardedly about herself and her story rather than have the camera observe her in her context. (The other main incident where that happens, significantly, is her confession at the end that she didn't want the baby that died in childbirth to be born.) This gesture to her uninflected experience of nature is a subtle but pointed assertion that the movie is authentic in the way it represents not only Cleo's experiences and story but also her interior thoughts and feelings. Simultaneously, we are observing her objectively and have access to her "true" subjectivity. The shot's visual agenda seems to simply present the beauty of the landscape in front of Cleo, but that simplicity is camouflage for how it also reinforces (not incidentally, using many of the same realism strategies as the forest fire immediately preceding it) that the film is a fitting and accurate depiction of her actual life. Notably, Cleo's subjectivity encompasses a life very different from Cuarón's own (a fictionalized version of Cuarón appears as one of the children in the film), and the viewer may have some qualms about accepting a bourgeois male filmmaker's version of it. The long take, lens flares, and slightly wobbly frame combine to create a visual language of authenticity. Showing the world not only through

Cleo's eyes but also through Cleo's sensory apparatus establishes the film's authority to represent her truth. As a point of comparison, we might look to *Avengers: Endgame* as a low-angle, backlit shot of the villain Thanos in the extreme foreground as he walks through an alien field (as in *Gladiator*), his hands brushing the sun-flecked thistles as a lens flares dramatically behind him (figure 2.27). Similarly, in *Black Panther*, as T'Challa's airship flies over Wakanda for the first time in the film, a shot from the ground shows the CGI stealth craft gliding across the landscape of the frame, backlit and flaring against the sun (figure 2.28). This is followed by the descent into the technologically cloaked city, likewise backlit by the sun and sparkling with flares. Again, in *Roma*, we experience Cleo's subjectivity as real, and the movie's depiction of it becomes her truth because we are used to CGI objects and environments presented to us as credible in a very similar way.

Fig. 2.27 *Avengers: Endgame* (2019): *Roma*'s intense backlighting and flares recall shots such as this in a Marvel movie to add credibility to fully CGI characters.

Fig. 2.28 *Black Panther* (2018): Likewise, *Roma*'s landscapes are lit similarly to the CGI landscapes in *Black Panther* and make us believe in the imaginary kingdom of Wakanda.

In other words, by combining the associative power of midcentury Bazinian realism with the visual reference to ILM realism, Cuarón creates throughout the film an extremely intense and convincing sense that we are "in" Cleo's life and her experiences. Interestingly, although downplaying the film's many digital effects in the publicity, Cuarón rhetorically placed digital aesthetics at the center of his visual strategies.[75] The director claimed he wanted to embrace rather than resist digital aesthetics in order to avoid dreamy nostalgia:

> There is a tendency to use digital to create a filmic look, and I have done this, but, on [Roma], we didn't want to emulate film, we wanted to embrace digital. The amazing dynamic range and resolution, the crisp, grain-less quality, I wanted to be unapologetic. And to be able to do the layering and have these amazing backgrounds with a combination of wide angles with shutters closed, more like what the eye would see.[76]

As Ariel Rogers has noted, digital video, due to its associations with CCTV, amateur filmmaking, and reportage, is another frequent aesthetic that cinema evokes as a marker of immediacy and authenticity.[77] Therefore, the trajectory to Cuarón's style of realism is a complicated composite: midcentury neorealism + ILM's effects version of New Hollywood realism + the evidence of digital capture = the ability to harness all the realisms to credibly represent Cleo's life. Or so the filmmakers calculate. Moreover, by equating "what the eye would see" with digital technology, Cuarón is rhetorically reducing the filter separating representation from real life. Again discursively, for Cuarón and his team, this composite realist aesthetic provides access to the maximum truth of his subject.

Briefly, we can see a similar approach in the folk horror film *Midsommar* (2019), in which a group of American and UK tourists attend an ancient Swedish village festival and slowly realize things are not as innocent as they seem. The intensely bright backlighting, long tracking shots, and lens flares employ the ILM realist aesthetics to reinforce "this crazy shit is really happening"—that the protagonists are really experiencing the unlikely and uncanny arcane rituals despite the film's escalating outlandishness (figure 2.29).

There are many more examples of noneffects films using ILM aesthetics for truth value. The 2018 *A Star Is Born*, again shot by Matthew Libatique, must quickly and decisively establish its director/star Bradley Cooper's character Jackson Maine as a bona fide music superstar. The

Fig. 2.29 *Midsommar* (2019): The intensely bright backlighting, long tracking shots, and lens flares employ the ILM realist aesthetics to reinforce the idea that the protagonists are really experiencing the film's incredible and uncanny arcane rituals.

film's opening number follows Maine in a handheld shot from the wings of the stage (as he washes down some pills with booze) to headline a huge outdoor concert hall. Shot similarly to previous rock documentaries, especially *Gimme Shelter* and *The Last Waltz* (1978), and referencing the photography of Kris Kristofferson's concert footage from *A Star Is Born* (1976, shot by Burnett Guffey), throughout the number Cooper is bathed in intensely colored stage lighting that he walks in and out of, backlighting his figure, with several kinds of lens flares filling the frame. These include unusually numerous flares in the same sequence: long, horizontal blue streak flares, white circles, multicolor bokeh background lights, as well as shimmering, gold sparkle flares dispersed around the frame (figure 2.30). The overflowing flare effects are also an expression of Maine's chemically induced subjective state, as the remainder of the film makes clear.[78] Once again, the ILM version of 1970s cinematography of handheld camera, backlighting, and lens flares serves to bring a sense of immediacy, spontaneity, and experiential subjectivity; perhaps most vitally, it also visually establishes at the outset of the film Cooper's authenticity and credibility as a performer. The actor's music superstardom is the film's special effect.

The 2018 Barry Jenkins film *If Beale Street Could Talk* selectively makes use of associations with the ILM aesthetic of blockbuster effects for a very different purpose. Rather than simple authenticity, this film—the bittersweet love story of African American love, injustice, and mass incarceration in the 1970s—deploys the ILM association with

Fig. 2.30 *A Star Is Born* (2018): The profusion of lens flares introducing Bradley Cooper adds credibility to a nonmusician as a rock superstar in a film where he appears alongside actual musical superstar Lady Gaga.

Fig. 2.31 *If Beale Street Could Talk* (2018): The sequence's elaborate lens flare evokes the fugitive beauty of flares in *Easy Rider*, suggesting we can believe that Tish and Fonny's future happiness could be real, if only for a moment.

expensive blockbusters to indicate moments of fantasy optimism. In the movie's most hopeful moment, lovers Tish (Kiki Layne) and Fonny (Stephan James) have finally found a landlord (Dave Franco) willing to rent to them as a couple so they can begin their life cohabitating together. They are on the rooftop of the building with the landlord, who is giving a warm speech about how he decided to rent to them because "I dig people who love each other." As the camera passes back and forth between them, a giant yellow multi-orb flare with an iridescent glow, brighter than the sun, dominates the upper portion of the frame (figure 2.31). Similar to *Easy Rider*, the extravagant flare here indicates the fugitive beauty of the couple's hopefulness that they will be allowed to live "normal" lives.[79] For a fleeting moment, it is real. Here, the movie surgically deploys the associations with ILM blockbuster aesthetics to allude to the staple of blockbuster themes—the fantasy of how one person (in this case, one couple) has the power to change the world—to demonstrate the opposite. Instead, hope, optimism, and individual will are as illusory, fantastic, and artificial as, for example, *Iron Man*'s or, in an earlier example, *Spider-Man*'s (2002) CGI-generated lens flares. We can see contemporary uses of flares for similar purposes in *Parasite* (2019) when Ki Woo enters the Parks' yard for the first time as if passing through a portal into an alternate universe.

In the Danny Boyle film *Yesterday* (2019), a mysterious global power failure causes most of the world to forget the Beatles, allowing Jack (Himesh Patel), a struggling singer-songwriter, to profit from the McCartney/Lennon songbook. It similarly deploys an intensification of lens flares to suggest a fantasy we want to believe is or could be true. In the film, because the Beatles never hit it big, John Lennon was subsequently never assassinated and lives anonymously in a cabin on the English coast. Late in the film, Jack visits Lennon (Robert Carlyle) and is convinced by him of the joys of a quiet, simple life over worldwide fame and fortune. In an image of pure wish-fulfillment fantasy that the Beatle is still in the world, the Lennon sequence is likewise shot with copious warm lens flares (which do not otherwise appear markedly in the film). Lennon is backlit with an otherworldly halo effect and bathed in golden light (figure 2.32). Strangely, like Tish and Fonny, the Lennon fantasy is first of all the fantasy of manifesting something into the world, like CGI

Fig. 2.32 *Yesterday* (2019): The flare adds credence to the alternative reality fantasy that John Lennon is still alive.

does, but conversely it is also the fantasy of the beauty of a "normal," unspecial life.

Again, it would be easy to claim that *Munich, Roma, A Star Is Born, If Beale Street Could Talk,* and others are generating visual rhetorical truth value simply by directly utilizing 1970s cinematography as a reference style. However, it is via the ILM aesthetic—the accumulations of references that continue to make the 1970s stylistic allusions contemporarily operative—that viewers' truth value associations are anchored, rather than via hazy memories of 1970s filmography. Again, we experience the character's subjectivity as real, and the movie's depiction of it becomes their truth, because we are accustomed to CGI objects and environments being presented to us as credible in a very similar way. As the *Roma* example especially stresses, the perceptual world-building of ILM's photoreal effect is not the world viewed of Stanley Cavell, with photography's privileged relationship to the "world" as we think we experience it. Instead, it reveals what has always been latent in cinema: the ability to create diegetic environments and perspectives of them wholesale with a combination of effects techniques. Moreover, these associations are powerful enough to extend to noneffects (or not obviously effects) films to create similar credibility effects and rhetorical expressivity. We might say these films look as true as 1970s role models such as *Five Easy Pieces, Gimme Shelter,* and *Medium Cool,* but perhaps also as true as *Iron Man* and *Star Wars: The Force Awakens.* This aesthetic almost literally builds in visual integrity and provides credibility on several levels. We can be comfortable simply believing what we see. And finally, it should give us pause that the marks of (white, masculinist) 1970s cinematography meant to disrupt a classical sense of seamless realism are entirely absorbed into a mental schema invoking photorealism and signaling the truth.

Conclusion

At the time of Lucasfilm's acquisition by Disney in 2012, indications were that the new parent company was not especially enthusiastic about bankrolling the legendary but expensive-to-run effects company. However, events foreshadowed how ILM had value in Disney's future. Disney began to develop the *Star Wars* universe's narrative intellectual property. It gave the go-ahead for Lucasfilm to develop a new trilogy of films in the *Star Wars* saga, with plans for other *Star Wars*–related anthology films to come.[80] This put ILM in a secure position as the keepers of that specific style, with a plan for potentially unlimited, high-profile effects work for the foreseeable future.

In addition, predating the sale, eventual corporate cousin Marvel Studios contracted with ILM for the launch of *Iron Man* in 2008, the first in its series of "Phase One" Marvel Cinematic Universe movies. This seemingly advantageous alliance had ambivalent consequences for ILM and its house style. By 2012, the success of those movies demonstrated the value of ILM's aesthetic as intellectual property beyond the *Star Wars* narrative. As chapter 5 will contend, the MCU version of the ILM style started with Jon Favreau's embrace of a very particular "analog" aesthetic for *Iron Man* and then, over the course of twenty-plus MCU films, streamlined into a formula that has purposefully drained the ILM aesthetic of its particularity. The aesthetic that has evolved might be called "blockbuster standardization" or, more uncharitably, "spectacular blandness." At the same time, through corporate might, the ILM version has slowly become the Marvel Studios version. This means that the very particular, precisely grounded, historically specific style that ILM spent decades refining remains the industry standard—but frequently in a less distinctive version. As seen in chapter 1, ILM's scale, reputation, and capitalization meant that other effects companies could not really compete with it. Instead, it took the resources of a global blockbuster franchise—not to mention the shared corporate parentage—to challenge ILM's dominance.

THREE

Retconning CGI Innovation

ILM's Rhetorical Dominance of Effects History

EVERY ONE OF THOSE MOVIES [*STAR WARS*, *TERMINATOR 2*, AND *JURASSIC PARK*] DID SOMETHING NOBODY ELSE THOUGHT COULD BE ACCOMPLISHED. AND THAT'S THE STORY OF ILM ITSELF.

—"RAIDERS, RAPTORS AND REBELS: BEHIND THE MAGIC OF ILM" (ABC VIDEO, 2015)

WE ALSO TALKED ABOUT THE POSSIBILITY OF USING SOME COMPUTER GRAPHICS [ON THE ORIGINAL *STAR WARS*]. I KNEW JOHN WHITNEY AND SOME OF THE OTHERS INVOLVED IN EARLY COMPUTER GRAPHICS AND THERE WAS A LOT OF THINGS GOING ON AT THAT TIME. SO WE DID SOME EXPERIMENTS WITH WIRE FRAME WHICH ARE ACTUALLY IN THE MOVIE SHOWING HOW TO GET INTO THE DEATH STAR AND EVERYTHING. THAT WAS VERY EARLY COMPUTER GRAPHICS—THE VERY BEGINNING.

OUT OF THAT IT BECAME OBVIOUS THERE WAS A FUTURE FOR THIS TECHNOLOGY. "THIS IS PRETTY CRUDE NOW BUT IN TIME. . ." SO I WAS ALWAYS INTERESTED IN IT AND I ALWAYS KEPT UP WITH WHAT JOHN WHITNEY AND A LOT OF THE OTHER PEOPLE ON THE COMPUTER SIDE WERE DOING.

—GEORGE LUCAS, QUOTED IN *CINEFEX*, 1996

LM did not become an empire of effects by accident. The company has thrived in large part through its image as always the first, always the most artistically fulfilled, always the most innovative, always the best among the effects houses. As the aspirational top of an industry with a great deal of fan mystique surrounding the rebels who made *Star Wars*, the company also flourished by taking advantage of the economy-of-genius model of creative labor to attract talent. While ILM indeed has a great deal to be proud of throughout its history of innovation, I contend that much of this unassailable image is in fact public relations retconning.

"Retconning" derives from fan culture and is shorthand for "retroactive continuity," a process by which new information changes or fills in the blanks of an established narrative, thereby imposing a new interpretation. In a prominent example, the spinoff film *Rogue One: A Star Wars Story* (2016) served as a feature-length retcon for what fans perceived as a plot hole in the original *Star Wars*: the Death Star's design flaw that allowed the Rebel Alliance to destroy it with a single, well-aimed proton torpedo. In *Rogue One*, filling in the perceived plot hole is the movie's narrative: it is reconceived as a purposeful fail-safe included secretly in the Death Star's design by the lead engineer in hopes his daughter will eventually make use of the information to help the rebels destroy the Empire's ultimate genocidal weapon. As we have seen in various franchise installments such as *The Mandalorian* (2019) and *The Falcon and the Winter Soldier* (2021) (both TV miniseries for the streaming service Disney+), as well as in non-Disney properties such as *F9: The Fast Saga* (2021) of the *Fast and Furious* series or the director's cut of *Justice League* (*Zack Snyder's Justice League*, 2021), retconning has become a powerful narrative tool for entertainment conglomerates to tighten narrative connections among the various strands of their multimedia diegetic universes.

Cinema history is also subject to retconning. Most academic and popular stories about the advent of digital effects in cinema include some version of the narrative that highlights Industrial Light & Magic's trailblazing innovation with CGI in the 1980s and early 1990s. As the first opening quote above puts it, ILM achieved "something nobody else thought could be accomplished." Like ILM's own version, academic narratives about cinematic CGI usually start with the 1982 planet terraforming simulation Genesis sequence in *Star Trek II: The Wrath of Khan*, followed by the 1985 Stained Glass Knight character in *Young Sherlock Holmes*, then accelerate through the triumphs of the watery pseudopod in *The Abyss* and the liquid metal T-1000 in *Terminator 2*, and climax in the huge worldwide success of digital effects technology's proof of concept: *Jurassic Park*'s dinosaurs.[1] But what if this fluid progression came from a history that is not only massaged, exaggerated, and bent—as we might expect from public relations? What if it is one that ILM and Lucasfilm invented after the fact? I contend that the accepted version is the result of George Lucas, Lucasfilm, and ILM retconning their own history to backdate their innovations and capabilities in digital technology in general and CGI in particular. As we will see, in order to maintain his image as a cinematic visionary, Lucas himself has frequently played the role of "retconner in chief" during interviews.[2] The Lucas quotes above are good examples of the kind of misleading technological foresightedness Lucas likes to take retrospective credit for while simultaneously claiming that he never cared about technology per se. This duality—speaking out of both sides of his mouth—allows him to play two sides of his latter-day persona, which consists of the artiste concerned with telling timeless stories not reliant on platform, medium, or era, in addition to the cutting-edge prophet boldly leading an entire industry into the future. Moreover, my research shows that Lucas and ILM, even as they clearly were reluctant to make the full break to digital at the production level, exploited the ambiguity of the term "digital" and used its aura to bring many different and actually disparate processes under one "visionary" image.

Lucas's statements such as the ones quoted above always start with a grain of truth. Lucas may well have had a general interest in the latest computer graphics innovations. Indeed, the wire-frame computer graphics he discusses did appear in *Star Wars* (1977), but the work was the result of an independent contractor: the experimental filmmaker Larry Cuba in his lab at the University of Illinois Chicago. The "we" in the quote implies that Lucas and his fledgling companies developed that work. In fact, Lucasfilm and ILM had nothing to do with the actual production of the digital Death Star specs, and no tests took place with ILM personnel. Cuba has said that the use of computer graphics was incidental to the Lucasfilm team in its use in the film.[3] However, the rhetoric from Lucas and Lucasfilm elides these significant details to bolster the aspirational mantra "only at ILM," as seen in the first quote.

Certainly, this is why powerful companies employ public relations strategies: by controlling their own narrative, they show themselves in the best possible light and eliminate unflattering or inconvenient details. However, it is important to carefully debunk this version because ILM's and Lucasfilm's self-produced PR discourse has stood in for factual history. Even more important, the most prominent examples from ILM-produced effects films form the basis of nearly all scholarly considerations of cinema's transition to the digital age. A more accurate historical accounting becomes paramount to a less manipulated version of the history of digital cinema. Scholars should look for the seams in the industry's, and especially ILM's, histories and discourses, in the same way we dissect their finished effects on screen. Scrutinizing the information the industry provides us is crucial to recognizing the act of retconning and the rhetorical blue-screen versions of events at work in these blockbusters and the industry that produced them.

Other scholars including Stephen Prince, Andrew Johnston, Tom Sito, and Wayne Carlson have provided academic histories of the emergence of CGI and how it was adopted by the movie industry and how that fit into broader contemporary trends in computing.[4] The feature-length documentary *The Story of Computer Graphics* (1999, produced for SIGGRAPH[5]), directed by Frank Foster and narrated by Leonard Nimoy, tells a non–cinema-centric story of the technological history of the development of computer graphics.[6] It starts with defense applications in the 1950s and wends through Ivan Sutherland's interactive wireframe Sketchpad in the 1960s, Renault engineer Pierre Bézier's Computer-Aided Design (CAD) and Computer-Aided Manufacturing (CAM) industrial design programs for curvature in the 1970s, and the Bell Labs communications collaborations with artists such as the Whitney brothers, Lillian Schwarz, and Stan Vanderbeek. It explores raster and vector graphics that came out of university research programs, especially at the University of Utah and Ohio State in the 1970s. The documentary introduces early cinema applications through smaller computer graphics companies including MAGI and Triple-I, as well as the prominent commercial graphics company Robert Abel and Associates, which worked on *Futureworld* (1976), *Looker* (1981), and *Tron* (1982), none of which gained much traction in the movie industry as a whole. Triple-I artists Gary Demos, Art Durinski, and John Whitney Jr. recount showing George Lucas test footage of X-wing Starfighters in 1979 they created to demonstrate "that you could do things [with CGI] as detailed as X-wing fighters," but Lucas did not bite.[7] The documentary then discusses the 1980s business applications of the mouse and desktop publishing, medical and science visualization, the marketing of the Macintosh personal computer, and off-the-shelf, high-powered Silicon Graphics (SGI) IRIS hardware. The documentary does not return to entertainment with Lucasfilm until the 1:13 minute of a 1:30 film, marking ILM's entry into the significant history of computer graphics with *Jurassic Park*. Although the film backtracks to Ed Catmull recounting the Genesis sequence and the computer group (Catmull emphasizes that the Lucasfilm computer group was never part of ILM and was "not interesting to the people at ILM") and Dennis Muren discussing the morph in *Willow* (1988), the placement in the film strongly suggests that, in the broader scheme of computer graphics, the Lucasfilm and ILM projects did not have a significant impact before the photoreal dinosaurs of the mid-1990s. The film implies that the photoreal breakthrough of *Jurassic Park* and the CGI achievements that followed in the 1990s were not possible until the computing power of the SGI workstations of the early 1990s, as well as the graphics software developed for it. In other words, from the late 1970s to the mid-1990s, Lucasfilm and ILM were responding to broader trends and developments in computer graphics, not initiating them. While *The Story of Computer Graphics* has been criticized as hardly all-inclusive and can be seen an advertisement for the activities of SIGGRAPH members, it is useful for demonstrating that technology in other fields and industries outside entertainment was needed before widespread use in cinema.[8] It also is hard to conclude that Lucasfilm or ILM had very much to do with initiating most of these innovations. The documentary is one specific useful counterpoint to Lucasfilm's overblown rhetoric.

The purposes of this chapter are to perform a thorough fact-check to establish the profusion of misinformation regarding ILM and to demonstrate how ILM's rhetorical spin has helped position it within the industry. One sees these Lucasfilm-authorized sources being cited as fact in academic studies, and ILM's digital triumphs have stood in for digital cinema as a whole in academic studies.[9] Much like mythical generalizations such as the one that *The Jazz Singer* (1927) was "the first sound picture," these modern myths should be contextualized—for example, the one that *Jurassic Park* was the blockbuster breakthrough for digital cinema. This gives us a more accurate picture of cinema's digital transition; this historical methodology also helps us see the limits of relying on firsthand testimony and interviews as hard evidence. Finally, scrutiny of ILM's rhetoric helps us understand how its complete control over how its own legend is interpreted played an important role in producing the industrial and aesthetic dominance described in the remainder of this book.

ILM History as Cinema History

ILM is the effects company we think we know the most about. It is the most prominent and successful effects company in history. Its lavishly illustrated coffee-table books, expensively produced television specials, DVD and Blu-ray extras, web videos, and frequent publicity releases have trumpeted its computer graphics innovation since the late 1970s. In this chapter, I contend that we actually know only the version of events that ILM has told, which is often highly misleading.[10] Moreover, I contend that ILM, despite its constant repetition of its triumphs with CGI, largely *resisted* CGI until after *Jurassic Park*. ILM deserves a great deal of credit for innovations in digital technology, notably software and hardware as well as open-source initiatives. However, it is not until well into the late 1990s, when ILM established itself as a CGI powerhouse, that it decided it had been a CGI powerhouse all along and retconned its history to make this so.[11]

That being said, part of the challenge of writing about ILM is to acknowledge what it actually achieved (which is considerable) while casting a skeptical eye on self-generated rhetoric. My research, based on comparing private or unpublished Lucasfilm materials with public-facing promotional materials, reveals discrepancies among sources intended for internal use versus external publicity—and even among its own materials.

This chapter will mostly focus on ILM's digital capabilities with CGI in the 1980s and 1990s, the period of its history that is most misrepresented. We see discrepancies about ILM's computer hardware capability, software development, and dedicated computer personnel, among other things. The goal is not to unmask ILM practitioners and Lucasfilm employees as frauds and liars. Instead, the purpose is twofold. First, scholars should not accept the ILM version of the story uncritically. Second, subjecting ILM's rhetoric to scrutiny reveals the unexpected resistance and challenges it faced as an entrenched corporate structure in the transition to digital technology. This revision troubles historical and technological trajectories in academic accounts that have relied on ILM's self-reporting. And ILM's public discourse has been aggressive in presenting itself as the best place to work, always on the cutting edge, and never with a false step. As in chapter 2, I propose not only denaturalizing ILM's style of realism to see its historical construction; I also insist that ILM's *history*—a straight line that passes from film triumph to film triumph—has seams and layers we can also scrutinize. While this rewriting of history did not alone *cause* ILM's aesthetic, industrial, and cultural dominance over the industry, its control of the historical narratives helped present this dominance as inevitable. Certainly, when the ILM aesthetic is able to pass unrecognized or as the natural outcome of things, it is easier to impose that aesthetic over the rest of the industry. However, for scholars, ILM's version of history as the indomitable industry leader conceals the fact that it was not always the innovator but instead was adapting the innovations of others in less prominent or less financially successful films. In this way, ILM's PR rhetoric imposes an interpretation on cinema history as a whole, keeping the ILM product front and center while downplaying or erasing the work of others.

ILM is able to bend history because it has produced and been the subject of far more media attention and output than any other effects firm. Ironically, ILM's exaggerations would seem unnecessary. It has without question developed game-changing technology and a style of photorealism that all others aspire to achieve. That being said, the self-reporting about its own history and ongoing accomplishments do not bear up under closer scrutiny. While other academics (Phil Rosen, Tom Sito, Michele Pierson, and John Belton) have noted inconsistencies and voiced skepticism with practitioner rhetoric in popular digital histories, I contend that the ILM version of history dominates accounts and perceptions, much more so than other scholars have noted.[12] The earliest scholarly work on digital technologies in film studies began primarily with ILM examples, most notably *Terminator 2* and *Jurassic Park*, in canonical 1990s articles and books by Warren Buckland, Michele Pierson, Lev Manovich, Stephen Prince, and others. ILM's versions of events, which frequently served as evidence of excellence, should be investigated.[13]

Academically, just as attention to on-screen effects has prioritized spectacular blockbuster examples over subtle or invisible effects, scholarly attention to effects should likewise scrutinize public rhetoric. Many accounts of effects practice do not query practitioner discourse and PR information.[14] Certainly, John Caldwell's caution to always engage in discourse analysis when dealing with practitioner and industry rhetoric goes double for the effects industry, which is just as selective and obfuscatory in the (seemingly more transparent) digital age as it was during the classical studio era.[15] Industrial public discourse from producers and practitioners about effects work is nearly always presented in idealized form through *Cinefex* articles, conference panels, and industry events, avoiding those inconvenient facts. For example, the Visual Effects Society's handbook characterizes the smooth workflows and easy camaraderie up and down the production hierarchy, but it is truly a fantasy text about an industry that is rife with labor disputes, overwork, and a lack of clout.[16] Similar to Lisa Bode's critique of fan-directed discourse on audience incredulity, the scholar must be incredulous about effects industry rhetoric, which constantly asserts, with a straight face, that actors are doing their own stunts and car chases were achieved practically.[17] I also agree with Hye Jean Chung that Hollywood blockbusters endeavor to create the illusion of seamlessness on all levels of production; as she points out, we must examine not only the layers of effects work on the screen that are made to be undetectable but also the layers of labor and geography the industry tries to erase.[18] Likewise, in the illusionistic world of effects discourse from the industry, we indeed must see the seams—the discontinuities that these entities prefer to gloss over.

ILM's power over its own rhetoric and its influence over the broader history of effects have been impressive. As established in chapter 1, ILM is the only effects company with the economic resources to endlessly promote itself on such a scale. However, rather than just take it as given, I want to be very specific as to how this rhetorical dominance functions. Fact-checking ILM is important because its version neglects the contributions of others, suppresses labor disputes within ILM and the industry as a whole, and, perhaps most significant, portrays its specific version of realist effects aesthetics as natural and inevitable.

ILM has been able to control the narrative that it invented digital effects and all its subsequent innovations because authorized ILM personnel frequently are the only ones telling the story; moreover, it has maintained very tight control over what is said about it and who is writing and speaking about it. Since the 1970s, ILM has been the primary subject of no less than three coffee-table books from high-profile commercial publishers (in 1986, 1996, and 2011).[19] All three were authorized by Lucasfilm—that is, written or cowritten by current or former ILM employees with the cooperation of the company. For comparison, there is one coffee-table book on Digital Domain from 2001, as well as a Weta-produced volume from 2015; there are no comparable publications for any other effects company, past or present.[20] Similarly, Lucasfilm has produced several ILM-focused feature-length documentaries designed to air on network and cable television, beginning in the early 1980s, full of famous talking heads such as Steven Spielberg (and one narrated by Tom Cruise), alongside commentary by ILM's effects artists.[21] No other effects company has been the subject of US network and cable specials anywhere close to that scale.[22] In addition, Lucasfilm has produced many behind-the-scenes featurettes for the numerous *Star Wars* saga DVD and Blu-ray releases, as well as for the ILM effects landmarks *Terminator 2, Jurassic Park*, and many others.[23] And finally, no other effects company has received a comparable amount of mass media journalistic attention, with dedicated features over the decades in national publications such as *Time, Newsweek*, the *New York Times*, the *Los Angeles Times*, and many more.[24] It must be noted that other effects companies have been barely covered in the popular press beyond brief mentions, except in times of great turmoil, such as the spate of bankruptcies in 2012–2013.[25] In order to maintain its focus, this chapter will emphasize information gathered from ILM-specific sources rather than fan-centered accounts surrounding the "making of" of movies such as *Star Wars*.[26]

In researching the rhetoric of these varied publications and productions, one is struck by the discipline across the company (especially after the 1980s) to maintain a consistent story of constant, industry-leading innovation, workplace harmony, and artistic success. Finding the contradictions among these in-house publications (such as the Lucasfilm yearbooks—described in the introduction—held in the Ransom Center at the University of Texas or other private materials) and more public aggrandizing discourse helps complicate the history that ILM promotes about itself.[27] The internal reporting can also demonstrate that the road to digitization that ILM purports was not so smooth. This allows us to support or refute claims about ILM and Lucasfilm's computer graphics capabilities over the crucial period from 1982 to 1991. As we shall see below, the lack of personnel reflected in the Lucasfilm yearbooks show us that, during that period, ILM did not significantly explore CGI beyond a handful of personnel and even underused the ones it had.

ILM did eventually dominate CGI and shifted to a largely all-digital production house. However, retrospective histories teleologically assert that, in the late 1980s and early 1990s, the whole facility intended to shift entirely to digital in a rational, purposeful way and began doing so as early as technologically possible. Much as Don Crafton describes the industrywide transition to sound from the 1920s to the 1930s, ILM's transition was a process of hedged bets, failed experiments, keeping up with competitors, and resistant personnel.[28] And while sound took about three to four years to take hold in the industry overall, it took ILM considerably longer for reality to catch up with its claims of an all-digital facility. The shift instead came in the mid- to late 1990s, when ILM was preparing for the *Star Wars* prequels (as well as the original trilogy's digitally enhanced special editions). Lucas finally put his full attention and encouragement during this time to motivate ILM's slow and uneven shift through the early 2000s.

The Popular Rhetoric

[T]HE [FRUITS] OF GEORGE [LUCAS]'S SPRAWLING EMPIRE OF SOUND, GAMING AND ANIMATION . . . TOOK ROOT IN OTHER ORCHARDS LIKE PIXAR, PHOTOSHOP, PRO TOOLS, AND THE AVID EDITING SYSTEM.

—JON FAVREAU, QUOTED IN *INDUSTRIAL LIGHT & MAGIC: THE ART OF INNOVATION* (2011)

I DON'T THINK I WAS THE ONE TO BE CONVINCED [ABOUT COMPUTER GRAPHICS]. I DON'T THINK I WAS EVER IN DOUBT OF IT. I MEAN I WAS SPENDING VAST SUMS OF MONEY ON THIS THING SO IT WASN'T THAT I HAD DOUBTS ABOUT IT, IT WAS REALLY TO CONVINCE ILM WHO WERE VERY MUCH AGAINST IT.

—GEORGE LUCAS, QUOTED IN *THE STORY OF COMPUTER GRAPHICS* (1999)

What is the overarching ILM narrative that it presents about itself in coffee-table books[29] and making-of featurettes?[30] Overall, Lucasfilm and ILM promote the narrative that the corporation, led by Lucas himself, invented and innovated in all aspects of digital filmmaking; from day one, they were working boldly toward that goal, even when others within the company and the industry resisted. This story is typically presented through rhetoric that seems plausible, as Lucas and the director and producer (and frequent ILM collaborator) Jon Favreau present it immediately above, but often it cannot be corroborated through historical research. Claims such as those above are typical of ILM's self-produced rhetoric in one especially notable way: exaggerating a grain of truth to arrange it into a revised teleological narrative. In Favreau's quote, each claim, in the forward of a handsomely illustrated 2011 coffee-table book celebrating ILM's thirty-plus years of achievements, is based on a version promoted by Lucasfilm histories but is not strictly true. To be clear, I do not believe Favreau is purposely repeating falsehoods, but he has learned the Lucasfilm story from the same familiar and unreliable sources. Briefly, it is true that Lucasfilm R&D invested in early versions of digital sound, editing, and gaming. However, Favreau's statement implies that the technologies that are now industry standards had roots in Lucasfilm even if they bore fruit in other orchards. He suggests Lucas's versions were direct forerunners to ProTools, Avid Editing, and Pixar. Granted, it is reasonable to claim that Lucas built an "empire of sound" with his THX theater systems and Skywalker Sound mixing facilities. However, the digital nonlinear sound and film editing systems Pro Tools and Avid were competitors to the (mostly) failed Lucasfilm R&D projects (SoundDroid and EditDroid), and the Lucasfilm projects did not precede them.[31] Likewise, nonlinear EditDroid was developed at Lucasfilm, but it was not the first and was not commercially successful.[32] ProTools sound design workstations likewise superseded Lucasfilm's SoundDroid to become the industry standard.[33] The games division (later known as LucasArts) made some semipopular adventure games such as *Maniac Mansion* (1987) and *Day of the Tentacle* (1993) and several based on *Star Wars* intellectual property, but they hardly anticipated or revolutionized the industry or were especially influential.[34]

Taking credit for ProTools and Avid is a misrepresentation at best. Pixar and Photoshop can make better claims, but it is hard for Lucas/ Lucasfilm to honestly claim full credit. Certainly, the team of computer graphics experts, including bona fide pioneers Ed Catmull, Alvy Ray Smith, John Lasseter, and others assembled at Lucasfilm in the early 1980s, later formed the animation giant Pixar. However, Lucas has said several times that he was uninterested in that group's efforts at computer-generated animation and did not support the ambitions to make animated films.[35] ILM effects supervisor John Knoll did invent Photoshop with his brother, Thomas, a professor at the University of Michigan. However, they developed it on their own time, and Lucasfilm never owned it or invested R&D in it. Perhaps most misleading, Favreau's quote appears in a book about ILM, not Lucasfilm. Not one of these "fruits" of "George's sprawling empire" originated at the ILM division of Lucasfilm.

The early examples of ILM's digital innovation conflate two aspects that confusingly merge the activities of Lucasfilm with ILM. This is in the fuzzy area of what is considered to be "digital" imaging. The Lucasfilm rhetoric treats all "digitals" as rhetorically the same, whether nonlinear editing, digital projection, software development, digital intermediate, computer-assisted motion control, or CGI. In this way, the rhetoric can imply that innovation in one area provides a halo effect around all the company's activities. These publications and productions exploit the space within what Tara Lomax claims is general slippage among Lucas the person and Lucas's various corporate and creative entities.[36] In that way, anything developed in connection with Lucas, Lucasfilm, or ILM, no matter how tenuous, is considered to be all in the family. However, Lucasfilm has been a sprawling concern with many diverse interests and projects; not all work in tandem, and occasionally they worked at odds. Moreover, Lucasfilm's Skywalker Ranch complex is spread over a significant geographical area. In this case, the R&D aspect of Lucasfilm was only very rarely in contact with the production side. Along with conflating all of Lucasfilm's activities with ILM's, throughout ILM's history, its rhetoric distorts the historical record on several interrelated fronts. It fudges the time line of events, exaggerates its technological foresight and capacity, claims precedent over others' innovations, makes misleading visual and narrative juxtapositions, conflates disparate technologies, and overstates successes. Again, this obfuscation is typical of public relations rhetoric, but it should not be typical of historical scholarship.

We can see ILM's founding myth as the source code for nearly all its later rhetoric, especially the claims about CGI. Previously I have written about ILM's heavy mythologizing around its founding for the original *Star Wars*, chronicling how a merry crew of inexperienced young rebel misfits banded together against the odds to buck the traditional system and make a totally new kind of effects movie that succeeded beyond their wildest dreams—because they dared to dream it.[37] This tale, of course, also tracks the *Star Wars* films' narratives. It also portrays ILM as a special kind of workplace, where passion and creativity count more than corporate conformity and profits. Lucas in 1984 expressed the casual attitude: "Give these guys enough pizza and beer and they can do anything!"[38] Likewise, these accounts ignore that most of the early technology (which ILM says was invented by these renegades attached to the original *Star Wars*) was in fact innovated by other companies. This includes motion control, which was used pre–*Star Wars* by experimental filmmakers such as the Whitney brothers as well as the producers of television commercials at Robert Abel and Associates, and the afore-mentioned computer graphics work from Larry Cuba.[39]

In this chapter, I will be granular about ILM's history circa 1982–1993, the period when ILM frequently points out how forward-thinking George Lucas and ILM were. The accumulation of seemingly minor misrepresentations will establish a rhetorical pattern. Throughout the retelling of its origins, ILM not surprisingly irons out inconvenient details that run counter to its story; the most inconvenient detail this chapter focuses on is ILM's constant repetition of its innovation in CGI. Much like the popular and academic narratives, ILM's public-facing rhetoric is enamored with the example of *Jurassic Park*. Consequently, ILM's PR machine decided that CGI—and specifically *Jurassic Park's* dinosaurs—is the kind of digital technology that best visualizes its inno-vation. This is despite the fact that ILM could very credibly crow about its innovations in crucial but lower-profile areas including digital com-positing, digital rotoscoping, and match-moving. While it is true that, by the end of the industrywide digital transformation, ILM remained the top effects company in the world with the most extensive capabilities, the process to get there was much more uneven.

My research shows that ILM, like many large, successful organiza-tions facing transformation, experienced resistance from within to dig-ital technology—and not just from conservative or fearful team mem-bers, as is often characterized. While R&D on digital technologies was ongoing at Lucasfilm, most people at ILM thought it had little to offer them and even contradicted their own self-image, as well as the image of ILM as a different kind of workplace that valued handcrafted artisanal creativity over corporate profits and efficiency. Most at ILM thought they were already on the cutting edge of a successful technological aesthetic of effects. Also, in the 1980s and 1990s, most did not think CGI had that much to contribute that could not be done more successfully with existing methods.

In the next section of the chapter, I examine three founding stories of the ILM transition to digital technology: the early-1980s CGI in *Star Trek II: The Wrath of Khan* and *Young Sherlock Holmes*; the CGI produced for two James Cameron projects, *The Abyss* and *Terminator 2: Judgment Day*; and the computer-generated dinosaurs produced for *Jurassic Park*. I focus on these stories because they consistently form the "proof" of the Lucas/Lucasfilm/ILM account of their long-standing cinematic digital foresight. As it concerns *Terminator 2* and *Jurassic Park*, it is important to have a clearer picture of two productions that figure centrally in nearly every scholarly account of digital cinema.

Star Trek II: The Wrath of Khan and Young Sherlock Holmes

We start this section with some rhetoric about CGI and visual effects, pulled from an ILM-produced cable TV documentary titled "Industrial Light & Magic: Creating the Impossible" (2010):

> **George Lucas:** And in the process of [forming the Computer Graphics Group], the Apple [personal computer] came out and Dennis Muren had said, "Gee, could I take six months off and just learn how to use this this Apple?" So he was the one that first put his foot in the water and learned what Ed [Catmull] and the guys were doing, and then that started the link so that I could transfer the technology that the computer division was developing over into ILM which is where it was meant to be. . . .
>
> **Narrator [Tom Cruise]:** Today's powerful computer-generated imagery owes its roots to this CG group who by 1982 were able to prove their various skills to create a sequence in *Star Trek II: The Wrath of Khan*. . . .
>
> **Jim Morris [ILM General Manager]:** And the minute Dennis Muren saw the types of things that could be done in computer graphics it led to Dennis using computer graphics to create the Stained Glass Man in *Young Sherlock Holmes*. . . .
>
> **Narrator:** The Stained Glass Knight was the first computer-generated character in a motion picture and the film was nominated for an Academy Award for best visual effects, a testament to the growing impact of computer technology.[40]

This narrative reinforces George Lucas's visionary credibility, Dennis Muren's quickness to recognize the power of CGI, and the industry's immediate recognition and reward of ILM's innovation. But first a quick fact-check: ILM supervisor Muren took his computer graphics sabbatical in 1990, six years after the debut of the Apple Macintosh, eight years after *Star Trek 2: The Wrath of Khan,* and five years after *Young Sherlock Holmes.* While Muren, mostly alone among ILM personnel, did demonstrate interest in the Graphics Group's activities, the link between the two groups did not go much further past him to ILM at large. It is true that CGI *was* produced for these films, but ILM did not produce them. The Graphics Group was a separate R&D division within the company and had very little overlap with ILM beyond Muren before it was sold off by Lucasfilm in 1986, almost immediately after the "triumph" of *Young Sherlock Holmes.* The film was indeed nominated for an Academy Award, but none of the Graphics Group members who produced the CGI for the Stained Glass Knight were among the four people named in the official nomination. These facts strongly suggest that Lucas could not foresee the Graphics Group's potential. Moreover, the always-on-the-cutting-edge ILM likewise ignored and even disdained significant advances in computer graphics in its own backyard.

A version of this triumphal narrative appears in every post-1995 retrospective history of ILM. It takes what was a complicated story of corporate divisions, technological specificity, and artistic intentions and streamlines it into a logical-seeming and easily understood trajectory toward an obvious teleological goal: the straight-line march toward CGI's takeover of the movie industry that Lucas, Lucasfilm, and ILM were leading. Lucasfilm histories are rightly proud of the fact it assembled a computer graphics dream team in the early 1980s, especially the enviable collection of computer graphics pioneers Ed Catmull, Eben Ostby, Bill Reeves, Alvy Ray Smith, and John Lasseter, who would eventually form the core of Pixar in the late 1980s.[41] While the technology that resulted from the digitally oriented R&D departments had greater (THX theatrical sound) and lesser (EditDroid digital editing) success in the broader industry and marketplace, it was genuinely forward thinking on the part of Lucas and Lucasfilm to invest in these areas.[42] Lucasfilm's Graphics Group did make groundbreaking progress that would reform the cinema industry as we know it. It produced some of the earliest animated effects sequences for feature films, and the entirely computer-animated short film *The Adventures of André and Wally B* (1984), in the early 1980s. Even more important, industry game-changing hardware and software were developed at Lucasfilm: Reyes, which would eventually become the industry-standard Renderman (three-dimensional shading architecture software); and the "Pixar" scanner, a prototype for scanning film into a computer and back out to film. However, the retellings do not highlight how Lucas (as well as ILM on the Lucasfilm production side) squandered nearly every opportunity with this computer graphics dream team. Lucas was focused on the Pixar scanner for effects use but found computer animation useless for his purposes. And more tellingly, they sold the Graphics Group off at exactly the time ILM could have most benefited from its expertise.

Verified with departmental information in the Lucasfilm yearbooks and other sources, Lucasfilm had by 1980 founded the Sprockets Systems division, designed to be the digitally oriented Research and Development division of Lucasfilm.[43] Although going by several different names both at the time and later (Computer Research and Development, Computer Division, The Graphics Project, and Computer Graphics Division), the Computer Graphics R&D Group was initially a division within Sprockets alongside the nonlinear editing project that would become EditDroid, as well as the digital sound projects that would become THX and Skywalker Sound.[44] Although the name of the Computer Graphics R&D group within Lucasfilm changed over time, the team itself did not change considerably until the sale to Steve Jobs. For clarity, I refer to the team led by Catmull as the "Graphics Group."

With the Graphics Group anxious to explore computer-generated images and digital animation for motion pictures, one would think CGI would be its main priority. Instead, Lucas assembled the Graphics Group with one goal in mind: to develop a film-to-computer-to-film scanning device, an apparatus that would eventually become the Pixar. Lucas has said that he found large portions of the filmmaking process cumbersome and time-consuming, and he was willing to invest significant funds to develop technology to make editing, sound, and special effects easier and less expensive.[45] For that reason, Lucas wanted the Graphics Group to focus on hardware, not software or production. As Lucas himself put it: "Doing just pure computer animation wasn't on the agenda."[46] These priorities affirm what Bob Rehak has said: for Lucas himself and Lucasfilm the corporate entity, the value of digital technology was not in what appears on the screen but in the "fundamental changes it enables in the production process."[47] The 1980s to 1990s ILM visual effects supervisor Richard Edlund likewise affirms: "[Lucas] doesn't look at technology as anything but a means to an end."[48] In the 1980s, Lucas did not see the Graphics Group's computer animation activities as having much value.

To repeat: none of this work was happening at ILM, which had its own facilities and completely different personnel a significant distance away from R&D.[49] Since the corporation's inception, ILM was the largest and most prestigious wing of Lucasfilm, working on high-profile effects films such as the *Star Wars* sequels and Steven Spielberg's blockbusters. The yearbooks show no ILM personnel before 1985 with a computer graphics job.[50] Nevertheless, examples in all the ILM-authorized accounts of its history claim the 1982 Genesis sequence and the 1985 Stained Glass Knight as ILM's triumphs. And it was not without the Graphics Group trying to catch Lucas's and ILM's attention. The Graphics Group members claim they had to develop the Genesis sequence on their own time and then aggressively pitch the Genesis sequence to Lucas for inclusion in *The Wrath of Khan*.[51] Additionally, only about three to five people from ILM were involved with the brief sequence of the Stained Glass Knight, and then only in an analog capacity.[52] The three-year gap between projects also makes it clear that the Genesis sequence did not lead to Lucas thinking of the group for other CGI sequences.

As this suggests, several voices point to Lucas's and ILM's disinterest in the Graphics Group's activities as a creative partner in production. Michael Rubin, who worked at Sprockets in the 1980s, describes the relationship between ILM and the Graphics Group as "separated by a cultural chasm" with rare interaction, something the Graphics Group complained about frequently.[53] Sprocket's CG systems programmer Tom Porter said: "There was no particular warmth [from ILM]. It was sort of like 'Hey, we're busy over here. We've got things to do. We've got *Raiders* and *ET* and *major motion pictures*."[54] Rubin suggests that the Graphics Group was irritated that ILM received all the attention, funding, and glory, while the Graphics Group was overlooked, especially by Lucas himself, who the group members said rarely visited.[55] As Alvy Ray Smith put it: "We kept waiting around for George to ask us to be in the movies, but he never came."[56]

Tracking the account of the Stained Glass Knight sequences across the coffee-table books demonstrates how the official history has claimed the Graphics Group's triumphs for ILM. Thomas Smith's version of the Graphics Group (called the Computer Research Division in *Industrial Light & Magic: The Art of Special Effects*) is the most thorough, in that it gives a great deal of credit to the Graphics Group's role in work on the Stained Glass Knight independent of ILM.[57] Smith credits the work of

Ed Catmull, John Lasseter, Bill Reeves, and Eben Ostby, all of whom were Graphics Group personnel, on the Stained Glass Knight. In fact, Dennis Muren is the only ILM employee to appear in that chapter in a book that is supposed to be about ILM's triumphs, once again conflating the two divisions.[58] And even though the script of the 2010 television special ratifies the Stained Glass Knight's success by noting its nomination for an Academy Award for Visual Effects, it was a nomination for the film overall. *None* of the artists from the Graphics Group were among the four names included in the nomination, which recognized only Dennis Muren (ILM), David Allen (stop-motion animator), and John Ellis and Kit West (physical effects and stunts).[59]

While Smith's account of CGI in 1986 is largely written in the future tense, outlining ILM's potential plans, the book by Mark Cotta Vaz and Patricia Rose Duignan, *Industrial Light & Magic: Into the Digital Realm* (1996), is keener to stake ILM's claim as CGI pioneers. In this book, the story has already shifted:

> The computer-generated stained-glass figure had been created at the nexus between the departure of the old Lucasfilm computer [graphics] division and the gearing up of ILM's CG division, a time of transition from purely research and development to actual motion picture production.[60]

This statement is vaguely defensible by virtue of the unclear nature of this "nexus," but it also retrospectively relates ILM's development of a computer graphics division to *Young Sherlock Holmes*, which ILM cannot claim to have instituted until after the film's production.[61] Even then, the ILM Computer Graphics Division in 1985 numbered two people, and up to 1989, as the yearbooks attest, computer graphics personnel never rose above ten.[62]

By 2011, in Pamela Glintenkamp's *Industrial Light & Magic: The Art of Innovation*, previous versions of the production of *Young Sherlock Holmes* are tweaked yet again. Under the entry "1985: *Young Sherlock Holmes*" is the following: "ILM's Computer Graphics Division is established to work on this film,"[63] which contradicts the more detailed account Smith portrayed fifteen years earlier.

A clearer picture of how computer graphics was regarded at Lucasfilm and ILM emerges when we consider contemporaneous accounts—the in-house Lucasfilm yearbooks from the mid-1980s into the early 1990s. The yearbooks barely mention the Genesis sequence or the Stained Glass Knight as year-end accomplishments.[64] Perhaps most tellingly, in the 1991 Lucasfilm yearbook, a twentieth-anniversary retrospective, no computer-generated sequences in any film, even the morph in *Willow* (1988), are mentioned as landmarks in a publication dedicated to memorializing Lucasfilm year-to-year milestones over the previous two decades.[65] As late as 1991, then, CGI is not promoted as the inevitable wave of the future. Instead, the future is represented fairly prosaically: entrepreneurial diversification efforts, through the newly formed LucasArts division, designed to exploit preexisting intellectual property, concentrating primarily on video gaming and the television series *The Young Indiana Jones Chronicles* (1992).

The image of ILM working full steam ahead toward a digital future already in the 1980s does not only come from retrospective histories. In fact, it is the juxtaposition of internal disregard and external hyping where we can demonstrate these publications as elaborate PR. If one reads press releases and industry reporting circa 1985 regarding *Young Sherlock Holmes*, ILM and Lucasfilm digital capabilities appeared prominently in the reporting, with the implication that these technologies were being used extensively by ILM. For example, the *Time* profile on ILM proclaimed: "Computers are also being used to create entire images from scratch."[66] One sees the company's continual efforts to contemporaneously appear future-looking, even though ILM's day-to-day operations were almost entirely focused on developing and practicing more or less traditional optical and physical techniques.

One may ask: Why shouldn't ILM claim the Graphics Group's work if it appeared in an otherwise all-ILM production? When one parses the public claims with internal or private material, it suggests nearly the opposite of the public rhetoric. Even though the Graphics Group had produced the Genesis sequence and the Stained Glass Knight, as well as *André and Wally B*, its brief from Lucasfilm was to make equipment. In fact, the ILM histories' greatest claim for technological foresight—assembling the top-flight computer graphics team in the early 1980s—is perhaps the most telling mark of its failure to anticipate the future or know what it had and leverage it. It shows how, in the 1980s, Lucasfilm and ILM ignored or undervalued computer graphics. Lucas said in 1999, while promoting the digital innovations of *The Phantom Menace*, regarding the Genesis sequence, that he was not "the one to be convinced."[67] The R&D computer graphics group claims that Lucas *did* need convincing. By its own account, the Graphics Group wanted very much to participate in production and fought to get its work into feature films.

And in 1986, when ILM says it was increasing CGI capacity for *The Abyss* and *Terminator 2*, Lucasfilm sold off its highly accomplished and experienced computer graphics division to Steve Jobs, which included the entire dream team.[68]

Moreover, it seems clear that the sale was not, as Lucas claimed, "so that I could transfer the technology that the Graphics Group was developing over into ILM which is where it was meant to be." Lucas may have invested a great deal of money in the R&D computer graphics team's project, but that does not mean the equipment performed as desired. In 1996, looking back on problems introducing digital technology to ILM at the time of *Willow* in 1988, Dennis Muren reported frankly on the "success" of the Graphics Group's major project, the Pixar scanning device:

> As with our other earlier attempts to use CG, we were limited by the capability of our output scanner. Probably one out of every ten times, if we were lucky, it worked—maybe one out of twenty. It would take a day to do each shot—then break down and be out of commission for a week or more.[69]

When Lucas put the Graphics Group on the market, he sought out buyers who would be chiefly interested in the hardware, not the Reyes software that would eventually transform the industry as Renderman. One problem with the Pixar Image Computer (PIC) in that era was that its innovations were still more potential than actual. Although the goal was to produce high-resolution images for the scientific visualization market, the machine was very expensive and quite slow. In 1985, the Graphics Group was nearly sold to Philips (for the PIC's potential as medical imaging technology) and then to General Motors (the PIC's potential for modeling objects in car design).[70] Only Apple was interested in realizing what the Graphics Group really wanted to do: feature animation. By all accounts, in the early to mid-1980s there was little foresight by Lucas or Lucasfilm, with the dogged exception of Dennis Muren, that CGI might be a viable future avenue. The Graphics Group was sold off for complex financial reasons but mostly because it had not fulfilled its original brief: producing a working and marketable film-to-digital-to-film scanner.[71]

In the 1980s and beyond, the Lucasfilm umbrella company invested heavily in R&D in digital technologies around editing, sound, and to a lesser degree computer graphics to create certain kinds of digital technologies that were supposed to make the filmmaking process easier and/or less expensive. For Lucas, CGI was a sideline at best: "To me, a laser printer was really more important—something we could use right away."[72] This is something that the Graphics Group failed to successfully deliver on, so Lucas sold it to Jobs.[73] The revisionist rhetoric now claims that the later developments at Pixar were a triumph of Lucas's vision, when all they really demonstrate is that almost no one at Lucasfilm in the mid-1980s saw the huge potential of computer graphics.

The Abyss and Terminator 2: Judgment Day

I HAVE FELT VERY STRONGLY THAT ILM SHOULD BE THE PLACE TO DO THIS WORK. WE HAVE BEEN ABLE TO REALLY FOCUS ON COMPUTER GRAPHICS, ESPECIALLY SINCE THE ABYSS. AND GEORGE LUCAS HAS REALLY SUPPORTED IT. ALL THE WAY BACK TO THE SECOND STAR WARS MOVIE [THE EMPIRE STRIKES BACK], GEORGE SAID THAT DIGITAL WAS THE WAY THINGS WERE GOING TO GO. WE'VE BEEN DOING THIS SINCE THE EARLY 80S.

—DENNIS MUREN, CINEFEX (1991)

TO CREATE THEIR CREATURE [THE PSEUDOPOD IN THE ABYSS] THE ILM TEAM NEEDED POWERFUL NEW TOOLS. THEY GOT THEIR TOOLS AND ULTIMATELY A STRATEGIC BUSINESS ALLIANCE WITH THE PURCHASE OF POWERFUL COMPUTER WORKSTATIONS PRODUCED BY SILICON GRAPHICS. AT THE TIME OF THE ABYSS, SGI, WITH AN ESTIMATED $167 MILLION IN SALES IN 1988, WAS JUST BEGINNING ITS SPECTACULAR RISE. BY 1993 THE COMPANY HAD GENERATED MORE THAN A BILLION DOLLARS AND ITS WORKSTATIONS HAD HELPED ILM ARTISTS PRODUCE THE IMAGINATIVE COMPUTER EFFECTS FOR DEATH BECOMES HER, TERMINATOR 2 AND JURASSIC PARK. THE DIGITAL TOOLBOX FOR THE ABYSS WAS ALSO ENRICHED BECAUSE OF AN AGREEMENT WITH ALIAS, A CANADIAN SOFTWARE COMPANY THAT PROVIDED CG WITH [A] PROPRIETARY MODELING AND ANIMATING SOFTWARE PACKAGE.

— VAZ AND DUIGNAN, INDUSTRIAL LIGHT & MAGIC: INTO THE DIGITAL REALM (1996)

While it is somewhat understandable that ILM would want to predate its digital capabilities both in the 1980s and in retrospective history, it may be surprising that ILM was still overstating accounts of its advances in CGI during the late 1980s and early 1990s, during a time when the division's CGI work was receiving a great deal of industry and popular attention. As for Muren's quote above,[74] we have already established that Lucas had hardly "been doing [computer graphics] since the early 80s," at least with any enthusiasm. However, dating ILM's sincere move toward CG to 1989–1991 seems plausible. Again, visual evidence and the renown of *The Abyss*'s pseudopod and the T-1000 of *Terminator 2* seem to make Muren's statement self-evident. However, my research suggests that despite these high-profile examples, the computer graphics group in ILM remained a niche group at ILM as a whole.

Admittedly, ILM really was doing innovative and impressive work in CGI; however, it was small-scale. Credit for innovative computer graphics work should also be given to the smaller, less prominent companies with most of their work in commercials and motion graphics imaging such as Robert Abel and Associates, MAGI, Triple-I, Digital Effects Inc, and later in the 1990s, Xaos and Kleiser-Walczak, among others.[75] At the same time, Rhythm and Hues (which largely grew out of Abel and Associates) was emerging as a company that would later become an effects rival known in CGI.[76] However, these companies' CGI output appeared in lower-profile and less financially successful films. ILM's CGI appeared in major films by James Cameron, a successful director of blockbusters, making it easier for ILM's PR machine to amplify its projects.

There is significant distortion in the retelling of how ILM's eye-popping CGI in *The Abyss* and *Terminator 2* came to be. Here is a composite version story as ILM tells it in several iterations: After the previous successful examples of the Genesis sequence and the Stained Glass Knight, George Lucas, Dennis Muren, and others at the company were convinced that computer graphics could be feasible for the kind of photoreal effects work ILM had been known for.[77] The Catmull-led computer group was sold in 1986 to become Pixar, having completed the necessary research and development to transfer the technology to ILM for production work.[78] Then, in 1986, ILM instituted its own computer group to focus on digital effects production.[79] Around the same time, Dennis Muren, intrigued by the possibilities for digital imagery as in the Stained Glass Knight sequence, took a year-long sabbatical to understand computer graphics, which led to the famous morphing sequence in 1988's *Willow*.[80] Now under the enthusiastic leadership of Muren and his "Mac Squad" of computer graphics artists and software engineers, ILM was ready to enter the digital age.[81] The ILM departments just needed the job to show off these new capabilities.[82] Around 1988, director James Cameron came to ILM with an idea for a previously impossible liquid creature he was planning for *The Abyss*. This project led to ILM's "major commitment to expand the CG Department in every way."[83] As the quote at the beginning of this section[84] claims, a historical confluence of technology, industrial cooperation, and opportunity came together to make the pseudopod and the T-1000 possible.

The story ILM provides about its CGI activity circa 1989–1991 is chock-full of specific details, dates, quotes, and examples and is supported by images of on-screen CGI results as well as pictures of computer workstations and server rooms. It reads logically and fluidly and seems to track with what we remember about the excitement those films generated for digital effects. Again, the motivation appears to bolster Lucas/ILM's visionary status in the industry. However, evidence suggests there was little enthusiasm for digital technologies at the company. As late as the 1989 yearbook, the President's Letter signed by Doug Norby announces "the beginning of phase three" at Lucasfilm, which one might imagine is about shifting the company toward digital technologies.[85] However, while he mentions many ongoing Lucasfilm and ILM endeavors, he does not mention digital technology at all. "Phase Three" is instead a conventional multimedia "diversification" effort away from feature-film production and toward commercial production, soliciting outside clients, retail outlets, and home entertainment. Clearly, the digital revolution that the PR machine is touting is not an especially top-of-the-mind priority for Lucasfilm executives.

Lucas likes to characterize the Catmull-led Computer Graphics Group as a logical R&D precursor to the ILM Computer Graphics Group. He also insists that selling off the R&D group and starting up the ILM computer graphics version was likewise a logical and planned step toward digitization. However, it is clear that the status of computer graphics in the late 1980s at ILM was hardly charging toward an imaginary digital age. One can track dedicated personnel for ILM's own computer graphics team in the yearbooks to verify (or not) ILM's commitment to CGI. The yearbooks confirm that ILM started the Computer Graphics department with two people, George Joblove and Doug Kay, in late 1985.[86] According to the 1985 yearbook, the separate Lucasfilm Computer Graphics Group, headed by Ed Catmull, numbered forty-one people the year before it was sold off, a number ILM would not achieve until *Jurassic Park*'s production.[87] None of the ILM team except Muren (who was more of a liaison) is confirmed to have worked directly on the CGI for *Young Sherlock Holmes*, since that work was done by the Lucasfilm Computer Graphics team.[88] In 1988, *Willow*'s computer graphics team consisted of six confirmed ILM employees.[89] *The Abyss* team in 1989 amounted to ten.[90] Even as late as 1989, ILM's overall personnel, according to the yearbooks, numbered about 270, meaning ILM's own Computer Graphics Group was about 4 percent of the ILM workforce.[91] Aside from the minimalist team, all accounts suggest it was a niche element within ILM, hardly the "wave of the future" for the rest of the company.[92]

Although the ILM new two-person computer graphics team in 1985 has been cited as evidence of changing priorities at the division, Joblove's and Kay's hiring does not appear to have "started the link" between ILM and the Computer Graphics team.[93] The two men had previously been the proprietors of a computer-generated motion graphics company in Los Angeles.[94] In fact, Joblove and Kay were not hired for CGI at all but instead brought in to work on an initiative that was more in line with Lucas's/Lucasfilm's actual priorities: digital compositing and wire removal work. A March 1986 item in the *Hollywood Reporter* states they were "named to head up Lucasfilm's ILM Co's newly created computer graphics division," but the same report cites they were hired to work on *Howard the Duck* (1986), not *Young Sherlock Holmes*. The yearbooks affirm that they did not start work until after *Young Sherlock Holmes* was completed.[95] Bringing outsiders into the fold appears to have been met with intense suspicion at ILM.[96] In other words, this reinforces the findings of the previous section: Lucas and Lucasfilm were uninterested in CGI as such but were very intent on developing digital rotoscoping (for wire removal work) and compositing, two techniques that would make effects work more efficient. I have not found any evidence that Joblove and Kay, despite being the only employees at ILM with significant experience in CGI, were involved even on the famous morphing sequence in *Willow*. They seem to have had very little to do with Muren until *The Abyss*, when they became part of the small CGI team for that movie as well as for *Terminator 2*. It was not obvious that their work was immediately applicable or that working on *The Abyss* was important enough to remove them from the prioritized wire removal project.

It does appear that Dennis Muren deserves credit for fighting nearly alone to introduce digital tools to Lucas and ILM, a battle that was much slower and more difficult than claimed in any of the rhetoric. The aforementioned Mac Squad was not established in the late 1980s for *Willow* and no earlier than 1990 after Muren's sabbatical between *The Abyss* and *Terminator 2*.[97] Muren admitted later: "Mainly [the Mac Squad] was Stuart Robertson, and we began doing a few shots for shows like *The Rocketeer* (1991) and *Memoirs of an Invisible Man* (1992)."[98] Robertson, who started at ILM in optical photography, was one of the first ILM employees Muren recruited to transition to digital effects. Various sources verify that the initial Mac Squad around the lead-up to *Terminator 2* was a very small team of about six to eight ILM personnel,[99] working on consumer-grade Macintosh computers and using largely off-the-shelf software, especially Photoshop, which had just hit the market.[100] Once again, the Mac Squad had its most important breakthroughs in digital compositing and rotoscoping (not CGI) in this era and received little public ballyhoo. As Doug Kay put it:

> At the time [digital compositing in] *Indiana Jones and the Last Crusade* didn't seem like a dramatic breakthrough, but in fact it was. We had finally realized a goal George Lucas had set way back when Ed Catmull started the first computer graphics group at Lucasfilm. We put it all together on this shot to create our first totally digital composite.[101]

Kay is asserting that both the Lucasfilm and ILM Computer Groups' priorities were invisible effects, and the CGI of the animated pseudopod sort was more of a sideline.[102]

Given the acclaim surrounding *Terminator 2*'s effects, PR rhetoric still overstates ILM's CGI capabilities. After *The Abyss*, CGI production did ramp up at ILM, but not quickly or in great numbers of personnel. To continue the popular version of the story: after the widespread fascination for the pseudopod in *The Abyss*, Cameron asked ILM to take on a bigger challenge—the liquid-metal T-1000 for *Terminator 2: Judgment Day*. According to Vaz and Duignan, this caused ILM to boost its hardware even further, to a capability that rivaled NASA:

> The *T2: Judgment Day* duty also required the ILM software engineers to develop new programs and a hardware setup of some 35 high powered Silicon graphics workstations. (In fact the capacities of SGI hardware were growing every year—effectively doubling in power and speed from year to year—thereby allowing high-end clients such as ILM and NASA to process the highest resolution images.)
>
> The volume of digital work also necessitated the CG Department expansion which involved not only installing the new SGI units but increasing the staff from 8 to more than 40 animators and software engineers. CG coordinator Judith Weaver recalled that "nothing this big had ever happened in the Department. There was a mad dash to set up and three weeks later it was humming." CG animators Steve Williams remembered it as "like a mass warfare effort."[103]

I do not know the hardware capabilities of NASA, but clearly evoking the comparison sounded impressive. Dennis Muren's (post-*Abyss*) sabbatical to teach himself about digital technology did lead to ILM being able to produce the forty-odd CGI shots for *Terminator 2*.[104] While the above quote asserts that forty people were hired for *Terminator 2* (compared to eight for *The Abyss*), Muren claimed in *Cinefex* that ILM's computer graphics crew grew to thirty-five people and that they bought eleven Silicon Graphics machines.[105] It is unclear exactly how many SGI machines ILM had at the time of *Terminator 2*, but the NASA-rivaling hardware was not mentioned in *Cinefex* and other coverage of *Jurassic Park*'s CGI development.[106] Although ILM does appear to have had some off-the-shelf SGI machines as of the *Terminator 2* production, I cannot find evidence that ILM began using SGI workstations with any consistency until *Death Becomes Her* (1992). Even then it was done sparingly, since ILM was still using the familiar Macs and Photoshop for much of the digital effects compositing and rotoscoping work.[107]

By 1990 ILM finally did have a reliably working input/output scanner, but it was still not the Pixar image scanner developed by Lucasfilm R&D.[108] According to Vaz and Duignan:

> During the late 1980s Eastman Kodak and ILM launched a joint R and D effort to build an input scanner for motion picture work that would improve on the existing in-house laser scanning system. After two years of development that trilinear multispectral high resolution CCD digital input scanner came online in time to contribute to another breakthrough: the digitally manipulated matte painting and sequence of 1990s *Die Hard 2*.[109]

Moreover, according to Stuart Robertson, the new scanner setup was still slow and buggy and continued to require the optical department to finish the digital matte shot. Traditional opticals would still be needed through the *Terminator 2* production.[110]

As for computer graphics personnel, information in the yearbooks (supplemented by other sources) points to thirty people, maximum.[111] Only eight members of the *Abyss* team later continued on to *Terminator 2*'s computer graphics and software team. Moreover, no more than twenty-three were regular ILM employees, and many appear to have been contingent workers hired only for the film.[112] Of the thirty confirmed on the *Terminator 2* graphics and software team, only seventeen stayed on at ILM to work on *Jurassic Park*; that computer team consisted of about forty people, suggesting a contingent and unstable workforce rather than the purposeful ramping-up for future work that eventually happened for the *Star Wars* prequels.[113]

Thus, we can see how the second quote at the beginning of this section formulates misleading rhetoric about ILM's digital capabilities in the time. Vaz and Duignan say: "To create [the pseudopod in 1989's *The Abyss*] the ILM team needed powerful new tools." The CGI team mostly used off-the-shelf Macs on *The Abyss*. "They got their tools and ultimately a strategic business alliance with the purchase of powerful computer workstations produced by Silicon Graphics." Neither of these things happened until 1993. "At the time of *The Abyss* SGI with an estimated $167 million in sales in 1988 was just beginning its spectacular rise and had helped ILM artists produce the imaginative computer effects for *Death Becomes Her, Terminator 2* and *Jurassic Park*." That may be true for SGI, but it does not make it true that ILM made use of those machines in any significant number on *Terminator 2*.[114]

The longer quote just above uses juxtaposition and compression of the time line to suggest a very fast transition to digital technology. "The volume of digital work also necessitated the CG Department expansion which involved not only installing the new SGI units but increasing the staff from 8 to more than 40 animators and software engineers." Both Joblove and *Terminator 2* CG shot supervisor Doug Smythe later affirm there were SGI servers and workstations used on *Terminator 2* (though both are vague on the number), but they appear to have been consumer models, not the ones specially designed in collaboration with ILM that would come later.[115] Suggesting that ILM was not constantly upgrading but making do, Smythe said this: "[The Mac system was] pretty crude and rudimentary but it worked for what we need to, and that basic idea was unchanged from the *Willow* days."[116] Also, the quote follows the assertion of personnel and equipment acceleration with: "There was a mad dash to set up and three weeks later it was humming" and "like a mass warfare effort." Again, the numbers are much lower than the juxtaposition and compression of time suggest. It sounds impressive when Eric Enderton, ILM software developer, echoes Vaz and Duignan:

> When I got there the CG group was 12 or 15 people and we had our meetings in the upstairs kitchen in C building. Then by the time I left it was almost the whole company—ILM had grown to 300 people and the great majority of that was CG.[117]

The yearbooks affirm that Enderton was hired in December 1989.[118] He left ILM after his work on *The Phantom Menace* in 1999. Enderton is reporting a rise of personnel over ten years, not, as implied, around the time of *Terminator 2*. Therefore, even in early 1990, when the *Termina-*

tor 2 production had already begun, there were still only about twelve or fifteen CG specialists, many of whom were contingent, which grew for the production to about thirty—an increase, to be sure, but not a "mad dash." Even in the late 1980s and early 1990s, neither ILM nor Lucasfilm can be seen to be moving forcefully toward a major CGI effort.

Jurassic Park and ILM in the 1990s

THE INDUSTRIAL PART OF THE ILM EQUATION CHANGED DRAMATICALLY DURING THE PERIOD 1990 TO 1993. THE COMPANY'S TRACK INTO THE DIGITAL REALM HAD SHIFTED INTO HIGH GEAR WITH THE COMPUTER GRAPHICS AND IMAGE PROCESSING SUCCESSES OF *TERMINATOR 2: JUDGMENT DAY* AND *JURASSIC PARK*. BY THE SPRING OF 1994, THE OLD PHOTOCHEMICAL OPTICAL PROCESS WAS COMPLETELY REPLACED . . .[119]

—VAZ AND DUIGNAN, *INDUSTRIAL LIGHT & MAGIC: INTO THE DIGITAL REALM* (1996)

TRADITIONAL MOVIE OPTICAL EFFECTS WERE SET ASIDE IN FAVOR OF THE NEW CG WAY OF DOING THINGS. ON JULY 8TH, 1993, INDUSTRIAL LIGHT & MAGIC COMPLETED ITS TRANSITION TO DIGITAL TECHNOLOGY BY SHUTTING DOWN ITS ANDERSON OPTICAL PRINTER.

—TOM SITO, *MOVING INNOVATION: A HISTORY OF COMPUTER ANIMATION* (2013)[120]

ILM still clings to *Jurassic Park* images in all its promotional materials, from 1993 to the present. That worldwide blockbuster event accomplished publicly for CGI what no other film was able to do before: prove that CGI could photorealistically represent living organisms. Moreover, *Jurassic Park*'s convincingly photoreal dinosaurs have become a synecdoche of digital innovation in the cinema, both in the popular imagination and in film and media studies itself. Every account of ILM justifiably puts the spectacular dinosaurs of *Jurassic Park* front and center. However, it must be pointed out that digital technology was only a small (albeit significant) part of what made this movie's effects so convincing. Moreover, ILM's digital future was hardly inevitable even as late as 1993. Nevertheless, as the quote above suggests, nearly all Lucasfilm rhetoric uses the visible triumph of *Jurassic Park* to mark when ILM "went digital." There is no refuting that *Jurassic Park* was important historically; neither are its most famous production details in doubt. However, retrospective histories frequently frame ILM's late 1980s and early 1990s digital work as warmups for the movie that fulfilled the destiny it had been working purposefully toward—ever since the early 1980s Graphics Group was instituted. Elements of this narrative contain aspects of truth but are shaped into a teleological version of the story in which ILM's digital triumph was both planned and inevitable.

Leading up to *Jurassic Park*'s release and immediately after the film's huge success and popular interest, ILM touted its impressive and unprecedented digital capabilities in the industry press and fan magazines such as *Cinefex* as well as profiles in popular news magazines such as *Time* and *Newsweek*.[121] Certainly one of the reasons Lucasfilm felt the need to shout about its so-called NASA-level technologies was that, for the first time in its fifteen-year history, ILM had serious well-funded rivals. Sony Pictures Imageworks, bankrolled by the consumer electronics giant, was founded in 1992. ILM's former client and collaborators James Cameron and Stan Winston started their IBM-funded effects company Digital Domain in 1993. Both companies promoted their companies' launches "into the digital realm." ILM was under pressure to remain the most cutting-edge effects company, and appearing innovative meant boosting the awareness of digital effects its small computer group had produced for previous films.[122]

The blockbuster performance of *Jurassic Park* bolstered ILM's cutting-edge image in the industry, where the PR machine boasted of the highest-powered computers, the savviest computer programmers, and the most advanced software. However, that was a PR illusion. The film was cleverly cobbled together with an artful mix of practical and traditional effects, with digital effects squarely in the minority. That being said, the success of *Jurassic Park* did lead to several changes at ILM and Lucasfilm. In 1993, the company grouped ILM and Skywalker Sound into a renamed subsidiary, Lucas Digital Ltd., and instigated the partnership with Silicon Graphics. However, despite *Terminator 2*'s popular success in 1991, ILM's digital capabilities had hardly accelerated between *Terminator 2* and *Jurassic Park*'s production in 1992–1993. Important hardware and software changes to make ILM go digital were also not put in place until after *Jurassic Park*.

Here is a brief account of what can be substantiated in ILM's self-told story surrounding *Jurassic Park*. Generally speaking, post–*Terminator 2* in 1991–1993, ILM continued developing invisible digital techniques and modestly advanced its production of CGI. It began acquiring a few more powerful Silicon Graphics workstations and the software to run them, and it began developing in-house imaging software. Indeed, as

Muren has claimed, SGI workstations were used on *Death Becomes Her*, but the majority of the film's impressive effects were achieved traditionally.[123] Again, these invisible effects enhanced ILM's (specifically, Dennis Muren's) style of photorealism, increased flexibility during filming, and made postproduction more efficient; they were all vital developments for effects work. These innovations were the necessary undergirding to *Jurassic Park*'s photorealistic effects. However, PR more or less ignored these invisible effects and instead primarily highlighted the digital dinosaurs (or let the viewer believe physical animatronics were also digital). Moreover, the facility had hardly "gone digital" in any overwhelming way. CGI was still a small sector of the company's output. CGI technology in the 1990s had been visually appropriate for liquid metal and cartoonish exaggeration but had yet to produce much that could be considered organic or naturalistic in the established ILM style. It that way, CGI in the early 1990s was far from being able to replace much of the physical work in miniatures and models or creature effects.

In fact, computer graphics were still so niche and limited in their application in 1992 that, as is fairly well known, Steven Spielberg did not initially plan on using digital effects for *Jurassic Park*.[124] It is also well known that, due in large part to rendering and storage capabilities in the early 1990s, there are surprisingly few computer-generated shots in the finished film—only about fifty, or about ten more than in *Terminator 2*. And even those few shots were split between ILM (thirty-seven) and the Tippett Studio animation house (fifteen).[125] Full credit should be also given to the impressive traditional analog and mechanical effects, especially the large-scale animatronics produced by Stan Winston's company that made up the great majority of the dinosaur effects shots for the film.[126] It should be emphasized that both the Stan Winston Studio and Tippett Studio, though historically close collaborators of ILM, were independent contractors, not made up of ILM personnel, or even largely working on-site at ILM.[127]

Like *Terminator 2*, *Jurassic* relied on a canny mix of large-scale mechanical effects cut together with a few digitally generated shots. Moreover, the effects' success relied on the ability to cut the several types of effects shots together as seamlessly as possible. However, the way the digital dinosaurs were produced echoed traditional techniques more than the future. They were produced largely through a hybrid CGI stop-motion process developed by animator Phil Tippett's famous Dinosaur Input Device (DID), a stop-motion puppet attached to digital sensors so Tippett could animate coordinates of the puppet's movement into a computer. The hybrid DID technique was an ingenious solution, appropriate to the capabilities of technology and personnel. The assembly of approaches reflects ILM's creative genius and ingenuity. It is also a good example of how ILM would approach digital technologies over the course of the 1990s and 2000s: fashioning digital versions of its well-honed analog processes to make them more efficient and better reproduce its photoreal in-house style in digital form.

Despite touting high-powered on-site computing and the people to use them, it appears that between the *Terminator 2* and *Jurassic* productions ILM and Lucasfilm were tiptoeing toward digital technology rather than charging ahead. ILM did not seem to increase hardware purchases, and it increased its computer graphics team from forty to a mere fifty. And only seventeen of those fifty had also worked on *Terminator 2*. In an April 1993 *Variety* article, ILM's PR machine claimed it already had seventy SGI workstations and strongly implied they were used for the *Jurassic* production.[128] Based on reporting during the actual production, this number does not seem likely. ILM's partnership with Silicon Graphics was not formalized until April 1993, after *Jurassic's* production. It is difficult to get reliable information about ILM's computing facilities in 1993, but very little of the reporting of the *Jurassic* production mentions the thirty-five SGI workstations Muren said were purchased for *Terminator 2*.[129] More likely, the seventy reported workstations were an order expected to be delivered to ILM in light of the collaboration, not the actual number on the ground and in use at ILM during the *Jurassic* production. ILM did indeed appear to use a hybrid of high-powered off-the-shelf imaging software (such as Alias and Softimage) on SGI workstations, and it did develop its own proprietary software, most importantly Viewpaint, which became an industry-standard 3D texturing tool that won an Academy Scientific and Technical ("Sci Tech") award in 1997.[130] As for personnel, Muren was the only person on the *Jurassic* production who would be in a key supervisory role over ILM's digital transition.[131] Important figures such as Roger Guyett, Ben Snow, Pablo Helman, Habib Zargarpour, and Hal Hickel had not yet been hired, and Photoshop coinventor John Knoll is nowhere to be found on the *Jurassic* credits list.[132]

Finally, Vaz and Duignan's assertion that "by the spring of 1994 the old photochemical optical process was completely replaced," echoed in Sito's text, should not be considered the synecdoche of ILM's digital transition.[133] It appears true that the optical department and its optical printers were largely decommissioned by 1994, and it does appear true that digital compositing and digital rotoscoping had proven themselves to be sufficiently effective and efficient to replace the traditional optical versions. However, since the early 1980s, Lucas had put a target on the back of analog opticals and rotoscoping, long among the most labor-intensive and aesthetically complex areas of effects work.

Another way to gauge ILM's CGI capabilities is by tracking its personnel. It does appear that circa 1993–1995 ILM did begin staffing up personnel with expertise in CGI and its support technology. Also, many of the longer-established effects personnel in opticals, matte painting, and other areas on the way out began transitioning to digital versions of their jobs or related jobs. Acceleration in hiring CGI artists and technicians was slow, initially. *Jurassic Park* had the highest number of ILM CGI crews to date, with forty to fifty people working on digital aspects of effects, up only modestly from about thirty-five to forty on *Terminator 2*. After the Silicon Graphics deal was established in mid-1993, the company did expand rather dramatically in digital capabilities and in percentage of workers working in CGI. In 1994–1995, digital effects technologies of various kinds and skill began to be treated not as a niche specialization with untested potential but instead as applicable to several different kinds of projects. ILM moved from deploying one smallish group of digital artists working on one big project with significant and visible digital technology such as *Jurassic Park* to different crews working concurrently. For example, ILM personnel connected to digital technologies on *The Mask* (1994, with actors enhanced by exaggerated animation plasticity) numbered about fifty of seventy-four total credited effects people. For *Forrest Gump* (utilizing photorealistic invisible effects), it was about sixty out of 103. For *Casper* (with expressive and acting CGI main character interacting with live-action cast), the digital crew represented about thirty of eighty-one. Cross-referencing the credited ILM crew members establishes that these three major ILM projects shared little if any of the same crew. This practice became more common as the 1990s continued. For example, on *Twister* there were about seventy-eight digital effects people on an ILM crew of 122, and in *Men in Black* (1997) about ninety-two were digital effects artists out of about 193.

In summary, Vaz and Duignan's 1996 book helps us compare ILM's hopeful 1990s digital rhetoric against the largely analog reality. Subtitled *Into the Digital Realm*, the book reveals how, even in 1996, the process of going all-digital was aspirational and piecemeal across departments at best. Extrapolating from the book's chapter contents about ILM's actual production, two-thirds to three-quarters of ILM effects activity was traditional analog effects. It is probably closer to 80/20 given that the authors use future tense frequently in discussing digital capabilities. A great deal of ILM's output in 1996 is in miniatures, models, art direction, the creature shop, and camera-based effects such as motion control. These effects remained firmly within the analog realm through much of the 1990s. This impression is backed up in other reporting, including in *Cinefex, American Cinematographer*, and trade papers, where one can gauge more thoroughly the proportion of analog effects work, since digital work remained prohibitively expensive and limited.[134] Therefore, while ILM continued to work on and highlight its effects for high-profile projects with CGI, the majority of its effects work was still mostly computer-assisted (at best) rather than computer-generated. Over the course of the 1990s, the process in these departments would be increasingly hybridized with digital technologies, but even up to and including *The Phantom Menace* (1999), much of ILM's work was still analog and physical.[135]

In other words, *Jurassic Park*, or any single movie example, cannot be taken as a synecdoche of cinema's digital transition, dazzling though it may be. Like everyone else in the business, ILM could not see the future and was sensibly hedging its bets. It just had more financial stability to weather its mistakes and missteps compared to other companies—as well as a PR apparatus to spin facts to its advantage.

Conclusion

ILM'S [1993] RETOOLING FOR THE DIGITAL REVOLUTION INCLUDED THE SWEEPING AWAY OF THE ARCHAIC TRAPPINGS OF THE INDUSTRIAL AGE. BY THE SPRING OF 1994 [PROPERTY MASTER] TED MOEHNKE . . . WAS COMBING THE COMPANY'S STORAGE BAYS CATALOGING AND AUCTIONING OFF OLD PROPS, INDUSTRIAL HARDWARE, AND MEMORABILIA. . . . WHAT WASN'T BEING SOLD OFF WAS BEING DISMANTLED DECOMMISSIONED OR . . . PUT ON DISPLAY.

THE NEW TECHNO WAVE WAS FELT WITH BRUTAL SUDDENNESS IN THE HALLS OF ILM. THE OLD MATTE PAINTING DEPARTMENT WHICH HAD ONCE HELD EASELS FOR BRUSH AND OIL WORK WAS REPLACED WITH COMPUTER HARDWARE AND PAINTING SOFTWARE SYSTEMS. THE OLD MOTION CONTROL CAMERA . . . HAD BEEN REMOVED AND PLACED BY SOME 20 CG

WORKSTATIONS. THE OPTICAL PRINTING DEPARTMENT . . . HAD BEEN VIRTUALLY ELIMINATED BY THE CCD SCANNER AND THE REST OF THE DIGITAL THROUGHPUT SYSTEM.

—VAZ AND DUIGNAN, *INDUSTRIAL LIGHT & MAGIC: INTO THE DIGITAL REALM* (1996)

WITH 450 PEOPLE AND 180 HIGH POWERED WORKSTATIONS—MORE THAN ANY OTHER ORGANIZATION EXCEPT NASA—[LUCAS'S] ILM IS BY FAR THE WORLD'S LARGEST EFFECTS HOUSE.

—*LOS ANGELES TIMES* (1995)

POINTING TO THE TWELVE OSCARS HIS GROUP HAS WON, MOST RECENTLY FOR 'DEATH BECOMES HER (1992),' [LUCAS] ADDED, "WE CHANGED THE FACE OF SPECIAL EFFECTS, WORKING FOR SIX YEARS ON A COMPLETELY DIGITAL PRODUCTION FACILITY."

—*VARIETY* (1993)

By now, the reader should be reading these innocuous quotes[136] with the skepticism they merit. Certainly, images of dinosaurs make a more exciting story than investment in specific kinds of computers and software. Nevertheless, we have little independent information about the effects industry, and what becomes evident is that we only know what it tells us, and what is provided in "the making-of" information and other PR-based rhetoric is selective. By extension, even quotes and information from outside journalistic and trade publications should be approached warily. Taking a granular historical approach to ILM's rhetoric and digital effects technologies shows that, despite self-serving histories touting specific films as watersheds, ILM and the industry's adaptation of CGI took place in staggers and lurches, not in a smooth line.

One might assert that ILM did the important things it claims: most prominently, it produced the eye-popping, game-changing effects in *Terminator 2* and *Jurassic Park*. However, it matters that ILM presents a massaged, more exciting version of history, because through repetition that story has become accepted reality. Moreover, ILM's aggressive but behind-the-scenes moves were made easier and more coercive by dint of its invincible image and rhetoric. Over the years, ILM has used this rhetoric to recruit talent, bolster its market position, and erase its rivals. And perhaps most important, the rhetoric has made ILM's own historical style seem natural and inevitable. Because ILM's in-house style is inevitable, any other style or approach that results in any different style becomes unacceptable, even a misrepresentation of reality.

Like any other technological transition the movie business has endured, the history of the transition to digital technology, and specifically the development of CGI, was not the continuous path to an obvious goal. When scholars see the seams in the industry's—and especially ILM's—histories and discourses, we not only recognize the act of retconning and the rhetorical blue-screen versions of events at work in these blockbusters and the industry that produced them; we also see cinema history more clearly.

Monsters Are Real

FOUR

ILM's International Standard of Effects Realism in the Global Marketplace

THE HOST MIGHT LOOK AS IF IT FOLLOWS THE CONVENTIONS AND EXCITEMENT OF THE PREVIOUS GENRE FILMS, BUT IT HAS SCENES THAT WE'VE NEVER SEEN IN WESTERN MOVIES BEFORE.

—SOUTH KOREAN DIRECTOR BONG JOON-HO

[THE GREAT WALL], INDEED, IS MY FIRST MOVIE TO HAVE THIS MANY MONSTERS IN IT—AND, ALSO, SO MANY VISUAL EFFECTS SHOTS.

—CHINESE DIRECTOR ZHANG YIMOU

Since the 1990s, ILM has capitalized on its industrial, cultural, and technological power to establish itself at the apex of the effects industry and thereby promote its in-house version of effects realism. This chapter and chapter 5 will consider the dissemination of the ILM aesthetic as a citational style frequently independent of ILM itself, both when ILM works directly on a project with other effects companies and also when it does not. Chapter 5 will consider how the ILM style has evolved beyond ILM through the Marvel Cinematic Universe. However, in this chapter I contend that the impact of the ILM aesthetic is not limited to the top-of-the-line Hollywood-style effects companies that can afford to compete with ILM, such as the houses described in chapter 1. ILM's aesthetic dominance is so complete that the ILM style has set expectations and a standard for effects aesthetics for nearly every filmmaking production that expects to play in the global marketplace. In effect, the industry standard that ILM has imposed on the major effects companies has solidified into what I am calling the "international standard of effects realism" (ISER). This heuristic term is admittedly awkward, but it unites the various approaches different filmmakers and productions take. It is a heuristic because most productions and effects companies do not recognize it as an explicit pressure exerted from outside. Most simply understand ISER not even as a style but implicitly as professional standards that lead to an agreed-upon realism.

Because ISER is largely unspoken does not mean it is imaginary; neither is it necessarily applied unthinkingly. As stated in chapter 2, ILM maintains its market dominance and differentiates its market position by promoting the contradictory promise of the most noticeably unnoticeable, perfectly imperfect effects that will also blow your socks off—effects only ILM can pull off. This has not meant the straightforward dispersal of the ILM house style. Instead, I contend that ISER is a kind of stereotype of the ILM house style. It represents the elements that can be formulated, streamlined, and distributed to partners. In other words, much of the basic stylistic approach is retained: the emphasis on a perfectly executed, seamless photorealism; anthropomorphic creature design; fast-paced, kinetic action; a hectic moving frame; the simulation of environmental effects picked up by camera lenses and filters; and, finally, "wow" moments of spectatorial wonder. What cannot be so easily replicated is ILM's expensive technological advantages as well as its well-honed aesthetic tradition and experience reaching back decades.

ISER is important to identify and name because, if global filmmakers outside Hollywood want their films to circulate in the global and especially North American markets, ILM's style is what they must aspire to, adopt, or, in some cases, slyly defy. In other words, ILM's initiatives to impose its style on the rest of the industry have become so successful that the style now operates more or less independently of ILM itself and can be used citationally. What I mean to convey is that filmmakers recognize the pressure to adopt ISER and use it for practical, rhetorical, or polemic purposes and meanings that ILM might not consider.

Nevertheless, while most of the global effects work still reinforces the industrial primacy of ILM style, this is not a dishearteningly centrifugal account along the lines of the Toby Miller and colleagues' "Global

Hollywood" model in which Hollywood dictates terms and the rest of the world snaps into line. While ISER is a vital reference point for these productions, we cannot identify this as simple cultural imperialism in a straightforward way.[1] The Global Hollywood thesis emphasizes the pressures exerted on global markets to conform to Hollywood standards and to adopt Hollywood practices. More vulgarly, it implies that filmmaking cultures in other markets either eagerly adopt US product unquestioningly or are otherwise powerless to resist. What this theory neglects is how other markets in the world might look toward adapting or resisting US product with a strategy in mind. Instead, it is better described along the lines of Miriam Hansen's vernacular modernism, where filmmakers adopt and adapt the globally dominant form to reach the widest audience possible as a way to comment on both hot-button social issues in an oblique way (often to avoid censorship) and also as metacommentary on the position of the global filmmaker in the face of Hollywood dominance.[2] For Hansen, Hollywood cinema, from the silent period on, was so popular around the world in part because of how it displayed up-to-date modernity and provided a vehicle for films to deal with modern issues that were not otherwise being discussed in the public sphere, such as women's economic precarity. As in Hansen's example of silent films made in Shanghai in the 1920s, I do not think these filmmakers who look to Hollywood for examples are doing so because they want to thoughtlessly or coercively adapt a popular model. What they want to say and how they want to show it are going to differ from film to film and from context to context, but this serves a purpose for the filmmakers. The adaptation of ISER serves what they want to say and present in various ways, whether to assert up-to-date technological facility, circulate on the global market, and/or register a resistance to Hollywood dominance.[3] ISER's powerful visual credibility is allegorized to a vision of the world that filmmakers use to show their own local audiences something specific, something that can also be understandable to international audiences accustomed to and expecting that style. As the examples below will illustrate, international filmmakers frequently use the framework of the Hollywood blockbuster or genre films by choice and shrewdly deploy an ISER aesthetic as a commentary on global filmmaking.

I contend that thoughtful users modify the ISER-imposed ILM style most meaningfully through savvy deployment of digital foregrounding. While ILM wants to wow the viewer with amazing photoreal effects, it takes care to downplay as much as possible that they are digital effects, what ILM refers to as the "digital curse." ISER, however, often strategically displays the digital object as an effect—a showy or impressive effect the production has achieved. What this means is accentuating the aesthetically or thematically relevant elements of the "digitalness" of the effects, including perfection, plasticity, algorithmic regularity, clean lines, and other aesthetic aspects associated with digital effects. I suggest that, to filmmakers, foregrounding digitalness can have two major but not always overlapping advantages: highlighting nationalistic technological prowess (see what we can do now, too!) as well as foregrounding the thematic potential in visible technology (see what using this technology means?).

The foregrounding of digital technology distinguishing ISER from the ILM house style has consequences beyond aesthetic expressivity. Moreover, many global filmmaking contexts link the ability to produce digital effects blockbusters explicitly to their competition with Hollywood and, by extension, the global economic superpowers. As the scholars Aynne Kokas and Rey Chow have argued within the context of China and mainland Chinese movie production, there has been much discussion in that country linking national pride with cinematic achievement. Kokas links Chinese president Xi Jinping's notion of the "Chinese Dream"—a globalized China brand as intellectual property—with the long-standing notion of Hollywood as the "dream factory" aspiring to a similar global cultural power. As Kokas put it: "When trying to build a global vision of the Chinese Dream, what could be better than turning to the *original* dream factory?"[4]

While the Chinese political rhetoric can be quite explicit in linking global economic power and the mastery of blockbuster-style digital technology, other national market contexts likewise see blockbusters as avatars of cultural power and influence. Likewise speaking of China, but less about governmentally proscribed factors Rey Chow skeptically links China's global economic ascendency with the mastery of technology, specifically Hollywood blockbuster technology:

> If China was once a subaltern among nations—enduring social inequality, disenfranchisement, and underrepresentation or unrepresentability—as a result of the globally mediated transactions of the 1980s, *it now talks back fluently and stares back proudly in languages and images of high tech, futuristic architecture, and finance capital.* This economic semiotic transfer is corroborated in the first decade of the

twenty-first century by blockbuster films . . . in which a masculinist moral universe
. . . is packaged for the big-budget screen with bestselling contemporary ingre-
dients like naturalized heterosexuality, fetishized female body parts, computer-
enhanced cinematography, and special effects.[5]

Chow describes the nationalistic market appeal of the blockbuster strategy in non-Hollywood productions. From a filmmaking approach, while
the impulse to demonstrate that one's culture is no longer subaltern
may be stronger in South Korea, say, than in France or the United Kingdom, all other national, geographic, and linguistic markets have been
faced with the cultural and economic domination of Hollywood since
at least the 1910s. In Chow's gendered formula, blockbuster films with
digital effects reinvigorate, effectively remasculinizing the subaltern film
culture (which is all of them) feminized by Hollywood domination.

In her book *Media Heterotopias*, Hye Jean Chung studies Hollywood's
discourses around creating "seamless" blockbusters.[6] She defines
"seamlessness" in industrial, aesthetic, and narrative terms, arguing that this rhetoric deployed by filmmakers, producers, executives,
and below-the-line workers alike aims to downplay the transnational
heterogeneity—and erase the transnational labor—that makes up a
Hollywood blockbusters' composite parts. I agree with Chung about the
rhetoric's political and polemic implications. What I aim to highlight,
however, is where in transnational production the effects are not invisible or seamless at all but designed to be seen *as* effects. Certainly, as she
points out, effects work very frequently has the contradictory job to be
seamlessly photorealistic and highly visible at the same time. However,
I contend that the non-Hollywood filmmaker's appropriation of ILM's
effects style is not often meant to be entirely visibly erased. Like Chung,
I see the digital monster in *The Host* (2006), to use an example common
to both of our studies, as a giant "visible seam" threatening the integrity
of cinematic space.[7] I agree that the seam represented by the monster
materializes the film's contradictory desires to be at the same time "Korean" and transnational. However, I interpret that seam as the visible
evidence that highlights the CGI monster's difference from Hollywood
blockbusters, not its merging with them.

Although rarely spoken about directly, as we can see from the quotes
that begin this chapter, the producers and filmmakers of global auteurist, genre, and blockbuster films are very aware of the need to abide
by the unspoken ILM version of ISER. While promoting *The Great*

Wall (2016), designed to be a model for Chinese-US blockbuster-scale coproductions (albeit funded primarily with Chinese money), the renowned Chinese auteurist director Zhang Yimou stated his concerns and his new considerations in working on a blockbuster scale:

> This, indeed, is my first movie to have this many monsters in it—and, also, so many visual effects shots. But this is also the first time I've made a Hollywood blockbuster, what we call a popcorn movie. The story actually came from American writers, and when my agents sent it to me, they weren't quite sure I'd even consider it. So I looked at it and there were certain elements that actually interested me. I'd never tried this before, and I always like to try something new, so why not give it a shot?[8]

While he speaks somewhat obliquely, it is clear from how production ensued that Zhang's evocation of Hollywood "popcorn movies" demonstrates how he also understands that an expensive, cross-border movie with "this many monsters" required the Hollywood-style effects and Hollywood cooperation that the movie exhibited. It did so most obviously by starring the Hollywood actor Matt Damon, but it also demonstrated its status by hiring the two most prestigious effects companies as the major vendors for the film: ILM and Weta. Zhang's long career and presence in international film festivals since the 1980s means he is accustomed to the world stage and savvy about how the grander scale of *The Great Wall*'s production would necessitate a modification of his previous, non–effects-heavy approach.

The global ambitions of South Korean director Bong Joon-ho's 2006 film *The Host* were trumpeted even more directly by one of the film's producers, Lewis Kim: "Our ambition was to deliver a high-end monster movie that will appeal to audiences worldwide. The way to guarantee the quality was to select the best effects elements from around the world."[9] Bong himself is more circumspect; like Zhang he uses similarly implicit but pointed language:

> The monster genre, excluding the Godzilla series from Japan, is in itself quite American. *The Host* might look as if it follows the conventions and excitement of the previous genre films, but it has scenes that we've never seen in Western movies before, like corpses lying around the group memorial where families are hugging each other, crying.[10]

Also like Zhang, Bong indicates he is altering *both* the aesthetic and subject matter of Hollywood blockbusters to suit his own purposes.

Likewise, global effects practitioners' rhetoric frequently follows the rhetoric of these auteurist directors. The trade and business press in the countries from which these films emerge often attest to the need for local effects companies to raise themselves to the level of Hollywood effects houses, specifically invoking ILM. UK houses Double Negative, The Moving Picture Company, and Framework speak from hindsight, having once been local effects houses that did in fact rise to the level of the top tier. DNeg CEO Matt Holben recalls the late 1990s and early aughts: "We could only aspire to have the R&D teams and vast resources that [the California houses] did." MPC's Christian Roberton, managing director of film, likewise uses Hollywood as a benchmark: "[Our success] has given us the confidence to go to the studios and guarantee that we can deliver to the same level as the California houses."[11]

The tone is more aspirational in other major film centers. At Prime Focus, an Indian American effects house, one executive lamented: "Most of the work is done [at the US branch] for Hollywood projects simply because India is not yet ready for the level of work international studios want."[12] Terrance Chang, producer on the John Woo film *Red Cliff* (2008), explained the need for an extensive US crew in terms of experience: "As good as crews can be in China, they have no experience [with] a movie of this scale, and I can't train people on the set"[13]—a sentiment echoed by producers for *The Great Wall* nearly ten years later.

The capability to produce large-scale effects across several production budgets changed significantly from the late 1990s to the 2010s. Following a historical trajectory from the early days of notable but modest digital effects work available to global productions in the 2000s to more global effects extravaganzas of the 2010s, the remainder of this chapter will trace how filmmakers in the global distribution marketplace use an ILM-derived ISER style both materially and rhetorically. These productions—including *The Host*, *The Great Wall*, and *Valerian and the City of a Thousand Planets* (2017)—frequently deploy ISER and simultaneously comment on it within their narrative thematics and aesthetic rhetoric. Later in this chapter, I explore ISER alternatives, including two Chinese examples, *The Mermaid* (2016) and *Wolf Warrior* (2015). However, I will not attempt an extensive study of local production (meaning filmmaking that is not meant for international distribution) of individual countries. It is beyond the scope of this chapter to attempt a market-by-market analysis. There are thousands upon thousands of effects companies around the world who work primarily on television commercials, video games, or web-based moving images. Although I believe they are also impacted by the ILM aesthetic, it is likewise beyond the scope of this study to bring them into the analysis. Certainly, most of the top-tier companies complete work on these and other ancillary media. And though there is some overlap, animation firms primarily tend to act within a different marketplace and labor pool. This chapter will mention some of the smaller regional effects companies that have worked on the films discussed. However, this chapter will focus more on the specific, effects-heavy, internationally distributed films more directly shaped by ISER pressures.

The Global Effects Industry

ILM's ability to assert aesthetic dominance over effects production outside Hollywood and Hollywood-style productions is and is not related to the "runaway production" the Hollywood effects business faced in the mid-2000s, transforming from a mostly California-based industry to one that is globally dispersed.[14] As described in chapter 1, in the mid-2000s, the major effects companies started opening effects branches in places that offered lower labor costs and tax incentives. Likewise, smaller companies appeared, subcontracting with the major companies and undertaking the copious but more rote effects work on blockbusters. Due to the greater ease in sharing large image files, these companies can be located anywhere. Government tax incentives and rebates led to the clustering of effects companies in Canada (especially Vancouver and Montreal), the United Kingdom, Australia, and New Zealand.[15] Regions with lower labor costs, including India, China, South Korea, and Malaysia, have also seen investments from US and European effects companies.[16] The low cost of entry means smaller independent boutique shops can be located far from any robust filmmaking context, including in Kosovo, Singapore, and South Africa.

Given this globalized dissemination of the VFX industry, one might easily conclude that the proliferation of Hollywood-style effects companies in locations around the globe would have created a parallel boom for effects work in the films being produced in those locales. In other words, a major Hollywood effects firm might open a new branch in Seoul, Chennai, or Shanghai, to cite examples with robust local filmmaking cultures. And one might assume that the local presence of these houses, through training programs and labor circulation, "lifts up" the quality and sophistication of the homegrown effects work to a global standard. By extension, the assumption might be that, if a major global filmmaker such as South Korean auteur Bong Joon-ho is making an effects-heavy film for global distribution, he would hire the same South Korean firms "lifted up" by the Hollywood firms in their midst. In fact, this scenario almost never plays out this way. John Swallow, VFX supervisor at Universal for fourteen years, articulated the problem in terms of resources: "Lots of people can get images 80 percent done. It comes down to having enough time to do that last 20 percent. And if shots are added, quality tends to suffer."[17] In other words, the industry believes that only the top tier has the scale to complete Hollywood-style work to Hollywood-style standards. This may or may not actually be true, but it certainly helps the top tier maintain its status.

More commonly, the Hollywood-style effects houses' presence in tax-incentive and low-labor-cost economic zones has instead reinforced a two-tiered system. This means that the global company works more or less in isolation on blockbuster Hollywood products, while smaller local firms have little or no contact with the top tier and work only on local products for local consumption. Moreover, most of the leadership is imported from the North American, European, and Australasian Hollywood-style companies. In other words, if Bong Joon-ho needs ISER effects so his movie can open at the Cannes Film Festival, he is largely going to have to use companies outside South Korea to make that happen.

One might cite the United Kingdom as an example for the way it reinforces this two-tiered pattern. From about 2008 to 2012, several articles in the trade press vaunted the so-called *Harry Potter* effect (discussed in chapter 1) on the London scene.[18] The eight-part film franchise did indeed attract a great deal of international talent to fill jobs, which in part led to a proliferation of top-tier effects companies opening branches in the area (including ILM in 2014[19]), as well as a robust second tier of companies. But whether the *Harry Potter* effect has had a broader impact on UK film production is debatable at best. The Hollywood-financed portions of the UK industry indeed benefited greatly from local top-tier effects companies (DNeg, Framestore, MPC) in high-budget films such as *Fantastic Beasts and Where to Find Them* (2016) and *Dunkirk* (2017), as well as occasionally in lower-budget effects-heavy films such as *Attack the Block* (2011) and *Ex Machina* (2014).[20] However, those Hollywood studio–funded productions are difficult to categorize as "local UK" productions, with the exception of the mostly UK-funded *Attack the Block*. Since the early 2010s, for UK-based, non–Hollywood-backed productions, if the filmmakers have a significant investment and are shooting for broad global reach or major awards attention, they typically can afford only to use a mix of top-tier and second-tier effects houses. Some examples of globally ambitious local UK output include *The Second Best Exotic Marigold Hotel* (2015, DNeg), *Paddington* and *Paddington 2* (2014 and 2017, Framestore), *Murder on the Orient Express* (2017, MPC), and *Darkest Hour* (2017, Framestore). More typically, UK-financed productions such as *Belle* (2013), *Mr. Turner* (2014), and *T2 Trainspotting* (2017) exclusively used second-tier (or lower) effects companies (BlueBolt, One of Us, Union, Milk). Other UK-based mid- and low-range productions hiring second-tier effects houses exclusively include *The King's Speech* (2010), *Anna Karenina* (2012), *Dredd* (2012), *About Time* (2013); *Trance* (2013), *Victoria and Abdul* (2017), *My Cousin Rachel* (2017), *Yesterday* (2019), *Tolkien* (2019), *Misbehaviour* (2020), and *Emma.* (2020).[21] London-based effects executives have conceded that, while the production of the *Harry Potter* films (2001–2011) was important to bringing international blockbusters to London, it took generous tax incentives to keep them there.[22]

Moreover, the impact of top-tier effects companies on local filmmaking cultures outside the United Kingdom has not been the "lifting up" benefit one might expect. As an instructive and more typical example of how top-tier effects companies work "offshore," ILM in 2012 formed a partnership with Beijing-based company Base FX.[23] The *Harry Potter* effect model assumes that if a top-tier effects company such as ILM opens a branch in Beijing, such a move would lead to the influx of international know-how and benefit the local labor pool of effects work. In theory, the local filmmaking culture's effects work would improve to follow international standards, and international Chinese auteurs would hire Base FX and related companies to work on films. In the Chinese context, little of this happened. The partnership with ILM stipulates that Base FX is contractually free to work with Chinese and independent productions. However, Base FX has very rarely done so and is, in practice, exclusive.[24] Likewise, Sony PI's Chennai branch (which closed in 2014) and Rhythm & Hues Malaysia (changed management in 2013) likewise had more or less exclusive relationships with their corporate owners and did not work on outside productions.[25]

Global Ambitions, ISER Effects

I contend that a consistent aspect of the dispersal of effects companies has been the homogenizing of an agreed-upon, consistent aesthetic standard that filmmakers tweak for specific needs. This section will consider examples from distribution categories I am calling the "global auteurist film," the "global genre film," and the "non-Hollywood international blockbuster." Where these categories overlap is on effects-heavy filmmaking made with the expectation of significant global consumption, whether through conventional cineplexes, the major festivals circuits, or global home-video distribution.

Again, the major category of global filmmaking that demonstrates the reach of the contemporary ILM-based international standard of effects realism is international films that feature significant effects work and expect to play beyond national or linguistic borders to a global audience. The auteurist effects film means a film designed to compete in a major international film festival, such as Cannes or Toronto, made by a global auteur.[26] "Global auteur" is defined here as a filmmaker who is recognized or styles himself or herself as a distinct filmmaking personality and whose films regularly play and compete in international festivals; the list includes, for example, Park Chan-wook, Alejandro González Iñárritu, Claire Denis, and Yorgos Lanthimos. The generic category frequently includes lesser-known filmmakers seeking to make an impact and gain international distribution at a festival or through video or streaming services, which usually means genres most closely associated with effects films, such as science fiction, fantasy, horror, and action films including *Attack the Block*, *The Raid: Redemption* (2011), and *The Babadook* (2014). The last category is the international blockbuster, which until recently was the exclusive domain of Hollywood. In this case, I do not include mostly Hollywood-funded productions such as the UK-based and -themed *Harry Potter* series and *Dunkirk*. Instead I am referring to films with a budget and scope comparable to Hollywood films but originating outside major Hollywood investment, such as *The Great Wall* (funded largely by Legendary, a subsidiary of the Chinese Wanda group) and *Valerian and the City of a Thousand Planets* (funded by EuropaCorp and partners).[27] Although most of these films have a significantly lower budget than, say, a *Star Wars* installment, the success of all of these films depends on adhering to more or less the same international standard for realism as the more expensive, Hollywood-funded blockbusters.

The dominance of the ILM-led ISER approach and the pressure on global effects houses have meant that, unlike these previous examples, a science fiction film from Korea, the United Kingdom, or South Africa must look more or less like a Hollywood science fiction film. Whether high-budget aspirational blockbusters or lower-budgeted projects, my research shows that non-Hollywood effects-reliant films directed by global auteurs such as Zhang Yimou, Ang Lee, Guillermo del Toro, John Woo, Yorgos Lanthimos, Lars von Trier, and many others were almost always under the visual effects supervision of one of the Hollywood-experienced top- or second-tier effects firms. And this is true despite some availability of local talent (which was only occasionally used and in a limited manner).

Historically, films outside Hollywood aiming for an international audience have featured cinematic subject matter and visual material not allowed or not encouraged by the Hollywood mainstream hegemonic practice. Traditionally, this has meant more nudity and explicit sex as in the midcentury art films by Ingmar Bergman, Federico Fellini, and Imamura Shohei or, more recently, the shock effects of violent and/ or sexual content of the festival/art house provocateurs such as Lars von Trier, Park Chan-wook, Catherine Breillat, and Julia Ducournau. Furthermore, the marketing strategy of genre appropriation for genre exportability has long been followed by global filmmakers seeking an international audience and distribution, from the serious-minded intensification of Sergio Leone's spaghetti westerns to the sincere but also winking melodrama of Pedro Almodóvar. These precedents have, however, been free and even critically encouraged to introduce a fresh visual aesthetic to the genre they are working in.

As a contrast to the global auteurs who deploy ISER, we may think of other auteurist filmmakers' making a virtue of limited means by accentuating the antinaturalism of their effects, as in the black-and-white sequence in Almodóvar's *Talk to Her* (2002), completed by local Spanish effects companies, which does revel in a creative but recognizably silly effects sequence; or Michel Gondry's purposefully craftsy, handmade effects in *The Science of Sleep* (2006); or the evident miniatures in Wes Anderson's *The Grand Budapest Hotel* (2014). In other words, these are meant as knowing postmodern winks at blockbusters that would otherwise be undermined by purposefully "bad" or cheesy effects. However, for many recent international genre filmmakers, such as Bong, del Toro, and *Attack the Block*'s Joe Cornish, there appears to be little or no virtue or strategic advantage in cheap-looking effects. Instead, if they want their films to visually rank alongside Steven Spielberg or Peter Jackson in their believable monsters, it means hiring Hollywood-caliber effects companies to complete the bulk of the work.

On the industrial side, around 2005, more and more films from international markets began making use of elaborate and visible visual effects. As *Time* magazine put it in a 2010 article:

> The global VFX industry has been fragmenting. It encompasses everything from [George] Lucas' 35-year-old state-of-the-art empire [Industrial Light & Magic] to months-old shops in India and China. Scott Ross, a former CEO of Digital Domain and general manager at ILM, estimates that VFX is a $1.35 billion industry, with the big five shops [Industrial Light & Magic, Weta, Digital Domain Sony Picture Image Works and Rhythm and Hues] each pulling in $80 million to $100 million a year and the many smaller shops taking in as little as $1 million.[28]

By 2005, nearly every reputable effects house anywhere in the world could competently complete basic photoreal effects work with standard equipment and a minimum of rendering power. This included, for example, basic digital compositing, rotoscope erasure of unwanted elements (such as wires), and virtual computer screens. Lower-tier companies could also handle simpler digital mise-en-scène objects such as automobiles and tanks, as well as natural elements such as fire and water, for contexts where off-the-shelf software was appropriate.

Top-tier houses were and are still needed where effects are necessarily visible: complex virtual environments and digital creatures or character design and animation. Research on South Korea's *The Host* (2006), mainland China's *Red Cliff* (2008), India's *Enthiran* [*Robot*] (2010), and many others confirms that films in this first wave provided very little benefit to local effects houses and vice versa.[29] For auteurist filmmakers in the international market, in fact, the opposite occurred. Rather than use local South Korean effects houses on *The Host*, director Bong hired prominent international effects houses Weta and the US-based Orphanage (now closed) almost exclusively to create his giant mutated beast, apparently to the chagrin of the local Korean marketplace.[30] The *Enthiran*/*Robot* production, touted as the most expensive in India's history up to that time, contracted its most visible effects with the Stan Winston Studio, now called Legacy Effects, in the United States.[31] Second-tier US and Canadian companies The Orphanage, Frantic Films, CafeFX, and Tippett Studio contributed to the bulk of the extensive battle sequences in Woo's *Red Cliff.*

Similarly, the majority of effects on Guillermo del Toro's Spain-set *Pan's Labyrinth* (2006) were produced by the US company CafeFX. And though shot primarily in South Africa, the South African director Neill Blomkamp's *District 9* (2009) made use of Weta, his mentor Peter Jackson's effects company.[32] Again, nearly all of these productions included some work from effects companies based in the director's home country. However, mainline companies—largely second-tier ones accustomed to working with major Hollywood productions—completed the majority of the effects. From the mid-2000s to the mid-2010s, the situation for local effects companies only saw minor changes. If anything, the rise of the non-Hollywood blockbuster only reinforced the need for international houses to produce within ISER. The greater the global ambitions, the more likely the production to hire the top-tier international houses. Early on in the mid-2000s, global auteurs turned to Hollywood-experienced effects companies but could not afford the top tier. By the mid-2010s, due to the rise of well-financed production companies outside the United States, two Hollywood-style global blockbusters, Zhang Yimou's *The Great Wall* (2016) and Luc Besson's *Valerian and the City of a Thousand Planets* (2017), could afford to hire the highest of high-end international effects teams—ILM and Weta—among several others in both cases.

Certainly, it should not be surprising that global filmmaking chases global tax incentives like everyone else or that the nationality of the director does not determine the location of the effects houses used. However, the pressure to adhere to ISER means that global auteurs, in order to get that "last 20 percent" of perceived Hollywood quality, consistently turn to Hollywood-experienced firms rather than local or cheaper companies who historically cannot afford to work within the same aesthetic expectations.

While I contend that all the films discussed in this section deploy ISER as developed by ILM, I do not suggest they all do it in the same way for the same reason or to the same effect or impact. These filmmakers and many others deploy ISER as a discourse rather than a blindly adapted standard forced on them. Namely, in the examples cited below, all use ISER as a strategy not only for their narrative and in order to circulate in the global marketplace but also as a way to comment on social issues and global filmmaking practices. With their invasion and colonization science fiction narratives, they are especially concerned with the dominance of the Hollywood blockbuster over all other film-making contexts. In this way, I contend that many filmmakers use the ISER aesthetic to strike back at Hollywood while seeming to conform to it.

ISER in Global Filmmaking

Bong, Zhang, Besson, and others want to compete on the same playing field as Hollywood blockbusters while adding meanings through effects in a way that Hollywood films would not consider, and they also display digital effects more flagrantly than ILM would likely do. Finally, these filmmakers evince a desire to show us how they use Hollywood's tools to critique Hollywood's dominance of the international market.

Bong's *The Host* is an especially ambitious early example of such blockbuster aesthetic appropriation. The film premiered at the Cannes Film Festival and also played the international film festivals in Toronto, New York, and elsewhere. As *Sight & Sound* said of *The Host* in relation to genre, director Bong engages not in a subversion of genre but in an embrace and reinvention of it.[33] Briefly, the film depicts the unexpected appearance of a giant monster on the bridge over the Han River in Seoul, attributed to the US military–led dumping of toxic chemicals. The monster runs amok, capturing the daughter (Ko Asung) of the hapless main character, Park Gang-Doo (Song Kang-ho), which triggers a rescue mission from her family. For *The Host*'s effects production, the primary energy went into designing and executing the movie's giant river monster. As with other movie monsters—from Frankenstein to Godzilla to King Kong—the creature also carried a great deal of the film's metaphoric heft.[34]

We get our first good look at the monster in a sequence where Park's daughter Hyun-seo is captured by the monster on the banks of the Han River where the family has a modest food truck. Through camerawork, staging, and lighting, we can see Bong's ambition to rival a Steven Spielberg movie, most specifically the previous year's Spielberg-directed *War of the Worlds* (2005) (figure 4.01). Both films use the look of unstabilized mobile handheld shots of the main actors in the foreground fleeing creatures advancing on them from behind, with very similar camera placements, lighting styles, and figure movements. It is also quite clear that the film's power and integrity depend on the visual credibility and

Fig. 4.01 *War of the Worlds* (2005): Tom Cruise running from the alien Tripods provides an important model for Bong's creature reveal in *The Host*.

actual scariness of the monster. Technologically, the monster is well integrated into the riverbank mise-en-scène by matching its lighting and atmospherics. And the monster moves logically and fluidly according to its character design's shape and bulk, in this case a kind of giant slug/fish/salamander hybrid. Unusually for a lower-budget film, the monster is on screen in full view for an abnormally long period of time in what is presented as full sunlight. More often, effects teams—even the most expensive ones—avoid full sunlight and instead hide the effects objects with obscuring techniques such as darkness, backlighting, lens flares, as well as shorter takes to move the eye around and not let it scrutinize the effects object too closely for too long. Here, the effects teams cleverly deploy the intensity of the sunlight as well as several other common ISER lighting and focus tricks to make viewers think they are seeing more of the monster than they really are. Park and his daughter Hyun-seo frequently appear at the top of the frame in medium close-up, with the monster advancing on them from the deep space. This allows the human figures in the foreground to be in sharp focus while the monster is slightly out of focus. The overall lighting is an intensely bright-yellow, blown-out, diffused sunlight, which causes background figures to lose definition through backlighting and creates planar distinctions through atmospheric haze (figure 4.02). While very much within ISER expectations, the effects nature of the creature is more evident than typical in an ILM production. The choice of a daylight attack suggests the filmmakers are (rightly) very proud of their monster and want to show it off as much as possible—a marketing tagline for the film is "Monsters Are Real"—and they even accentuate their impressive animation effects achievement with slow motion.

While also featuring an invasion/attack narrative and hewing closely to the aesthetics used in *War of the Worlds*, the monster in *The Host* as an effects object and in effects sequences creates resonances that differentiate it from the Spielberg film. Rather than being from outer space, the monster here is portrayed (not unlike Godzilla) as the product of environmental pollution, in this case caused by the American military having dumped classified chemicals unthinkingly into the Han. The resulting giant, pitiless, sludgy mutation attacks and devours random South Koreans along the riverbanks, punishing them for their collusion with American interference. In this way, the monster in *The Host* plays both sides. It satisfies the South Korean audience's desire for locally produced products in the style of Hollywood spectaculars, and it also provides a metaphoric reprimand for acceding to the demands of outside American interests and values and, moreover, for demanding such monsters through market forces. It is as if to say, "See the monster you've created? The monsters *are* real"—and they can be defeated. Through its effects object, *The Host* is able to demonstrate to the rest of the world through the festival circuit and home video that South Korean filmmaking can compete technologically and aesthetically in the global marketplace. Also, the film demonstrates how the production does not

Fig. 4.02 *The Host* (2006): Bong's creature fits within the expectations of the international standard of effects realism to play in the international market.

blindly or thoughtlessly follow the external threat of ISER; instead it takes the foreign "pollution" and in turn uses it to speak to its own specific South Korean context.

The Host is among the early wave of international genre pictures that made use of the lower price and greater availability of international-standard effects services, albeit for a relatively modest number of effects shots and with a limited budget. By the mid-2010s, it became possible for international productions to begin to aspire to grand, Hollywood-style blockbusters, with similar 2,000-plus effects shot counts. The two primary examples are The Great Wall and Valerian and the City of a Thousand Planets, which go well beyond the modest effects program of The Host with the goal of competing with, finding an alternative to, and aesthetically surpassing Hollywood blockbuster output. In the case of The Great Wall, the film takes the template of an epic fantasy spectacle such as the Lord of the Rings franchise films (2001–2003), especially in the elaborate use of creature design and animation, set and environmental extension, crowd-building, and the climactic siege/battle sequence. However, it presents a blockbuster displaying Chinese nationalistic values such as altruism, collectivism, and honor, in contrast to Western (Hollywood) greed and rapacious capitalism. In Valerian's multitude of creature design and animation, character morphing, detailed world-building, and kinetic action sequences, Besson sees your Star Wars and then raises the stakes in imagination, fantasy, and narrative risk-taking. Tellingly, both films use the same major Hollywood-style effects companies (ILM and Weta) alongside Canadian shops Hybride and Rodeo that their Hollywood models use. Even in seeking to create an alternative for or improvement on Hollywood blockbusters, the productions feel they need to realize an outsized spectacle that is grounded in the expectations of ISER to play across various international audiences, including the US market.

Renowned Chinese art film director Zhang Yimou made his mark with international successes Raise the Red Lantern (1991) and House of Flying Daggers (2004). The ambitious and epic The Great Wall announced its global aspirations not only through its expense and scale but also by casting Hollywood action star (and globally bankable) Matt Damon, along with Willem Dafoe and Game of Thrones (2011–2019) alum Pedro Pascal among the lead roles. The production likewise cast older and newer Chinese superstars, including Andy Lau and Tian Jing, as well as several young male teen idols to increase East Asian appeal.[35]

Rather than what might be called a historical epic with expectations of factual accuracy, *The Great Wall* is pure historicized fantasy. In the film, Damon and Pascal, who play Western mercenaries William and Tovar, are looking for China's fabled gunpowder in a loosely historicized past (styled to evoke the Song Dynasty circa 1000 AD). They encounter the Nameless Order, a crack team of defenders along a Great Wall much like the existing one on China's historical northern border. After overcoming the initial distrust of the Chinese defenders and forming an alliance with guard Commander Lin Mea (Tian Jing), William and Tovar join the fight against the monstrous creatures (Tao Tei, based on a beast from Chinese mythology) that periodically attack the wall. East and West combine know-how to take on and eventually defeat the swarming hordes of terrifying beasts. As this account of the narrative suggests, the *Lord of the Rings* films, with fortified battlements, giant armies of clashing humans and beasts, and acrobatic derring-do, provide appropriate templates for the effects program in Zhang's film.

The *Lord of the Rings* films portray a fellowship of distinct, individual human (and humanlike) characters who join forces to face off against an army of a mindless, undifferentiated, evil beasts. Like the *Lord of the Rings* movies, *The Great Wall* stages an abstracted, easily grasped Manichean narrative in starkly visual terms. As Kristen Whissel has described, both films deploy intensified verticality to stage a clash of cultures as a historical moment of truth, where good must triumph over evil.[36]

The battle where we see the monstrous Tao Tei en masse for the first time begins with an extravagant display of the digitally rendered cinematic environment: the (virtual) camera sweeps past enormous sheer walls with huge doors, indicating scale through (pointedly male and female) human soldiers. Verticality is emphasized by the pulleys that raise captives William and Tovar in an elevator-like cage up multiple levels of battlements until they reach the top of the wall, where the camera pulls back to a long shot with rows upon rows of soldiers along the twisting top of the wall, along with various giant catapults and other imposing weapons. The sense of battle readiness then intensifies through a lengthy montage sequence of soldiers springing into action, ready, in formation to do their expected duty. All of this is witnessed in cutaways by the awestruck William and Tovar. Attention then shifts to waiting for the beasts' arrival, as the film cuts around to the various divisions as they stand poised and alert. Finally, the Tao Tei funnel swiftly

Fig. 4.03 *The Great Wall* (2017): The humans' side consists of a well-organized and exquisitely trained army who fight not only fiercely but with martial artistry.

through the valley toward the wall. In response to the general's signal, the bright-blue drum corps starts pounding orders through their rhythm, prompting a well-coordinated team to set off fireballs from the catapults, which the camera follows as they explode among the Tao Tei. Scarlet-clad archers let off an impossibly thick hail of arrows, which the camera follows in *Matrix*-style "bullet time" until they connect with a creature's flank.[37] Some Tao Tei fall, but they continue to advance in immense numbers. Frequent cuts to long shots emphasize the scale of the attack (figure 4.03).

As the onslaught continues, the cerulean-armored, female Crane Division leaps balletically into action, diving from parapets hanging from cords. They fiercely stab at the wall-crawling Tao Tei with their lances, but empty, bloody hoops metonymically represent their sacrificial numbers. The Tao Tei queen, shielded by a force of paladins, barks transmitted orders to her throng, which they receive as if by radio waves. A few individual Tao Tei breach the top of the wall, so we can see them fight the Nameless Order in close combat. William and Tovar are released from their bonds, in time for William to show his archery and fighting skills and save the life of the general's son. The Spaniard Tovar even gets to break out a bit of toreador skills in fighting the beast, waving a red cape so that William can kill it. After a lengthy pitched battle, the queen inexplicably signals a retreat, and the Tao Tei rush back to the depths of the valley, pulling their dead and injured along with them. The Nameless Order regroups for the next fight, with some new information about their Western captives. The sequence is conceived and edited similarly to the Battle of Helm's Deep in *The Lord of the Rings: The Two Towers*, with sweeping camera moves that highlight scale in long shots and in plummeting virtual tracking shots, rapid cutting between the two sides picking up pace for suspense, and an emphasis on both sides' strategic coordination. In other words, as demonstrated in this early battle, *The Great Wall*'s effects strategies and priorities emphasize the expanded scale and size, height, and expanse available to the movie.

At one point in the film, Andy Lau's strategist (described in the press releases as "alchemist, intellectual and technological innovator"[38]) characterizes the Tao Tei as "greed unchecked," "devouring all meat" in their path. Moreover, the conception of the effects and the technological aesthetics used to depict them draw significant differences between the two sides. The hordes of lizardlike Tao Tei are seemingly made up of pure algorithm, which systematically swarm in formation as they attack (figure 4.04). As the ILM VFX supervisor put it: "Zhang Yimou wanted [the Tao Tei] to move in specific formations and form patterns."[39] Their appearances attacking the Great Wall are regular as well, occurring predictably every sixty years.

In contrast, the human multitude, instead of an unthinking, automated digital mass, is frequently seen in medium shot to demonstrate pointedly that they are not digitally generated (film promotion bragged of 500-plus costumed extras).[40] The Chinese Nameless Order troops are a color-coded, well-trained, disciplined crack force, instilled with ideals of duty and the honor of protecting their homeland. They are masters of the most advanced knowledge and technology (including gunpowder) available to them. Importantly, although many human troops and most of the Great Wall environments are digitally generated, only the Tao Tei

Fig. 4.04 *The Great Wall* (2017): By contrast, the Tao Tei monsters attack as if they are controlled by computer algorithms; their digital nature is foregrounded.

attacks are represented as markedly CGI, perhaps even in a dated way. The filmmakers took a good deal of care to make the Tao Tei move and swarm in a more artificially "computerized" manner, while the humans are more thoughtfully deliberate and specific. For example, while the Great Wall itself was completely digitally generated (no location shooting at the real landmark took place), the production built a great deal of sets to be tactile, depicting interior areas of the wall to a very grand scale and intricate detail.[41] We never see a lair or social structure for the Tao Tei, which makes them seem to be materializing out of nowhere. Weta Workshop, again renowned for its detailed costumes, props, and sets in the *Lord of the Rings* franchise, designed and executed the elaborate weapons and armor worn by the principal cast and the hundreds of extras. Though carefully designed with appropriate zoomorphic forms and movement and even decorative impressions on their bodies, the Tao Tei are otherwise indistinguishable from each other. The only personality traits they display are mercilessness and relentlessness.

Moreover, unlike the Tao Tei, human activity is carefully rendered as eminently skillful and artistically expressive. The Tao Tei's movements, especially as a mass, are too regular and mathematically formulated to read as conventionally ISER-realistic, which works with crowd-generating software (most famously Weta's Massive software developed for the *Lord of the Rings* films) to avoid a too-regular algorithmic look. By contrast, the blue-coded Crane Division divers are a good example of the human fighters' representation as skillful and regimented but also possessed of human artistry. The Cranes plummet at the Tao Tei as if Olympic platform divers, swooping gracefully on cords as they complete irregular, bungee-like trajectories with long spears, alighting gracefully back on the parapets. While likely not as efficient as a killing squad, they are indeed spectacular as cinematic objects.

Nevertheless, the Nameless Order is an analog multitude fighting a digital multitude and losing. Enter the Western partners. Matt Damon's European mercenary William is welcomed (at least provisionally) among the Nameless Order because he displays a similar physical prowess and improvisatory bravery. He flaunts his archery skills several times, most showily by pinning a teacup to a column with three arrow shots, and later leaps blindly through the fog to confront the Tao Tei in direct combat. The Nameless Order also welcomes and quickly adopts his Western knowledge of magnets and new fighting strategies. However, William's weakness comes in his admission to Commander Lin Mea that, unlike her, he is fighting for money and self-interest, not for honor and country. His character arc is to become more like the Nameless Order soldiers who selflessly devote themselves to China's (and by extension humanity's) overall good by not allowing the Tao Tei to reach populated areas where their access to human nourishment would make them unstoppable.

After East and West work together to allay the Tao Tei threat, William and Lin Mea, now promoted to General of the Northern Armies, go their separate ways. She thanks him and praises him as "more similar than I thought" in the end; despite some very mild flirting, she does not urge him to stay. In other words, Westerners may have many amazing skills, and the Chinese can learn from them, but only to fortify Chinese ways, which they will keep in the future.

As in Kokas's and Chow's earlier observations, *The Great Wall* demonstrates what Chinese authorities say they want for demonstrating their political, economic, and cultural ascendency to their own people and the world. The film features a world-renowned director in Zhang Yimou, an epic cast of both digital and human thousands, the glorification of an albeit fantastic history and patrimony, and of course a positive message about China's power and its responsible wielding of it. As a copartnership with Universal and other US investors with the Chinese production company Legendary, Zhan Haicheng of China Film Group said the movie brought together the "best of China and [the] U.S." and was a "real co-production," though he called it a "very American film."[42] Zhan continued: "The outlook from the beginning was, this is an international, English-language movie with Matt Damon and monsters, and it speaks to a specific demographic, and it happens to have Chinese themes."[43] And indeed, *The Great Wall* was reasonably successful in China, making $175 million, while decidedly less so in North America, where it made $45 million.[44]

Although a Chinese-based effects house, the ILM-affiliated Base FX, was employed on the production, the bulk of the effects were contracted to Western and Anglophone houses, mostly ILM and Weta but also Hybride of Montreal, Animal Logic of Australia, and Ghost VFX of Denmark.[45] Despite the nationalistic triumphalism of the film's themes and portrayal of Western "help" as useful but ultimately incidental, the film's epic scale, spectacle, and naturalistic fantasy elements would not have been possible without mainline Western effects houses and would not have been marketable as a "Chinese blockbuster" globally, as we will see with other Chinese examples below, without those houses' adherence to ISER.

Finally, the Tao Tei monsters are represented much like the way many science fiction films represent robots and artificial intelligence: scarily clever, adaptable, efficient, and heartless. Human environments such as the Great Wall itself were digitally generated but within ISER expectations. The Tao Tei lizards display a more fanciful, more "digital" character. What differentiates the sides is artistry and responsibility. *The Great Wall* does not display a fear of technology but rather the unthinking and greedy uses of technology. *The Great Wall* is about demonstrating that, programmatically, we (i.e., China) have the technology, and we can wield that technology with artistry and skill. We take things from the world that we use carefully, but we also give them back, and we give them back better. We do things mindfully; it is not just about capitalistic profits.

The 2017 film *Valerian and the City of a Thousand Planets* likewise was an attempt by the well-known French director and filmmaking mogul Luc Besson to compete with Hollywood at a like scale. *The Great Wall* and *Valerian* both use ISER-style effects from Hollywood effects houses but twist them to create a discourse about Hollywood's previously unchallenged place at the top of the economic and cultural blockbuster pyramid. A hypothetical and impolitic Luc Besson might call *The Great Wall* simply a cut-and-paste *Lord of the Rings*. He might uncharitably hit *The Great Wall* with a common charge against Chinese cultural and industrial productions: China is good at imitation but not innovation.[46] Certainly, more fairly, *The Great Wall* marries Zhang Yimou's aesthetic discernment to Western blockbuster templates and formulas. Besson in his film, while understanding that it needs to fit within the high-production value of ISER expectations, wants to imagine a European alternative to Hollywood. Using French *bande dessinée* source material, Besson and his team work to out-imagine the Hollywood space operas it recalls. Based on a beloved and long-running French series of graphic novels, *Valerian* introduces Valerian (Dane DeHaan) and Laureline (Cara Delevigne), twenty-eighth-century intergalactic operatives for the Human Federation who must go to Alpha, the titular City of a Thousand Planets, to unravel a mystery about the destruction of a civilization of "Pearl" beings with covetable resources, and uncover the conspiracy that surrounds it, to avoid a similar devastation of the universe.

Like *The Great Wall*, *Valerian* casts Anglophone leads with blockbuster credentials (though not as solid as Damon's), shoots with an

English-language script, and promotes a particular cultural patrimony through what might be called "cultural-nationalist intellectual property." Rather than the *Lord of the Rings* films, *Valerian* has in mind Hollywood space operas of the *Star Wars* variety, specifically, the looser, more variegated original 1977 *Star Wars* than the more homogenized and tightly controlled sequels that followed it. The film is action-paced and episodic in the extreme as Valerian and Laureline race among the detailed environments of the "thousand planets" and from effects set-piece to effects set-piece, encounter pop singer Rihanna as a shape-shifting performer in an illicit cabaret, a civilization of beings as elegantly elongated as Giacometti sculptures and iridescent as pearls, and many more intergalactic species of zoological or humanoid (or occasionally aqueous or gaseous) forms.

Not surprisingly, this production required more effects work than any non-Hollywood film had ever attempted. The production contracted an almost identical set of effects houses as *The Great Wall* (ILM, Weta, and Hybride, plus Base FX and Rodeo FX). *Valerian* was the largest effects film (Besson brags of 2,734 effects shots several times in the Blu-ray extras) and at a reported $178 million budget, the most expensive film ever made outside Hollywood, through an elaborate international coproduction led by Besson's own EuropaCorp and the Chinese investment company STX.

In many ways, *Valerian*'s effects approach tracks with many other Hollywood productions. Most of the multitudes of creatures were created through motion-capture technologies and used the two companies, ILM and Weta, most associated with creature triumphs in the past. And the majority of creatures display zoomorphically or anthropomorphically appropriate movement: elongated Pearls sashay with the grace and elegance of fashion models (many of the reference actors in motion-capture suits were in fact fashion models). The bottom-heavy Boulan-Bathor of the Red Zone's motion-capture models were large bouncer–size humans to capture the appropriate gait and relationship to gravity. All digital characters are integrated seamlessly into their intricately designed bluescreen environments.

And although the creature work cannot be faulted from an ISER perspective, one senses a certain exaggeration of all aspects of the effects work that makes them especially obvious and palpably digital, frequently with qualities that recall and even highlight prominent digital techniques. For example, Bubble, the shape-shifting character is voiced

Fig. 4.05 *Valerian and the City of a Thousand Planets* (2017): Rihanna's polymorphic character Bubble is a morph-as-character, constantly metamorphosing with a digital wipe.

and often embodied by the Barbadian superstar pop singer Rihanna. She appears as a "glampod" alien working as a burlesque performer who takes the form of whatever is going to be most alluring to the customer watching, so sometimes she looks like Rihanna in different erotic archetypes: the sexy nurse; the French maid; the ponytailed uniformed schoolgirl; a fishnetted Sally Bowles (complete with bowler hat); and a 1970s afroed roller girl. Her "costume changes" come in the form of the smooth transition of the morph, such as a rapid full-body wipe timed with a hoop or the miming of a striptease. Her dance moves are supplemented by invisible transitions to head-replaced body doubles with more gymnastic, pole-dancing, and aerial skills than Rihanna likely possesses (figure 4.05). In other words, this two-and-a-half-minute display is designed to exhibit reasons to use morphing in European (sexier) ways the PG-rated Hollywood blockbusters would not likely encourage; they also come thick and fast to demonstrate creativity with the technique. It is pure flaunting, signaling that the *Valerian* production team can use the technology extravagantly and with abandon. While the film does not explore the problematics of doing so on the Black sexualized female body (emphasized by a feathered "native" costume and gyrating dance midway through), the sequence fits neatly into the movie's effects aesthetic, which values the densely packed, busily moving layered mise-en-scène to show off not only what the production can do but what it can imagine doing.

Other elements of the story are practically living effects technologies, albeit with a satirical edge. Take, for example, the movie's MacGuffin everyone is chasing—the last replicator creature from the Pearl home world. Like a miniature digital renderer, this small lizard/hamster hybrid can replicate anything endlessly by ingesting it by mouth and then extruding it from the other end. Moreover, the film's climactic feel-good ending involves simulated world-building as civilization-saving. The movie ends with the story of how the previously technologically primitive Pearls, after hiding out on Alpha, found they could access all the knowledge of all these civilizations, giving them the tools to rebuild their own destroyed civilization in simulacrum form. With help from the replicator creature, the Pearls are restored to their "natural" environment through a virtual-reality technology that closely resembles digital matte simulation software.

In fact, layering and layers, and a whole host of them, are perhaps the driving metaphorical strategy for *Valerian*'s effects and action. Characters in the mise-en-scène not only shapeshift; they are coated with various materials, have iridescent skin tones, pass through permeable membranes, and hide themselves inside other creatures in at least two separate instances. In one of the most ostentatious sequences, Valerian himself crashes through ten separate enclosed environments amassed together on the city-planet, highlighting the vast strata of possible environments to show and imagine what the City of a Thousand Planets implies. Besson is not just world-building and world-rebuilding (as in the Pearl homeland); he is multiverse-building, all in one three-minute sequence. And the film piles on in this way throughout. The long opening montage sequence episodically explains how Alpha grew from a small, Earth-based space station by welcoming group after group after group of new alien arrivals to be home to its thousand planets. The (separate) marketplace planet where Valerian and Laureline take possession of the coveted replicator creature exists simultaneously on three different planes of existence: the physical plane of the desert planet, the virtual-reality simulation of the market that the visitors experience through headgear, and the cloaked one that Valerian uses to hide himself from both the other two. In other words, *Valerian* deploys the typical uses that effects are put to use in most other movies, makes them conform to the international standard of effects realism, but dials them all up to eleven to create an imaginative wonderland of such excessive profusion that even Hollywood would consider it over the top.

In order to make his *bande-dessinée* come to life in accordance with his vision, Besson tweaked well-worn ISER routines. Besson ordered the teams to part from one very typical ISER effects practice: the atmo-

Fig. 4.06 *Valerian and the City of a Thousand Planets* (2017): Director Luc Besson demanded ILM remove its usual atmospherics from the space images so that the cinema image would more closely resemble the *bande dessiné* source material.

spheric haze added to environments to simulate planar depth. Because the Jean-Claude Mézières drawings in *Valerian*'s source material feature crisp, sharp lines, he forbade all the effects companies to use the ILM-derived trick that is standard procedure every time they create a digital environment (figure 4.06). As the film's overall VFX supervisor Scott Stokdyk put it:

> As a vfx artist, you rely on atmosphere as a major tool in your arsenal to fill in the volume between the camera and the background. It helps with depth cues and gives a richness to the environment.[47]

As Rodeo FX supervisor François Dumoulin said: "It was really odd. We were unlearning twenty years of putting atmosphere in shots."[48]

Although ILM VFX supervisor Phillippe Rebours faced resistance from his crew, he demonstrated ILM's ability to freestyle with the director's wishes and still create an effect not too far off ISER expectations:

> I remember the artist saying, "How are we going to get the scale?" And my answer was, "with lighting." Instead of using atmosphere, we added dark areas and bright areas. We also unified areas by illuminating them with colored light. You still see that you have variations of colors in the scene, but you're simplifying the palette, and everything becomes more homogeneous. On top of that we would add color accents to be sure that the image was not becoming monochromatic.[49]

This approach implies that Besson wanted to see everything in crisp detail, not just suggest it in hazy outline—like a pen and ink drew it, not like a camera photographed it. The style certainly is designed to respect the French source material but is also a way that flaunts Besson's auteurist creativity and mastery of the digital blockbuster.

The Besson team wants to be sure *Valerian* is not corporate plug-and-chug like his perception of Hollywood blockbusters, churning out a new but identical Marvel superhero movie every six months or so. Instead, *Valerian* takes the resources and technology of a Hollywood blockbuster and infuses it with a European esprit, one that does not simply aim to match Hollywood in its scale but surpass it in imagination, creativity, and design élan. In this way, *Valerian* does not just seek to turn Hollywood tools and skills against itself; it seeks to use them with an inventiveness Hollywood would never allow and could never conceive.

While *The Host* makes metaphoric hay out of its limited effects budget, the less restrained splendors of *The Great Wall* and *Valerian* increase the impact of what it means to appropriate Hollywood tools for their own use. These examples that adapt the ISER aesthetic are able to straddle the potentially diverging desires of conforming to global blockbuster expectations while at the same time subtly playing up the productions' mastery of and surpassing of Hollywood-style digital technology.

Global Alternatives

As we have seen, filmmakers who expect their films to play in the global and especially the North American market do not have much leeway in veering very far from ISER effects aesthetics. Nevertheless, many filmmakers do not simply acquiesce to the style thoughtlessly; they manage to make use of the dominant aesthetic for thematic meaning or other purposes. These films are useful to demonstrate how ISER is a choice and that other choices are possible. These films and others display an approach to plasmatic creature design and animation, set extensions, and action and comedy set-pieces that reveals how the Hollywood-based ISER is first a stylized convention and not an inevitable effects style.

For films that do not expect to travel globally and only need to please local audiences, alternative aesthetic choices do exist. Prominent mainland Chinese hits such as *Wolf Warrior* (2015) and *The Mermaid* (2016) will serve as my primary examples, but others include Indian science fiction and historical epics such as *Robot* and *Baahubali 2: The Conclusion* (2017) and Chinese/South Korean fantasy films including *The Monkey King* (2014 and its sequels) and *Mr. Go* (2013). These films' elaborate effects programs avowedly or implicitly want to make films with blockbuster-size effects shot counts but primarily for local or regional audiences. And while most of these filmmaking contexts are certainly limited by budget and time, I contend that there is a choice being made not to conform to the look of Hollywood films. Interestingly, unlike the previous category of film, which I contend creates a specific discourse about "center-periphery" technological and cultural interaction, these examples are largely unconcerned with the Hollywood gaze, even if they are looking at Western forms and genres.

How and under what criteria can we determine that this alternative style is not just botched effects? Most Western viewers accustomed to and expecting Hollywood-style ISER would rate the effects in films such as these (which, again, are not made for international distribution) as categorically "bad." Edges between composited areas are frequently evident, digital characters and doubles' movements are often rubbery, resolution of detail (such as hair) is low, and in digital set extensions, the computer's geometry is unvarying. In sum, everything about these effects screams "digitally generated" or "cartoony"—that is, everything Hollywood-style effects companies try to avoid. Western viewers would likely write off this look to the cheapness of the production or technical amateurishness. As we will see with the example of Dexter Studios below, many Asian effects houses, especially in South Korea, avowedly want to be considered "as good as" Hollywood ISER effects companies. However, the fact that they do not conform to ISER should not be seen as a contradiction or a mockery of those goals. Instead, I believe that they are making exactly the style of effects they want to make for their markets and that the evident digital foregrounding—even pushing into cartoonishness—is in various ways part and parcel of that style. Emphasizing the digitalness of the effects emphasizes the very presence of digital effects and the filmmakers' ability to manipulate the technology to their own purpose. As a quick example, we might think of Stephen Chow's 2004 *Kung Fu Hustle*, a playful post-*Matrix* Hong Kong reappropriation of digitally enhanced wire-fu. For example, in the final fight when Chow's character has become the very Bruce Lee–like "The One," he launches himself far above the ground, pushes off a soaring eagle to go higher, and serenely reverse-dives back to Earth, transforming into a fireball as he reenters the atmosphere to finish off his opponent. That film's aesthetic pastiches and exaggerates *The Matrix*'s weightless acrobatics in increasingly outrageous and even ridiculous action sequences to demonstrate that Hollywood can't beat Hong Kong at its own game.

Again, an instructive counterexample to the international standard of effects realism includes Chinese films made for national or regional markets, with little interest in international or Western consumption. In other words, prominent filmmakers of popular crowd-pleasers, especially in China, often want effects that look digital—and obviously so. Stephen Chow's *The Mermaid* and Wu Jing's *Wolf Warrior* were both overwhelming successes in Chinese theaters. *The Mermaid* was the biggest moneymaker in Chinese box-office history, only being displaced by *Wolf Warrior*'s sequel in 2017.[50]

Stephen Chow, director of *The Mermaid*, goes beyond subtle digital foregrounding to fully embrace the animated potential (some might say "cartoonish" potential) of digital technology in a way that is only rarely attempted in Hollywood films. And this is especially true beyond what Michele Pierson has called the early days of digital technology's "wonder years" of the 1990s and early 2000s, when Hollywood filmmakers were keen to show off the industry's digital technology potentials in films such as *The Mask* (1994) and *Casper* (1995).[51] For Western audiences, Chow's films fit in easily with this wondrous early digital aesthetic. With his earlier cult favorites *Shaolin Soccer* (2001) and the aforementioned *Kung Fu Hustle*, Chow's films delighted Western viewers with a total disregard for naturalistic physics in obviously digitally enhanced wire work. As described earlier, the turn of-the-millennium trend for digital effects–heavy films that flaunted digitally generated characters and environments and defied naturalistic gravity, such as *The Matrix* (1999), *Gone in 60 Seconds* (2000), *Crouching Tiger, Hidden Dragon* (2000), and *Spider-Man* (2002), was more or less depleted in Hollywood by about 2005 when *Batman Begins* and *Iron Man* were released. And broadly speaking, such overtly exaggerated digital displays were nearly totally unacceptable by the time *The Dark Knight* and *Iron Man* appeared in 2008, setting a trend for Marvel-style photorealism at least through the next decade.

While Hollywood ISER shifted, Stephen Chow's approach to digital effects did not significantly change over that time. Rather than "evolve" with Hollywood-style effects to be more photorealistic, the effects in *The Mermaid* remain just as cartoony and blasé about naturalistic Earth physics as his earlier films. I contend that it is not simply because of cost or technical amateurness, as the Western viewer might assume; it is an aesthetic strategy to play up the cute animated aspect of the film's merpeople and highlight their cinematic artificiality to demonstrate his idiosyncratic, expressive control over the technology.

The Mermaid is an eco-fable about a group of merpeople hiding in a part of the sea that is being destroyed by commercial development. The merpeople elect to send Shan (Jelly Lin), a beautiful female, as a "honey pot" (as the translation calls it) to seduce Liu Xuan (Deng Chao), the wealthy property developer targeting their ecosystem. Naturally, they fall in love. Much hilarity ensues, followed by a surprisingly brutal assault on the merpeople.

How do *The Mermaid*'s effects defy ISER? As in the example of *Warcraft* (2016) in the introduction, the effects style, based on the cartoonish *World of Warcraft* video games, attempted to reconcile the expectations of Blizzard, the video game company, and ISER. It is clear that *Warcraft*'s animated orcs are very carefully executed within ISER expectations. Also as discussed in the introduction, they have detailed hair, skin texture, and armaments—all thoroughly designed to be size- and weight-appropriate for the warlike creatures they are. Moreover, their faces express complex emotion, and their bodies move within expectations of the physics of a creature with a strong, hulking mass.

The Mermaid, however, is blithely unencumbered by such ISER expectations, including the usual effects refinements: shading figures so that they merge with their environments, intricate detail, movements that would be zoologically appropriate to their type, and moving within expectations of earthly physics. Design of the fishy tails in *The Mermaid*'s titular creatures, for example, make little attempt to imagine an if-Mermaids-existed-in-real-life-and-if-they-were-photographed ISER ideal, such as carefully detailed scales, naturalistic colors, and zoomorphic movement. Instead, they are defiantly animated to be "cute" and elastic rather than true-to-life, with brightly colored, iridescent scales (more like a sequin dress representing fish scales than anything fish would actually have), and movement that has a Tex Avery–style exaggerated dexterity. They also make little attempt to smooth out the transition from human to fish body, where one sees a kind of indistinct blurriness in the waist area where the CGI begins (figure 4.07).

As a more specific example, the extravagant way the merpeople, led by the militant Octopus man (played by Show Lo), leave their sanctuary in an abandoned freighter to send Shan to meet developer Liu Xuan

Fig. 4.07 *The Mermaid* (2016): Evident CGI compositing between Shan's fish and human halves suggest the filmmakers' disinterest in the international standard of effects realism.

Fig. 4.08 *The Mermaid* (2016): Slapstick antics of the merpeople indicate a cartoonish fantasy world unencumbered by photorealist expectations.

for a date helps exemplify the film's cartoonish effects aesthetic. One by one the merpeople catapult themselves out of the ship's hold. The Octopus is first, in a medium shot, roaring "Kill Liu Xuan!" as he hurls himself out of the hold, up and away from the camera to a long shot. Bellowing all the while, he then flies out a hole in the ship, through a waterfall; his tentacles undulate behind him until he bounces off an inner tube to brace his fall. Next comes the heroine, Shan, whose catapulting flight is viewed first from the front, then as if from the point of view of a Go-Pro camera mounted just behind her, following the same path as the Octopus (figure 4.08). Three more mermen follow in rapid succession, the sound accentuating the rhythmic snapping action of the catapult. The point of the sequence is less for the merpeople to get from point A to point B than to do so in a comically roundabout fashion, as in the classic Warner Bros. cartoons. Sound effects add to the comical effect. The Octopus lets out a gonzo scream, and his shell breastplate jingles as he soars. The wind whistles and zips around Shan. The catapult's crack recalls a rubber band's snap, and the merpeople make a squishy smack as they hit the inner tube. Visually and sonically, the sequence has a punchy visual rhythm (long, long, short-short-short) that humorously contrasts with the triumphant choral score playing on the soundtrack. In other words, it is not "failed realism" of "bad" effects but laughing with the merpeople's silly antics, as one might with Homer Simpson's or Wile E. Coyote's many violent bodily mishaps.

For Chow, digital effects help extend his physical slapstick comedy to new realms. Chow has long proclaimed and demonstrated an affinity with silent movie comedians, especially Buster Keaton (in his movies where he appears, he performs slapstick with a similarly stone face) and Charlie Chaplin.[52] *Kung Fu Hustle* in particular pays homage to *City Lights* (1931). Chow's films are also more interested in using digital technology to highlight live-action cinema's relationship to animation, to a degree that even Hollywood feature-length animation rarely approaches. In an Eisensteinian sense, Chow is approaching the pure plasmatic live-action body.[53]

In *The Mermaid*, we might detect some thematic and even subtle political meaning in emphasizing the animated movie-bodies of the merpeople. The penetration of the film's eco-message depends on the very careful strategic approach to the effects. In other words, how do the filmmakers produce sympathy for "bottom-feeding" sea creatures among viewers who might not otherwise have it, except by turning the sea creatures into adorable and silly, and also animated, human-animal hybrids? The movie takes advantage of the association with no-stakes physical animation humor in the first part of the movie, to endear the viewer to the merpeople's cute silliness. Our feelings of endearment to the merpeople makes especially brutal and wrenching the film's climatic battle, when a paramilitary force from the developer's company machine-gun down the merpeople in their sanctuary. The cute merpeople that we've experienced as make-believe cartoons we now must experience as fleshy beings in pain. And not unlike a film such as *Who Framed Roger Rabbit?* (1988), we as viewers feel bodily sympathy for the disregard that the greedy developers are showing for their lives. *The Mermaid* does not want to hide the effects but instead depends on the very fact that viewers habitually create emotional connections to animated characters in a way that they might not to "real" sea creatures or even to human ones. The film seems to ask: If you can be made to feel something for patently unreal cute movie characters such as Shan and Octopus, why not actual sea creatures whose very real habitats are being threatened by development and pollution? This non-ISER style of effects work also allows the film to toe the line by providing nonovert social ecological criticism that would likely be censored by mainland Chinese officials. *The Mermaid* and other effects-heavy Chow films demonstrate how his particular approach to effects serves as a showcase for his ridiculously outrageous imagination—a kind of auteurist vision that would not be served by more conventionally realistic styles.

The Mermaid made $527 million in mainland China, three times more than the solidly successful *The Great Wall*.[54] Despite its huge mainland and Hong Kong success, *The Mermaid* goes against China's ambitions for promoting popular blockbuster cinema as an example of its cultural power. Besides being a Hong Kong–produced film with implied criticism of mainland China's environmental policies (although portrayed as the act of a greedy company), *The Mermaid* was also much more successful than either *The Great Wall* or more faithful historical war films of the kind China would prefer to be blockbusters, along with the version of history it wants depicted. In fact, *The Mermaid's* lowbrow slapstick comedy genre is the polar opposite to the "prestige" type of film China has preferred to promote: epic historical war films.[55]

A movie that may seem to provide a middle ground to Chinese authorities is 2015's *Wolf Warrior*, a militaristic action film that blends popular action and nationalistic pride in the style of the *Rambo* (1982–2019) series of films. Many Hollywood filmmakers and effects artists (such as *Iron Man* director Jon Favreau; see chapter 5) state that one of the purposes of perfectly rendered photorealism is that it doesn't distract the audience by "obvious" or "bad" effects; instead the viewer can be more fully absorbed into the cinematic world and also its themes. *The Mermaid's* huge success suggests that realistic effects, at least for Chinese audiences, are not necessarily a requirement for audience investment. But can it apply to films outside of the looser expectations for comedy? In both *The Mermaid* and *Wolf Warrior*, an elaborate and visible effects program is an important part of attracting viewers, although not always with the same motivations. In the case of *Wolf Warrior*, the last thing the production seemed to want was to hide the use of digital effects. However, if *The Mermaid's* use of digital technology plays into realizing

Chow's personal vision of slapstick antics, and *The Great Wall* exhibits Zhang's mastery of aesthetic distinction and discrimination, then *Wolf Warrior* takes yet another tack in foregrounding its digital effects. Similarly to *The Great Wall*, *Wolf Warrior* instead flaunts digital technology as part of a larger demonstration of military, economic, and cultural might. *Wolf Warrior* is a film made primarily for Chinese audiences and not for export as an expression of patriotic (and even jingoistic) pride. As such, it does not have to adhere to ISER the way *The Great Wall* does in order to play in the North American market or use it to present a point of contrast. And also unlike *The Great Wall*, international coproductions are not thematized in a positive light. In *Wolf Warrior*, foreign influence is a nefarious phenomenon to be studied and mastered—but also resolutely repulsed.

As we saw with *The Great Wall*, the Chinese government sees Chinese popular filmmaking within a context of demonstrating its political, economic, and cultural ascendency to its own people and to the outside world. How do effects technology and aesthetics help with this endeavor? Joshua Neves characterizes the Chinese attitude toward cinematic effects technology as playing into a dynamic of what he calls "Southern FX." As he puts it:

> Southern FX signals the formative role played by special effects cinema in conjuring Asia as a site of the primitive, the excessive, and the monstrous as well as more recent transformations in not only technologies of production and postproduction (the *making of* special effects) but also distribution forms and platforms. These contact zones put on display V/FX's worldmaking capacity— including its designs beyond the image.[56]

In other words, the display of effects by Chinese filmmakers, as well as their production and distribution into theaters, get Chinese filmmaking into the fight. And it is a fight that is deeply nationalistic and tinged by memories of Western colonialism. As Neves points out, mobilization of the monsters of the Godzilla and King Kong sort have served historically as contact zones between East and West. In contrast to *The Host*, *Wolf Warrior* is, to paraphrase Rey Chow, not speaking back to Western hegemony but is speaking to its own people translated into the popular language they want to hear. Certainly, *Wolf Warrior* is an unsubtly nationalistic film, in which glorious Chinese troops, led by super-soldier hero Leng Feng (Wu Jing, also the director), must repel Western mercenaries fighting for a drug lord. The climax of the film sees Leng fight against a British mercenary (martial arts star Scott Atkins), who tries to remove Leng Feng's uniform patch with the Chinese flag that says, in English (and not Chinese), "I fight for China." After dispatching the foreign invader, Leng triumphantly puts the patch back on his sleeve and rejoins his compatriots with Schwarzenegger-style bravado.

An example of the digital-on-display effects comes about a half an hour into the film, in the wolf attack that gives the protagonist his nom de guerre. Hero Leng Feng begins the film in disgrace and under arrest in the brig. This is due to having gone rogue by disregarding orders and shooting a hostile without authorization. After being recommissioned by Commander Long Xiaoyun (Yu Nan) for the Wolf Warrior Detachment, the "special force of the special force," as the movie's dialog describes it, with the "best weapons" that "simulate tactics of foreign special forces," Leng Feng must reincorporate himself as a useful member of the Chinese armed forces. The very obviously digitally rendered nighttime wolf attack is also significant narratively, where the movie demonstrates that Leng has overcome his disgrace and earned the right to lead the Wolf Warrior Detachment. We first see the dimly silhouetted pack of twenty to thirty wolves coming over a ridge in a row, their eyes reflecting the light, surrounding the small detachment of troops huddling in a circle (figure 4.09). The wolves attack the troops and scamper back in retreat. At the climax of the sequence, Leng faces off with and defeats the alpha wolf by bayonetting the beast as it leaps. By the end of the sequence, rather than the "lone wolf" he began as,

Fig. 4.09 *Wolf Warrior* (2015): The nighttime setting silhouettes the CGI wolves assembling for an attack.

Leng rises through combat and camaraderie to the role of alpha. Even more, by defeating the wolves, Leng shows himself as more wolf than the wolves. Now he is fit to defend his homeland against the foreign mercenaries.

The CGI effects in the film are not only used to generate giant wolves for the hero to defeat (in order to earn his nickname); they also simulate hi-tech computer screens, military hardware (especially aircraft), and troops and place its hero in outrageous stunts. A Western viewer might think a movie with such a nationalistic, Rambo-style agenda would want its effects as much up to the international standard as possible—that is, as blended and realistic as possible—to beat the Westerners at their own game. Instead, the film's other effects make the wolves' digitalness as evident as possible and again serve to proclaim the act of digital rendering by Chinese companies as politically and culturally significant as the military hardware and troops that the effects render.

The wolf attack effects sequence appears in the film after a series of conventionally ISER physical and visual effects sequences designed to show off Chinese military might and capabilities: helicopters, tanks, drones, antiaircraft weapons, automatic firearms, as well as a sophisticated remote command center manned by computer techs with video imaging and digital simulations in real time. As part of the film's rhetoric of Chinese capabilities, the elaborate wolf attack links the effects work to the display of military capabilities. However, the demonstration is not meant to impress both Chinese and Western audiences, as in *The Great Wall*. Instead, the display of effects capabilities is to impress Chinese audiences with technological mastery over the natural world. The wolves' movements are fairly naturalistic in that they move in ways one would expect real wolves to move: crouching, leaping, and gripping with their teeth. The effects artists have given much attention to the rendering of their fur. In other words, they successfully suggest a very elaborately choreographed wolf attack. However, from a Western perspective—compared to, say, the bear attack sequence in *The Revenant*—as effects objects the CGI wolves are rather schematic and obviously digital (figure 4.10). In other words, although one gets the idea of wolves from the fur simulation and motion animation, they are less finely detailed and more obviously composited than the expectation for animal rendering in ISER. However, I contend that it is more important to show the wolves as evidently digital, as a metaphorical extension of technological might. The film displays the CGI wolves as simulations

Fig. 4.10 *Wolf Warrior* (2015): A close up of the CGI wolf exhibits its status as a CGI object.

against which the Chinese sharpen their skills and readiness, but then they use the same technology and skills to do things their own way.

It would be disingenuous and chauvinistic to suggest that this production would make ISER wolves if it had the time and money. The other digital work, such as the green-screened computer displays in the control room, are fairly seamless. Unlike *The Great Wall*, it is a relatively low-budget production using small, Beijing-based effects houses.[57] However, I contend that the blatantly CGI wolves play into an overall rhetoric of pride in Chinese capabilities and readiness. And if the Wolf Warrior Detachment "simulates tactics of foreign special forces" to keep regular troops sharp, the sequence creates a rhetoric about how the Chinese movie industry tests itself against ISER but does not necessarily copy it.

The alternative effects style of these movies can be seen as extensions of Asian cinema's long stylistic heritage of Hong Kong wire-fu action films and the popularity of Japanese- and South Korean–style anime. Many other Asian films would make interesting test cases for alternative effects styles, such as South Korea's baseball-playing gorilla film *Mr. Go* and the popular Chinese mythological fantasy series *The Monkey King* (2014–2018). One could also examine other successful filmmaking cultures that are not made to compete in the Western global market, most notably India and Nigeria.[58] These examples of locally or regionally successful effects films also definitively demonstrate the narrowness of aesthetic possibilities in ISER. Western executives such as Ian Smith who want to partner on Chinese productions such as *The Great Wall* speak condescendingly about Chinese production by asserting that "it would be good for the Chinese film industry to learn more of the language and syntax of storytelling that is currently shared by European and American film makers."[59] However, Hollywood productions could learn from the way that Chinese films successfully serve regional audiences with alternative aesthetics.

Conclusion

I end this chapter on what may or may not be a hopeful note: digital effects that had previously been economically unfeasible for local productions are now bringing attention and exportability to various countries' genre output. This is especially true with science fiction films, but also in other effects-heavy genres, including fantasy, martial arts, and historical epics. The economic exportability of genre in general, and science fiction/fantasy in particular, has provided a venue for productions worldwide to insert their own local products into the transnational economy of the Hollywood blockbuster. In effect, films such as *The Host* and *The Great Wall* are creating a product with comparable production values and therefore analogous exchange values while at the same time deploying the same high-tech tools to tell stories, air concerns, and create fantastic environments that chime with their "home" audience.

Finally, whether these global films adapt or reject ISER, I reiterate that we cannot understand this as simple Global Hollywood cultural imperialism in a straightforward way. Instead, as in vernacular modernism, the adaptation of ISER serves what filmmakers want to say and present in various ways. For global auteurs, it presents a powerfully credible but allegorized vision of the world that they use to show their own local audiences something specific and that also can be understandable to international audiences accustomed to that style. Alternatively, productions can demonstrate their technological and cultural cosmopolitanism by adopting and adapting visible effects in a display of digital mastery. It is not a coincidence that many of these productions make use of traditional thematic preoccupations of science fiction, including the alien invasion and technology-created monsters. However, although in the science fiction tradition the protagonists in the film must fight to defeat these invaders, to the filmmakers *The Host*'s tagline is true: the Monsters Are Real. And they are turning them on their masters.

FIVE

That Analog Feeling

Disney, Marvel Studios, and the ILM Aesthetic

PHOTOREALISM IS *ALWAYS* WHAT WE STRIVE FOR, WHETHER WE'RE IN
WAKANDA OR ASGARD.

—VICTORIA ALONSO, MARVEL STUDIOS EXECUTIVE VICE
PRESIDENT FOR PHYSICAL PRODUCTION

[MARVEL STUDIOS'] APPROACH TO VISUAL EFFECTS COULD BE
DESCRIBED—ALMOST PARADOXICALLY—AS "MUST BE WORLD-CLASS"
AND "MUST BE SECONDARY TO THE STORY."

—JAKE MORRISON, VISUAL EFFECTS SUPERVISOR ON *THOR*,
THE AVENGERS, ANT-MAN, AND THOR: RAGNAROK

In Iron Man's first major sequence in *The Avengers* (2012), Tony Stark soars onto his penthouse deck at Stark Tower. There, an apparatus (dubbed by the ILM effects team as the "car wash") removes his suit part by part, which we see from various angles and shot scales. He then enters the penthouse apartment to share an intimate moment with Pepper Potts, his business and life partner. Here, what I will describe as the "MCU effects approach" turns what could be a very spectacular display of Stark technology into an almost offhand nonevent. As carried over from *Iron Man*, the digital double suit is given personality in part by placing bright lights

Fig. 5.01 *The Avengers* (2012): In what the effects team dubbed the "car wash," robotic hands remove Tony Stark's Iron Man suit automatically and fluidly. Much like the effects themselves, the display is so nonchalant and naturalized that the audience no longer experiences either as spectacle.

at his eye, heart, hand, and foot points, thereby drowning out and softening the other details of the suit in most of the sequences. Stark Tower lights up with bright blue lights as he approaches, and strikingly, the brightest lights in the frame as the car wash takes off his suit besides the eyes and the heart are the art deco lights outlining the Chrysler Building. The first part the apparatus takes off is his faceplate, then we see an extreme wide shot of the platform from above, then close-ups of his breastplate and all the other complex, metallic, spinning, moving parts that we as viewers must take on faith would function logically in such a way. The robotic "helper" arms—an elaboration of devices we have seen in the previous *Iron Man* movies—smoothly, automatically, and efficiently remove parts as Tony strides forward, hiding everything away in compartments below deck until they are needed again without an explicit command from him. The interior of his penthouse is likewise filled with bright, fluorescent lighting elements, including a heads-up holographic display on a large screen and other lights suggesting tech; even the conversation pit is outlined in fluorescent lights (figure 5.01). While this sequence seems to be a gee-whiz sequence of technology, it plays like an ideal depiction of the effortless machinery of the Marvel effects program, integrating effects objects such as a digital double, machinery, a large skyscraper, and a city environment. Rather than having the camera gape at this technology, we as viewers absorb it quickly as a new innovation at Stark Industries. But also, like Tony, we as viewers do not have to think about it; it just happens. It is a cinematic and capitalistic commonplace that cinema is always reinventing itself by producing greater and greater cinematic marvels to wonder at. However, I contend that the Marvel Cinematic Universe, in some ways the most successful franchise in cinema history, is completely uninterested in that approach.

Conveniently, the altered Marvel Studios model for contracting effects work looks a lot like the plot of *The Avengers*: several far-flung personalities with various special talents are brought together by a larger organization with mysterious inner workings and motivations. Led by a project point-person, these personalities have to work together, pooling their abilities into a consistent working method for a harmonious result, motivated by the greater good—at least ideally.[1] Moreover, the rival but collaborating effects companies' rhetoric tries to project the image that these kinds of arrangements produce a result much like the fractious bunch of superheroes in the film—a loose confederation of equals with an important job working together to save or, in this case, generate the world. Despite effects artists' rhetoric lauding Marvel Studios for its collaborative spirit and openness to a variety of voices, the actual economics of the effects business is slightly less magical, and the effects houses superpowers are not always so harmonized.[2] Even in the plot of *The Avengers*, and especially in *Captain America: Civil War* (2016), when the teams of superheroes split into factions and fight one another, this assemblage does not always work smoothly.

The Marvel Studios model also necessitates shared aesthetic goals. But where does Marvel Studios' shared sense of "good" or "world-class" effects come from? When Disney acquired Industrial Light & Magic via the Lucasfilm purchase in 2012, it also secured the intangible value that had accrued to the ILM house style. As stated earlier, industry insiders believed at the time that Disney would spin off the unprofitable and expensive-to-run ILM. However, that did not happen. While the most visible and obvious value of Lucasfilm to Disney was and remains the lucrative *Star Wars* intellectual property, it appears that Disney's plans for making use of ILM's aesthetic extended beyond the *Star Wars* universe.

As part of shoring up its movie assets, Disney had acquired Marvel Studios in 2009, after the immense success of *Iron Man* in 2008. One of Disney's major priorities would clearly be to exploit the synergy between its corporate cousins by cementing the association between ILM's powerful brand of realism with the multifilm potential of Marvel's superhero universe. The combination of Marvel Studios and Lucasfilm proved remarkably lucrative. Disney's control of the North American theatrical release box office grew in 2012 from an already substantial share of about 15 percent to about 40 percent by 2020, producing 80 percent of the top box-office hits of 2019, until COVID-19 disrupted the business. As the lead house producing the majority of the effects for *Iron Man* and *Iron Man 2*, ILM set the aesthetic for what Marvel Studios called "Phase One" of the Marvel Cinematic Universe, which included *Iron Man* (2008), *The Incredible Hulk* (2008), *Iron Man 2* (2010), *Thor* (2011), and *Captain America: The First Avenger* (2011).[3] Of course one cannot solely attribute Disney's phenomenal growth to ILM. However, I would contend that the ability to harness the power of the ILM aesthetic is an underrated factor in the overall success of Disney's live-action box-office domination.

ILM established an international standard of effects realism that exerted soft power to encourage or coerce other effects companies and productions to adopt the aesthetic. The ILM style over the years accommodated the photorealistic house style evident in signature franchises such as the *Star Wars* films, *Jurassic Park*, *Harry Potter*, and *Transformers*. ILM also produced striking but more eccentric effects for films such as *Willow*, *Death Becomes Her*, *Forrest Gump*, *Casper*, *The Great Wall*, and *Warcraft*. Under Disney, the MCU has had remarkable success in co-opting the previous, somewhat flexible ILM effects style and streamlining and narrowing it into a fairly strict set of parameters for effects companies to follow.

As part of the Lucasfilm acquisition, ILM maintained its value to Disney in part because it had already successfully positioned itself rhetorically and industrially as an aesthetic that, around the world, had come to mean simply a byword for "realistic." However, to become the MCU house style, the ILM aesthetic would need modification. Most notably, the ILM style needed to be standardized and streamlined to fit into an elaborate production pipeline. I contend that Marvel Studios' effects aesthetic is an extension of its overall risk aversion.[4] It also reflects Marvel Studios' well-known (and even bragged about) moviemaking-by-corporate-committee production process, where every film and every moment is massaged or "plussed" for maximum appeal. In all areas of production, whether it be the music, the script, the costuming, or other aspects, Marvel Studios does not get in the way of narrative delivery while striving for an aesthetic of least objection.[5]

This corporate standardization is understandable: a cohesive movie franchise requires consistent aesthetics. MCU movies are full of digital characters and objects interacting with live-action photography, so working in tandem with cinematography and art direction, they need to deploy an effects strategy to cue viewers that every new film is an extension of the previous films and is a part of what they've seen and accepted before. However, the MCU aesthetic strategy changed gears from earlier blockbuster franchises in one important way. Previously, in awe-inspiring fantastical world-building projects of blockbusters discussed by Thomas Elsaesser, Michele Pierson, and others, movie franchise stories tended toward the archetypical ("boy goes on a quest to rescue a princess"), and filmmaking energy was placed where the aim was to wow the viewer with new sights and sounds. But the MCU from the beginning was more narratively motivated: producers sought to animate the density of an already-existing comics world in cinematic form, bringing what Jason Mittel calls "complex televisual narrativity" to serial cinema.[6] In other words, with all the resources of a string of $100–200 million blockbusters, the MCU created a complex multipart narrative world that brings to life the Marvel universe in all its dense intricacy. The filmmaking priority is now keeping the audience focused on the narrative and characters, rather than on imaginary world-building.

Fostering an expensive and risky superhero universe and protecting its considerable investment meant responding to an amalgamation of fan complaints about digital effects over decades to arrive at what might be called a crowdsourced notion of the "best effects." One of the major complaints motivating Disney's and Marvel Studios' aesthetic decisions appears to be a response to the widespread popular rhetoric about how "bad" CGI "takes the viewer out of the movie." As an example, we see hundreds of fan-driven articles and videos with clickbait titles such as "6 Reasons Modern Movie CGI Looks Surprisingly Crappy," an existing listicle on the fan site Cracked.com. Illustrated with gifs and racking up more than 1.5 million page views, the article gives reasonable-sounding criticism: "Lack Of Visual Restraint Makes Gravity Act Like A Cartoon; Color Grading Makes Everything Look Like A Fantasy; CGI Was Originally Used As A Last Resort; Most Films Forget That A Camera Needs To Physically Exist; Modern Movies Forget We Can Tell When

Something Looks Fake; and Big Effects Sequences Are Supposed To Be Treated With Awe."[7] These dictates—emphasizing naturalism, restraint, and plausibility—are representative of how amateur online criticism reiterates ahistorical and scientistic notions to attack the perceived aesthetic paucity of CGI, providing commonsensical "reasons" CGI cannot represent anything "real" in effects-driven movies. Leaving aside the vast majority of undetectable digital effects in movies that these commentators do not notice, the popular rhetoric asserts a we-know-real-when-we-see-it aesthetic that seems to loosely and arbitrarily correspond with a notion of lived experience of the phenomenal world. As described in chapter 2, it is an aesthetic based primarily on a nostalgic memory for the late 1970s and early 1980s ILM aesthetic. This criticism also insists that a restrained approach to effects, used sparingly only when necessary, shot with reference to a physical camera, and that never looks stylized or stands out as "fake" should be the goal of contemporary blockbusters. And as we shall see, that formula is a good way to describe the aesthetic deployed by Marvel Studios for the MCU. Producers justify this direction by doubling down on and making true the long-standing practitioner cliché that effects should primarily serve the narrative and the characters.

However, it is worth noting that this tasteful "restraint" in the amount of CGI used is an illusion, and denial and downplaying of CGI amount to effective public relations, since MCU films have as much or more CGI than other blockbusters. We can see many examples of recent productions within and outside the MCU that deploy the rhetoric of "grounded" realism. For example, movies such as *Star Wars: The Force Awakens* (2015) or *Spider-Man: Homecoming* (2017) have been praised for their adherence to a restrained use of effects and an emphasis on physical locations and props.[8] For *The Force Awakens*, promotional behind-the-scenes videos released online stressed the production's location shooting and physical props such as BB-8 and downplayed the film's significant greenscreen work.[9] However, as ILM visual effects supervisor Roger Guyett emphasized, there were 2,100 effects shots in the film, and much of the highly touted location shots (such as Rey's desert home planet Jakku) were entirely reconstructed digitally.[10] As Guyett put it: "Our job is to do this massive visual effects movie but make it look as though somehow or another it wasn't that." And: "It might be more work to actually make it feel like it's less effects shots than *The Phantom Menace*. . . . That's the trick."[11] *Spider-Man: Homecoming*'s effects were especially well received in the Marvel Universe. It was praised as a "down to earth" approach to Spider-Man (*The Verge* even called the $175M blockbuster "a great little movie") while nevertheless featuring a minimum of 1,500 effects shots.[12] Likewise in *Homecoming*, Sony PI VFX supervisor Theodore Bialek said his brief was to "keep it relatable and grounded. It should all look cool of course, but never lose sight that the story and our characters should remain front and center."[13] Similarly, Dan DeLeeuw, visual effects supervisor on *Captain America: The Winter Soldier* (2014) asserted: "Marvel was always pushing to make the movie better, to make every moment the best and biggest it could be—and that's how we wound up with 2,500 visual effects shots in a 'grounded' 1970s thriller."[14] In other words, Guyett, Bialek, and DeLeeuw are admitting that these films must make use of as many or more digital effects while at the same time appearing not to do so. Or, as ILM stated in the 1990s, it must dispel the "digital curse" that has accrued to movies that have been deemed too obviously digitally generated. These films were simply more skillful in hiding the large amount of CGI deployed while promoting them as more physically based. And perhaps most important, this approach habituates viewers over the course of the series, conforming perfectly to what they have aggregated as fan expectations of a grounded photoreal aesthetic.

Though ultimately hugely successful, this aesthetic approach was not inevitable. The aesthetic joining of Marvel and ILM may initially have been a fluke (albeit one that suited Disney's interests) that began as a kind of personal directorial predilection. When the director Jon Favreau was conceptualizing the look for *Iron Man*, he spoke very directly and unambiguously about his preference for a specific kind of "analog," or predigital, effects over obvious CGI. Acknowledging that the execution of Iron Man's superpowers would require a great deal of CGI, he nevertheless wanted *Iron Man*'s effects to exhibit what he called "flawless photorealism."[15] Favreau in this era and beyond is frequently quoted as disliking what I call the "faith in the animated" trend in CGI that had been dominant since the mid-1990s. This earlier, elastic, physics-less style of CGI initially helped serve as a demonstration and attraction of digital technologies' cinematic attraction potential. However, in promotional interviews, Favreau criticized this style in detail and at length, instead admiring the ILM-produced effects films of his youth, most prominently the original *Star Wars* trilogy and Steven Spielberg 1980s crowd-pleasers such as *E.T.*

I contend that it is difficult to overestimate the impact Favreau's personal preferences have had on blockbuster aesthetics. *Iron Man* was indeed a huge worldwide hit, along with the even greater financial success of *Iron Man 2* shortly thereafter. Once Disney took over from Paramount and began producing the MCU films in 2010, it doubled down on Favreau's *Iron Man* style. From *The Avengers* on, the Marvel Studios version of the ILM style set the basic template for effects aesthetics across the MCU. Before the MCU films, ILM had set the style for effects realism and strongly encouraged other companies to adapt their style. What was initially an unspoken but ILM-led standard up to about 2010, what I call the "ILM style of effects realism," Disney co-opted by way of Marvel Studios into a style that all effects companies had to adopt to compete for jobs.

These aesthetic choices have had major consequences for the industry. It is worth remembering that in 2012, as described in chapter 1, the effects business was in turmoil and even on the brink of collapse. Marvel Studios' effects production shift made a certain financial and organizational sense at the time, but in fact it had considerable impact on the style of effects employed in those films. The narrowing of effects aesthetics was consequential in the way that it shifted production conventions in hiring effects houses for Disney's post-2010 production of MCU films. Instead of four or five first- and second-tier effects houses being contracted on an effects blockbuster (as had been standard practice since the late 1980s), Disney sought to limit its investment in any single financially unstable effects house. MCU productions going forward would split the effects jobs among a larger and larger number of effects houses across the industry, from sizable top-tier companies such as ILM and Weta on down to tiny houses with ten employees scattered around the world. Notably, *The Avengers* employed twenty-plus houses, which would become the MCU practice from then on.

By some accounts, it could be said that Disney came along to save the day by producing several giant effects spectacles a year, all of which employed twenty or more effects companies, bringing a much-needed stabilization to the industry. However, this stability has come at a cost. Under the hegemonic aegis of Disney, Marvel Studios' adoption of the ILM style for the MCU has forced the entire effects business to adapt to the Marvel Studios style—even ILM itself. In other words, Marvel Studios adapted a version of the ILM style of effects realism across the MCU and, through directly applied economic might, concretely made that style into the industry standard. Similar to the international standard of realism described in chapter 4, Disney took the ILM style and modified it to its own uses. However, it developed its own distinct version.

What do I mean in referring to the MCU's version of the ILM style? Throughout its history, ILM has performed innovation, with a see-what-we-can-do-now approach to effects. A constituent part of the ILM house style has been its relentless self-promotion. Most notably, the MCU formula has meant a hard turn away from what Michele Pierson calls the "wonderment" approach of showing off effects as effects, especially CGI as CGI. This turn away from wonder would seem like a counter-intuitive claim, due to the massive battle scenes, exotic creatures, and futuristic technology on display in the MCU. However, to keep the emphasis on narrative and character, the MCU producers evidently do not want the viewer to spend any time being "wowed" by its effects; instead the viewer should simply accept the world it encounters as natural.[16] In other words, it leans on the photorealism techniques of ILM while deemphasizing styles that would call attention to themselves as noticeably innovative or spectacular. The Marvel Studios aesthetic is instead antispectacular, even purposefully featureless or quotidian.

Obviously, "unspectacular" and "featureless" are not the words MCU producers and filmmakers use in their public rhetoric. Neither would those terms seem to apply to blockbuster films chock-full of expensive and elaborate action sequences. However, they purposefully do not want the effects sequences to read as amazing effects sequences but instead as matter-of-fact extensions of the narrative context. The word Favreau and team used most often when discussing *Iron Man*'s style of effects is "grounded," which is only marginally more meaningful than "realistic." Extrapolating from the discourse, the term is typically used to mean that: (1) Movement and weight should mimic earthbound physics as if shot by a live-action camera; (2) shots with camera movements should resemble those that physical cameras could feasibly make; and (3) digital effects objects should have a real-life physical reference point.[17] Elements that emphasize camera reality are not radically different from the ILM house aesthetic. However, the Favreau/MCU approach narrows the parameters considerably. Favreau's version of effects realism was also attractive to Marvel and Disney producers because it hearkened back to familiar and beloved existing intellectual property. Now, the new MCU version of the ILM style is to bring the analog circa 1980 to the present, as if the goal were to make a perfect replica of a familiar beloved classic such as *The Empire Strikes Back*, only with digital tools. For the MCU aesthetic, it means re-invisibilizing digital effects by stylistically turning back the clock to a nostalgic time before digital effects.

In order for *The Avengers*, the sixth MCU film, to resonate, viewers would need to have absorbed, at least vaguely, a great deal of narrative information and character development from the previous films. They would also need to take in a great deal more to push the MCU into new areas of expansion. The recognizable and repeatable aesthetic formula orients the viewer to the MCU across multiverses and story lines. At the same time, they dissipate the input of any one particular creative voice.[18] This minimization of the display of effects *as* effects is a major way that Marvel Studios has minimized the ILM dominance over the effects industry, using ILM's tools against itself by not allowing ILM to show off what makes it distinct as ILM in the industry's biggest blockbusters.

It is worth emphasizing that Favreau's proposed *Iron Man* style was meant to contrast with the more plastic style of early 2000s CGI and return to the familiar look of ILM's analog effects of in the 1970s and 1980s. As VFX supervisor Janek Sirrs put it: "[In *Iron Man*] there were no magic powers, or forces from another planet. Everything was grounded in reality."[19] In other words, ramping up digital technology and application nevertheless means an explicit turning away from the more fanciful approach to effects work in the late 1990s and early 2000s that played with notions of gravity, permeability, and malleability. In this way, Favreau's approach was similar to Christopher Nolan's in DC's Batman franchise, starting with *Batman Begins* in 2005 and crystalizing into a marked aesthetic with *The Dark Knight* in 2008. Both films were very similarly characterized in their directors' and collaborators' discourse in terms of returning to an aesthetic of photorealism; the main differentiation between them is that Nolan, as a film purist, fetishizes actually shooting on film (frequently large-format IMAX) and using physical effects as often as possible and CGI as sparingly as possible to achieve his look. While rhapsodizing in public about the materiality of built miniatures, Favreau was more or less happy for ILM to produce effects that looked as if they were physical effects shot on film but were in fact produced digitally. I am not interested in arguing that one approach is more "authentic" than another or ends in a more "authentic" result. Both are as reliant on rhetoric as actual production methods to sell their realism effect. However, while the Nolan approach has been undoubtedly influential, the Favreau approach has proven to get a similar result with a more sustainable production model for expensive blockbusters. The Favreau approach allows MCU productions to actually increase the typical amount of CGI per film while removing much of the perception of the digital curse.[20] Just as important, the Favreau approach maintains similar production pipelines as the earlier animated-looking films of the early 2000s. Nolan's film-based approach may provide him with auteurist virtue-signaling but is prohibitively expensive and too labor-intensive to turn into a broader kind of standardized production.

Iron Man: "That Analog Feeling"

A LOT OF SUPERHERO MOVIES LOSE SIGHT OF THE FACT THAT THEY HAVE TO KEEP THINGS PHOTOREAL—BECAUSE THE LESS REAL THE ACTION IS, THE MORE YOU SUBCONSCIOUSLY DETACH YOURSELF EMOTIONALLY FROM THE STORY. MOVIES ARE AN EMOTIONAL MEDIUM, AND WHEN YOU CREATE A LAYER OF ARTIFICE BETWEEN YOU AND THE AUDIENCE, YOU LOSE THE CONNECTION WITH THAT. SO MAINTAINING REALISM WAS AN OVERALL STRATEGY THAT WE STAYED TRUE TO THROUGHOUT THE MAKING OF [IRON MAN].

—JON FAVREAU, DIRECTOR OF IRON MAN AND IRON MAN 2

In launching a new superhero franchise, director and longtime effects film superfan Jon Favreau[21] finally got the chance to work with ILM, the company that, as he put it, formed many of his earliest and most powerful cinematic memories.[22] In reference to designing the effects for *Iron Man*, Favreau stated explicitly that "I loved *Star Wars* . . . [it] was life changing for me" and that *Iron Man* should evoke the style of that era of effects.[23] Favreau's public references to the 1970s and 1980s indicates a nostalgic belief that the 1980s films of his youth were more real, because his young self experienced them that way. When he says that the more recent CGI films "subconsciously detach [you] emotionally from the story," he means that they evoke the wrong style of realism. Favreau resists the style that Lev Manovich characterized, referring to 1990s CGI as "computer vision," or the cyborg eye: a futurist, smoothly executed hyperrealism, more perfect than human vision.[24] Favreau seeks an optical look that cues human camera vision but by actually using computer vision: a contradictory optical cyborg eye. In other words, he is making a computer-made version of the long-standing, influential, and powerful version of the aesthetic that ILM developed in the 1980s.

Favreau's conception of the optical cyborg eye is especially appropriate for *Iron Man*'s high-tech superhero, whose POV we often experience through his helmet's heads-up display. However, this effect aesthetic has permeated the entire MCU film series, regardless of director. When Victoria Alonso, vice president of postproduction at Marvel Studios when *Iron Man* was made, can say in 2018 (nineteen movies into the MCU) as Marvel Studios' VP of physical production, "photorealism is *always* what we strive for, whether we're in Wakanda or Asgard," she is using terminology and an aesthetic approach set in place by Favreau and ILM for the first *Iron Man* in 2008.[25] For Alonso and Favreau, ILM's historical photorealism is the most appropriate aesthetic for the MCU; as Favreau's quote asserts, he believes it places the emphasis on the audience's connection to the Marvel superhero characters so that the audience is invested in their adventures. The viewer should not be scrutinizing the effects or be dazzled by blockbuster spectacles, which distract from the broader story. And in order for the MCU to work, the audience must follow a fairly intricate series of personalities and alliances in order to sell future movies featuring assembled teams. For this reason, the particulars of the story details count, and the design and action priority is on the real person (or humanoid) in the superhero suit, even if (or especially if) that suit is in fact entirely digitally generated.[26]

Alonso's and Favreau's discursive insistence on using the term "photorealism" could be passed by without comment because it perhaps seems obvious or commonsensical that this is what their approach would be. However, in the mid-2000s, when Marvel planned the inauguration of the MCU, Favreau was bucking the dominant, animated-looking aesthetic trend of CGI. The VFX supervisor for Favreau's *Zathura: A Space Adventure* (2005) described the director's disdain of that aesthetic: "He doesn't like the aesthetic of CG when it's recognizable as such; whereas he doesn't mind being able to spot the miniature, because he finds charm and warmth in that aesthetic."[27] Favreau wanted *Iron Man* to return to the nostalgically warm style that for himself and others would be experienced as more powerfully immersive in the narrative. For *Iron Man*, an adherence to the ILM style—specifically the 1980s ILM style of photorealism—would obtain, in Favreau's words, "that analog feeling that we were going for."[28] His personal biases were apparently shared by other influential filmmakers. In 2008, the one-two punch of *Iron Man* and *The Dark Knight* turned the tide in effects trends toward a faith in a predigital photorealism that has continued at least through the early 2020s.[29]

When one analyzes his public discourse on the effects aesthetic for *Iron Man*, it is not hard to believe that Favreau has been reading *Cinefex* and absorbing its rhetoric since the 1980s, since his discourse about photorealism strongly resembles that of ILM artists dating back to that era.[30] And whether or not such is the case, he has been professing his love for analog effects ever since one of his movies appeared in its pages.[31] For example, in discussing what specific techniques remove the "CGI curse" from CGI objects to achieve the analog feeling he was looking for, his wording resembles Dennis Muren's, ILM's most prominent architect of its style of photorealism. Here is Favreau:

> I constantly asked myself, "what would it really be like to photograph this if it was a real event?" . . . Sometimes you miss a bit of action. Sometimes you don't frame it properly and the camera lags behind. We would make things look practical by not having everything in focus, not always having the right lens or having the camera in the right place. We also made the lighting in the plates a bit imperfect, letting elements blow out or fall off. All of those little things had the cumulative effect of making you feel as if you were witnessing something real, rather than CG.[32]

Compare Favreau's words to a Muren quote in the 1990s about the realistic imperfection aesthetic that he helped develop the 1980s for *Star Wars*. Muren is discussing the ILM photoreal aesthetic that made miniatures and models "read" as if full-sized spacecrafts were being shot by a single camera pass for the original *Star Wars* trilogy:

> I tried to inject a sense of personality in each ship, as if there were a real person inside flying it. I also tried to give an obvious hand held look to some of the shots—like there was actually a cameraman there who was having trouble following the action.[33]

In other words, the specific aspects of ILM 1970s and 1980s photorealism Favreau absorbed, likely from *Cinefex*, emphasize elements from ILM's rhetoric: highlighting the act of filming by a person to inject human imperfections such as camera wobble, purposeful misframing and focus mistakes, and lighting artifacts in the shooting. And it is worth noting that, with Muren's work on the original *Star Wars* trilogy, the elements suggesting photorealism are also *added* as a stylistic element, not inherent in the analog predigital shooting. In Favreau's version, these historically stylized digital effects (experienced by 1970s and 1980s audiences as technologically novel and visually spectacular) become the uninflected "natural" way to make artificially "too-perfect" CG imagery appear photorealistic.

To be more specific, Favreau refines what he means by "photorealism" when he makes another reference to 1980s physical miniature work. In comparing what he aspired to in *Iron Man*'s flying sequences to those in *Top Gun* (1986), he contrasts what he wants with the aerial action film *Stealth* (2005).[34] Favreau puts his finger on what does and does not work in those sequences for him:

> [For the dogfight footage] . . . rather than putting virtual cameras anywhere, we [on *Iron Man*] always had our camera shooting from a platform. . . . We actually sent airplanes up to do maneuvers. We had a whole aerial unit so we could get all the idiosyncrasy of the camera work, the lenses and the lens flares, the scratches and condensation, all the things you saw in *Top Gun* and didn't see in *Stealth*, which was a similar type of story, but told through the tools of CG. *Stealth* moved the camera around in a very dynamic way; but you felt connected to the action in *Top Gun*, viscerally, in a way you didn't feel in *Stealth*. I felt that my responsibility was to make this dogfight action as photoreal as possible, not necessarily as *dynamic* as possible.[35]

Per Favreau's instructions, the *Iron Man* effects team was to sacrifice the greater flexibility and potential dynamism that CG affords and proceed as if virtual cameras were never invented. Instead, there is an emphasis on the realism effect of human-operated cameras and the mistakes that actual cameras provide over the impossibly clean perfection and impossible viewpoints associated with CGI. And again, Favreau insists that the audience's almost subliminal association of the 1980s style of effects as "more real" photorealism holds the key to CGI providing fresh emotional impact for an audience tired of too-perfect, "inauthentic" CGI.

Sacrificing visual dynamism meant downplaying ILM's trademark never-before-seen innovative spectacle. In *Iron Man* and subsequent MCU productions, technological spectacle is fully grounded in an intense narrative event. The effects are marshalled in a way that we are not supposed to perceive them or think of them as effects. In *Iron Man*, the borrowed ILM strategy, even though largely produced by ILM itself, appears to always be at a restrained remove. For example, *Iron Man* does not present its effects with the gaping-at-the-effects-object strategy ILM-led films such as *Jurassic Park*, *Transformers*, and *Pacific Rim* enjoy.[36] By that, I mean the trope of characters in the mise-en-scène standing open-mouthed or fleeing in terror from the display of the effects object. Instead, *Iron Man* dispenses largely with "wow" moments to present a world already formed where superheroes happen to be, rather than a world rocked by fresh spectacle. Diegetic spectators in MCU films may well respond to effects objects, as in *The Avengers* when New York City crowds cower in terror before an alien onslaught, or as in *Avengers: Age of Ultron* when Sokovians panicked as their country is lifted into the air, but the technological visual spectacle of these cataclysms are prioritized first as intense narrative events.

Iron Man: The Shellhead in the Suit

The extreme amount of digital effects in these films may make the attempt to suppress the audience's awareness of CGI seem perverse. Similar to how the assemblage of Marvel superheroes in the narrative of *The Avengers* parallels its accretion of effects companies in its production, the construction and display of Tony Stark's Iron Man armored suit likewise narratively echoes its effects production context.

For example, a central problem that the *Iron Man* production faced is that its hero was encased in a helmeted suit for large portions of the movie, and the suit had to be a digital double for much of the time. Nevertheless, the movie's attraction needed to be Robert Downey Jr.'s acerbic Tony Stark as Iron Man the character and his origins, not the suit that encases him. As a genius inventor, his personality defines his powers, rather than the other way around. The effects reflect that priority by enlivening the digital double and adding personality not only to the movements of the suit and frequent cutaways to Downey's face inside the suit (and his voiceover) but also in how the suit is lit and placed in an environment. The primary way to characterize the CGI suit and to tie it to its environment comes out of the ILM effects photorealistic lighting playbook, where one uses lighting to strategically emphasize or deemphasize elements of the effects object and the mise-en-scène. For the effects object, the goal is to highlight the shape of the effects object while veiling the details through backlighting, particulate or mist in the air, or quite simply the obscurity of darkness. To place it photorealistically in a mise-en-scène, effects artists add cinematographic lighting artifacts such as lens flares to move the eye around instead of fixing on the effects objects or extra-bright lighting elements such as computer-screen graphics, likewise to distract the eye. Cinematographers (here

Fig. 5.02 *Iron Man* (2008): The strong lights at Iron Man's eyes, heart, and hands aid in the digital double's characterization and also attract the eye away from the effects object.

Matthew Libatique) include similar kinds of lights on the set to tie the spaces together. However, the filmmakers also design the effects and set lighting to enliven and personify the CGI suit. Fitting in with Favreau's and Marvel's priorities for narrative over spectacle—even when we are supposed to experience the suit as the spectacle, such as in its first test flight—the animators use lighting to emphasize the person in the suit rather than the suit itself (figure 5.02).

Even though the development of Iron Man's armor is a major plot trajectory in the film, *Iron Man* introduces the suit and later exhibits it in an almost offhand manner. The first Iron Man suit (the "Mark 1") debuts while our titular superhero-to-be, billionaire arms dealer, and tech giant Tony Stark is being held captive by a group vaguely reminiscent of al-Qaeda/ISIS who are also mercenary fighters in a desolate Middle East landscape. The bulky, crude, steel-colored body armor made from scrap metal is introduced, à la the monster in *Frankenstein*, piece by piece in a barely visible darkened cave. Here, the suit is not an attraction in and of itself but a prototype that serves an immediate purpose: Tony's escape. Most of the details are lost in darkness, with only a few highlights glinting off the pitted and grooved roughness of the minimally reflective metallic surface, so that the outline of a metal suit is suggested without providing us a good look at it.

In the sequence when Stark fights his way out of the cave in the suit—the first time we see it in action—the editing cuts as if the suit is moving too haphazardly to be framed properly. Moreover, the bright flares from his weapon distract our vision. All of these strategies obscure the suit itself, placing emphasis on Stark's attempts to control it and operate it as he is fighting his captors. We can also contrast this sequence to, say, the opening of the first *Transformers* film. The all-CGI Transformer effects object attacking the military base is similarly revealed in parts and during nighttime with light flashes but is in fact gradually revealed in a full, wide "hero" shot, flaunting the impeccably photoreal CGI object. The Iron Man Mark 1 suit (a combination of Stan Winston physical elements and CGI-animated elements) is never fully revealed in a wide shot and is left as junk in the desert in pieces. Evidently a beta version, it is unimportant in and of itself.

When Stark returns from his captivity, we see him build the new, more sophisticated suit in his Malibu workroom/garage. The iconic suit pointedly emerges as it is built, nonchalantly and organically in the narrative. As such, before Stark actually uses the suit, it is lit to match the other metallic hardware in the room. While the Mark 1 was concealed by dark lighting and a matte, metallic surface, as well as rapid editing and other distractions, we see the Mark II Armor in sufficient lighting, as well as Stark's process, in great detail, of putting it together via manipulation of a computer display and performance testing. Throughout, Stark refines the look and movement of the suit through a multilayered display that resembles animation software displays in Autodesk Maya.

Practical lighting around the set provides visual models for how the new suit will be lit as well as spatial and depth cues. In every shot, we see extra-bright fluorescent elements in the mise-en-scène providing hard, white light from above, and also points of intense light scattered around the frame and pooling under the various hardware in the workshop. The utility look of the lights reflects Stark's near-surgical focus, alongside his workshop's functional, smooth concrete walls and matte, dark rubberized floors. The uncluttered clinical setting is also all the better to show off his bitchin' motorcycle and car collection. But even more emphatically, the number of similarly metallic physical items are on the set for subtle visual comparison with the suit elements (which in this first episode were again created through Stan Winston studio–designed physical suits, all-CG suits, or a combination of the two). The suit is designed to seem of a piece with Stark's gearhead collection (figure 5.03). The metal on the likewise red-and-yellow suit and the finish on his cars are exactly the same, selling the physical realness of the suit. In other words, his suit is not only as real as the cars; it is ordinary as the cars—

Fig. 5.03 *Iron Man* (2008): Iron Man's digital suit is lit to look as physical as Tony's other mechanical "toys," such as his sports-car collection and computer monitors.

or at least as ordinary the 1932 vintage Ford Roadster, from which he gets the suit's color scheme, or a nearly $200,000 Audi R8—things that exist in the real world.

Later appearances of the suit visually downplay the actual suit and play up Stark's narrative experience of it. The suit finally becomes enlivened and embodied by Stark's character when he takes the Mark II Armor (importantly, all CGI while in flight) for its first test flight in darkness; once again, the nighttime lights suggest the outline of the suit more than the tactile details. The suit is largely backlit, with a few glinting highlights suggesting the metallic finish. Rather than lens flares as light artifacts designed to move the eye away from the details of the effects object, we instead see hard points of white light, recalling the fluorescent globes in Stark's workroom. He frequently zips out of the frame like he is moving too fast and too erratically for a physical camera to frame him professionally.

But beyond the frequent cutaways to Stark's face inside his helmet, what visually turns the suit into the Iron Man character is the extra-bright lights on key parts of his suit. The brightest light in the frame comes from Stark's eyes, the palms of his hands, and the soles of his feet (when flying); but even brighter is the artificial power source in his chest that also serves as his heart. These concentrated fields of light simply, if abstractly, accentuate the most characterizing aspects of his humanity and his agency, selling the idea of an actual person in the suit. Additionally, there are often a few other haloed lights scattered around the mise-en-scène. To compare again to the wonderment presentation of effects objects in the *Transformers* films, once we are in the air we are not treated to fetishistic close-ups of suit details as in the lengthy sequences of interlocking pieces and gears turning in the giant Transformers' shift from car to robot. Moreover, even though he is flying over the Santa Monica Pier and swoops into downtown Los Angeles, spectators' notice of him is reduced to a reaction shot of a mildly surprised child on a Ferris wheel and a momentarily frightened swerving motorist. There is none of the awestruck gaping and pointing that are a staple of the *Transformers* films, the *Jurassic Park* films, and other ILM signature franchises.

When we do finally see the Mark II Armor in full daylight, when Stark takes it to Afghanistan to fight for civilian villagers, the lighting scheme takes advantage of the opposite lighting phenomenon to nighttime: overly harsh Middle East desert sunlight. An intensely yellow glow backlights Iron Man's figure in some cases, and the sandy particulates in the air raised in the dustup blur out the details of the suit. Still, the power lights from the suit, especially the anthropomorphizing eye and heart lights, drown out even the desert noontime sun. (figure 5.04)

Favreau's "grounded photorealism," modeled on ILM's 1980s style of highlighting the effect of the human camera operator's mistakes, is designed to provide that analog feeling to a largely CGI production. However, neither version is based on anything natural, and they are not an inevitably realistic style. Both derive from what has cinematically read as real: cultivated and simulated mistakes and chance, in contrast to perfect CGI smoothness. And in this case, the optical cyborg eye makes a perfect blending of old-school nostalgic aesthetics and up-to-date digital

Fig. 5.04 *Iron Man* (2008): The effects team takes advantage of the intense Middle East overhead light and dusty atmospherics to display and also camouflage the CGI Iron Man suit at the same time.

capabilities. And like the original *Star Wars* trilogy's influence over the future of ILM's style for subsequent decades, the style of effects adapted for *Iron Man* has had a profound effect on the entire run of Marvel movies.[37] The economic power of Marvel Studios has had an acute effect on the industry more broadly, extending the ILM aesthetic even further.

The Avengers and the Marvel Effect

The ILM aesthetic is one that global effects companies have long looked to as a level of aspirational excellence. Disney and Marvel Studios may have had the plan to implement a version of the ILM style across their MCU films, but that does not mean the effects industry was prepared to accommodate them. How, then, did Disney take over the effects industry via the MCU? And how did the effects industry cope with this new reality?

The incentive to adapt to the MCU was especially attractive in 2011, when effects artists were striking in picket lines outside the Academy Awards and working to organize into a labor union, protesting their poor working conditions and unpaid contracts.[38] Perhaps not coincidentally, at the same time in 2011, Disney's actions began to consolidate the effects industry. Marvel Studios had proven the viability of its MCU "Phase One" and was gearing up to launch *The Avengers*. This film was not only the culmination of Phase One's efforts to introduce the main characters and several secondary characters that form the narrative core of the MCU; it was the first wholly Disney-produced film in the series.

But first, the roiling effects industry stood in Disney's way of ensuring a stable pipeline for these effects-dependent films. Disney's and Marvel Studios' strategies to protect their burgeoning franchise from the volatility of the effects industry took several forms. The first crucial move was to split up the effects job among as many companies as possible to avoid production disruptions by one effects company's bankruptcy, ballooning the companies per film to more than twenty. The producers then further split up the job. Rather than award entire sequences to a given company, the effects companies' contributions were divided into discrete assets. Top-tier houses such as ILM or Weta would still complete the most complicated aspects, such as the helicarrier in *The Avengers* or acting motion-captured characters such as Hulk, while more rote work such as backgrounds and cleanup were handled by smaller, less established houses. This means the elements of a major action sequence could have been worked on by ten or so different companies in, for example, San Francisco, Wellington, Paris, Chennai, Vancouver, Montreal and Singapore. Marvel Studios instituted another effects production shift. Rather than appointing a visual effects supervisor who was employed by a particular company for each film, Marvel Studios hired an independent supervisor to wrangle the many far-flung companies' shots and make sure they were aesthetically coherent. It also instituted effects quality and efficiency control at the corporate level. Instead of answering to a single creative personality, such as George Lucas in the *Star Wars* series (or, traditionally, the film director), Marvel Studios appointed an executive VP of postproduction to oversee the visual effects supervisor and ensure the workflow was on track and achieving the Marvel look.

The Avengers demonstrates practically how this industrial strategy played out in a crucial MCU film. Considering some of the specific aspects of *The Avengers* production not only provides an instructive example for how Marvel Studios has industrially transformed much of the effects industry; it also displays how the MCU absorbed Favreau's *Iron Man* version of ILM's lineage of realist aesthetics into the contemporary Marvel superhero blockbuster. *The Avengers* would feature about 2,000 effects shots, the highest number of effects shots in a Marvel movie yet. That would overwhelm even the biggest and most efficient effects company on its own. Most of the Paramount-produced MCU Phase One films had followed the example of previous big-budget, high-effects blockbusters since the late 1980s and through the 1990s: hire two or maybe three big effects houses to complete the majority of the shots and let them subcontract more as needed to a handful of smaller, friendly companies. This procedure had worked satisfactorily for most of the Phase One films. However, when *Iron Man*'s 900-plus effects shots increased in *Iron Man 2* to about 1,350, Marvel Studios saw the limitations and financial dangers of that model. Faced with an even higher effects shot count for future installments, alongside the volatility of the industry, Marvel Studios took what at the time seemed to be an extreme new route for the effects on *The Avengers*: assemble and assimilate.

As a "team-up" movie bridging the MCU's Phases One and Two, the effects look of *The Avengers* not only had to mesh within itself but also recall all the previous films of Phase One. Again emphasizing narrative consolidation, director Joss Whedon, like several directors in the MCU, was previously best known as a television director and showrunner.[39] In line with Favreau's example and Marvel Studios' expectations, Whedon referred to the film's overall style, as "insanity grounded in reality."[40] Further reinforcing the Marvel Studios' stated priorities of narrative continuity over spectacle, Jeff White, VFX supervisor at ILM, said of Whedon: "[Joss is] going to keep the visual effects working for the story and character development and not the other way around."[41]

To accomplish this, Marvel Studios hired Janek Sirrs as the overall project visual effects supervisor. Because Sirrs's signature was identified as "a very strong photorealistic aspect, marked by clarity and a lack of fussiness,"[42] he would seem to be compatible with Whedon's and, more importantly, Marvel Studios' vision. Sirrs's job was to organize the workflow of twenty-plus houses to realize a coherent effects whole. Sirrs had previously contributed to the MCU as visual effects supervisor on *Iron Man 2* and had previously worked as visual effects supervisor for the Coen brothers and Christopher Nolan. Like Sirrs, most of the vendors had worked on previous Marvel superhero films, and then had to work with each other as they traded "assets," or what they call "digital effects elements," back and forth with one other (much as in the film itself).[43]

On production for *The Avengers*, as with *Iron Man* and *Iron Man 2*, ILM was the most central of the twenty-plus companies working on the film, completing nearly a third (about 700 shots) of the overall effects shot count.[44] Weta handled 400 shots. Moreover, ILM originated most of the film's major assets, which were then handed off to other companies to modify. ILM's in-house motion capture (iMo-Cap) and digital double rigs (iClone, Lightstage, and Mova) provided the data for digitally generated stunt doubles and performing digital characters.[45] ILM designed and digitally built the exterior helicarrier on which much of the film's first act takes place. Finally, it also built in the computer the twelve blocks of New York City where the film's climactic battle would take place.[46]

Like *Iron Man*, we see much of the same photorealistic strategizing implemented for *The Avengers*. For example, the movie needs to showcase the Hulk, the film's most important re-debuting digital character, after two previous, minimally successful solo outings. Like the Mark 1 Iron Man suit, the Hulk is first introduced in the dark bowels of the helicarrier, with only backlighting from bright lights to suggest his form in parts before we see the full character. Moreover, Hulk's introduction takes place in a very fast-paced fight sequence with the Hulk charging through the space in rapid cutting showing him from different angles and shot scales. The first hour of *The Avengers* takes place at night in darkness, making the connection to the obscuring effects strategies in *Iron Man* all the more evident. Sequences in the first hour of *The Avengers* are lit very similarly to the dark interiors punctuated with very bright fluorescent lights in Tony's workroom as he built the Mark II Armor. Throughout we can see the backlighting, flares, erratic camera framing, motion blur, focus blur, and spatializing light depth effects that characterize the contemporary standards for photorealist effect.

ILM effects elements then go through a complex process whereby it shares its assets with other companies to complete effects frames and then effects sequences, eventually brought together by the Marvel Studios–appointed visual effects supervisor. However, the effects process is far from over at this point. As Victoria Alonso elaborated:

> There's a term we use a lot that Walt Disney used, which is "plussing." We are trying to plus the movie every day. If the story is not being told in the right way, there's a minus there that we need to turn into a plus. How do we plus it? Sometimes it means that we have to tear it apart to put it back together. . . . I always say that as filmmakers, we detach with love. We love our stories, but we detach from them as if they are somebody else's story. We also have a group of creatives that look at it, and we're all incredibly hard with each other. We will go in and *shred* a movie, which is hard for some writers and directors.[47]

In the same interview, Alonso also cheerfully admits to demanding changes up to the last possible minute if the movie is, in her words, "not working." While it has never been unusual for producers to go over the heads of directors when it comes to controlling the design and look of effects objects, Marvel Studios and Disney formalized and complicated their systems of oversight, not surprisingly to ensure that all MCU products conform to corporate expectations. Purportedly, up to 2015, Marvel Studios put MCU films past a "creative committee," a Marvel Comics–based panel of executives to give notes to maintain the Marvel brand. Filmmakers Patty Jenkins and Edgar Wright reportedly exited their MCU projects largely due to this layer of control, and it has led to major frustrations for those who completed their projects, including James Gunn and Joss Whedon.[48] However, although the creative committee has been disbanded, the Marvel creative process is still very centralized at the producer level, as Alonso's characterization in 2018 suggests.[49]

As the Marvel executive with a visual effects producer background and now as the person in charge of physical production, Alonso's initiatives have had significant impact on the effects industry overall. Crediting her as the architect of Marvel's effects production strategy, *Variety* reported it this way when she was installed in the high-level job: "At Marvel she is known for finding creative ways to control vfx costs and for building a global vfx pipeline for the company."[50] Alonso's efforts have had an upside to the effects business. Marvel Studios' standardization across the effects industry has done an efficient job stabilizing the volatile industry. While the Marvel Studios model is not completely different from how some blockbuster effects movies had been produced in the past, it certainly represents an organizational intensification across several vectors. In addition, VFX supervisors also laud Alonso's putting into practice a model of collaboration that effects teams have long asked for. ILM VFX supervisor Ben Snow reports that on MCU films the effects team is finally being brought in earlier and more centrally as part of the creative team: "Previously, I was used to being shoved into the corner of a shared trailer and scrabbling for a position at video village! With Marvel Studios . . . I never have felt as supported on set as I do on their films."[51] Other effects supervisors praise the more streamlined workflow and insist that the Marvel executives are open to collaborative voices, especially when those voices help to "plus" the product.[52] While not contradicting their statements, it is worth a reminder that visual effects artists' public rhetoric is obliged to take an accommodating tone.

Alonso's rhetoric fits in to the perception of collaborative unity reflected in the films' superhero team-ups: "It's a team effort to keep the cohesiveness of the look and to hold everyone to a delivery date— especially considering how we change our minds at the end of the day."[53] Nevertheless, even in statements meant to project cheerful enthusiasm regarding the filmmaking's teamwork, one senses the strain put on the effects teams expected to implement last-minute changes.

When Marvel Studios adapted the ILM aesthetic as the template for the MCU, and then employed all the world's effects companies across twenty-plus films, it enforced its version of the ILM aesthetic into a mandatory style to which all companies had to adhere. Moreover, Marvel via Disney carried a much bigger stick than ILM on its own ever had to coerce the effects companies to fall in line with its aesthetic: the promise of steady, consistent work for the next several decades. Consequently, the MCU effects aesthetic also became a conventional bar that, as of about 2012, any effects company was forced to clear technologically in order to work on a major blockbuster such as a Marvel film. As long as the company could produce effects up to Marvel's standard, it did not matter if that company was a huge firm in California with a storied history or a tiny startup out of Finland. It is worth noting that, while more companies can clear the bar with less financial layout than in the past, it is still a barrier to many companies around the world.

The Marvel Studios Aesthetic in the MCU

Across the MCU, the Marvel Studios aesthetic initiated by *Iron Man* and *Iron Man 2*, and then solidified through subsequent movies, features a series of visual cues linking the production design, cinematography, and effects aesthetics. Director of photography Libatique designed the cinematography in *Iron Man* to enliven the mise-en-scène and create depth cues with points of intense lights; this also was instrumental in creating a pattern of lighting that would smoothly integrate the effects object—initially the Iron Man suit, but eventually the pattern for all major effects objects—into a live-action frame. Put alongside the effects lighting strategies (backlighting, particulates, lens flares) as well as editing "reveal" patterns and other strategies, this consistent, easily replicated formula streamlines effects production across the multitude of effects houses working on the many films; everyone understands Marvel's expectations, which do not change a great deal from film to film.

As Alonso put it, "whether in Asgard or Wakanda," or for *Guardians of the Galaxy* (2014), *Thor: Ragnarok* (2017), or *Shang-Chi and the Legend of the Ten Rings* (2021), all MCU film productions take pains to ensure the viewer is oriented to the MCU from the jump by repeating visual information patterns established and reinforced by earlier films. Moreover, whether On-Earth or Off-Earth, these films may have distinctive art direction for product differentiation, but they maintain consistent effects aesthetics. As in *Iron Man*, nearly every single MCU film begins in a dark environment punctuated with hard shafts of directed light and/or intense points of intensely colored fluorescent lights. *The Avengers*, for example, continues in this dark environment pattern for the first hour of the film. And when the films emerge from the darkness into light, the lighting does not necessarily become more naturalistic. Similar to *Iron Man*'s sequences in Afghanistan, in *Thor*'s sequences, set in the New Mexico desert, daytime exteriors are frequently overlit with intense backlighting and particulates in the air, creating a haze over the image.

Nearly all the MCU films start with the *Iron Man* template and then, having established that we are in the familiar Marvel universe, either continue in that vein or expand from there to more fantastic locales that are variations or exaggerations of the now-expected grounded photorealistic aesthetic.

Spider-Man: Homecoming provides an example of how later MCU films play with, modify, and even thematize the aesthetic formula established in Phase One while at the same time staying within expectations. We also see how the production design, cinematography, and effects work together to unify the MCU. The sixteenth MCU film since 2008 and the third reboot of the character since 2001, *Homecoming* places emphasis on Spider-Man as "your friendly neighborhood Spider-Man," dispensing with origins and stressing his teen-outsider relatability. In costume, Peter Parker's jerky motion appears less naturalistically fluid than other digital doubles, and somewhat lighter than gravity, but that is naturalized through the act of web-slinging and, more characteristically, Peter's awkward adolescent physicality. His narrative trajectory is to progress from untrained naïf taking down bicycle thieves in Queens to being worthy of joining the more worldly and accomplished Avengers team. The film's aesthetic trajectory mirrors this.

The movie opens in familiar MCU territory: villains in a dark warehouse punctuated by bright light elements largely embedded in the alien tech and hard shafts of light. We then cut to the classroom, where Peter's low-def iPhone video reviews his involvement in the previous *Captain America: Civil War*, to contrast with his banal, quotidian high-school existence in Queens. While past movies such as *Iron Man* purported to show superhero action within a "grounded" reality, *Homecoming* takes that groundedness to even more featureless, ordinary extremes. Peter's everyday Queens life, even when dressed in the bright-red Spider-Man suit and thwarting crimes, is presented as naturalistically and unexceptionally as possible, in flat daylight, unstylized, lit as evenly as a John Hughes teen movie (figure 5.05).[54] However, when his world intersects with the world of the Avengers, whether in Tony Stark's realm or that of the villains, the style reverts to the dim interiors with brightly lit highlights of the now familiar Marvel MCU (figure 5.06). In *Homecoming*, the MCU is now figured as the more extraordinary reality to which normcore Peter wants entry. By the end, when he defeats Michael Keaton's Vulture at Coney Island, the design has once again reverted to the MCU's familiar nighttime palette: Vulture's wings and eyes glow

Fig. 5.05 *Spider-Man: Homecoming* (2017): When Peter Parker is in his high school classroom, the style of filming is conventional and evenly lit, suggesting his teenage quotidian life.

Fig. 5.06 *Spider-Man: Homecoming* (2017): When Parker's life intersects with that of the Avengers, as here at Stark Enterprises, the lighting shifts to one more aligned with the other films of the Marvel Cinematic Universe, a world of sleek technology with high-contrast lighting and fluorescent hot spots.

green, with the Coney Island neon-lit rides decorating the backdrop. Peter's world has become Marvelized because he's completed his arc of becoming worthy to join the Avengers (which he then does in *Avengers: Infinity War* [2018]). Peter's change in the world is reinforced at the end. Even when he's walking the halls of his previously unremarkable, flatly lit high school, dusty particulates in the air and the intensely blown-out background lighting now create a backlighting effect introducing the newly minted hero in the more typical MCU style.

The patterning continues in the characters' designs, where saturated primary colors accentuate their comic book–style silhouettes while remaining naturalistic. Digital character design usually is dark with intense light and/or color elements, the heroes in undiluted strong colors (such as red for Iron Man and green for Hulk) and the villains appearing more acidic, such as Loki, or Yellowjacket in *Ant-Man* (2015). Most humanoid characters (whether their costumes and makeup are physical or digital) have a Jack Kirby–inspired design that is largely neutral with brightly colored accents, such as Loki's steel-colored armor with acid-green accents, Drax's dark pants and bare, olive-colored chest with dark red scarification marks, or Black Panther's purple energy network over his dark-colored suit. While their animated movements are mostly in accordance with Earth gravity, they sometimes use exceptional strength or power to leap higher or faster than normal humans could, but still as if impacted by some amount of Earth physics.

Elsewhere in the MCU, major digital effects objects and characters are introduced either gradually, to familiarize the audience to them as effects objects, or nonchalantly, to suggest they naturally fit in next to human characters. The overall design effect is that of the ordinary world if a bit more extraordinary, but not too exaggerated or stylized. It is highly rationalized and patterned to reinforce its extraordinariness. For example, similar to the Mark 1 suit in *Iron Man* and Hulk's introduction in *The Avengers*, the Leviathan ships attacking New York in *The Avengers* appear first in silhouette as shapes, then in a dimly lit, quickly edited sequence of effect object fragments, then in backlit full form, and only briefly in full sunlight.

Rocket and Groot, the two fully digital acting characters introduced in *Guardians of the Galaxy*, are presented for the first time in that film with no particular fanfare. The strategy is clearly that the viewer is to simply accept and not think too much about the inclusion of two of the oddest characters in the MCU—a talking racoon-like creature and an anthropomorphized tree. They are introduced via Rocket's voiceover in a city plaza on the planet Xandar in sparkling sunlight. Rocket makes snarky comments about the succession of humanoids he is scanning through a transparent tablet, the roving camera finally landing on his laughing face as he addresses Groot. They are intended to be understood by the viewer as materially solid and physically coherent as any other human we have just seen, with no concealing lighting effects or other visual distractions. They are in fact introduced with considerably less drama than the other eventual crewmates: Peter Quill, Gamora, and Drax. In other words, a talking racoon and a sentient tree? Think nothing of it.[55]

Off-Earth, as *Guardians* suggests, the design of environments, characters, and action has more license to be unusual. The metallics are shinier, the color palette more expansive, the movement less gravity-based, the characters less anthropomorphic, and the environments more fanciful and bizarre. Also, as in the *Guardians* films, the more the film leans toward comedy, the quirkier the design and whimsical palette. *Thor: Ragnarok* takes this liberty to an extreme, with its candy-colored trash planet, Sakaar, where Thor and Hulk reunite. Certainly, this visual variety ensures a certain product differentiation so that the formula is neither too obvious or becomes stale.

One might be wondering at this point: But what about *Doctor Strange* (2016) and its puzzle box–style folding of city environments and mystical metaphysicality? And doesn't *Ant-Man* feature a lengthy trippy sequence in the quantum realm? A surprising aspect of most MCU films is that they feature at least one fantastical sequence where the grounded formula of photorealistic logic is temporarily suspended. Counterintuitively, these strategic escape-from-rationality sequences provide a way to reinforce the "rightness" of the normal world as depicted by the effects program in the majority of the film. These sequences are most often portrayed in the narrative largely as unpleasant episodes our heroes must escape from (*Ant-Man*, *Black Panther*), rationalized as bad or repressed memories (*Captain America: Winter Soldier*, *Avengers: Infinity War*), and frequently engineered by villains (*Spider-Man: Far from Home* [2019], *Captain Marvel* [2019], *Avengers: Age of Ultron*, *Doctor Strange*). Not incidentally, it is also another way the MCU adopts strategic selections of the ILM effects aesthetic. The *Star Wars* films nearly always feature a dreamlike, Force-induced, uncomfortable sequence where the hero confronts the irrational: for example, Luke's training dream/hallucination in *Empire Strikes Back*, where he sees his own face in Darth Vader's helmet, or Rey's montage of imagery when she touches Luke Skywalker's lightsaber in *The Force Awakens*. In both cases, characters—and, it seems, viewers—breathe a sigh of relief when these interludes of irrationality are left behind for the "real" world. I suggest that *Doctor Strange* takes this rationale and thematizes it into a feature-length film, where his arc is to achieve mastery over such irrational forces.

Conclusion

For some critics, fans, and even filmmakers, Disney's and Marvel's turn to a photoreal grounded aesthetic based on narrative motivation in effects may be seen as an important corrective to the nearly completely animated digital spectacles of the *Transformers* sort. Professional critics and fans frequently disparage these franchise films for being insufficiently narratively rich, in addition to expressing their distaste for elaborate effects sequences where obviously CGI creations wreck CGI landscapes.[56] However, the consequences to this Marvel-imposed economic stability include discouraging any alternative styles. Further, this homogeneity means any styles outside of these films are judged as "wrong" or "bad," as we see with examples of deliberate alternative styles such as *Warcraft* and *The Mermaid*.

The "grounded" effects aesthetic of the MCU was developed in part to respond to popular fan charges of "crappy"—obviously CGI—effects in blockbuster films of the 2000s. The Marvel style has been successful in conventional terms. The films have helped Disney dominate world box office. Critics and fans respond favorably to the MCU output, and moviegoers appear to find its look and subject matter uncontroversial. As various Reddit forums attest, the MCU is not immune from criticism for its effects.[57] However, no MCU film has been met with the controversy that surrounded *Star Wars: The Last Jedi*'s (2017) or *Star Wars: The Rise of Skywalker*'s (2019) narrative and aesthetic choices. And it is controversy that the MCU production process has been set up to avoid.

Marvel's rise as the world superpower of the effects business also had the consequence of diminishing ILM's influence. In the past, for a movie such as *The Avengers*, ILM would have played the role of lead effects house, with one of its own employees as the film's credited lead VFX supervisor. Today, ILM answers to the Marvel-hired VFX supervisor. The Marvel Studios configuration has made ILM just one effects company among many—albeit a privileged favorite. But ILM is far from falling into irrelevance. After the post-Disney purchase of Lucasfilm, the new associates announced and began producing an extensive slate of *Star Wars* spinoffs modeled on the MCU's theatrical release schedule. Even if that schedule was scaled back, as Disney turns its attention to the Disney+ streaming platform, ILM remains the lead house for all the movies and serials in the *Star Wars* universe and will likely continue to be.

However, as the *Star Wars* universe expands, its importance to Disney's intellectual property has meant that is being subsumed into the Disney management production style. As the renowned sound designer and longtime Lucasfilm collaborator Ben Burtt has observed about the new slate of *Star Wars* movies, with criticism similar to Roger Deakins around the Marvel movies:

> It wasn't always easy working with George [Lucas], but at least it was one voice. And you could get his attention and have your say and present something and get a yes or a no. But it was just one person you had to get past. Not *banks* of different people who want to have a say.[58]

And like Marvel movies and Favreau, also a top executive developing *Star Wars* properties such as *The Mandalorian*, Disney's Lucasfilm team has crowdsourced a very specific version of the *Star Wars* aesthetic that must be followed.

Most relevant to effects as a creative endeavor, Disney's hegemony also discourages the long-standing "aesthetic innovation model" of the effects industry, wherein R&D innovation not only is strived for on a technical level but also is displayed as spectacle and production value.[59] As I have discussed elsewhere, at any given time there has been a relatively narrow range of possibilities for high-end effects aesthetics. However, as Michele Pierson, Brooks Landon, Albert de Valley, and Richard Matby have suggested, one of the economic raisons d'être for blockbuster movies was to put the money on the screen, to show "what movies can do now" and give spectators a reason to go to the theater to witness the new technical wonders.[60] Ambitious effects houses saw incentives to develop software and techniques that would produce effects spectacle for the sake of showing off their prowess as well as expanding their visual storytelling potential. *Jurassic Park*'s photoreal dinosaurs were not only presented in the film as remarkable photorealistic effects objects; they were gawked at by amazed characters in the mise-en-scène, cueing the audience's equally awed response. The Wachowskis and VFX supervisor Jon Gaeta introduced bullet time in *The Matrix* as an effects spectacle that also described the contours of the world they were building.[61] And in *Pacific Rim*, Guillermo del Toro encouraged the ILM team toward a non-naturalistic, exaggerated lighting in the kaiju fights to create an operatic heightened tone, a style that clearly influenced the Warner Bros. MonsterVerse franchise, especially *Godzilla vs. Kong* (2021).[62] In other words, the introduction of fresh effects approaches helped fuel product differentiation and set trends for less ambitious and less expensive blockbusters down the line, bolstering visual effects as a creative sector.

Since the 1970s blockbuster era kicked into high gear, filmmakers and effects artists have insisted in their rhetoric that the story is what is important and that the effects are there to support it. Frequently these artists' show-stopping spectacles contradicted such statements. What is striking is that the MCU films actually do everything they can to transform this disingenuous rhetoric into practice for the screen. And they have done it by reorganizing how big-budget, effects-heavy films had been contracting effects work since the 1980s. Marvel's influence on the effects industry—the Marvel Effect—has meant there is much less economic incentive to provide innovative or diverse effects imagery. In the Avengers Initiative, individuals are vulnerable, but the collective is strong, and no doubt this is the image Disney and Marvel Studios want to encourage. While admittedly it is self-serving rhetoric, claiming to strive to outdo the other guy has been an R&D motivation that has kept the effects industry vital and has made it a magnet for creatives since the 1980s.[63] If there is no ILM to act as a beacon to those ambitious newcomers, then the effects industry loses its luster and becomes more like any other service. In an industry that is woefully unrecognized and unremunerated for its efforts, the Marvel Effect makes effects artists more anonymous and unrewarded than ever.

Unreal Engine

ILM in a Disney World

WE COULD GO ON MAKING "STAR WARS" FOR THE NEXT 100 YEARS.

—GEORGE LUCAS IN 2012, AFTER ILM'S SALE TO DISNEY

Delineating the contours of the ILM aesthetic is important to denaturalizing it so that it does not go by unnoticed. However, one must also recognize the ideological implications of a style of realism in popular cinema that clings so tightly to a 1970s New Hollywood model. What does it mean that for most effects practitioners and filmmakers their unthinking notion of perceptual realism is (a version of) 1970s New Hollywood realism? And how does this connect to the future of ILM in the context of the Disney conglomeration?

The ILM house aesthetic was originally conceived as a way to photorealistically match the cinematography, editing, and staging of films from filmmakers in George Lucas's New Hollywood peer group. That style was originally developed to oppose "slick" Hollywood professionalism and also bring New Wave and cinema verité aesthetics into the themes of what Thomas Elsaesser would refer to as the pathos of failure and the unmotivated hero in American cinema.[1] In both the American and global contexts, a major trait of this style (as in the example of *Medium Cool*) was to lay bare the camera and draw attention to the act of filming as well as to the presence of the filmmaking team through staging and editing. This approach chimed with the effects goals associated with the first *Star Wars*. That 1977 film strove for an abraded "used future" in miniatures and models, in the look of a handheld camera (actually computerized motion control), as well as a dynamic and slightly jagged editing style. This style also complemented what Jeff Menne calls New Hollywood's "economy of genius," discussed in chapter 1, in which the early ILM team banded together to feel as if they were making something not only fresh and original in the face of Old Hollywood but also filmmaking suffused with handmade honesty.

It is somewhat surprising that in the rise of digital technology in the 1990s and early 2000s this New Hollywood aesthetic would remain viable. Modeling digitally generated effects material on the 1970s was a clever way to ground this new technology in an era that retained the cachet of a culturally agreed-on visual authenticity and artistic integrity. However, while New Hollywood used to stand unthinkingly for artistic candor and rugged independence, in light of the Time's Up and #MeToo movements spotlighting the historical treatment of women in Hollywood, it is looking more and more like out-of-touch macho Boomerism. Just as we should unmask the ILM aesthetic as a highly stylized reality effect, we need to see it and the New Hollywood realism it is based on as the perspective of a certain kind of perception—one that is mostly white, mostly straight, and mostly male.

As recent scholarship, especially by Maya Montañez Smukler, has reinforced, the New Hollywood boys' club and the histories of New Hollywood have not been welcoming to nonwhite non-male perspectives.[2] The women interviewed in Peter Biskind's influential popular chronicle of the era, *Easy Riders, Raging Bulls*, are portrayed largely as disgruntled first wives, even though Biskind hardly mentions that many of them, such as Marcia Griffin Lucas, Polly Platt, and Toby Carr Rafelson, were important (and frequently uncredited) artistic collaborators with their more lauded former husbands.[3] Even during the 1970s, the (rare) female directors Elaine May and Barbara Loden cast a self-conscious and even baleful eye on the ability of the New Hollywood form of realism to represent women's subjectivities.[4] Neither can director's realism be taken as straight representations of a "more authentic" reality. Take the example of the lens flare in *The Heartbreak Kid* at the moment Cybill Shephard's character, Kelly, is introduced. As in *Easy Rider*, it seems to indicate Kelly's association with nature's beauty. However, it also can be read as a monster reveal, appearing at the moment when she begins to wreak (self-imposed) havoc on Charles Grodin's life.

Similarly, as I have demonstrated with examples both within and outside mainstream practice, filmmaking teams from marginalized groups and those outside Hollywood tend to use the traits associated with the ILM New Hollywood realism style more self-consciously. Speaking very generally, marginalized filmmakers (meaning, in light of lopsided filmmaking demographics, anyone not a white man) and non-Hollywood filmmakers already are more likely to "see through" the ILM international style of realism. As discussed in chapter 4, based on their public statements, Bong Joon-ho and Zhang Yimou clearly see the dominant form of Hollywood realism as a style that they are participating in and self-consciously adapting to their purposes. Likewise, in the example in chapter 2 discussing *If Beale Street Could Talk*, Barry Jenkins's use of the lens flare to indicate fleeting hopefulness that the doomed pair will be able to live together as a normal couple is at the same time a devastatingly impossible fantasy. We can compare that to *Yesterday*, where the flare instantiates an especially Boomer-friendly fantasy of an encounter with a still-alive John Lennon. In another register, "afro-pessimist" films such as *Sorry to Bother You* (2018) play with codes of realism and science fiction to comment on the limitations of both for Black creatives.

In most mainstream cases, the reality being evoked is one with which the filmmakers are aligned. This approach to ILM's realism has been reinforced rather than questioned by *Star Wars* superfans J. J. Abrams and Jon Favreau, who have been the major creative forces in ILM's Disney conglomeration period—Abrams as director of *Star Wars* episodes VII and IX and Favreau as the creator of the Disney+ series *The Mandalorian*. Under Disney, ILM has had to shift from the (albeit problematic) 1970s economy of genius and adapt itself to Disney's conglomerated nostalgia machine.

When Disney acquired Lucasfilm in 2012, it was evident to business analysts that the conglomerate's goal was to take advantage of the lucrative *Star Wars* intellectual property and the franchise's loyal, built-in fan base.[5] Although ILM was not one of the more attractive parts of the deal, Disney's announcement that it planned to release a new *Star Wars* movie every two to three years meant that, for the time being, ILM's role as the custodian of the *Star Wars* aesthetic legacy would be secure. While it was not confirmed to be the case, the spate of movie franchise plans (a Boba Fett origin story, an Obi-Wan Kenobi prequel, writers hired for unspecified trilogies) suggested a ramping-up of the *Star Wars* film series to what Disney clearly hoped would be an MCU-style release schedule of maybe even two to three *Star Wars* movies each year. However, the financial underperformance of *Solo: A Star Wars Story* (2018), released only five months after the fan-divisive *The Last Jedi*, led to an announcement by then–Disney CEO Bob Iger that Disney had miscalculated with their *Star Wars* plans; henceforth, *Star Wars* movies would be rarer and therefore more special.[6] These corporate release strategies indicate a crisis of representation that needed solving.

Then, in 2019, Disney+ released *The Mandalorian*. The immediate runaway hit series for Disney's new streaming service helped begin the *Star Wars* shift away from feature films toward streaming series. However, the COVID-19 pandemic's closing of movie theaters in March 2020 for nearly a year and a half, as well as the huge success of the second season of the series, hastened the announcement in late 2020 that Disney would be intentionally moving *Star Wars* productions largely toward streaming. At the annual investors meeting in December 2020, Disney announced it was putting into production ten new *Star Wars*–based live-action and animated series along with other one-off movies and assorted *Star Wars*–related projects.

As entertainment journalists such as *Variety*'s Adam B. Vary and others quickly noted, Disney was finally appearing to succeed in making over the *Star Wars* franchise into the Marvel Cinematic Universe: an intricately interconnected series of narratives that relied to some degree on the viewers' awareness of other properties.[7] Plans to "culminate in a climactic story event," à la *The Avengers*, cemented the comparison. *Mandalorian* creator Jon Favreau (alongside longtime Lucasfilm animation chief Dave Filoni) cited as crucial his experience with the MCU in informing *The Mandalorian*'s production style and approach.[8]

These corporate machinations represented a kind of good news for ILM, in that it would be busy with *Star Wars*–related projects for the foreseeable future. This meant a stability at the heart of Disney's plans it had not enjoyed since the corporate takeover. Less positively, it appears to also mean a similar kind of freezing in carbonite of the ILM aesthetic, something similar to that experienced with the MCU. In fact, while ILM had previously prided itself on an emphasis on dazzling innovation combined with a flexibility to accommodate whatever style it was called to produce, it can be argued that the *Star Wars* universe under Favreau is experiencing a streamlining of the ILM style into a solidification of the historical 1970s and 1980s *Star Wars* look.

This style includes more than visual references to the original *Star Wars* trilogy. Chapter 5 described how Favreau, Disney, and Marvel Studios began to take advantage of ILM's status as the industry leader in order to base the MCU aesthetic on a version of the ILM historical house style, beginning with the first two *Iron Man* films. The MCU's aesthetics of "grounded photorealism" takes a version of the predigital ILM house style as a goal, placing its primary priority on narrative integration rather than effects spectacle for its own sake, as well as downplaying the look of digitalization by limiting its more animated potential.

The aesthetic used for *The Mandalorian* is something even more limited: it is *Star Wars* circa the original trilogy. Motivated similarly as with *Iron Man*, Favreau wanted to recapture the wonder that *Star Wars* had ignited in his teenage self.[9] Again, this did not only mean characters and plots. Getting that old *Star Wars* feeling hinged on a fairly literal replication of the aesthetic of the original trilogy. Discourse from *The Mandalorian* production emphasizes an old-school approach to effects: physical effects (especially the Baby Yoda puppet); physically built miniatures; and even some Phil Tippett–produced stop-motion and motion-control shots by John Knoll.[10] Even when digital technology was used to tweak the physical rubber masks, puppets, or miniatures, Favreau insisted that the effect maintain the "charming" limitations of the more traditional techniques: digitally animated Blurrgs should look "puppety," Quarren masks should look a little rubbery, and so on.[11] In this way, Favreau is yet again mixing the state-of-the-art digital technology with traditional techniques in order to give *The Mandalorian* a seemingly "authentically" physical and optical *Star Wars* look; but he is still happy to finesse it with digital technology so that the result is not *too* 1980.

Despite a well-publicized use of traditional techniques, the real core of how *The Mandalorian* production achieved this "updated circa 1980" look was through an elaborate digital effects technology that the industry somewhat confusingly calls "virtual production." *The Mandalorian* production calls this setup "the volume," a giant LED screen environment that is a functional equivalent of rear-screen projection (although the actual technologies are quite different) as a kind of real-time compositing, using game-engine technology developed by Epic's Unreal Engine. *The Mandalorian* production shot more than 50 percent of its first season on a stage surrounded not by bluescreens but instead by giant, high-definition LED screens that "composited" in real time, and it was completed on the set at the time of principal photography.[12] Unlike bluescreen environments, the principal photography and composited footage would have an as-if-shot-on-location lighting aesthetic.

Through this setup, the in-house ILM photorealism priorities of "as if shot by human camera operator" and its 1970s-inflected lighting effects would be not only preserved but also enhanced. Once again "photorealism" was the term used to describe this new production method's aesthetic goals. ILM visual effects supervisor Richard Bluff described this photorealism as a minimally manipulated mise-en-scène:

> We had to put photography on the screen that you wouldn't question so people could focus instead on whether or not this idea was going to work. [In the test footage] . . . there was no artist intervention with that content and no interpretation of the lighting. [The location footage] was a real environment that looked completely photographic.[13]

As is often the case in effects discourse, the word "photorealism" is doing a lot of descriptive heavy lifting. Here, "real" is equated not only with photography; it is the ability of minimally manipulated location footage to serve as a real-time composite and also be read through the camera as normal principal photography footage. Instead of complex algorithms and built-from-scratch CGI environments, the magic comes from what appears to be simple, unmanipulated location photography looking exactly like what it is. Previously, photorealism meant the perfect digital replication of (or a stylization of) camera reality. Here it is the ability for photographed real locations to act as real locations, fine-tuned by digital manipulation. Once again, we can see how the term "photorealism" and the aesthetics it is meant to describe, as well as the technology that produces it, are historically fungible.[14]

The rhapsodic fan response to *The Mandalorian* suggests that Disney-owned Lucasfilm finally succeeded in satisfying its finicky fans.[15] Fan approval is typically characterized in story terms: fans are getting the characters and kinds of old-school *Star Wars* narratives they long craved—but had not yet gotten—in the Disney era. However, I contend that much of the gratification in *The Mandalorian* derives from ILM's success in replicating the look of the original trilogy as directly as possible. The MCU has endeavored to normalize "grounded" photorealistic effects as narrative events and play down pure spectacle. Counterintuively, ILM brings back the "wow" of its brand by using contemporary technology to make *The Mandalorian* look just like 1980.

However, instead of "wow—here's what ILM's technology can accomplish now," it is "wow—that looks and *feels* just like the original *Star Wars* trilogy." The ILM spectacle is that old *Star Wars* feeling through that old *Star Wars* style. Furthermore, bringing back a more literal historical version of the ILM style for *The Mandalorian* and presumably its offshoots also demonstrates how, for its Disney masters, it is not keeping the ILM house style updated that will keep ILM relevant; instead it is its ability to deliver the *Star Wars* version of the ILM style. For Disney's nostalgia-based approach to intellectual property, nothing could be more ideal.

Appendix

List of Films Mentioned in the Text

2001: A Space Odyssey (1968)
A Star Is Born (1976)
A Star Is Born (2018)
About Time (2013)
The Abyss (1989)
Ace Ventura: Pet Detective (1994)
The Adventures of André and Wally B. (1984)
Alvin and the Chipmunks (2007)
American Graffiti (1973)
Anaconda (1997)
Anna and the King (1999)
Anna Karenina (2012)
Ant-Man (2015)
Apocalypse Now (1979)
Astro Boy (2009)
Attack the Block (2011)
Avatar (2009)
The Avengers (2012)
Avengers: Age of Ultron (2015)
Avengers: Endgame (2019)
Avengers: Infinity War (2018)
The Aviator (2004)
Baahubali 2: The Conclusion (2017)
The Babadook (2014)
Babe (1995)

Babe: Pig in the City (1998)
Badlands (1973)
Batman Begins (2005)
The Battle of Algiers (1966)
Beauty and the Beast (2017)
Belle (2013)
Black Panther (2018)
Bob & Carol & Ted & Alice (1969)
Bohemian Rhapsody (2018)
Bringing Up Baby (1938)
Bumblebee (2018)
Butch Cassidy and the Sundance Kid (1969)
Captain America: Civil War (2016)
Captain America: The First Avenger (2011)
Captain America: The Winter Soldier (2014)
Captain Marvel (2019)
Casper (1995)
Cats (2019)
Cinderella (2015)
City Lights (1931)
Clash of the Titans (1981)
Close Encounters of the Third Kind (1977)
Cockfighter (1974)

Cocoon (1985)
Contact (1997)
Crouching Tiger, Hidden Dragon (2000)
The Curious Case of Benjamin Button (2008)
Curious George (2006)
Daddy's Home 2 (2017)
Dante's Peak (1997)
The Dark Knight (2008)
Darkest Hour (2017)
Dawn of the Planet of the Apes (2014)
Day of the Tentacle (1993)
Days of Heaven (1978)
Deadpool (2016)
Death Becomes Her (1992)
Death Proof (2007)
Die Hard 2 (1990)
District 9 (2009)
Doctor Strange (2016)
Doctor Who [TV series] (1963–1989, 2005–present)
Drácula (1931, dir. George Melford)
Dracula (1931, dir. Tod Browning)
Dredd (2012)
Dune (1984)
Dunkirk (2017)
E.T. the Extra-Terrestrial (1982)
Easy Rider (1969)
Emma. (2020)
Ender's Game (2013)
Enthiran (trans. *Robot*) (2010)
Evan Almighty (2007)
Ex Machina (2014)
F9: The Fast Saga (2021)
The Falcon and the Winter Soldier (2021)
Fantastic Beasts and Where to Find Them (2016)
The Fast and the Furious film series (2001–):
    The Fast and the Furious (2001)
    2 Fast 2 Furious (2003)
    The Fast and the Furious: Tokyo Drift (2006)

Fast & Furious (2009)
Fast Five (2011)
Fast & Furious 6 (2013)
Furious 7 (2015)
The Fate of the Furious (2017)
F9 (2021)
The Fifth Element (1997)
Five Easy Pieces (1970)
Forrest Gump (1994)
Frankenstein (1931)
The French Connection (1971)
Frozen (2013)
Frozen II (2019)
Futureworld (1976)
Game of Thrones (2011–2019)
Geostorm (2017)
Gimme Shelter (1970)
Gladiator (2000)
The Godfather (1972)
The Godfather: Part II (1974)
Godzilla (1954)
Godzilla (1998)
Godzilla (2014)
Godzilla vs. Kong (2021)
The Golem (1920)
Gone in 60 Seconds (2000)
The Goonies (1985)
The Graduate (1967)
The Grand Budapest Hotel (2014)
Gravity (2013)
The Great Wall (2016)
The Green Mile (1999)
Greenland (2020)
Gremlins (1984)
Grindhouse (2007)
Guardians of the Galaxy (2014)
Harold and Maude (1971)
Harry Potter film series (2001–2011)
    Harry Potter and the Sorcerer's Stone (2001)
    Harry Potter and the Chamber of Secrets (2002)
    Harry Potter and the Prisoner of Azkaban (2004)

Harry Potter and the Goblet of Fire (2005)

Harry Potter and the Order of the Phoenix (2007)

Harry Potter and the Half-Blood Prince (2009)

Harry Potter and the Deathly Hallows: Part 1 (2010)

Harry Potter and the Deathly Hallows: Part 2 (2011)

The Heartbreak Kid (1972)

Heavenly Creatures (1994)

The Host (2006)

House of Flying Daggers (2004)

How the Grinch Stole Christmas (2000)

Howard the Duck (1986)

Hugo (2011)

Hulk (2003)

The Hunger Games (2012)

The Hunger Games: Catching Fire (2013)

If Beale Street Could Talk (2018)

The Incredible Hulk (2008)

Independence Day (1996)

Indiana Jones and the Last Crusade (1989)

Indiana Jones and the Raiders of the Lost Ark (1981)

Indiana Jones and the Temple of Doom (1984)

Iron Man (2008)

Iron Man 2 (2010)

Iron Man 3 (2013)

Jack the Giant Slayer (2013)

Jaws (1975)

The Jazz Singer (1927)

The Jungle Book (2016)

Jurassic Park (1993)

Jurassic World: Fallen Kingdom (2018)

King Kong (1933)

The King's Speech (2010)

Kong: Skull Island (2017)

Kung Fu Hustle (2004)

The Last Waltz (1978)

Life of Pi (2012)

The Lion King (2019)

The Lobster (2015)

Logan's Run (1976)

Looker (1981)

Lord of the Rings film series (2001–2003):

The Lord of the Rings: The Fellowship of the Ring (2001)

The Lord of the Rings: The Two Towers (2002)

The Lord of the Rings: The Return of the King (2003)

The Lost World (1925)

The Lost World: Jurassic Park (1997)

Love Story (1970)

M*A*S*H (1970)

Mad Max: Fury Road (2015)

Maleficent (2014)

The Mandalorian (2019)

Maniac Mansion (1987) [video game]

The Mask (1994)

The Matrix (1999)

Medium Cool (1969)

The Meg (2018)

Melancholia (2011)

Memoirs of an Invisible Man (1992)

Men in Black (1997)

The Mermaid (2016)

Metropolis (1927)

Midnight Cowboy (1969)

Midsommar (2019)

Misbehaviour (2020)

Mission: Impossible—Fallout (2018)

The Monkey King (2014)

Monsters, Inc. (2001)

Mr. Go (2013)

Mr. Turner (2014)

The Mummy (1999)

Munich (2005)

Murder on the Orient Express (2017)

My Cousin Rachel (2017)

Nashville (1975)

Night at the Museum (2006)

Nosferatu (1922)

Oblivion (2013)

Once Upon a Time. . . In Hollywood
    (2019)

Pacific Rim (2013)

Paddington (2014)

Paddington 2 (2017)

Pan's Labyrinth (2006)

Parasite (2019)

Pearl Harbor (2001)

Pirates of the Caribbean film series
    (2003–2017):
    Pirates of the Caribbean: The Curse of
        the Black Pearl (2003)
    Pirates of the Caribbean: Dead Man's
        Chest (2006)
    Pirates of the Caribbean: At World's
        End (2007)
    Pirates of the Caribbean: On Stranger
        Tides (2011)
    Pirates of the Caribbean: Dead Men
        Tell No Tales (2017)

Poltergeist (1982)

Pride and Prejudice (2005)

The Raid: Redemption (2011)

The Rain People (1969)

Raise the Red Lantern (1991)

Rambo film series (1982–2019)
    First Blood (1982)
    Rambo: First Blood Part II (1985)
    Rambo III (1988)
    Rambo (2008)
    Rambo: Last Blood (2019)

Red Cliff (2008)

The Revenant (2015)

The Rocketeer (1991)

Rocketman (2019)

Rogue One: A Star Wars Story (2016)

Roma (2018)

The Rules of the Game (1939)

The Science of Sleep (2006)

The Second Best Exotic Marigold Hotel
    (2015)

Shampoo (1975)

Shang-Chi and the Legend of the Ten
    Rings (2021)

Shaolin Soccer (2001)

Shrek (2001)

Slumdog Millionaire (2008)

Snow White and the Huntsman (2012)

Solo: A Star Wars Story (2018)

Sorry to Bother You (2018)

Spider-Man (2002)

Spider-Man: Far from Home (2019)

Spider-Man: Homecoming (2017)

Star Trek (2009)

Star Trek Beyond (2016)

Star Trek: Generations (1994)

Star Trek Into Darkness (2013)

Star Trek II: The Wrath of Khan (1982)

Star Trek: The Motion Picture (1979)

Star Wars film series (1977–2019):
    Star Wars: Episode IV—A New Hope
        (1977)
    Star Wars: Episode V—The Empire
        Strikes Back (1980)
    Star Wars: Episode VI—Return of the
        Jedi (1983)
    Star Wars: Episode I—The Phantom
        Menace (1999)
    Star Wars: Episode II—Attack of the
        Clones (2002)
    Star Wars: Episode III—Revenge of
        the Sith (2005)
    Star Wars: Episode VII—The Force
        Awakens (2015)
    Star Wars: Episode VIII—The Last
        Jedi (2017)
    Star Wars: Episode IX—The Rise of
        Skywalker (2019)

Stargate (1994)

Starlog (1976–2009)

Starman (1984)

Starship Troopers (1997)

Stealth (2005)

The Story of Computer Graphics (1999)

The Sugarland Express (1974)

Super 8 (2011)

T2 Trainspotting (2017)

The Taking of Tiger Mountain (2014)

Talk to Her (2002)

Terminator 2: Judgment Day (1991)

Terminator 3: Rise of the Machines (2003)

Terminator Salvation (2009)

The Thing from Another World (1951)

Thor (2011)

Thor: Ragnarok (2017)

Titanic (1997)

Tolkien (2019)

Top Gun (1986)

Toy Story (1995)

Trance (2013)

Transformers film series:

    Transformers (2007)

    Transformers: Revenge of the Fallen (2009)

    Transformers: Dark of the Moon (2011)

    Transformers: The Last Knight (2017)

    Transformers: Age of Extinction (2014)

Tron (1982)

Twister (1996)

Umberto D. (1952)

Valerian and the City of a Thousand Planets (2017)

Van Helsing (2004)

Victoria and Abdul (2017)

War of the Worlds (1953)

War of the Worlds (2005)

Warcraft (2016)

Who Framed Roger Rabbit? (1988)

Willow (1988)

Wolf Warrior (2015)

Wolf Warrior 2 (2015)

X-Men Origins: Wolverine (2009)

X-Men: Apocalypse (2016)

X-Men: Days of Future Past (2014)

Yesterday (2019)

The Young Indiana Jones Chronicles (1992)

Young Sherlock Holmes (1985)

Zack Snyder's Justice League (2021)

Zathura: A Space Adventure (2005)

Notes

Introduction

Epigraphs: *With 450 people* . . . : Martha Groves, "Digital Yoda: George Lucas at Entertainment's High Tech Edge," *Los Angeles Times*, June 4, 1995; *ILM does more business* . . . : Richard Wolkomir, "High-Tech Hokum is Changing the Way Movies Are Made," *Smithsonian*, October 1990; Favreau quote: Foreword to Pamela Glintenkamp, *Industrial Light & Magic: The Art of Innovation* (New York: Abrams, 2011); Spielberg quote: Groves, "Digital Yoda"; *Can anybody catch ILM?* . . . : Carl DiOrio, "Tech Talk," *Hollywood Reporter*, June 4, 1998.

1. Disney on its own accounted for 33 percent of the American box office in 2019, and its acquisition of Fox brings Disney's market share up to nearly 40 percent. Adam B. Vary, "Disney Explodes Box Office Records With $11.1 Billion Worldwide for 2019," Variety.com, January 2, 2020, https://variety.com/2020/film/box-office/disney-global-box-office-2019-1203453364.

2. According to the Academy's rules, the burden of proof is on the side of the animated feature. To qualify in the category of Animated Feature:

> In an animated film, animation must figure in no less than 75 percent of the picture's running time. In addition, a narrative animated film must have a significant number of the major characters animated. If the picture is created in a cinematic style that could be mistaken for live action, the filmmaker(s) must also submit information supporting how and why the picture is substantially a work of animation rather than live action.

Oscars.org, "Animated Feature Film Award—Additional Resources," Rules & Eligibility, Oscars, www.oscars.org/oscars/rules-eligibility.

3. Josh Rottenberg, "'The Lion King': Is It Animated or Live-action? It's Complicated," *Los Angeles Times*, July 19, 2019. Misha Mihailova presented the paper "Virtually Unchanged: The Lion King (2019), Quantified Nostalgia, and Disney's Animated Denials" at the Society of Cinema and Media Studies 2021 online conference that more thoroughly deals with these issues concerning *The Lion King*.

4. According to Favreau, he "slipped in one single shot that we actually photographed in Africa to see if anyone would notice"—the film's very first shot. Ryan Lattanzio, "Here Is the One Real Shot in 'The Lion King' Remake," Indiewire.com, July 28, 2019, www.indiewire.com/2019/07/the-lion-king-live-action-shot-1202161574.

5. David S. Cohen, "'War of the Worlds': Blockbusters Take Toll on F/x Shops," *Variety*, May 25, 2007.

6. Reportedly, Disney does not list ILM's revenue (or lack of) or market share in their annual report. See, for example, https://thewaltdisneycompany.com/app/uploads/2020/01/2019-Annual-Report.pdf. Around the year 2000 it was estimated that ILM accounted for over 50 percent of the market share in the effects business, but again, it is difficult to verify. www.strategy-business.com/article/15151?gko=98b82.

7. David Bordwell, Janet Staiger, and Kristin Thompson, *The Classical Hollywood Cinema: Film Style & Mode of Production to 1960* (New York: Columbia University Press, 1985); Tino Bailo, *Grand Design: Hollywood as a Modern Business Enterprise, 1930–1939*, vol. 5 (Berkeley: University of California Press, 1995); John Thornton Caldwell, *Production Culture: Industrial Reflexivity and Critical Practice in Film and Television* (Durham: Duke University Press, 2008); Jennifer Holt and Alisa Perren, eds., *Media Industries: History, Theory, and Method* (Hoboken: John Wiley & Sons, 2011); Toby Miller et al., *Global Hollywood 2* (London: Bloomsbury Publishing, 2019).

8. I am using the formulation "special/visual effects" following the example of Kristen Whissel, who provides a lengthy justification based on the historical instability of the terms in Charles Keil and Kristen Whissel, eds., *Editing and Special/Visual Effects: Behind the Silver Screen* (New Brunswick: Rutgers University Press/Academy of Motion Picture Arts and Sciences, 2016), 12–15.

9. Stanley Cavell, *The World Viewed: Reflections on the Ontology of Film* (Cambridge: Harvard University Press, 1979); Laura Mulvey, *Death 24x a Second: Stillness and the Moving Image* (London: Reaktion Books, 2006); D. N. Rodowick, *The Virtual Life of Film* (Cambridge: Harvard University Press, 2009).

10. Or even "cosmopolitan artlessness," as Charles Acland puts it. Charles R. Acland, *American Blockbuster: Movies, Technology, and Wonder* (Durham: Duke University Press, 2020), 191. Richard Maltby, *Hollywood Cinema* (Hoboken: Blackwell Publishing, 2003); David A Cook, *Lost Illusions: American Cinema in the Shadow of Watergate and Vietnam, 1970–1979*, vol. 9 (Berkeley: University of California Press, 2002); Justin Wyatt, *High Concept: Movies and Marketing in Hollywood* (Austin: University of Texas Press, 1994).

11. Stephen Prince, *Digital Visual Effects in Cinema: The Seduction of Reality* (New Brunswick: Rutgers University Press, 2011); Lev Manovich, Roger F. Malina, and Sean Cubitt, *The Language of New Media* (Cambridge: MIT Press, 2001).

12. For examples, see the "bullet time" deployed in *The Matrix*, morphing in *Terminator 2*, and impossible virtual camera moves frequently used in David Fincher movies such as *The Game* (1997), *Fight Club* (1999), and *Panic Room* (2002).

13. Warren Buckland, "Between Science Fact and Science Fiction: Spielberg's Digital Dinosaurs, Possible Worlds, and the New Aesthetic Realism," *Screen* 40, no. 2 (1999): 177–192; Geoff King, *Spectacular Narratives: Hollywood in the Age of the Blockbuster* (London: I. B. Tauris, 2000); Michele Pierson, *Special Effects: Still in Search of Wonder* (New York: Columbia University Press, 2002).

14. Kristen Whissel, *Spectacular Digital Effects: CGI and Contemporary Cinema*

(Durham: Duke University Press, 2014); Dan R. North, *Performing Illusions: Cinema, Special Effects and the Virtual Actor* (New York: Wallflower Press, 2008); Lisa Bode, *Making Believe: Screen Performance and Special Effects in Popular Cinema* (New Brunswick: Rutgers University Press, 2017); Lisa Purse, *Digital Imaging in Popular Cinema* (Edinburgh: Edinburgh University Press, 2013); Aylish Wood, *Digital Encounters* (London: Routledge, 2007).

15. Bordwell, Staiger, and Thompson, *The Classical Hollywood Cinema*; J. D. Connor, *The Studios After the Studios: Neoclassical Hollywood (1970–2010)* (Stanford: Stanford University Press, 2015); Maltby, *Hollywood Cinema*; Wyatt, *High Concept*.

16. Acland, *American Blockbuster*, 12; Kristin Thompson, in *The Frodo Franchise: The Lord of the Rings and Modern Hollywood* (Berkeley: University of California Press, 2007), mentions the role of Weta Digital in the *Lord of the Rings* films, but the company is not the focus of her study.

17. J. P. Tolette, *The Mouse Machine: Disney and Technology* (Champaign: University of Illinois Press, 2010).

18. LeiLani Nishime, *Undercover Asian: Multiracial Asian Americans in Visual Culture* (Champaign: University of Illinois Press, 2014); Adilifu Nama, *Black Space: Imagining Race in Science Fiction Film* (Austin: University of Texas Press, 2010); Tanine Allison, "Blackface, *Happy Feet*: The Politics of Race in Motion Capture and Animation," in *Special Effects: New Histories/Theories/Contexts*, edited by Dan North, Bob Rehak, and Michael S. Duffy (London: Bloomsbury Publishing, 2015), 114–126; Kara Keeling, *Queer Times, Black Futures* (New York: New York University Press, 2019); Eliza Steinbock, *Shimmering Images: Trans Cinema, Embodiment, and the Aesthetics of Change* (Durham: Duke University Press, 2019); Cáel M. Keegan, *Lana and Lilly Wachowski* (Champaign: University of Illinois Press, 2018).

19. Manovich, Malina, and Cubitt, *The Language of New Media*; Sean Cubitt, *Digital Aesthetics* (London: Sage, 1998); Steven Shaviro, *Post Cinematic Affect* (Winchester: John Hunt Publishing, 2010); Judith Halberstam and Ira Livingston, eds., *Posthuman Bodies* (Bloomington: Indiana University Press, 1995); and Shane Denson, *Discorrelated Images* (Durham: Duke University Press, 2020).

20. Ariel Rogers, *Cinematic Appeals: The Experience of New Movie Technologies* (New York: Columbia University Press, 2013), and Matt Rothman, *On the Screen: Displaying the Moving Image, 1926* (New York: Columbia University Press, 2019); Hye Jean Chung, *Media Heterotopias: Digital Effects and Material Labor in Global Film Production* (Durham: Duke University Press, 2018); Bob Rehak, *More Than Meets the Eye: Special Effects and the Fantastic Transmedia Franchise* (New York: New York University Press, 2018); Michael Curtin and John Vanderhoef, "A Vanishing Piece of the Pi: The Globalization of Visual Effects Labor," *Television & New Media* 16, no. 3 (2015): 219–239; Leon Gurevitch, "The Straw That Broke the Tiger's Back?,"in *The Routledge Companion to Labor and Media*, edited by Richard Maxwell (New York: Routledge, 2015), 190–201, 190. Aylish Wood, *Software, Animation and the Moving Image: What's in the Box?* (New York: Springer, 2014).

21. Prince, *Digital Visual Effects in Cinema*.

22. Manovich, Malina, and Cubitt, *The Language of New Media*.

23. I'm following the term coined by art historian Alois Riegl, frequently trans-

lated as "will to art," expressing a consistent style of expression within the spirit of an age.

24. Claire Clouzot, "The Morning of the Magician: George Lucas and *Star Wars* (1977)," in *George Lucas: Interviews*, ed. Sally Kline (Jackson: University Press of Mississippi, 1999), 58.

25. This is likewise what Phil Rosen calls "digital mimicry" or "the capacity of the digital to imitate such pre-existing compositional forms of imagery." In Philp Rosen, "From Change Mummified," in *Film Theory and Criticism: Introductory Readings*, 8th ed., edited by Leo Braudy and Marshall Cohen (Oxford: Oxford University Press, 2016), 814.

26. Lev Manovich, "Digital Cinema and the History of the Moving Image," in *Film Theory and Criticism: Introductory Readings*, 8th ed., edited by Braudy and Cohen, 725.

27. Although much more digital manipulation was used in the film than its promotion suggested. Carolyn Giardina, "How 'The Revenant's' VFX Team Brought That Bear to Life," *Hollywood Reporter*, February 3, 2016, www.hollywoodreporter .com/behind-screen/how-revenants-vfx-team-brought-861157.

28. One might compare it with the bear Baloo in 2016's *Jungle Book*, voiced by Bill Murray. While adhering to photoreal aesthetics generally speaking, the fact that the bear anthropomorphically talks and sings takes him out of the expectations of strict realism and puts him into the realm of the "cute," closely associated with animation.

29. A. A. Dowd, "There's Nothing Immersive (or Fun) About This World of *Warcraft*," AVClub.com, June 8, 2016, https://film.avclub.com/there-s-nothing -immersive-or-fun-about-this-world-of-1798188048; Chris Nashawaty, "'Warcraft': EW Review," *Entertainment Weekly*, June 8, 2016, www.ew.com/article/2016/06/08 /warcraft-ew-review.

30. Sianne Ngai, *Our Aesthetic Categories: Zany, Cute, Interesting* (Cambridge: Harvard University Press, 2012), 91.

31. ILM historically has had a fractious relationship with cuteness. In the self-serious *Star Wars* universe, cuteness is constantly evoked for merchandising purposes but apparently is only tolerated by fans in droids. Teddy bear–like Ewoks have long been the focus of fan ire, as was the child actor Jake Lloyd as young Anakin Skywalker. Even more strongly, see, for example, the meticulously animated but much derided Jar Jar Binks in *The Phantom Menace*, among the first all-acting CGI characters. In that film, Jar Jar's bouncy elasticity read as too cute and therefore trivial in the context of the *Star Wars* universe (not to mention the troublingly stereotypical racialization evoked by Jar Jar's characterization and stereotypically Caribbean accent.)

32. Mainland Chinese audiences were also more familiar with the video game than North American audiences. Patrick Frater, "10 Reasons Why 'Warcraft' Opened Six Times Bigger in China Than in the U.S.," *Variety*, June 13, 2016, https://variety .com/2016/film/asia/ten-reasons-why-warcraft-opened-six-times-bigger-in-china -than-in-the-u-s-1201794300.

33. Apart from my own work on ILM, I was only able to find one other academic article directly about ILM: Miguel Angel Fuertes, "Industrial Light & Magic:

La Informática Al Servicio Del Cine," *Cuadernos Hispanoamericanos* 596 (February 2000): 37–39. The only existing book-length treatments of ILM are coffee-table books written or cowritten at the behest of Lucasfilm by former or current employees: Rob Bredow and Ron Howard, *Industrial Light & Magic Presents: Making* Solo: A Star Wars Story (New York: Abrams, 2019); Glintenkamp, *Industrial Light & Magic: The Art of Innovation*; Thomas G. Smith, *Industrial Light & Magic: The Art of Special Effects*, 1st ed. (New York: Ballantine Books, 1986); Thomas G. Smith, *Flashback: From Notes and Memory*, limited ed. (n.p.: Graham and Malone Press, 2018); Mark Cotta Vaz and Patricia Rose Duignan, *Industrial Light & Magic: Into the Digital Realm*, 1st ed. (New York: Ballantine Books, 1996).

As to Lucasfilm, most academic articles are not about Lucasfilm in any detail but about legal or other issues: Kristen Elisabeth Bollinger, "A New Hope for Copyright: The U.K. Supreme Court Ruling in *Lucasfilm Ltd. v. Ainsworth* and Why Congress Should Follow Suit," *Journal of Intellectual Property Law* 20, no. 1 (Fall 2012): 87–119; Patrick Brodie, "*Star Wars* and the Production and Circulation of Culture Along Ireland's Wild Atlantic Way," *Journal of Popular Culture* 53, no. 3 (June 2020): 667–695; Charlotte Courtois, "Jouer Dans L'Espace Urbain Capitaliste De Disneyland Avec the Secret of Monkey Island: Monkey Island 1 & 2," *Géographie & Cultures*, no. 109 (March 2019): 99–118; Henry Lydiate, "What Is Art? A Brief Review of International Judicial Interpretations of Art in the Light of the UK Supreme Court's 2011 Judgment in the *Star Wars* Case: Lucasfilm Limited v. Ainsworth," *Journal of International Entertainment & Media Law* 4, no. 2 (January 2012): 111–147; Richard Ravalli, "George Lucas Out of Love: Divorce, Darkness, and Reception in the Origin of PG-13," *Historian* 78, no. 4 (Winter 2016): 690–709; Pippa Rogerson, "Conflict of Laws—Foreign Copyright Jurisdiction," *Cambridge Law Journal* 69, no. 2 (July 2010): 245–247; Tim Vollans, "The Empire Strikes Back? Lessons from the Supreme Court's Judgment in *Lucasfilm Limited and Others (Appellants) v. Ainsworth and Another (Respondents)* [2011] UKSC 39, July 2011," *Journal of International Commercial Law & Technology* 7, no. 3 (July 2012): 276–81.

Similar to the case with ILM, publications about Lucasfilm tend to either be memoirs, profiles primarily of Lucas himself, and/or promotional material authorized by the company: Charles Champlin, *George Lucas: The Creative Impulse: Lucasfilm's First Twenty-five Years* (New York: Harry N. Abrams, 1997); Bill Kimberlin, *Inside the Star Wars Empire: A Memoir* (Guilford: Rowman & Littlefield, 2018); J. W. Rinzler, Charles Lippincott, and Peter Jackson, *The Making of Star Wars: The Definitive Story Behind the Original Film: Based on the Lost Interviews from the Official Lucasfilm Archives*, 1st trade paperback ed. (New York: Ballantine Books, 2007); Phil Szostak and Rick Carter, *The Art of* Star Wars: The Force Awakens (New York: Abrams, 2015); Mark Cotta Vaz and Shinji Hata, *From Star Wars to Indiana Jones: The Best of the Lucasfilm Archives* (San Francisco: Chronicle Books, 1994).

I have omitted reference to the scores of popular press books profiling George Lucas, such as those by Dale Pollock, Karina Longworth, and many others unless cited elsewhere.

34. Will Brooker, *Using the Force: Creativity, Community and Star Wars Fans* (Bloomsbury Publishing, 2002); Tara Lomax, "'Thank the Maker!': George Lucas,

Lucasfilm, and the Legends of Transtextual Authorship across the Star Wars Franchise," in Sean Guynes and Dan Hassler-Forest, *Star Wars and the History of Transmedia Storytelling* (Amsterdam: Amsterdam University Press, 2017), 35–48. Rebecca Harrison, *The Empire Strikes Back* (London: British Film Institute, 2020).

35. Okun about *Cinefex*:

I love [the writers at *Cinefex*] dearly and they are good friends, but none of their stories talk about reality. All their stories talk about "we met with the director, we presented our idea, he loved it, we shot it, presented it, and we are the best buddies we go out drinking now." . . . I said "well, we are gonna tell the truth, right?" Tell the truth of how I presented 35 versions to Roland [Emmerich] of what the stargate was and he ended up firing me . . . and then he hired me again. . . . And [*Cinefex*] said "we are not interested in that story." . . . As a result of all this PR that it's all just fun and games, there is no hard work involved, it's really cool stuff, you get to hang out with really cool people, there is no trial and error, there are no failures, we bred a group of people that are like "hey, this will be fun . . ." [and not work]. Jeff Okun, personal interview with the author, Encino, CA, August 8, 2015.

36. In order of the number of articles, with a representative proportion:

Selected ILM press: Richard Zoglin, "Lights! Camera! Special Effects," *Time*, June 16, 1986; Thomas G. Smith, "Reel Illusion," *OMNI*, June 1987; David Kaplan, "Secret Lair of the Jedi, Grain, and Green Slimers," *New York Times*, July 2, 1989; Wolkomir, "High-tech Hokum"; Julie Lew, "FILM; Invisibility Is More Than Meets the Eye," *New York Times*, February 23, 1992; "Believe in Magic," *Newsweek*, June 14, 1993; "How to Make a Ghost," *Newsweek*, February 27, 1995; Ian Austen, "A Galaxy Far, Far Away Is Becoming Fully Digital," *New York Times*, May 25, 2000; Rick Lyman, "Down to the Sea in Chips; Computers Open a Virtual World of Effects to Filmmakers," *New York Times*, June 20, 2000; Marco R. della Cava, "Lucas: The Titan of Tech," *USA Today*, February 23, 2001; "Do You Believe in Magic? For 'Eragon,' Creating a Realistic Dragon Was a Tricky Task," *Washington Post*, December 13, 2006; David Elliott, "Digitalize Me Hearties, Digitalize! It Took More Than 250 Wizards to Create the Effects for 'Pirates of the Caribbean: At World's End,'" *San Diego Union-Tribune*, May 27, 2007; Dave Itzkoff, "Jar Jar Binks, Coming at You in 3-D," *New York Times*, September 30, 2010; Melena Ryzik, "Drawing Board For a Digital Age," *New York Times*, February 16, 2012; Kahn Howie and Dan Winters, "Inside the Magic Factory," *Wired*, June 2015; Dave Itzkoff, "How 'Rogue One' Brought Back Familiar Faces," *New York Times*, December 27, 2016; Nathalia Holt, "The Women Behind the Force," *New York Times*, February 12, 2017; Gina McIntyre, "Hyperspace in Your Face; The 'Solo' Visual Effects Team Puts the Millennium Falcon through Its Paces. It Proves To Be a Wild Ride," *Philadelphia Inquirer*, February 22, 2019; Josh Rottenberg, "The New Way to Turn Back the Clock; De-aging Methods Used in 'The Irishman' Could Change the Face of Acting," *Toronto Star*, January 11, 2020.

Selected Digital Domain Press: Sharon Waxman, "Wizards of Ah! More Than Ever, Hollywood's Special-Effects Experts Are Calling the Shots," *Washington Post*, July 05, 1996; Michel Marriott, "Project Virtual Funk: The Digitizing of James Brown," *New York Times*, April 13, 2000; Michael McCarthy, "Animated Cyber-Performers Take the Center Stage in Ads Special Effects Create Walking, Talking 'People,'" *USA Today*, June 2, 2000; Dave Itzkoff, "A Method Performance, All Right," *New York Times*, January 4, 2009; Ethan Smith, "Rapper's De-Light:

Tupac 'Hologram' May Go on Tour," *Wall Street Journal*, April 17, 2012; Ben Fritz, "Hollywood Visual-Effects Firms Fade to Black," *Wall Street Journal*, February 23, 2013; Mekado Murphy, "Fighting in Zero Gravity Just for Practice," *New York Times*, October 20, 2013.

   Selected Weta Digital Press: Mike Snider, "'Rings' Takes Special Effects to Another Level," *USA Today*, February 11, 2004; Patricia Cohen, "Perfecting Animation, Via Science," *New York Times*, December 30, 2010; Michael Cieply and Brooks Barnes, "New Zealand Wants a Hollywood Put on Its Map," *New York Times*, November 24, 2012; Chris Suellentrop, "Tantalizing Potential Outpaces Reality," *New York Times*, March 9, 2015; Roslyn Sulcas, "Andy Serkis, Caesar the Ape, Has a Message for the Academy," *New York Times*, July 6, 2017; Mekado Murphy, "'Mortal Engines': How the Filmmakers Created a Roaming London," *New York Times*, December 14, 2018; Mekado Murphy, "Questions About 'Gemini Man?' We Have Answers," *New York Times*, October 11, 2019; Julia Jacobs, "'Call of the Wild' Casts a Digital Star. Is He a Good Dog?" *New York Times*, February 23, 2020.

   Selected Rhythm and Hues Press: Stuart Elliott, "The Media Business: Advertising; Coke Takes a Bearish Approach to Its New Winter Campaign," *New York Times*, July 7, 1993; Kris Goodfellow, "Mayday! Mayday! We're Leaking Visuals! A Shakeout of the Special Effects Houses," *New York Times*, September 29, 1997; Joel Kotkin, "Grass-Roots Business; Norma Desmond Had It Wrong: The Picture Makers Got Small," *New York Times*, May 23, 1999; Mekado Murphy, "A First Mate Bares His Fangs," *New York Times*, November 18, 2012; Mallory Pickett, "Why Hollywood's Most Thrilling Scenes Are Now Orchestrated Thousands of Miles Away; The Money Issue," *New York Times*, May 4, 2017.

   Selected Sony Pictures Imageworks Press: Neil Strauss, "50's Sci-Fi Camp Goes High-Tech; Icky Giants That Hop, Fight and Think," *New York Times*, November 10, 1997; Sharon Waxman, "Cyberface," *New York Times*, October 15, 2006; David M. Halbfinger and Andrew Ross Sorkin, "Sony Said to Be Pondering Partial Sale of Movie Units," *New York Times*, October 31, 2007; Charles Solomon, "How the 'Spider-Verse' Animators Created That Trippy Look," *New York Times*, December 25, 2018.

37. Interviews with Academy members conducted by the Academy museum constitutes another important source, but the museum's delayed opening and recent COVID-19 research travel restrictions have meant I have not yet been able to gain access to them.

38. Lucasfilm yearbooks are found in the Thomas Smith Papers, Container 20, folders 1–10, at the Ransom Center at the University of Texas, Austin.

39. Tom Smith, personal correspondence via email with the author, January 2018.

40. Smith, personal correspondence.

41. For examples of less strictly authorized discourse, see Michael Rubin, *Droidmaker: George Lucas and the Digital Revolution* (Gainesville, FL: Triad, 2005); Richard Edlund in Richard Natale, "Richard Edlund: Magician of the Silver Screen," *Los Angeles Herald-Examiner*, December 7, 1984; Smith interview with the author, 2018; Larry Cuba interview with Andrew Johnston, Iota Center, July 23, 2010; Peter Kuran interview with the author, August 5, 2011; Chris Casady interview with the author, June 21 and 24, 2010.

Chapter 1: ILM Versus Everybody Else

Epigraphs: Lucas quote: Paula Parisi, "George Lucas' 'THR salutes ILM: George Lucas' Magic Lamp: Why the Famed Producer Director Pulled Together the Enormous Talent and Resources of ILM," *Hollywood Reporter*, April 9, 1991; Ross quote: Jack Egan, "How Ross Came to Rule the Roost," *Variety*, July 28, 2003.

1. Similar to accounts of the videogame industry described by Ergin Bulut, *A Precarious Game: The Illusion of Dream Jobs in the Video Game Industry* (Ithaca: Cornell University Press, 2020).

2. Thomas Schatz, "New Hollywood, New Millennium," in *Film Theory and Contemporary Hollywood Movies*, ed. Warren Buckland (New York: Routledge, 2009), 19–46.

3. Miller et al., *Global Hollywood 2*.

4. Jeff Menne, *Post-Fordist Cinema: Hollywood Auteurs and the Corporate Counterculture* (New York: Columbia University Press, 2019).

5. Menne, 111.

6. As I have argued elsewhere, the 1970s and 1980s effects business likewise followed the pattern of other "below-the-line auteurs" (in cinematography, sound design, editing, etc.), attempting to establish a similar kind of "economy of genius" for the growing effects work sector around figures such as Douglas Trumbull and John Dykstra, whose status as creative genius innovators served as inspiration. Julie Turnock, "Special Effects: Auteur Renaissance, 1968–1980," in *Editing and Special Visual Effects: Behind the Silver Screen*, volume edited by Charles Keil and Kristen Whissel, series ed. Jon Lewis (New Brunswick: Rutgers University Press/Academy of Motion Picture Arts and Sciences, 2016), 116–128.

7. Nancy Rivera Brooks, "Mouse of Babes," *Los Angeles Times*, July 10, 1996.

8. See blogs created by industry professionals such as Effects Corner and Scott Ross's VFX Soldier.

9. Bill Gilman, interview with author, Los Angeles, CA, July 12, 2007; Jean Pierre Flayeux, interview with author, February 28, 2018, via Skype; Simon Marinof, interview with author, June 26, 2018, via Skype.

10. "PDV" means "Post, Digital, and Visual" effects sector, an Australian term. Amy Ratelle, "Chris Carter—Digital Beings: An Opportunity for Australian Visual Effects," *Animation Studies*, February 6, 2014, http://journal.animationstudies.org /chris-carter-digital-beings-an-opportunity-for-australian-visual-effects.

11. For discussions of labor under media convergence, see Henry Jenkins, *Convergence Culture: Where Old and New Media Collide* (New York: New York University Press, 2006); Chuck Tryon, *Reinventing Cinema: Movies in the Age of Media Convergence* (New Brunswick: Rutgers University Press, 2009); Bulut, *A Precarious Game*; Catherine McKercher and Vincent Mosco, eds., *Knowledge Workers in the Information Society* (Lanham, MD: Lexington Books, 2007); James Bennett and Niki Strange, eds., *Media Independence: Working with Freedom Or Working for Free?* (New York: Routledge, 2015); Miranda J. Banks, "The Picket Line Online: Creative Labor, Digital Activism, and the 2007–2008 Writers Guild of America Strike," *Popular Communication* 8 no. 1 (2010): 20–33; Chase Bowen Martin and Mark Deuze, "The Independent Production of Culture: A Digital Games Case Study," *Games and Culture* 4,

no. 3 (2009): 276–295. Greig De Peuter, "Creative Economy and Labor Precarity: A Contested Convergence," *Journal of Communication Inquiry* 35, no. 4 (2011): 417–425; Steven Jay Tepper, "Creative Assets and the Changing Economy," *Journal of Arts Management, Law, and Society* 32, no. 2 (2002): 159–168.

12. Even in the high studio era when the major studios had in-house effects departments, a majority of effects workers were employed on contingent contracts, and the studios frequently contracted with outside independent optical, title, and effects houses (many of them run by former studio employees) to do effects work. See Julie Turnock, "Before Industrial Light and Magic: The Independent Hollywood Special Effects Business, 1968–1975," *New Review of Film and Television Studies* 7, no. 2 (2009): 133–156. Julie Turnock, "'Uninhibited, Thorough, and Wild Thinking': Reconsidering the Studio Era through Special Effects," Society for Cinema and Media Studies, International Conference, Seattle, March 2014.

13. Scott Squires, "Effects Corner" blog, posted April 18, 2013, http://effectscorner.blogspot.com/2013/04/visual-effects-guilds.html#.VO89X2ZyeOU.

14. From the VES website: www.visualeffectssociety.com/about.

15. Julie Turnock, "Patient Research on the Slapstick Lots: From Trick Men to Special Effects Artists in Silent Hollywood," *Early Popular Visual Culture* 13, no. 2 (2015): 152–173.

16. Turnock, "Patient Research."

17. Turnock, "Before Industrial Light and Magic."

18. While ILM's official history (www.ilm.com/about-us) puts their founding in 1975, the actual company under that name was not incorporated until 1978. See Turnock, *Plastic Reality*, 131.

19. Weta Workshop preexisted Weta Digital by more than ten years. A note about nomenclature: the origins of the name "Weta" vary in its corporate press releases. Most often, the company traces the name to a particularly fearsome insect found only in New Zealand, which appears as "Weta." At a certain point, there was an attempt to turn the name into an acronym, presented as "WETA" for "Wingnut Effects and Technical Allusions." This appears to be an attempt to join the preexisting Weta name with Jackson's Wingnut production company. The all-caps acronym did not appear to have caught on. Alex Ben Block, "WETA Physics," *Hollywood Reporter*, November 9, 2009.

20. Cook, *Lost Illusions*; Prince, *Digital Visual Effects in Cinema*; Maltby, *Hollywood Cinema*; Thomas Elsaesser, "The Blockbuster: Everything Connects, but Not Anything Goes," in *The End of Cinema as We Know It: American Film in the Nineties*, edited by J. Lewis (New York: New York University Press, 2002) 11–22; David Bordwell, *The Way Hollywood Tells It: Story and Style in Modern Movies* (Berkeley: University of California Press, 2006); Acland, *American Blockbuster*.

21. See Julie Turnock, *Plastic Reality: Special Effects, Technology, and the Emergence of 1970s Blockbuster Aesthetics* (New York: Columbia University Press, 2015), and Turnock, "Before Industrial Light and Magic."

22. Wolkomir, "High-tech Hokum"; see also Donald Chase, "War of the Wizards," *American Film* 7, no. 8 (1982): 52–59; Susan Witty, "The Masters of Special Effects," *Geo* (June 1983): 42-; Thomas G. Smith, "Reel Illusions."

23. See Turnock, *Plastic Reality*.

24. For example, see the authorized ILM histories: Vaz and Duignan, *Industrial Light & Magic: Into the Digital Realm*; Glintenkamp, *Industrial Light & Magic: The Art of Innovation*; and Thomas G. Smith, *Industrial Light & Magic: The Art of Special Effects*.

25. Dream Quest sometimes also appears as DreamQuest, Dreamquest, and later DQI. See Turnock, *Plastic Reality* for a more thorough discussion of these companies.

26. John Swallow, interview with the author, July 21, 2006. While ILM was working on the *Indiana Jones* movies, the *Star Wars* sequels, etc., Apogee was making *Lifeforce* and *Zapped!*.

27. Trumbull sold Future General to Richard Edlund in 1982, which was then renamed Boss Films.

28. Twenty for *The Abyss*. Don Shay, "Dancing on the Edge of the Abyss," *Cinefex* 39 (August 1989): 46; Ian Failes, "The Tech of 'Terminator 2'—An Oral History" vfxblog.com, August 23, 2017, https://vfxblog.com/2017/08/23/the-tech-of-terminator-2-an-oral-history.

29. Matt Rothman, "H'wood Enters Digital Domain," *Variety*, February 26, 1993; Carl DiOrio, "Sony Fx Gets Its Own Place," *Hollywood Reporter*, August 31, 1996.

30. Rothman, "H'wood enters Digital Domain;" "Exec Shuffle," *Variety*, September 29, 1994; Variety Staff, "Ken Ralston Tops Fx Unit at Sony Pix," *Variety*, September 6, 1995.

31. Carl DiOrio, "THR E-mail," *Hollywood Reporter*, June 8, 1998.

32. DiOrio, "THR E-mail."

33. "In 1996 Disney purchased DreamQuest Images, which later became Secret Lab, but it closed 5 years later." Richard Verrier and Ben Fritz, "Visualizing Disney's Deal," *Los Angeles Times*, November 1, 2012.

34. DiOrio "THR E-mail."

35. See Turnock "Before Industrial Light and Magic."

36. Ad, "ILM," *Hollywood Reporter*, March 8, 1985.

37. Rothman, "H'wood enters Digital Domain."

38. Weta Workshop, "Weta Workshop," press kit 2004, in the Herrick Library Clipping Files.

39. Rhythm & Hues, "Rhythm and Hues," "Babe" press releases 1995 and "Babe II" press release 1998, in the Herrick Library Clipping Files.

40. SPI, "Anaconda" press release 1997 and "Stuart Little" press release 2002, in the Herrick Library Clipping Files "Sony Pictures Imageworks."

41. Rothman, "H'wood enters Digital Domain."

42. "The start-up cost could be as high as $20 million, reportedly the budget for IBM's own digital studio." Rothman, "H'wood enters Digital Domain."

43. Rothman.

44. Rothman.

45. King, "The Hottest Movies Have the Coolest Effects," *Wall Street Journal*, November 14, 1994.

46. Paula Parisi, "Monster Job for Digital Domain," *Hollywood Reporter*, October 7, 1994.

47. Rothman, "H'wood enters Digital Domain."

48. Ron Magid, "Cause and FX," *Hollywood Reporter*, December 3–9, 2002.

49. See Turnock, "Before ILM" and *Plastic Reality* for more on Abel and Associates.

50. Rhythm & Hues, "Rhythm and Hues" and "Babe" press releases.

51. "Payroll is now slightly less than 200 at the company." Carl DiOrio, "Rhythm & Hues Effect Layoffs," *Hollywood Reporter*, April 12, 1996.

52. Vaz and Duignan, *Industrial Light & Magic: Into the Digital Realm*, 283.

53. Jonathan Weber, "The Force Is Still with Him: Lucas Showcases Gadgets to Show He Remains King of Special Effects Hill," *Los Angeles Times*, April 8, 1993.

54. Groves, "Digital Yoda." These numbers (and the NASA comment, which appears in other ILM PR materials) were almost certainly supplied by ILM and should be understood as PR.

55. Parisi, "THR salutes ILM."

56. Parisi, "THR salutes ILM."

57. Parisi, "THR salutes ILM."

58. See various lists of "worst CGI of all time" as examples, including Joel Golby, "Worse Than Cats? The Biggest CGI Disasters in Cinema," *Guardian*, July 19, 2019, www.theguardian.com/film/2019/jul/19/worse-than-cats-the-biggest-cgi-disasters-in-cinema; Ann Casano, "Really Bad CGI That You Have to See to Believe," Ranker, September 3, 2020, www.ranker.com/list/bad-cgi/anncasano; and Joshua Rothkopf and David Ehrlich, "The 10 Worst CGI Special Effects in Movie History," Timeout, June 9, 2015, www.timeout.com/newyork/movies/the-10-worst-cgi-special-effects-in-movie-history.

59. The article reported that the unit's profit is "much below" [Sony Pictures Entertainment's] target of 10 percent. Claudia Eller, "Sony Pictures Seeks Buyer for Half of Digital Unit," *Los Angeles Times*, November 1, 2007.

60. Carl DiOrio, "WB's Sarnoff Morphs to Sony," *Hollywood Reporter*, March 5, 1997.

61. Paul Karon, "Sony Digital f/x Shop Gets a 'Hollow' Deal," *Variety*, July 20, 1998.

62. Carl DiOrio, "Ralston Re-ups, Claims 'Island,'" *Hollywood Reporter*, December 18, 1998; Marc Graser, "Sony Imageworks Taps F/xers Legato, Thomas," *Variety*, June 21, 1999; Carl DiOrio, "Sony Fx Gets Its Own Place," *Hollywood Reporter*, August 31, 1996.

63. Rex Weiner, "Exec Sees No Windfall on 'Titanic,'" *Variety*, May 23, 1997.

64. Carl DiOrio, "Titanic a Wash for DD Fxers," *Hollywood Reporter*, May 23, 1997; DiOrio, "THR E-Mail;" Paul Karon, "Domain Shrinking: F/X House Makes 54 Staffers Disappear," *Variety*, October 9, 1997.

65. Rex Weiner, "Exec Sees No Windfall on 'Titanic,'" *Variety*, May 23, 1997.

66. Karon, "Domain Shrinking."

67. Rex Weiner, "Cox, IBM Ready to Connect with Digital Domain," *Variety*,

February 26, 1996; "DD Inks Link with CSI Digital," *Variety*, October 21, 1996; Carl DiOrio, "DD, K-L get German Effects House," *Hollywood Reporter*, December 18, 1998. It is unclear if DD bought Chennai-based PentaMedia outright, but it called it in press releases a "collaboration." Nyay Bhushan, "DD, PentaMedia of India in Pic Pact," *Hollywood Reporter*, March 15, 2000; Eric Olson, "Digital Domain Enters Germany," *Variety*, December 21, 1998.

68. Carl DiOrio and Josh Chetwynd, "Cameron Sinks Board Role at DD," *Hollywood Reporter*, August 20, 1998.

69. DiOrio, "Tech Talk."

70. At this time John Hughes was touting a return to profits after a red ink crisis in the year after *Babe*. DiOrio, "Tech Talk."

71. Marc Graser, "Fox to Sell Visual f/x Division to R&H," *Variety*, March 4, 1999.

72. Marc Graser, "Rhythm & Hues Drums Up Own Slate," *Variety*, December 15, 1999.

73. Graser, "Rhythm & Hues Drums Up Own Slate."

74. Graser, "Rhythm & Hues Drums Up Own Slate."

75. THR staff, "Rushes," *Hollywood Reporter*, October 23, 1997.

76. "Correction: ILM has around 1000 staffers working on fx for its pics. Information was incorrect in Tues' paper;" "Corrections," *Variety*, June 16, 2000.

77. Marc Graser, "ILM Will Make Magic for Hulk, Next Potter," *Variety*, October 10, 2001.

78. DiOrio, "Tech Talk"; Benedict Carver, "Ralston to Helm Jumanji 2," *Variety*, June 3, 1999.

79. Susan Faludi, *The Terror Dream: Fear and Fantasy in Post-9/11 America* (New York: Macmillan, 2007); Tom Pollard, *Hollywood 9/11: Superheroes, Supervillains, and Super Disasters* (New York: Routledge, 2015).

80. Marc Graser, "F/x Heavy Tentpoles are Coming to Light," *Variety*, August 16, 2002.

81. Caroline Chapain and Tadeusz Stachowiak, "Innovation Dynamic in the Film Industry: The Example of the Soho Cluster in London," in *Creative Industries in Europe: Drivers of New Sectoral and Spatial Dynamics*, edited by Caroline Chapain and Tadeusz Stryjakiewicz (New York: Springer, 2017), 65–94, 90.

82. Nick Lacey, *Introduction to Film* (London: Macmillan International Higher Education, 2016), 137.

83. Chapain and Stachowiak, "Innovation Dynamic in the Film Industry."

84. Filmworks Staff, "Rhythm & Hues: Special Effects Powerhouse Offers Insight into VFX Industry," August 15, 2012, http://filmworks.filmla.com/2012/08/15/rhythm-hues-special-effects-powerhouse-offers-insight-into-vfx-industry.

85. Chapain and Stachowiak, "Innovation Dynamic in the Film Industry."

86. From government websites: "The Advantages of Montréal," VFX Montréal, http://vfx-montreal.com/why-montreal-2; "Film Tax Relief," British Film Commission, http://britishfilmcommission.org.uk/plan-your-production/tax-reliefs/; and "Ministry of Finance," British Columbia, www.sbr.gov.bc.ca/documents_library/bulletins/cit_011.pdf.

87. Adam Dawtrey, "Soho Vfx Biz Arises from Potter's Spell," *Variety*, February 28, 2011.

88. Dawtrey, "Soho Vfx Biz Arises from Potter's Spell."

89. Michael Cieply and Brooks Barnes, "New Zealand Wants a Hollywood Put on Its Map"; Leon Gurevitch, "The Straw that Broke the Tiger's Back?"

90. Graser, "F/x Heavy Tentpoles are Coming to Light."

91. David Cohen, "Building a Legacy," *Variety*, February 14, 2005.

92. A 2017 Reddit debate does a good job of exemplifying the fan dislike of the CGI in the prequels and even demonstrates an emerging reappraisal: "Bad CGI in the Prequels," Reddit, www.reddit.com/r/StarWars/comments/66ywlp/bad_cgi_in _the_prequels.

93. David Cohen, "Is the Force Still with Him?" *Variety*, February 13, 2005.

94. Cohen, "Is the Force Still with Him?"

95. Cohen, "Building a Legacy."

96. Cohen, "Building a Legacy."

97. Magid, "Cause and FX."

98. While Jar Jar Binks in *The Phantom Menace* predates Gollum and is roughly concurrent with the digitized Yoda in *Attack of the Clones*, neither character was created with motion capture, a technique that for various reasons ILM was slow to embrace. Yoda in *the Phantom Menace* was operated in the theatrical release version as a puppet by Frank Oz, but later, in home video releases, he was replaced by a digital version.

99. Magid, "Cause and FX."

100. Magid, "Cause and FX."

101. Jerry Beck, "Weta Evolves into Global Giant," *Variety*, November 13, 2006.

102. Peter Calder, "Workshop Taps Local Talents," *Variety*, December 16, 2002; Cieply and Barnes, "New Zealand Wants a Hollywood Put on Its Map."

103. Matt Nippert, "Inside Wellywood: How NZ Taxpayers Forked Out $575 Million for Hollywood to Film Here," *New Zealand Herald*, June 30, 2018, www.nzherald .co.nz/business/news/article.cfm?c_id=3&objectid=12072876; Ben Heather, "A Heavenly Trajectory: 20 Years of Weta," Stuff.co.nz, October 4, 2014, www.stuff.co .nz/entertainment/film/10579617/A-heavenly-trajectory-20-years-of-Weta.

104. Ann Donahue, "Digital Piracy: With 'Caribbean' and 4 Other Effects Noms, Could This Be ILM's year?" *Variety*, January 8, 2004.

105. Carolyn Giardina, "Rhythm & Hues Sets Up Malaysian Shop," *Hollywood Reporter*, May 22, 2008.

106. Marc Graser, "Meeper Intros Sony CG Toon Unit," *Variety*, February 28, 2002.

107. Marc Graser, "CG Shops Set to Tackle Toon Territory," *Variety*, February 28, 2002.

108. In fact, the only feature animation project produced by an effects company was ILM's *Rango* (2011), still ILM's only feature animation release.

109. Sheigh Crabtree, "DD Lays Off 17, Adds Motion Graphics Dept," *Hollywood Reporter*, April 3, 2001; Marc Graser, "Title Graphics Enter Digital's Domain," *Variety*,

August 12, 2002; Sheigh Crabtree, "DD Nukes Market," *Hollywood Reporter*, July 12, 2002.

110. As well as former Microsoft exec Carl Stork, former Sims Snowboards chair John C. Textor, and Jonathan Teaford, formerly of GE Capital Services, as part of "Wyndcrest Holdings." David S. Cohen and Ben Fritz, "Digital Domain Docks with Bay," *Variety*, May 16, 2006.

111. Which turned out not to be true.

112. Sheigh Crabtree, "Bay Master of Domain in VFX Stunner," *Hollywood Reporter*, May 16, 2006.

113. "VFX Business," Scott A. Ross, http://scottaross.com. Ross stopped updating his blog about fx issues in 2012. He is still active on fx issues on Twitter, as @DrScottRoss. For more intraindustry effects debates, see also VFX Soldier, vfxsoldier.wordpress.com, and @VFXSoldier.

114. Cohen, "War of the Worlds."

115. Tom Schatz, "Seismic Shifts in the American Film Industry," in *American Film History: Selected Readings, 1960 to the Present*, edited by Cynthia Lucia, Roy Grundmann, and Art Simon (Hoboken, NJ: Wiley, 2015), 187; for a more journalistic take, see Mark Harris, "The Day the Movies Died," *GQ*, February 10, 2011.

116. Cohen, "War of the Worlds."

117. Cohen, "War of the Worlds."

118. David S. Cohen, "'War' Is Hell for F/x Shops," *Variety*, May 22, 2006.

119. Cohen, "'War' Is Hell for F/x Shops," *Variety* 22 May 2006

120. Cohen, "War of the Worlds."

121. Cohen, "War of the Worlds."

122. Piecemealing did not originate in this era, but has long been associated with lower budget productions (*Honey, I Shrunk the Kids* (1989), for example).

123. Cohen, "War of the Worlds."

124. Cohen, "War of the Worlds."

125. Cohen, "'War' Is Hell for F/x Shops."

126. For more on the peripatetic nature of effects work, see Gurevitch, "The Straw that Broke the Tiger's Back?," 190.

127. Neonmarg, "Killer Schedules: Behind that Variety Story," posted on Jun 26, 2007, www.fxguide.com/modules.php?name=News&file=article&sid=439.

128. Nyay Bhushan, "Frameflow in Sony's Imageworks Fold," *Hollywood Reporter*, February 22, 2007.

129. David Cohen, "Imageworks Looks to Rule F/x Field," *Variety*, June 17, 2009.

130. Cohen, "Imageworks Looks to Rule F/x Field."

131. Carolyn Giardina, "California VFX Houses Fight to Stay Alive," *Hollywood Reporter*, February 4, 2011; David Cohen, "'Spirit of Openness' ILM, Imageworks Tout Toon Software," *Variety*, August 10, 2011; Dave McNary, "Animators Mull Union Offer," *Variety*, April 23, 2012.

132. Though they retain some presence in Culver City, California, ". . .housing more than 700 artists." Francois Marchand, "Sony Pictures Imageworks Unveils New Vancouver Headquarters," *Vancouver Sun*, July 10, 2015.

133. Michael Bay, "Digital Domain," Michael Bay website, www.michaelbay.com /2012/09/08/digital-domain.

134. Karen Idelson, "DD Pacts with Reliance: Post Partners Clock in with Global Plan," July 12, 2011; David Cohen, "DD Expands to Vancouver," *Variety*, October 6, 2009; David S. Cohen, "Domain Expands to China," *Variety*, December 15, 2011.

135. David S. Cohen, "Can Ailing Fx House Fix Woes in Post?" *Variety*, September 12, 2012.

136. Cohen, "Can Ailing Fx House . . . ?"

137. The full name of the Chinese company is Beijing Galloping Horse. David S. Cohen, "It's Time to Fight the Fangs of Finance," *Variety*, October 11, 2012.

138. This *Variety* article gives a minutely detailed account of the deal: David S. Cohen, "VFX Firm is Now 'Well-Funded,' but Its Future in L.A. Is Clouded," *Variety*, July 29, 2013.

139. Patrick Frater, "Digital Domain Remains on the Sick List," *Variety*, September 1, 2014.

140. Though this is very tentative: Patrick Frater, "Digital Domain Holdings Reports $64 Million in Losses," *Variety*, March 30, 2017.

141. Giardina, "Rhythm & Hues Sets up Malaysian Shop;" David S. Cohen, "Hues Hops to Canuck Shop," *Variety*, May 27, 2011;" David S. Cohen, "F/X House in Taiwan Deals," *Variety*, January 2, 2012 [possibly 2010, smudged stamp].

142. David S. Cohen, "Offshore Vfx: a Matter of Perspective," *Variety*, August 30, 2012.

143. See Curtin and Vanderhoef, "A Vanishing Piece of the Pi," for more detail.

144. David S. Cohen, "El Segundo-Based Company Sold as Layoffs Loom Around Vfx Biz," *Variety*, March 29, 2013.

145. David S. Cohen, "Rhythm & Hues Bankruptcy Reveals Vfx Biz Crisis," *Variety*, February 12, 2013.

146. David S. Cohen, "R&H Hoping for Fast Exit from Bankruptcy," *Variety*, February 10, 2013.

147. David S. Cohen, "Prana Wins Auction for Rhythm & Hues," *Variety*, March 28, 2013.

148. According to *Variety*: "[R&H] had about 1,400 employees before layoffs and bankruptcy began this past weekend. The layoffs are estimated at around 200." David S. Cohen, "Rhythm & Hues Bankruptcy Reveals Vfx Biz Crisis."

149. Cohen, "Prana Wins Auction for Rhythm & Hues."

150. Although its IMDB page suggests there is an entity named "Rhythm and Hues" doing work for mostly television, including *Game of Thrones*, it is unclear what that company's relationship is to the prior company. Gabey Goh, "Rhythm & Hues Malaysia to Fly Solo Under New Identity," Digital News Asia, May 23, 2013, www.digitalnewsasia.com/digital-economy/rhythm-and-hues-malaysia-to-fly-solo -under-new-identity.

151. David S. Cohen, "ILM at Center of Vfx Storm," *Variety*, May 28, 2007.

152. David S. Cohen, "ILM Finds Beijing Base," *Variety*, May 24, 2012; Carolyn Giardina, "California VFX Houses Fight to Stay Alive;" Alex Rittman, "Lucasfilm's ILM Opens London Studio," *Hollywood Reporter*, October 17, 2014; Leo Barraclough,

"Industrial Light and Magic Opens R&D Division in London," *Variety*, October 15, 2014. Creating 200 jobs: Robert Mitchell, "'Star Wars' Films 'A Gift for a VFX Company' as Industrial Light & Magic Opens London Studio," *Variety*, October 16, 2014.

153. Verrier and Fritz, "Visualizing Disney's Deal."

154. Verrier and Fritz, "Visualizing Disney's Deal"; *Variety* Staff, "Disney Likely to Treat Lucasfilm Like Pixar," *Variety*, November 8, 2012.

155. Curtin and Vanderhoef, "A Vanishing Piece of the Pi."

156. Film Works Staff, "Rhythm & Hues: Special Effects Powerhouse Offers Insight into VFX Industry."

Chapter 2: Perfect Imperfection

This chapter expands on Julie Turnock, "The ILM Version: Recent Digital Effects and the Aesthetics of 1970s Cinematography," *Film History: An International Journal* 24, no. 2 (2012): 158–168.

Epigraph: Muren is discussing the 1995 film *Casper*. "Movie Magic: When It Comes to Special Effects, Dennis Muren Has Done It All," *Wall Street Journal*, September 15, 1995.

1. "Lucasfilm, and more specifically the *Star Wars* franchise, fits perfectly within the Disney portfolio of intellectual properties," Disney press release, "Disney to Acquire Lucasfilm Ltd.," October 12, 2012, www.thewaltdisneycompany.com /disney-to-acquire-lucasfilm-ltd. Industry analysis has deemed this financial move a huge success on the part of the Disney conglomerate: Sarah Whitten, "Disney Bought Lucasfilm Six Years Ago Today and Has Already Recouped Its $4 Billion Investment," CNBC, October 30, 2018, www.cnbc.com/2018/10/30/six-years-after -buying-lucasfilm-disney-has-recouped-its-investment.html.

2. For examples of this kind of evaluative rhetoric, such as *Star Trek* director J. J. Abrams on emulating *Star Wars*, see Joe Fordham, "A New Enterprise," *Cinefex* 118 (July 2009): 42; also see *District 9* director Neil Blomkamp as quoted in the *District 9* DVD extras. For negative judgment of *Clash of the Titans*, see Gillian Flynn, "Men and Myth," *Entertainment Weekly*, May 14, 2004, 28; and Owen Gleiberman, "'Clash of the Titans': Are Special Effects Less Special in the CGI Era?" *Entertainment Weekly*, April 1, 2010; and on *Dune*, which they call "a bad acid trip that refuses to end," see *Entertainment Weekly*, March 16. 2012, 9.

3. Prince, *Digital Visual Effects in the Cinema*.

4. For a nuanced discussion of the visual illusion of motion, see Scott Richmond, *Cinema's Bodily Illusions: Flying, Floating, and Hallucinating* (Minneapolis: University of Minnesota Press, 2016).

5. Harrison Ellenshaw, "Creating Matte Paintings for EMPIRE," *American Cinematographer* (June 1980): 608.

6. For more effects artists rhetoric along this line, see Jody Duncan, "The Unusual Birth of Benjamin Button," *Cinefex* 116 (January 2009). For discussion of water simulation tools, see Jordan Gowanlock's "A History of Simulation 'FX': How Dynamic Simulation Tools See and Manage the World" (PhD diss., Concordia University, 2017).

7. There were 600 visual effects shots in *Hulk*, 440 with character animation, lasting approximately 37 minutes of screen time. Joe Fordham, "*The Hulk*: Green Destiny," *Cinefex* 94 (July 2003): 126.

8. Fordham, "A New Enterprise," 83.

9. See more statements by Krasser and others supporting this approach: Fordham, "A New Enterprise," 94–99.

10. Fordham, "A New Enterprise," 85; Muren's full quote: "As soon as you put [Hulk] in a shot, you're no longer looking at the whole frame—you're looking at the effect. It was like a neon sign."

11. Muren's work for *Close Encounters* was under Douglas Trumbull, not ILM, but Muren was also working for ILM on *Star Wars* at roughly the same time. See Turnock, *Plastic Reality*, for more detail on these 1970s ILM obscuring strategies.

12. The article mentions several other strategies to "de-green" the Hulk. Fordham, "A New Enterprise," 85–86.

13. Fordham, "A New Enterprise," 84.

14. For accounts of negative fan reaction to Lee's *Hulk*, see Keith Phipps, "The Successful Failure of Ang Lee's *Hulk*," thedissolve.com, April 28, 2015, https://thedissolve.com/features/movie-of-the-week/1006-the-successful-failure-of-ang-lees-hulk; and "Why Did the First Two *Hulk* Movies Fail?," Reddit, January 8, 2015, www.reddit.com/r/movies/comments/2rr7sp/why_did_the_first_two_hulk_movies_fail.

15. Fordham, "A New Enterprise," 80.

16. As articles report about ILM's work on later Marvel films in which the Hulk appears, most notably in *The Avengers*, ILM seems to have been haunted by what it considered the failure of the Ang Lee Hulk character and worked up more strategies to make him fit the mise-en-scène better. Jody Duncan Jesser, "The Avengers Initiative," *Cinefex* 130 (July 2012): 83–88.

17. For an account of unspoken practitioner assumptions of an earlier historical era, see James Lastra, *Sound Technology and the American Cinema: Perception, Representation, Modernity* (New York: Columbia University Press, 2000).

18. This composite comes primarily from discourse in special-interest publications *American Cinematographer*, *Cinefex*, and *Cinéfantastique* and a few assorted popular press publications including *Time*, *Newsweek*, *Omni*, and *Entertainment Weekly*, among others.

19. Turnock, *Plastic Reality*.

20. Turnock, *Plastic Reality*.

21. Although typical of the digital era, of course neither *Jurassic Park* nor ILM is the originator of the "wondering at an effects object" sequence, as *King Kong*, *The Ten Commandments*, *Close Encounters of the Third Kind*, and many others prove.

22. For representative fan discourse, see Jordan Maison, "Why People Can't Enjoy the VFX in the Star Wars Prequels," cinelinx.com, July 14, 2014, www.cinelinx.com/movie-news/movie-stuff/why-people-can-t-enjoy-the-vfx-in-the-star-wars-prequels, and Reddit threads such as: www.reddit.com/r/StarWars/comments/66ywlp/bad_cgi_in_the_prequels.

23. Jody Duncan, "The Man in the Iron Mask," *Cinefex* 114 (July 2008): 59–60.

24. This also made the motion a detachable effects element in of itself. For more, see Turnock, *Plastic Reality*.

25. Don Shay, "Of Ice Planets, Bog Planets, and Cities in the Sky: Interview with Richard Edlund," *Cinefex* 2 (August 1980): 4–23, 12.

26. "Effects Photography for Empire: Interview with Dennis Muren," *American Cinematographer* (June 1980): 588.

27. For further articulation of Edlund's and Muren's photoreal aesthetic, as deployed on *Star Wars* and *The Empire Strikes Back*, see Ricard Edlund, "Special Visual Effects for *Empire*," *American Cinematographer* (June 1980): 552; Paul Mandell, "Tauntauns, Walkers, and Probots," *Cinefex* 3 (December 1980): 4–41; Don Shay, "Of Ice Planets, Bog Planets, and Cities in the Sky," 4. See also Paul Mandell, "Richard Edlund: 2nd Effects Cameraman," *Cinéfantastique* 7, no. 1 (1978): 17–18; and Paul Mandell, "Dennis Muren: First Effects Cameraman," *Cinéfantastique* 7, no. 1 (1978): 21–24.

28. Muren is discussing the 1995 film *Casper*. "Movie Magic: When It Comes To Special Effects, Dennis Muren Has Done It All," *Wall Street Journal*, September 15, 1995.

29. For more on the role of the director vs. the effects artist, see Julie Turnock, "'The True Stars of *Star Wars*?': Experimental Filmmakers in the 1970s and 1980s Special Effects Industry," *Film History* 26, no. 4 (2014): 120–145.

30. One might differentiate between the business-oriented New Hollywood Tom Schatz delineates in a longer time period from the 1960s through the 1990s, versus the more critical aesthetic New Hollywood also referred to as the "Hollywood Renaissance," "American New Wave," and "the Film School Generation," among others, confined largely to 1967–1980. All of these terms have their own problematic associations. Because determining what is or is not comprised by these terms is not my argument, for the sake of simplicity I will refer here primarily to the critical aesthetic dimensions of New Hollywood. For discussions on the term "New Hollywood," see Steve Neale, "The last good time we ever had?': Revising the Hollywood Renaissance," *Contemporary American Cinema* (2005): 90–108; Thomas Schatz, "The New Hollywood," *Movie Blockbusters* (2003): 15–44; Thomas Elsaesser, Noel King, and Alexander Horwath, *The Last Great American Picture Show: New Hollywood Cinema in the 1970s* (Amsterdam: Amsterdam University Press, 2004); Peter Krämer, *The New Hollywood: From Bonnie and Clyde to Star Wars* (New York: Columbia University Press, 2006).

31. Bradley Schauer, "The Auteur Renaissance 1968–1980," in *Cinematography*, edited by Patrick Keating (New Brunswick: Rutgers University Press, 2014), 85.

32. Cited in Bradley Schauer, "The Auteur Renaissance 1968–1980," in *Cinematography*, edited by Patrick Keating (New Brunswick: Rutgers University Press, 2014), 86.

33. See Turnock, *Plastic Reality*.

34. Although the more stabilized rig on the Steadicam later made a version of this style more accessible to more camera operators, Gareth Brown's technology was not introduced until 1975 and was not used in a feature film until *Paths of Glory* in 1976.

35. To use the influential Owen Roizman cinematography from *The French Connection* (1971) as an example, the ILM style makes use of the handheld and unstabilized moving camera shots in many of the chase sequences but does not frequently imitate that film's frequent use of zooms, a more difficult effect to replicate in motion control or miniature work. For more on *The French Connection* and its aesthetic "environment of uncertainty," see Nathan Holmes, *Welcome to Fear City: Crime Film, Crisis, and the Urban Imagination* (Albany: SUNY Press, 2019), 99–102.

36. Even the Universal and Sony logos of 2018–2019 that play before films feature the ILM look: backlighting, lens flares, atmospherics.

37. These historical and contemporary uses of lens flares are discussed by Vilmos Zsigmond, ASC, and Charles Clark, ASC, in an interview in *American Cinematographer* in 1974, "The Moving Camera," *American Cinematographer* (June 1974): 688–689. Also, before the 1960s, *American Cinematographer* has many ads and articles for professionals and amateurs on how to avoid lens flares. *American Cinematographer* (April 1948): 136, for the Kodak Ektar lens promised to reduce lens flare; William Stull, "Non-Glare Coating Makes Lens One Stop Faster" *American Cinematographer* (March 1940): 108; Clifford Harrington, "Filming with Filmorama," *American Cinematographer* (December 1955): 718.

38. Specific lens flares go by many different names. For the sake of simplicity, I will mostly be discussing flares generally as a category unless it is useful to specify them.

39. Interestingly, a quick instance of lens flaring happens in Tarkovsky's *Solaris* (1971), when the virtual camera is imitating the landing onto the orbiting Solaris space station. As the camera tracks in, a brief series of flares sparkles around the landing pad.

40. Turnock, "The Auteurist Special Effects Film: Kubrick's *2001: A Space Odyssey* and the 'Single Generation Look,'" in *The Hollywood Renaissance: Revisiting American Cinema's Most Celebrated Era*, edited by Peter Krämer and Yannis Tzioumakis (New York: Bloomsbury Academic Press, 2018), 71–90. Kubrick, however, was less concerned with suggesting the presence of a verité-style live camera operator.

41. For more on *2001's* specific influence on the *Star Wars* effects production, see Turnock, *Plastic Reality*.

42. While effects in *Close Encounters* were produced by Douglas Trumbull's Future General (ILM did not yet officially exist at the time of CE3K's production), several key ILM personnel, especially Dennis Muren and Bruce Nicholson, were instrumental to that film's effects. Also, Zsigmond recounts that the producers of *The Sugarland Express* wanted to cut or reshoot the lens flare behind Goldie Hawn's head in the famous traveling pullback shot, but Spielberg "was very strong and said, 'I love it.' From that point on everybody loved it." "The Moving Camera," *American Cinematographer* (June 1974): 698.

43. Shane Denson discusses digital lens flares as marks of the posthuman in digital imagery. Shane Denson, "Crazy Cameras, Discorrelated Images, and the Post-Perceptual Mediation of Post-Cinematic Affect," in *Perspectives on Post-Cinema: An Introduction*, edited by Shane Denson and Julia Leyda (Sussex, UK: Reframe

Books, 2016), 193. See also Nick Jones on art historical precedent against "transparent" reality. Nick Jones, *Spaces Mapped and Monstrous: Digital 3D Cinema and Visual Culture* (New York: Columbia University Press, 2020), 45.

44. Dan North, "Super 8: Victory Through Lens Flare, Spectacular Attractions," September 3, 2011, https://drnorth.wordpress.com/2011/09/03/super-8-victory -through-lens-flare; Katie Bird, "Updated! Lens Flare, Indexicality, and J. J. Abrams, Special Affects," last modified May 20, 2013, www.fsgso.pitt.edu/2012/01/lens-flare -indexicality-and-j-j-abrams.

45. As this 2016 video essay by Phil Edwards suggests: "We've Reached Peak Lens Flare," www.youtube.com/watch?v=_IesAvesFUo.

46. I do not have any information to suggest that it is not happening "for real" (though I suspect at much slower speeds than it seems in the film), know if the flares are profilmic or added digitally.

47. See, for example, popular press discourse about how much of Tom Cruise's stunts were done "for real," a claim I find extremely dubious. Ben Kenigsberg, "Tom Cruise's Most Dangerous Stunts in 'Mission: Impossible,'" *New York Times*, July 30, 2018, www.nytimes.com/2018/07/30/movies/mission-impossible-fallout-stunts-tom -cruise.html; Trey Williams, "Did Tom Cruise Really Do All the Stunts in 'Mission: Impossible—Fallout'?" *Wrap*, July 28, 2018, www.thewrap.com/tom-cruise-stunts -mission-impossible-fallout.

48. Wexler details how he in fact did light this shot artificially to create the naturalistic aesthetic (as well as other technical details of the shoot) in Herb Lightman, "The Filming of Medium Cool," *American Cinematographer* (January 1970): 25.

49. Edlund, "Special Visual Effects for *Empire*," 565.

50. Edlund.

51. It is worth noting that an emphasis on an image's photographic aesthetic is not a mark of the optical/digital divide, since the practice at ILM long predates the 1990s. See Turnock, *Plastic Reality*.

52. Effects in *The Empire Strikes Back* are the most frequently cited as influential in the year 2000 roundup of effects artists in *Cinefex*. Don Shay and Jody Duncan, eds., "Twenty Questions," *Cinefex* 80 (January 2000): 25.

53. Also Arthur Hiller's *The Crazy World of Julius Vrooder* (1974).

54. Also, the stop motion animation technique called "Go-Motion" (which Phil Tippett and others at ILM developed for *Empire*) enhanced the naturalistic irregularity of the motion. Shay, "Of Ice Planets, Bog Planets, and Cities in the Sky." For more on the history of Go-Motion, see Turnock, *Plastic Reality*.

55. Vaz and Duignan, *Industrial Light & Magic: Into the Digital Realm*, 227–229.

56. Glintenkamp, *Industrial Light & Magic: The Art of Innovation*, 80.

57. See also Victor Kemper's (credited) cinematography in Elaine May, dir., *Mikey and Nicky* (Hollywood, CA: Paramount Pictures, 1976).

58. Bokeh effect is defined by Wikipedia and Merriam-Webster as "the aesthetic quality of the blur produced in the out-of-focus parts of an image produced by a lens," and as "the way the lens renders out-of-focus points of light."

59. The storybook look may have been purposeful and was in line with other literary adaptations of the era, such as the *Lord of the Rings* films.

60. Benjamin Wright, "The Auteur Renaissance, 1968–1980: Editing," in *Editing and Special Visual Effects: Behind the Silver Screen*, volume eds. Charles Keil and Kristen Whissel, series ed. Jon Lewis (New Brunswick: Rutgers University Press/ Academy of Motion Picture Arts and Sciences, 2016): 103–115.

61. Meredith Geagan-Breiner and Kyle Desiderio, "How Marvel Movies Are Actually Created Years Before Production Begins," Insider.com, January 29, 2021, www.insider.com/marvel-plans-movies-action-scenes-years-before-filming-previs -visualization-2021-1.

62. See Benjamin Wright, "The Auteur Renaissance, 1968–1980: Editing," 103–115.

63. Or, if one prefers a more international heuristic, the *Nosferatu* (1922) and *Golem* (1920) pattern, which breaks down similarly. For more elaborated discussion on the aesthetics of Dracula versus Frankenstein, see also Robert Spadoni, *Uncanny Bodies: The Coming of Sound Film and the Origins of the Horror Genre* (Berkeley: University of California Press, ca. 2007), 73 and 109. See also Bode, *Making Believe*.

64. Effects-heavy silent Weimar cinema, by contrast, tended toward the Frankenstein/Golem reveal, as with robot-Maria in *Metropolis* (1927) or the dragon in *The Nibelungen* (1924). The original *Godzilla* follows the Dracula reveal, appearing for the first time abruptly over a rise.

65. Chewbacca, by contrast, is introduced in *Star Wars* casually, as just another character. However, in *Solo: A Star Wars Story* (2018), Chewbacca is initially introduced as "the beast," and his reveal is treated as that of a dangerous monster, gradually in parts emerging out of the darkness, along with dramatic backlighting.

66. In the 1997 special edition version of the film as well as the one available on Disney+, several full-figure Wampa scenes have been added to the sequence.

67. For example, Muren on how matte line position is determined by where the attention is going to be: "The [matte] is usually repositioned so that it *does* fit in the area where your *eye* looks. That's consciously done by the printer operators for each shot" [emphasis original]. Mandell, "Tauntauns, Walkers, and Probots," 13.

68. Discussed more thoroughly in Turnock, *Plastic Reality*.

69. See Buckland, "Between Science Fact and Science Fiction"; Dan North, "The Spielberg Effects," *A Companion to Steven Spielberg* 16 (2017): 389.

70. Although the anxieties it is addressing are different, the Frankenstein approach in the CGI reveal could be seen as a strategy similar to Mulvey's description of the aesthetics of Oedipal scopophilia, where the female body is introduced in parts in order to manage anxieties around gazing at the desirable female image. See, for example, the introduction of Marlene Dietrich in *Blonde Venus* (1932), Rita Hayworth in *Gilda* (1946), and Uma Thurman in *Pulp Fiction* (1994).

71. See, in the discussion of *Transformers: Revenge of the Fallen* (2009), the emphasis on matching the cinematography to the needs of the effects crew in Jay Holben, "Robots Run Rampant," *American Cinematographer* (August 2009): 54–57; for an extreme case, see the discussion of *Avatar*'s (2009) problems matching effects with cinematography in Jay Holben, "Conquering New Worlds," *American Cinematographer* (January 2010): 35–47.

72. Turnock, "The ILM Version" (2012).

73. Despite the director's lifelong acquaintanceship and accounts of long talks with the woman Cleo is based on, Liboria Rodríguez, a director of a different age, gender, social class, and language can only imagine her experience. Marcela Valdes, "After 'Gravity,' Alfonso Cuarón Had His Pick of Directing Blockbusters. Instead, He Went Home to Make 'Roma,'" *New York Times*, December 12, 2018.

74. Accounts of precisely what effects were used in these scenes are scarce, although, according to *The Hollywood Reporter*, "in fact, the majority of the $15 million film, . . . involves some degree of visual effects work, according to VFX supervisor Dave Griffiths." Carolyn Giardina, "How 'Roma's' Visual Effects Team Created That Intense Ocean Sequence," *Hollywood Reporter*, December 18, 2018.

75. "Ghostly Past: *Roma*," *British Cinematographer* 91, January 2019, https://british cinematographer.co.uk/alfonso-cuaron-roma.

76. Bill Desowitz, "Alfonso Cuarón's Black-and-White 'Roma' Was a Cinematic Master Stroke," Indiewire, November 16, 2018, www.indiewire.com/2018/11/alfonso -cuarons-black-and-white-roma-was-a-cinematic-master-stroke-1202021233.

77. Ariel Rogers, *Cinematic Appeals: The Experience of New Movie Technologies* (New York: Columbia University Press, 2013), 92–96.

78. For contrast, when Lady Gaga's Ally appears onstage with Maine for the first time to sing "Shallow," we also see a profusion of lens flares, most notably the large ring flare at the end of the song, but they are less erratic and more subtle. The aesthetic effect relies more on the concentrated intensity of the colored lighting effects to create an emotional "falling in love" effect through the lighting.

79. Similarly, we see flared lighting effects, especially extravagant backlighting, at other (briefly) hopeful moments in the film, when Regina King's character arrives in Puerto Rico to find Fonny's accuser, and the moment when Fonny and Tish's baby is born.

80. Disney also opened *Star Wars* theme park attractions in Disneyland and Disneyworld, which both opened in summer 2019.

Chapter 3: Retconning CGI Innovation

Epigraphs: "Raiders, Raptors and Rebels: Behind the Magic of ILM," ABC.com, 2015. www.youtube.com/watch?v=fmFSbWL_4d0&t=904s; *We also talked about the possibility . . .* : Don Shay, "30 Minutes with the Godfather of Digital Cinema," *Cinefex* 65 (March 1996): 62; *I don't like technology very much . . .* : Vaz and Duignan, *Industrial Light & Magic: Into the Digital Realm*, 238.

1. In addition to the coffee table books by Smith, Vaz and Duignan, and Glintenkamp, see the feature-length television specials produced since 1999: John Kroll, dir., "From *Star Wars* to *Star Wars*–The Story of Industrial Light & Magic" (Fox, June 15, 1999); Leslie Iwerks, dir., "Industrial Light & Magic: Creating the Impossible" (Starz Encore, 2010); "Raiders, Raptors and Rebels: Behind the Magic of ILM," ABC.com, 2015. See also bonus feature discs for the *Star Wars* special editions (1997).

2. Another significant example of Lucas/Lucasfilm historical retconning is the erasure of Lucas's first wife, Marcia Griffin Lucas, in her role as editor for the original trilogy and as his creative partner up to 1983. Griffin Lucas won an Academy Award for editing on *Star Wars*. Before their divorce, Lucas gave his wife a great deal of credit as creative collaborator, and she appeared prominently in the Lucasfilm yearbooks in various roles. After their divorce in 1983, virtually no reference to Griffin Lucas was made in any official Lucasfilm publication.

3. Cuba generated the simulation using the GRASS system at the University of Illinois Chicago campus, a system developed by Tom DeFanti at Ohio State, according to http://design.osu.edu/carlson/history/timeline.html. See also Larry Cuba, Alternative Projections Oral Histories, interview by Andrew Johnston, July 23, 2010.

4. Andrew Johnston provides the most academic cinema-focused account, emphasizing the artistic, cinematic, and entertainment industry applications of the technologies described in the SIGGRAPH documentary. Andrew Johnston, "The Rise of Computer-Generated Imagery, 1965–1989," in *Animation*, edited by Scott Curtis (New Brunswick: Rutgers University Press, 2019), 209–243. Wayne Carlson's and Tom Sito's books are very detailed histories of computer graphics, but as to Lucasfilm and ILM activities, they both unfortunately fall into a similar trap as other sources, using Lucasfilm-generated "facts" for their accounts. Wayne Carlson, *History of Computer Graphics and Animation* (Columbus: Ohio State University Pressbooks, ca. 2013); Tom Sito, *Moving Innovation: A History of Computer Animation* (Cambridge: MIT Press, 2013).

5. Special Interest Group on Computer Graphics and Interactive Techniques, an industry group.

6. Frank Foster, *The Story of Computer Graphics*, Frank Foster Films, 1999, video, 1:32:17, www.frankfosterfilms.com/portfolio/the-story-of-computer-graphics -full-feature-film-documentary.

7. Foster, *The Story of Computer Graphics*, at :45. Carlson recounts this episode as Lucas having commissioned the tests. Carlson, *History of Computer Graphics and Animation*, 329.

Lucas assembled his own Computer Graphics group shortly thereafter, but as we shall see, its purpose was to build equipment, not to make X-wing Starfighter graphics.

8. The film was funded by SIGGRAPH, the Association for Computer Machinery, Intel, *Computer Graphics World* magazine, and Sony Pictures Entertainment, among others. Richard Winn Taylor, for example, grumbled in an interview with me how the documentary "leaves out so much." Richard Taylor, interview by author, Marina del Rey, CA, July 18, 2007.

9. One sees these books cited frequently by many academics and scholars, and books used in educational contexts, including Sito, *Moving Innovation*; Pierson, *Special Effects*; Prince, *Digital Visual Effects in Cinema*; as well as Norman Klein, *The Vatican to Vegas: A History of Special Effects* (New York: The New Press, 2004); and Rama Venkatasawmy, *The Digitization of Cinematic Visual Effects: Hollywood's Coming of Age* (Lanham, MD: Lexington Books, 2012).

10. Barbara Klinger, *Beyond the Multiplex: Cinema, New Technologies, and the Home* (Berkeley: University of California Press, 2006); Jones, "Seamless Composites? VFX Breakdowns and Digital Labour."

11. For example, in 1999: "As early as the late 70s . . . Lucas developed a small in-house digital department at ILM. . . and encouraged that handful of computer wizards to stretch the envelope of digital effects for feature films, both artistically and technologically." Jody Duncan, Kevin H Martin, and Mark Cotta Vaz, "Heroes Journey," *Cinefex* 78 (July 1999): 74–77.

12. Prince, *Digital Visual Effects in Cinema*; Pierson, *Special Effects*; Phil Rosen, *Change Mummified: Cinema, Historicity, Theory* (Minneapolis: University of Minnesota Press, 2001); John Belton, "Digital Cinema: a False Revolution," *October* (2002): 98–114.

13. Manovich, Malina, and Cubitt, *The Language of New Media*; Buckland, "Between Science Fact and Science Fiction;" Michele Pierson, "No Longer State-of-the-Art: Crafting a Future for CGI," *Wide Angle* 21, no. 1 (1999): 29–47. Stephen Prince, "True Lies: Perceptual Realism, Digital Images, and Film Theory," *Film Quarterly* 49, no. 3 (1996): 27–37; Sean Cubitt, "Le Réel, c'est l'impossible: The Sublime Time of Special Effects," *Screen* 40, no. 2 (Summer 1999): 123–130.

14. Prince, *Digital Visual Effects in the Cinema*.

15. Caldwell, *Production Culture*.

16. Jeff Okun, personal interview with author, August 8, 2105; Jean Pierre Flayeux, personal interview with author, February 28, 2018, via Skype.

17. Bode, *Making Believe*.

18. Chung, *Media Heterotopias*.

19. Smith, *Industrial Light & Magic*; Vaz and Duignan, *Industrial Light & Magic: Into the Digital Realm*; Glintenkamp, *Industrial Light & Magic: The Art of Innovation*. Thomas G. Smith, as stated elsewhere, was general manager of ILM from 1980–1985. Vaz is a freelance effects author, but Duignan worked at ILM for twenty years in executive and marketing positions. Pamela Glintenkamp was employed by Lucasfilm from 2001 to 2003 and was the producer of the Lucasfilm History project.

20. Piers Bizony, *Digital Domain: The Leading Edge of Digital Effects* (New York: Watson-Guptill Publishing, 2001); Weta, *The Art of Film Magic: 20 Years of Weta* (New York: Harper, 2014).

21. The feature-length television specials produced by ILM include, "The Making of Star Wars . . . as told by C-3PO and R2-D2," originally aired on September 16, 1977, on ABC, www.youtube.com/watch?v=FSuDjjlIPak&t=83s; "From Star Wars to Star Wars—The Story of Industrial Light & Magic," Fox, June 15, 1999; "Industrial Light & Magic: Creating the Impossible" (Starz Encore, 2010); "Raiders, Raptors and Rebels: Behind the Magic of ILM," ABC.com, 2015.

22. I am omitting American TV specials primarily about specific movies that include effects information and am instead focusing on specials about ILM.

23. Notably, these specials about the effects in the films produced by ILM are largely trademarked as Lucasfilm productions, not by the releasing studios.

24. Zoglin, "Lights! Camera! Special Effects." In a search of the popular press

articles primarily about specific effects companies since 1992, ILM represents nearly four times (forty) more articles in newspapers and newsmagazines than the next highest number of articles: Digital Domain with fourteen, Weta with eleven. The remainder average about five. No other company appears on its own in either *Time, Newsweek,* or *USA Today,* for example. See endnote 36 in introduction for a thorough list of citations.

25. Most thorough of these Lucasfilm histories is Michael Rubin's *Droidmaker.* Rubin, who worked for Lucasfilm in the Droid Works (editing) division in the 1980s, was given access to a great deal of valuable company memos and other primary resources. However, he is writing from the perspective of Sprockets R&D rather than ILM, so his description tends to favor that side. As a contented former employee, he remembers his time fondly there and frequently interprets motivations in a positive light.

For more on Rhythm and Hues and Digital Domain bankruptcies, see: *Variety* Staff, "Rhythm & Hues Bankruptcy Reveals Vfx Biz Crisis," *Variety,* February 12, 2013, https://variety.com/2013/film/news/rhythm-hues-bankruptcy-reveals-vfx-biz-crisis-1118066108; Carolyn Giardina, "Revealing 'Rhythm & Hues: Life After Pi' Doc Exposes Grief, Anger and Troubled Business," *Hollywood Reporter,* February 26, 2014, www.hollywoodreporter.com/behind-screen/revealing-rhythm-hues-life-pi-682526; George Szalai, "Digital Domain Files for Chapter 11 Bankruptcy," *Hollywood Reporter,* September 11, 2012, www.hollywoodreporter.com/news/digital-domain-chapter-11-bankruptcy-383839. See also *Time* magazine's reporting on the effects houses' bad times: Rebecca Keegan, "Hollywood's VFX Shops: Trouble in Boom Times," *Time,* May 21, 2010, http://content.time.com/time/magazine/article/0,9171,1990803,00.html.

26. Discourse that includes accounts of ILM activity that abounds in the many *Star Wars*–specific film coffee-table books and popular publications, as well as in biographies of George Lucas, will be referred to only when they depart from the company line in the ILM-specific material listed above. Rinzler, Lippincott, and Jackson, *The Making of Star Wars: The Definitive Story Behind the Original Film;* Dale Pollock, *Skywalking: The Life and Films of George Lucas* (New York: Da Capo Press, 1999); Michael Pye and Lynda Myles, *The Movie Brats* (New York: Holt, Rinehart & Winston, 1979).

27. As a particularly strong example, in the yearbooks we can see evidence of strife and conflict within ILM—for example, about the crunch time to finish *Howard the Duck.* Lucasfilm Ltd. Yearbook 1986, Thomas G. Smith Papers, 20.5, Ransom Center, University of Texas, Austin; Lucasfilm Ltd. Yearbook 1987, Thomas G. Smith Papers, 20.6, Ransom Center, University of Texas, Austin.

28. Donald Crafton, *The Talkies: American Cinema's Transition to Sound, 1926–1931,* vol. 4 (Berkeley: University of California Press, 1999).

29. Pamela Glintenkamp, foreword to *Industrial Light & Magic: The Art of Innovation.*

30. Frank Foster, *The Story of Computer Graphics* (1999), www.frankfosterfilms.com/portfolio/the-story-of-computer-graphics-full-feature-film-documentary.

31. For more on EditDroid versus Avid, see Deron Overpeck, "The New Hollywood, 1981–1999: Editing," in *Editing and Special/Visual Effects*, edited by Charlie Keil
and Kristen Whissel (New Brunswick: Rutgers University Press, 2016), 129–141; and
the documentary by Tom van Klingeren, dir., "The EditDroid, Rise and Fall," 2014,
www.youtube.com/watch?v=z99wO2utddo]. For more on SoundDroid, see Rubin,
Droidmaker, 445–446, 450–551. For more on ProTools, see Jay Beck and Vanessa
Theme Ament, "The New Hollywood, 1981–1999," in *Sound: Dialogue, Music and
Effects*, edited by Kathryn Kalinak (New Brunswick: Rutgers University Press, 2015),
107–132.

32. Overpeck, "The New Hollywood, 1981–1999: Editing," 132–133.

33. Beck and Ament, "The New Hollywood, 1981–1999," 137.

34. Douglas Brown, "To Disney Infinity and Beyond—Star Wars Videogames
Before and After the LucasArts Acquisition," in *Disney's Star Wars: Forces of Produc-
tion and Promotion*, edited by William Procter and Richard McCulloch (Iowa City:
University of Iowa Press, 2019), 123–135.

35. For example, in Foster, *The Story of Computer Graphics*; "Industrial Light &
Magic: Creating the Impossible" (Starz Encore, 2010); and Don Shay, "30 Minutes
with the Godfather of Digital Cinema," *Cinefex* 65 (March 1996): 62.

36. Lomax, "'Thank the Maker!'"

37. Turnock, *Plastic Reality*.

38. Lucas, Yearbook 1984, 12.

39. Turnock, "Before Industrial Light and Magic."

40. "Industrial Light & Magic: Creating the Impossible" (Starz Encore, 2010),
www.youtube.com/watch?v=PBRoi09nV7w, starting at about 12:00.

41. Catmull "joined Lucasfilm in 1979" and Smith "joined Lucasfilm in 1980."
According to the first Lucasfilm yearbook in 1982 (20.1 Lucasfilm Ltd. 1982 Yearbook), Ostby first appears in 1983 ("joined LFL [Lucasfilm Ltd] in Jan 1983"), and
Lasseter appears in 1984 ("LFL since Nov '83"), verifying they were Lucasfilm employees by those years.

42. Jordan Gowanlock explores Lucasfilm's relation to broader trends in what
he calls Hollywood's "R&D complex" in his book *Animating Unpredictable Effects:
Nonlinearity in Hollywood's R&D Complex* (London: Palgrave Macmillan, 2021).

43. Lucasfilm Ltd. Yearbook 1982, Thomas G. Smith Papers, 20.1, Ransom Center, University of Texas, Austin, 4.

44. Per the yearbooks, in 1982 it was the Computer Research and Development
group within the Sprockets division; in 1983 it was called Computer Graphics within
the Computer Division; in 1984, it was The Computer Graphics Project within the
Computer Division; in 1985, called variously The Computer Group, the Graphics
Group, The Computer Graphics Division; in 1986, the Computer Division was gone,
with remaining research groups being their own divisions: Games was its own division, Sound was once again called Sprockets, and Droidworks was the editing group.

45. Don Shay, "30 Minutes with the Godfather of Digital Cinema," *Cinefex* 65
(March 1996): 65.

46. Shay, "30 Minutes with the Godfather of Digital Cinema," 62.

47. Rehak, *More Than Meets the Eye*, 93.

48. Groves, "Digital Yoda."

49. Rubin, *Droidmaker*, 197 and 258; Catmull in Foster, *The Story of Computer Graphics*, at about 1:13.

50. Thomas G. Smith Collection, Ransom Center, container 20, folders 1–10.

51. Alvy Ray Smith in Foster, *The Story of Computer Graphics*, at about 1:15; Sito, *Moving Innovation*, 159.

52. Rubin, *Droidmaker*, 247 and 257; Catmull in *Story of Computer Graphics* (1999) about 1:16, www.frankfosterfilms.com/portfolio/the-story-of-computer -graphics-full-feature-film-documentary. ILM apparently believed the feeling was mutual. According to George Joblove: "[ILM could see] that the Graphics Group wanted to go off by themselves without a lot of interaction." Rubin, 409.

53. Rubin, *Droidmaker*, 409.

54. Rubin, *Droidmaker*, 243 (original emphasis). Sito tells a similar story, Sito, *Moving Innovation*, 158.

55. Rubin says Lucas rarely ever visited the Graphics department, which irritated Alvy Ray Smith, and which was also located a long way away from most of the other Lucasfilm divisions. Rubin, *Droidmaker*, 217.

56. Rubin, *Droidmaker*, 241.

57. Smith, *Industrial Light & Magic*, 211–214.

58. Smith, 211–214.

59. Quotation from "Industrial Light & Magic: Creating the Impossible" (Starz Encore, 2010). The first three are all ILM division employees, and the last a UK physical effects freelancer who had worked with ILM several times previously. Although this could also indicate an instability in the category regarding computer generated effects in the 1980s.

60. Vaz and Duignan, *Industrial Light & Magic: Into the Digital Realm*, 193.

61. *The Hollywood Reporter* in 1986 notes the hiring of George Joblove and Doug Kay from Los Angeles in March as "named to head up Lucasfilm's ILM Co's newly created computer graphics division," to work on wire removal technology on *Howard the Duck*. Duane Byrge, "Kay, Jablov [sic] Lead ILM Unit," *Hollywood Reporter*, March 12, 1986. In 1986, as Michael Rubin put it, "wire removal was a big deal," both to ILM and the industry as a whole. Rubin, *Droidmaker*, 476.

62. In the 1985 yearbook no computer graphics artists are listed in the ILM section. The 1986 yearbook lists Edward Gronke (Computer Services), George Joblove (co-supervisor computer graphics department), Doug Kay (co-supervisor), Lincoln Hu (computer graphics), John Luskin (computer animation programmer), Jay Riddle (computer graphics), and Bruce Wallace (computer graphics), which is six out of about 225 employees; 20.4 Lucasfilm Ltd. (Yearbook) 1985, 20.5 Lucasfilm Ltd. (Yearbook) 1986.

63. Glintenkamp, *Industrial Light & Magic: The Art of Innovation*, 22. Glintenkamp's account of ILM's first 20 years is careful to separate ILM's digital work from its practical and optical work, but since her history is based on oral history interviews, some revisionism from within the company is evident.

64. The Genesis sequence is not mentioned in the 20.1 Lucasfilm Ltd. 1982 Yearbook. The Stained Glass Knight merits a brief mention in 1985, 20.4 Lucasfilm Ltd. (Yearbook) 1985: 30 Lucasfilm Yearbook 20.6. Genesis and the Stained Glass Knight are mentioned in one line each in Lucasfilm: The 1987 Yearbook, 10th Anniversary: 8.

65. 1991 Twentieth Anniversary Yearbook, 20.10 Lucasfilm.

66. Zoglin, "Lights! Camera! Special Effects;" Smith, "Reel Illusion;" Kaplan, "Secret Lair of the Jedi, Grain, and Green Slimers;" Wolkomir, "High-tech Hokum"; David A Kaplan et al. "Lights! Action! Disk Drives," Newsweek, July 22, 1991; Richard Corliss, "They Put the ILM in Film," Time, April 13, 1992.

67. Foster, The Story of Computer Graphics, at about 1:15.

68. Rubin, Droidmaker, 402–406.

69. Don Shay, "Dennis Muren—Playing it Unsafe," Cinefex 65 (March 1996): 108.

70. For Ed Catmull's account of the Graphics Group's sale, see Edwin Catmull, Creativity, Inc. (New York: Random House 2014), 38–44.

71. Rubin, Droidmaker, 402–406.

72. Shay, "30 Minutes with the Godfather of Digital Cinema," 62.

73. Rubin, Droidmaker, 394.

74. Jody Duncan, "The Once and Future War," Cinefex 47 (August 1991): 58.

75. These computer graphic companies worked on feature films: Triple-I (Westworld, Looker, Tron), MAGI (Tron), Digital Effects Inc (Tron), Xaos ("Liquid Television," Lawnmower Man), Kleiser-Walczak (Star Gate, special exhibition ride films like "In Search of the Obelisk" at the Luxor Resort in Las Vegas, designed by Douglas Trumbull).

76. Rhythm & Hues Coca-Cola Polar Bears TV ads first appeared in 1993.

77. "Industrial Light & Magic: Creating the Impossible" (Starz Encore, 2010), starting at about 12:00, www.youtube.com/watch?v=PBRoi09nV7w.

78. "Industrial Light & Magic: Creating the Impossible" (Starz Encore, 2010), starting at about 12:00.

79. Vaz and Duignan, Industrial Light & Magic: Into the Digital Realm, 111.

80. Lucas quoted in Foster, The Story of Computer Graphics, at about 1:15; Lucas in "Raiders, Raptors and Rebels: Behind the Magic of ILM."

81. Vaz and Duignan, Industrial Light & Magic: Into the Digital Realm, 119.

82. Lucas quoted in The Story of Computer Graphics, at about 1:15.

83. ILM president Jim Morris in Vaz and Duignan, Industrial Light & Magic: Into the Digital Realm, 195.

84. Vaz and Duignan, Industrial Light & Magic: Into the Digital Realm, 195.

85. 20.8 Lucasfilm Ltd. (Yearbook) 1989, 1. As to technology, the President's Letter only mentions the establishment of LucasArts, the videogaming and educational division. 20.9 Lucasfilm Ltd. (Yearbook) 1989.

86. 20.4 Lucasfilm Ltd. (Yearbook) 1985, 37–38.

87. 20.4 Lucasfilm Ltd. (Yearbook) 1985, 23.

88. Although ILM veteran Jay Riddle claims to have learned computer anima-

tion from Lasseter while he was still in the Computer Graphics group. From Ian Failes, "The Tech of 'Terminator 2'—An Oral History," https://vfxblog.com/2017/08/23/the-tech-of-terminator-2-an-oral-history.

89. Those six were: Hu, Joblove, Kay, Les Dittert, Luskin, and Smythe.

90. Those team members were: Anderson, Dippe, Hu, Joblove, Knoll, Luskin (who only worked on *The Abyss* at ILM), George McMurry (who only worked on *The Abyss* at ILM), Riddle, Smythe, Steve Williams, and Rosenbaum.

91. Lucasfilm Ltd. Yearbook 1989, Thomas G. Smith Papers, 20.8, Ransom Center, University of Texas, Austin.

92. Shay, "Dennis Muren—Playing it Unsafe," 108; From Ian Failes, "The Tech of 'Terminator 2.'"

93. Rubin implies Joblove's and Kay's hirings indicate changing priorities around computer graphics at Lucasfilm toward production. He writes: "Soon Joblove and Kay became the interface between ILM and the Computer Group." That may have been the intention, but he also writes: "There was a chasm between C Building [The Computer Group and the other R&D departments] and D Building [ILM] and it was wider than the diminutive parking lot," 407–409.

94. "We . . . established a new Computer Graphics dept headed jointly by Doug Kaye [sic] and George Joblove." In the same yearbook, Joblove and Kay list their employment start dates as 4/85. Lucasfilm Ltd. Yearbook 1985, Thomas G. Smith Papers, 20.4, Ransom Center, University of Texas, Austin, 3, 37–38.

95. Byrge, "Kay, Jablov [sic] Lead ILM Unit."

96. Tom Smith, personal correspondence via email with the author, January 2018.

97. Vaz and Duignan, *Industrial Light & Magic: Into the Digital Realm*, 280; Shay, "Dennis Muren—Playing it Unsafe," 108.

98. Shay, "Dennis Muren—Playing it Unsafe," 108. Vaz and Duignan reconcile the discrepancy by suggesting that *Terminator 2* monopolized the SGI machines, while the Macs were used on less prominent shows such as *The Rocketeer* and *Memoirs of an Invisible Man*. Vaz and Duignan, *Industrial Light & Magic: Into the Digital Realm*, 119.

99. Pulling from *Cinefex*, credit sequences, and oral histories, other unconfirmed Mac Squad members in addition to Stuart Robertson included Dippé and Riddle. Muren's team for *The Abyss* included Scott E. Anderson (animator), Dippé (animator), Hu (animator), Joblove (animator), Luskin (animator), Riddle (supervisor), Smythe (software), Steve Williams (animator), Stephen Rosenbaum (animator), and possibly also Knoll (designer) and George McMurry (video image).

100. Vaz and Duignan, *Industrial Light & Magic: Into the Digital Realm*, 119; Shay, "Dennis Muren—Playing It Unsafe," 108; Vaz and Duignan, *Industrial Light & Magic: Into the Digital Realm*, 72.

101. Vaz and Duignan, *Industrial Light & Magic: Into the Digital Realm*, 139.

102. *The Abyss* did nevertheless represent a proud moment for Joblove and Kay, whose skills were finally being used up to their potential:

Instead of just producing quiet little elements or wire removal and things you didn't see, the pseudopod [in *The Abyss*] was the key featured sequence and it got great publicity. There was tremendous pride felt inside the Department and it was a high point of my professional career when ILM picked up the Academy Award for this work.

Vaz and Duignan, *Industrial Light & Magic: Into the Digital Realm*, 200.

103. Vaz and Duignan, *Industrial Light & Magic: Into the Digital Realm*, 204. Glintenkamp's description compresses this to: "The work on this film requires a significant expansion of ILM's computer graphics Department. Millions of dollars are invested in new hardware and software." Glintenkamp, *Industrial Light & Magic: The Art of Innovation*, 25–26.

104. Jody Duncan, "The Beauty in the Beasts," *Cinefex* 55 (August 1993): 60.

105. Duncan, "The Once and Future War," 6.

106. Duncan, "The Beauty in the Beasts."

107. Vaz and Duignan, *Industrial Light & Magic: Into the Digital Realm*, 211 and 213.

108. Vaz and Duignan claim that the Pixar output scanner was used on *Terminator 2* (115), but then later they seemingly conflate the Pixar and the Kodak CCD scanner, which were different devices:

> The computer graphics department however had an advantage going into the *Terminator* challenge: the old laser light ILM Kodak prototype input scanner had been replaced by the new trilinear multi color high resolution CCD digital input scanner which had begun being developed in January 1988 and received its first feature film workout for *Die Hard 2*.

Vaz and Duignan, *Industrial Light & Magic: Into the Digital Realm*, 200.

109. Vaz and Duignan, *Industrial Light & Magic: Into the Digital Realm*, 115. Lincoln Hu, Michael MacKenzie of ILM, and Glenn Kennel and Mike Davis of Eastman Kodak won a Science and Technology award from the Academy in 1994 for their joint development work on a linear array CCD (Charge Coupled Device) film input scanning system.

110. Stuart Robertson:

> The drawback with digital is that it's still very slow. . . . Optical by comparison, can process that same amount of info in a 24th of a second. Because of the comparatively slow, but much more precise nature of digital processing, we found it worked very well to scan in different pieces, composite them digitally, then scan the result out to film. . . . So we were getting the best of both optical and digital.

Mark Cotta Vaz, "Maximum Impact," *Cinefex* 45 (February 1991): 65.

111. Yearbook 1991, IMDB.com.

112. Seven of the confirmed *Terminator 2* crew did not continue working at ILM after the film, but I cannot be sure what the hiring statuses of the others were.

113. Based on a composite of numbers counted from IMDB.com, *Cinefex*, and Failes.

114. Muren does not talk about using SGI machines on *Death Becomes Her*: "I reasoned if we could get a shot 90 percent right our artists could take the shot go into our Mackintoshes and use Photoshop to paint out any flaws." Vaz and Duignan, *Industrial Light & Magic: Into the Digital Realm*, 209.

115. Doug Smythe: "We had a few SGIs from before that were much smaller, but we got the really powerful 340 VGXs, so the morph team, we all got those massively powerful [machines]." Quoted in Failes, "The Tech of 'Terminator 2.'"

116. Failes, "The Tech of 'Terminator 2.'"

117. Eric Enderton (computer graphics software developer), ILM's first software developer. 91 yearbook hired Dec 89; 20.10 Lucasfilm 1991 Twentieth Anniversary Yearbook. From Ian Failes, "The Tech of 'Terminator 2."

118. 20.10 Lucasfilm 1991 Twentieth Anniversary Yearbook.

119. Vaz and Duignan, *Industrial Light & Magic: Into the Digital Realm*, 17.

120. Sito, *Moving Innovation*, 258.

121. Corliss, "They Put the ILM in Film"; David Kaplan, "Believe in Magic," *Newsweek*, June 14, 1993; Bill Brownstein, "The Making of Jurassic Park Offers Insights into Movie Magic," *Gazette* (Montreal, Quebec), September 20, 1993.

122. Lucas and others refer to these new competitors a lot in interviews in the early to mid-1990s. Matt Rothman, "ILM, SGI Form Alliance Against Sky-high Sci-fi," *Variety*, April 8, 1993; Rothman, "H'wood enters Digital Domain."

123. Kevin H. Martin "Life Neverlasting" *Cinefex* 52 (November 1992): 57.

124. Nearly every account of *Jurassic Park*'s production reports the story of Spielberg's plans to use Go-Motion and his being convinced by Muren with a CGI test that digital dinosaurs were feasible. Vaz and Duignan, *Industrial Light & Magic: Into the Digital Realm*; Duncan, "The Beauty in the Beasts," 42–95; Ron Magid, "Effects Team Brings Dinosaurs Back from Extinction," *American Cinematographer* (June 1993): 46–52; "Industrial Light & Magic: Creating the Impossible" (Starz Encore, 2010); and *Jurassic Park* DVD extras.

125. According to *Cinefex*, the computer graphics assignment was divided between Tippett Studio and ILM. Tippett animated fifteen shots for two major sequences: the T-Rex attack on road, and the stalking velociraptors in the kitchen. ILM did thirty-seven shots: revealing the browsing brachiosaurs, the gallimimus herd stampede with the T-Rex, and the climactic battle between the T-Rex and the raptors. Duncan, "The Beauty in the Beasts," 60.

126. Duncan, "The Beauty in the Beasts."

127. Muren boasts of a telecommunication link between San Rafael (ILM) and Berkeley (Tippett Studio). Duncan, "The Beauty in the Beasts," 60.

128. This number would have come from ILM, not from independent reporting on *Variety*'s part, since there is no indication the reporter was on-site in Northern California. Rothman, "ILM, SGI Form Alliance Against Sky-high Sci-fi."

129. Where Muren bragged about the SGI workstations for *Terminator 2*, neither he nor anyone else brings them up in contemporary *Jurassic Park* coverage. Duncan, "The Beauty in the Beasts." Failes's oral history from 2018 recounts SGI machines in use, but some of the artists get their dates confused in the twenty-fifth anniversary retelling. The "making of" video on the 2000 DVD shows a computer room purported to be at ILM, which according to the website sgistuff.net is full of PowerSeries systems, most of which have VGX graphics. However, the picture is vague, and one cannot see how many units are in the room; neither is there any clear indication of the actual date of the images. "Hollywood: Jurassic Park," sgistuff

.net, last modified November 12, 2019, www.sgistuff.net/funstuff/hollywood/jpark
.html. The 1995 *Making of Jurassic Park* documentary (www.dailymotion.com/video
/x2ymqb4) narrated by James Earl Jones features Dennis Muren in a server room
full of SGI boxes, but it appears that the archival footage comes from after the
production of *Jurassic Park*.

130. Ian Failes, "Viewpaint: ILM's Secret Weapon on *Jurassic Park*," 2018, https://
vfxblog.com/viewpaint. John Schlag, Brian Knep, Zoran Kacic-Alesic, and Tom Williams received a Sci-Tech award for Viewpaint in 1997. They also developed Sock
(originally for *Terminator 2*), as well as Enveloping, and began using Softimage off
the shelf. The only reference I can find to Alias being used was in tests, and then it
was off-site. Duncan, "Beauty in the Beasts"; Failes, "Viewpaint."

131. *Variety* reported in December 1993 that forty people were brought in to ILM
for computer graphics, twenty-five from outside, fifteen from within. Andy Marx,
"ILM Plans More Light and Magic Tricks," *Variety*, December 16, 1993.

132. Roger Guyett's first job at ILM was *Casper*, Pablo Helman was hired for *Lost
World: Jurassic Park*, Hal Hickel was hired for *Lost World: Jurassic Park*, Habib Zargarpour was hired for *The Mask*, and Ben Snow was hired for *Star Trek: Generations*
and *Casper*.

It appears that in the years 1989–1993, Knoll was not working significantly on
The Abyss or at all on *Terminator 2* and *Jurassic Park* because he was traveling around
the region trying to find an investor in Photoshop, which Adobe licensed in April
1989 and shipped version 1.0 in February 1990. Knoll continued concentrating on
Photoshop through version 3.0, which was released in November 1992. Jeff Schewe,
"Ten Years of Photoshop: The Birth of a Killer Application," *PEI: Photo Electronic
Imaging Magazine*, February 2000, 16–25; *Start Up Memories: The Beginning of Photoshop* (2011), www.youtube.com/watch?v=EtzFvRjrvXM.

133. Sito, *Moving Innovation*, 258.

134. In *Cinefex*, one can gauge the actual amount of CGI being produced for
mainstream films on ILM projects and those of other companies. See Shay, "Dancing on the Edge of the Abyss"; Adam Eisenberg, "Ghostbusters Revisited" [on *Ghostbusters 2*], *Cinefex* 40 (November 1989): 4–45; Susan Dayton, "Backyard Odyssey" [on
Honey, I Shrunk the Kids], *Cinefex* 41 (February 1990): 34–67; Jody Duncan Shannon,
"A Dark and Stormy Knight" [on *Batman*], *Cinefex* 41 (February 1990): 4–33; Paul
Roberts, "Ego Trip" [on *Total Recall*], *Cinefex* 43 (August 1990): 4–33; Vaz, "Maximum Impact"; Peter Sorensen, "Cyberworld" [on *Lawnmower Man*], *Cinefex* 50 (May
1992):4–74; Mark Cotta Vaz, "A Knight at the Zoo" [on *Batman Returns*], *Cinefex*
51 (August 1992): 22–74; Debra Kaufman, "Effects in the Vertical Realm" [on *Cliffhanger*], *Cinefex* 54 (May 1993): 30–53; Jody Duncan, "The Making of a Rockbuster"
[on *The Flintstones*], *Cinefex* 58 (June 1994): 34–65; W. C. Odien, "The Rise and Fall
of Norville Barnes" [on the *Hudsucker Proxy*], *Cinefex* 58 (June 1994): 66–85; Jody
Duncan, "From Zero to Hero" [on *The Mask*], *Cinefex* 60 (December 1994):46–69;
Estelle Shay, "Quick Cuts: Sub Plots"[on *Crimson Tide*], *Cinefex* 62 (June 1995): 11–16;
Mark Cotta Vaz "Cruising the Digital Backlot" [on *Mission: Impossible*], *Cinefex* 67
(September 1996): 90–105.

135. "Everything has been geared to do the next 'Star Wars' with a reasonable

amount of money," Lucas said. "The announcement, said several Lucas executives, was not in response to Jim Cameron's recent deal with IBM to create Digital Domain, a special effects company." Rothman, "ILM, SGI Form Alliance Against Sky-high Sci-fi"; Rothman, "H'wood Enters Digital Domain."

136. *ILM's [1993] retooling . . .*: Vaz and Duignan, *Industrial Light & Magic: Into the Digital Realm*, 237; *With 450 people . . .*: Groves, "Digital Yoda"; *Pointing to the twelve Oscars . . .*: Rothman, "ILM, SGI Form Alliance Against Sky-high Sci-fi."

Chapter 4: Monsters Are Real

Epigraphs: Bong Joon-ho quote: Magnolia Pictures press packet, Herrick Library, 12; Zhang Yimou quote: Bob Strauss, "How Zhang Yimou Built 'Great Wall' with Matt Damon," *Los Angeles Daily News*, February 15, 2017.

1. Miller et al., *Global Hollywood 2*.

2. Miriam Bratu Hansen, "The Mass Production of the Senses: Classical Cinema as Vernacular Modernism," in *Disciplining Modernism*, ed. Pamela L. Caughie (London: Palgrave Macmillan, 2009), 242–258.

3. Though filmmakers demonstrating evident resistance to Hollywood blockbusters is also perhaps a requirement for critical success on the festival market.

4. Aynne Kokas, *Hollywood Made in China* (Berkeley: University of California Press, 2017), 4. Kokas also provides a photo of public advertising in Shanghai 2013 linking the Chinese Dream and cultural output, equating "Chinese Spirit, Chinese Images, Chinese Culture, Chinese Representation" (21).

5. Rey Chow, *Entanglements, or Transmedial Thinking about Capture* (Durham: Duke University Press, 2012), 172. Thanks to Joshua Neves for this citation.

6. Chung, *Media Heterotopias*, 2–3.

7. Chung, *Media Heterotopias*, 119.

8. Strauss, "How Zhang Yimou Built 'Great Wall' with Matt Damon."

9. Patrick Frater, "Koreans Hope F/X Make a Monster Impression," *Variety*, November 17, 2005.

10. Magnolia Pictures press packet, Herrick Library, 12.

11. Dawtrey, "Soho VFX Biz Arises from Potter's Spell."

12. Aminah Sheikh, "Indian Firm Behind Visual Effects in Avatar," *Business Standard* (Mumbai), December 20, 2009.

13. Fionnuala Halligan, "Prepare for Battle," *Screen Intl*, July 15–28, 2005.

14. Miller et al., *Global Hollywood 2*; Curtin and Vanderhoef, "A Vanishing Piece of the Pi"; Gurevitch, "The Straw That Broke the Tiger's Back?," 190; David S. Cohen, "Blockbusters Take Toll on F/X Shops," *Variety*, May 25, 2007; Ted Johnson, "Visual-Effects Artists Urge Tariffs to Fight Runaway Production," *Variety*, August 6, 2014; Ellen Wolff, "Core California FX Companies Find Success Despite Exodus of Many Rivals," *Variety*, June 8, 2016.

15. For academic accounts of the effects business's economic troubles, see Curtin and Vanderhoef, "A Vanishing Piece of the Pi," and Gurevitch, "The Straw That Broke the Tiger's Back?"; Charles R. Acland, "An Empire of Pixels: Canadian Cul-

tural Enterprise in the Digital Effects Industry" and Gillian Roberts "Cross-Border Film Adaptation and *Life of Pi*," both in *Reading Between the Borderlines: Cultural Production and Consumption Across the 49th Parallel*, edited by Gillian Roberts (Montreal: McGill-Queens University Press, 2018), 143–170; 225–242.

For a more approachable format, see the Freakanomics podcast "No Hollywood Ending for the Visual-Effects Industry," February 22, 2017, http://freakonomics.com /podcast/no-hollywood-ending-visual-effects-industry, for a largely accurate account that is particularly detailed about global tax incentives.

16. Curtin and Vanderhoef, "A Vanishing Piece of the Pi," and Gurevitch, "The Straw That Broke the Tiger's Back?" are informative. The tax incentive and low labor areas historically wax and wane. South Korea is less of a "low cost labor" area than it was in the early 2000s.

17. Ellen Wolff, "VFX Good Enough? Sez Who?," *Variety*, March 2, 2011.

18. Adam Dawtrey, "London's CG Houses Share Digital Wealth," *Variety*, November 10, 2008; Diana Lodderhose, "Framestore Looks at Bigger Picture," *Variety*, Jan 17–23, 2011; Dawtrey, "Soho VFX Biz Arises from Potter's Spell"; Rob Mitchell "State of the Art Stays the Course in Soho," *Variety*, February 21, 2017.

19. David S. Cohen, "'Star Wars,' 'Avengers' Spawn ILM London's Expansion," *Variety*, February 12, 2014.

20. In other words, despite the presence of top-tier houses locally, UK effects production acts very similarly to effects production elsewhere. Similar to Bong Joon-ho or Zhang Yimou, depending on the budget, UK productions hire top-of-the-line for the more complicated work but from the second tier or below for supporting effects.

21. These lower-tier UK effects houses also act as support houses on Hollywood blockbusters, but their primary work is clearly prestige television and streaming, such as *The Crown*.

22. Mitchell, "State of the Art Stays the Course in Soho." Similarly, one can see the impact on the global dispersal of effects companies in a handful of other filmmaking examples. Two EU-based effects companies experienced in Hollywood productions, Pixomondo (based primarily in Germany) and Buf (based in France), brought their experience to European productions such as *Melancholia* (2011) and *The Lobster* (2015), respectively.

Conversely, some companies have pursued more regional work as a path to growth. South Korean Dexter Studios, a company formed in the 2010s to produce the giant baseball-playing gorilla for the Chinese-South Korean coproduction *Mr. Go*; and Tsui Hark's *The Taking of Tiger Mountain* (2014) and *Journey to the West: The Demons Strike Back* (2017). Dexter has become the go-to production house for many Chinese language productions because, as *Variety* put it, Dexter provides "an optimal balance of quality that is better than local Chinese firms and price that is lower than the top U.S. or antipodean houses." Patrick Frater, "Korea's Dexter Sets Up Beijing VFX Unit," *Variety*, November 28, 2013.

As for the Canadian context, Charles Acland contends that what is usually characterized as "runaway" (from California) has been at best a mixed bag for the

Canadian VFX industry, what he describes as "sustained precarity," where the presence of international effects houses in Vancouver and Montreal works primarily to the benefit of public relations rather than the workers. Acland, "An Empire of Pixels: Canadian Cultural Enterprise in the Digital Effects Industry," 143–170, and Roberts, "Cross-Border Film Adaptation and *Life of Pi*," 225–242.

Effects production in Australia is discussed briefly in Ben Goldsmith, Susan Ward, and Tom O'Regan, *Local Hollywood: Global Film Production and the Gold Coast* (Brisbane: University of Queensland Press, 2010); South Africa's film service industry to global science fiction filmmaking is the subject of Jessica Dickson's PhD dissertation, "The Making of 'Hollywood's' Apocalyptic Aesthetic in South Africa," August 2021, Harvard University.

23. Cohen, "ILM Finds Beijing Base"; Matthew Scott, "Base FX @ 10: A Crazy Dream Became China's Leading VFX Studio," *Variety*, June 7, 2016.

24. The mainland Chinese production *Monster Hunt* (2015) is an exception. Matthew Scott, "Base FX @ 10."

25. Patrick Frater, "Sony Flows into India F/X," *Variety*, February 21, 2007. Although articles announcing these partnerships frequently claim the subsidiary will "continue to service third-party productions," it appears, as with Base FX, they did so only very rarely. See also Rachel Abrams, "Rhythm & Hues Seeks Coin for Int'l Expansion," *Variety*, October 11, 2012.

26. By "compete" I mean not necessarily the festival main competition but the marketplace for attention and distribution.

27. Legendary Entertainment is a somewhat complex example, since the company is officially located in Burbank and frequently coproduces Hollywood blockbusters such as *Kong: Skull Island* and *Jurassic World*. See also Charlie Michael, *French Blockbusters: Cultural Politics of a Transnational Cinema* (Edinburgh: Edinburgh University Press, 2019).

28. Keegan, "Hollywood's VFX Shops: Trouble in Boom Times."

29. The shuttering of Rhythm and Hues's Asian branches in 2010 appears to have meant other Asian companies picked up some of their workers, but the impact on local production is unclear.

30. Darcy Paquet, "CG Shops Tout Their Chops: Korea Leads Asia in VFX, Starts Charge on H'wood," *Daily Variety*, February 8, 2008.

31. The *Robot* production also hired South Korean and Hong Kong companies, along with a few Indian companies.

32. Pip Bulbek, "The Jackson Effect," Hollywood Reporter, November 25, 2011.

33. Nick Roddick, "Red River," *Sight and Sound* (December 2006): 34.

34. For a thorough discussion of *The Host* along different theoretical lines, see Chung, *Media Heterotopias*.

35. Referred to by the production as "'little fresh meat,'" or Chinese heartthrobs, who appeal to young Chinese women. Julie Makinen, "With $150-million 'Great Wall,' Legendary Aims to Bridge U.S.-China Film Gap," *Los Angeles Times*, July 2, 2015.

36. Whissel, *Spectacular Digital Effects*.

37. For more on bullet time, see Purse, *Digital Imaging in Popular Cinema*; and Bob Rehak, "The Migration of Forms: Bullet Time as Microgenre," *Film Criticism* 32, no. 1 (2007): 26–48.

38. Makinen, "With $150-million 'Great Wall,' Legendary Aims to Bridge U.S.-China Film Gap."

39. Vincent Frei, "The Great Wall: Samir Hoon, VFX Supervisor—Industrial Light & Magic," ArtofVFX.com, March 8, 2017, www.artofvfx.com/the-great-wall -samir-hoon-vfx-supervisor-industrial-light-magic.

40. ILM VFX Supervisor Samir Hoon: "The Wall set could fit about 500 extras in costume," Frei, "The Great Wall."

41. As can be seen in Frei's Art of VFX video, "The Great Wall: Samir Hoon," www.artofvfx.com/the-great-wall.

42. Makinen, "With $150-million 'Great Wall,' Legendary Aims to Bridge U.S.-China Film Gap."

43. The *Los Angeles Times* then editorializes: "If 'The Great Wall' proves to be the global blockbuster it's designed to be, it could serve as a model of cross-Pacific collaboration for years to come. . . . But if it flops, it may be a dispiriting signal that the long-sought holy grail of bringing together Hollywood and Chinese talents to create hybridized film juggernauts is beyond the grasp of even one of the most as-tute operators in the industry." Makinen, "With $150-million 'Great Wall,' Legendary Aims to Bridge U.S.-China Film Gap."

44. Data from Boxofficemojo.com

45. Frei, "The Great Wall."

46. See, for example, the business study by George S. Yip and Bruce McKern, *China's Next Strategic Advantage: From Imitation to Innovation* (Cambridge: MIT Press, 2016: 12–14.

47. Graham Edwards, "Symphony of Colors: *Valerian and the City of a Thousand Planets*," *Cinefex* 154 (August 2017): 80.

48. Edwards, "Symphony of Colors," 93.

49. Edwards, "Symphony of Colors," 86.

50. Patrick Frater, "'The Mermaid' Becomes Highest-Grossing Film Ever in China," *Variety*, February 22, 2016; Patrick Frater, "'Wolf Warriors II' Takes All-Time China Box Office Record," *Variety*, August 7, 2017.

51. Pierson, *Special Effects*.

52. As Chow has said: "'Charlie Chaplin is my all-time favourite, alongside Buster Keaton." Kaleem Aftab, "Stephen Chow: Hong Kong Hustler," *The Inde-pendent*, July 9, 2013, www.independent.co.uk/arts-entertainment/films/features /stephen-chow-hong-kong-hustler-295387.html.

53. Sergei Eisenstein, *On Disney*, edited by Jay Leyda (London: Methuen, 1986); Anne Nesbet, *Savage Junctures: Sergei Eisenstein and the Shape of Thinking* (London: I. B. Tauris, 2003).

54. From Boxofficemojo.com.

55. "In this respect [*Wolf Warrior 2*] has proved a far more successful piece of propaganda than the official propaganda film *The Founding of an Army* which was

released in Chinese theaters on the same day and has grossed only $50.3 million." Frater, "'Wolf Warriors II' Takes All-Time China Box Office Record."

56. Joshua Neves, "Southern Effects: *Kaiju*, Cultural Intimacy, and the Production of Distribution," *Cultural Critique*, no. 114 (Winter 2022, 127–152).

57. Both Chinese productions of various kinds tend to use South Korean houses—and not Chinese houses—for more elaborate effects productions, such as Dexter Digital's work on *The Monkey King* and its sequels.

58. The Indian business press reports on Western effects activity in India. According to Malhotra: "Most of the work is done [in the US] for Hollywood projects simply because India is not yet ready for the level of work international studios want." Aminah Sheikh, "Indian Firm Behind Visual Effects in Avatar," *Business Standard* (Mumbai), December 20, 2009. See also Anu Thapa, "Haunting Bollywood: Gender, Genre, and the Supernatural in Hindi Commercial Cinema," *Historical Journal of Film, Radio and Television* 38, no. 1 (2018): 219–220.

59. Patrick Frater, "China Is the New Hollywood, Says James Schamus," *Variety*, April 17, 2016. Variety reports the panel discussion as a paraphrase of Smith's comments.

Chapter 5: That Analog Feeling

Epigraphs: *Photorealism is always what we strive for* . . . : Jody Duncan, "Q&A: Victoria Alonso," *Cinefex* 158 (April 2018): 23 [emphasis in original]. The *Cinefex* article describes Alonso as, alongside Kevin Feige (President of Marvel Studios from 2007–) and Lou D'Esposito (Marvel Studios co-President, 2009–) as the "three legged stool upon which [Marvel Studios] rests." Duncan, "Q&A," 17; *[Marvel Studios'] approach to visual effects* . . . : Graham Edwards, "The Marvel Effect," *Cinefex* 158 (April 2018).

1. The Visual Effects Society's handbook is a document that usefully outlines what the industry would consider the "best practices" for effects production. However, even Jeffery Okun, a coeditor of the handbook, admits it describes how the industry would like the practices to be more so than the actual conditions on actual film productions. *VES Industry Standard VFX Practices and Procedures*, edited by Jeffrey Okun and Susan Zwerman (Waltham, MA Focal Press 2010); Jeffery Okun, personal interview with the author.

2. Edwards, "The Marvel Effect."

3. Paramount had produced the films of Phase One, up to *The Avengers*, which was the first MCU film produced by Disney. Previously, ILM did not produce effects for the other Phase One films: *The Incredible Hulk* (2008), *Thor* (2011), and *Captain America: The First Avenger* (2011).

4. It is important to note that this is not simple financial risk aversion but also aversion to any controversy. As Derek Johnson has contended, Marvel Studios has exhibited a canny understanding and plays to fan culture, largely by sticking to some amount of established Marvel Comics canon. Derek Johnson, "Cinematic Destiny: Marvel Studios and the Trade Stories of Industrial Convergence," *Cinema Journal* 52, no. 1 (2012): 1–24.

5. See, for example, this video essay on the Marvel Symphonic Universe on the YouTube channel Every Frame a Painting by Taylor Ramos and Tony Zhou: www.youtube.com/channel/UCjFqcJQXGZ6T6sxyFB-5i6A; and see composer Mark Mothersbaugh's comments on the same topic, "'Thor' [Ragnarok] Composer Knew Marvel Scores Sounded Similar, So He Decided to Change That," *Hollywood Reporter*, November 3, 2017, www.hollywoodreporter.com/heat-vision/thor-ragnarok-composer -acknowledges-marvel-scores-sound-same-1054503.

6. Jason Mittel, *Complex TV* (New York: New York University Press, 2015), 18.

7. David Christopher Bell, "6 Reasons Modern Movie CGI Looks Surprisingly Crappy," Cracked.com, May 12, 2015, www.cracked.com/blog/6-reasons-expensive -films-end-up-with-crappy-special-effects. I follow the site's style of capitalizing every word in the headings.

8. Bryan Curtis, "The Turn Against Digital Effects," *New Yorker*, January 20, 2016, www.newyorker.com/culture/cultural-comment/the-turn-against-digital -effects; Peter Rainer, "'Star Wars: The Force Awakens' Is the Best Movie in the Series Since 'Empire Strikes Back," *Christian Science Monitor*, December 16, 2015, www.csmonitor.com/The-Culture/Movies/2015/1216/Star-Wars-The-Force-Awakens -is-the-best-movie-in-the-series-since-Empire-Strikes-Back; Ty Burr, "Review: Launch of "'Star Wars: The Force Awakens' Takes the Faithful Full Circle," December 15, 2015, www.bostonglobe.com/arts/movies/2015/12/15/the-force-with-star-wars-the -force-awakens/KyOQ1W4zeMyVDncrIirp5M/story.html.

9. See the "Behind the Scenes Featurettes for *The Force Awakens*" on YouTube: www.youtube.com/watch?v=A8qXj3ALyyU; This approach was repeated for *The Last Jedi*: www.youtube.com/watch?v=N2gB8eqEV9o; See Curtis, "The Turn Against Digital Effects."

10. Guyett said explicitly: "The trick was trying to make it all as integrated as possible – really blurring the line between the practical and digital." Vincent Frei, "Star Wars Episode VII—The Force Awakens: Roger Guyett," artofvfx.com, February 29, 2016, www.artofvfx.com/star-wars-the-force-awakens-roger-guyett-overall-vfx -supervisor-2nd-unit-director-ilm.

11. This interview with Guyett spends a good deal of time parsing what is CG and what is practical on *The Force Awakens*, as well as the reasoning behind it. Peter Scrietta, "The Force Awakens Had More CG Visual Effects Shots Than The Phantom Menace," slashfilm.com, January 14, 2016, www.slashfilm.com/force-awakens -visual-effects.

12. Kwame Opam, "Spider-Man: Homecoming's VFX Lead Unpacks the Secrets of the Staten Island Ferry Scene," theverge.com, July 14, 2017, www.theverge.com /2017/7/14/15973770/spider-man-homecoming-ferry-scene-visual-effects. The number of effects shots on this film does not appear in the usual coverage in sources such as *Cinefex*. Cobbling together a total from the Art of VFX website (artofvfx.com) comes up with about 1,500; considering it does not cover all the houses involved on the film, a safe guess would be close to the Marvel Studios usual of about 2,000 effects shots.

13. Vincent Frei, "Spider-Man—Homecoming: Theodore Bialek," artofvfx .com, July 26, 2017, www.artofvfx.com/spider-man-homecoming-theodore-bialek-vfx

-supervisor-sony-pictures-imageworks. The "grounded" rhetoric continues through the MCU films, most markedly in the Russo brothers' films. For example, Russell Earl, ILM VFX supervisor on *Captain America: The Winter Soldier*, reports: "The brothers wanted everything to be grounded in reality." Jody Duncan, "Captain's Orders," *Cinefex* 138 (July 2014): 49.

14. Duncan "Captain's Orders," 49.

15. Duncan, "The Man in the Iron Mask," 59; see also: Jody Duncan, "MCU: The Big Bang," *Cinefex* 158 (April 2018): 28. For *Iron Man* (2008): "Favreau's approach . . . was to maintain a standard of absolute photorealism throughout, with vfx shots designed to look as if they were shot with a real camera, with all the attendant mishaps and errors."

16. As Whissel and others have convincingly argued, spectacle and narrative do not necessarily need to be seen as incompatible or in competition with each other.

17. Extrapolated from *Cinefex* articles: Duncan, "The Man in the Iron Mask," 56; Jody Duncan, "Batman Grounded" [on *The Dark Knight*], *Cinefex* 115 (October 2008): 62–88; Jody Duncan, "Iron Clad" [on *Iron Man 2*], *Cinefex* 122 (July 2010): 32–61; Joe Fordham, "God of Thunder" [on *Thor*], *Cinefex* 126 (July 2011): 14–38; Duncan Jesser, "The Avengers Initiative," 64–91; Duncan, "Q&A: Victoria Alonso," 17–23; Graham Edwards, "Black Panther," *Cinefex* 158 (April 2018): 54–82; Edwards, "The Marvel Effect," 84–98.

18. Many creatives complain about Marvel's lack of interest in artistic individuality. As cinematographer Roger Deakins has asserted, rather than rely on the skills of a single camera directed by a director of photography, "studios often rely on second units to pick up the filming of various scenes. Marvel Studios is notorious for working this way. One reason the MCU has lured new indie talent behind the camera is because the studio has second unit teams working on the action scenes." Zack Sharf, "Roger Deakins Refused to Shoot 'Blade Runner 2049' the 'Sloppy' Way Hollywood Studios Expect," Indiewire.com, April 8, 2020, www.indiewire.com /2020/04/blade-runner-2049-roger-deakins-refused-second-unit-1202223652/?fbclid =IwAR2EaktjEHe2kTqW2NJoc-fZypQKuqsWbOL4JrxSqr2XT5hvF0q64_2E4G8.

19. Joe Fordham, "Starting Over" [on *Batman Begins*], *Cinefex* 103 (October 2005): 90–92; see also Duncan, "Batman Grounded" [on *The Dark Knight*], 62–88, for similar rhetoric.

20. Duncan, "The Man in the Iron Mask" [on *Iron Man*], 59. For more uses of the term "digital curse," see Jody Duncan, "Star Wars II: Attack of the Clones: Love and War," *Cinefex* 90 (July 2002): 90.

21. The quote is from Duncan, "The Man in the Iron Mask" [on *Iron Man*], 59.

22. Duncan, "Iron Clad" [on *Iron Man 2*], 61.

23. Duncan, "Iron Clad" [on *Iron Man 2*], 61.

24. Lev Manovich, "Digital Cinema and the History of the Moving Image," in *Film Theory and Criticism: Introductory Readings 8th Edition*, ed. Leo Braudy and Marshall Cohen (Oxford: Oxford University Press, 2016), 725.

25. For some examples of blaming a movie's faults on its "bad" effects see, Corey Hutchinson, "The MCU Has a CGI Problem," Screenrant.com, February 19, 2018, https://screenrant.com/mcu-bad-cgi-black-panther-marvel-movies-special-effects;

and "In Your Opinion, What Has Been the Worst Moment of CGI or Greenscreen in the MCU?," Reddit, July 25, 2017, www.reddit.com/r/marvelstudios/comments/6pft9g/in_your_opinion_what_has_been_the_worst_moment_of; Noah Berlatsky, "Infinity War's Thanos Proves CGI Supervillains Are a Terrible Idea," The Verge, March 16, 2018, www.theverge.com/2018/3/16/17130846/infinity-wars-trailer-thanos-cgi-supervillains-mcu-characters.

26. Beginning with *Iron Man 2* in the MCU, most suits are digitally generated. As Favreau said: "We found ourselves replacing the practical suit a lot with CGI in the last movie anyway." Duncan, "Iron Clad," 34.

27. Joe Bauer, in Jody Duncan, "Joe Bauer on Zathura," *Cinefex* 105 (April 2006): 23–28.

28. Duncan, "The Man in the Iron Mask" [on *Iron Man*], 73.

29. This emphasis on photographic realism and is also consistent with the related trend of more kinetic action movies at the time, in films such as the Paul Greengrass–directed Jason Bourne films (2004, 2007) and the Daniel Craig James Bond series, beginning with *Casino Royale* (2006).

30. In 2012, he was still publicly demonstrating his support of *Cinefex* on social media. Jon Favreau (@Jon_Favreau), "Cool iPad app for digital version of *Cinefex* magazine. http://itunes.apple.com/us/app/cinefex/id512379220?mt=8," Twitter post, November 12, 2012, https://twitter.com/Jon_Favreau/status/268157478800355330.

31. Duncan, "Joe Bauer on *Zathura*," 23.

32. Duncan, "The Man in the Iron Mask" [on *Iron Man*], 59–60.

33. Shay, "Dennis Muren—Playing It Unsafe," 102. See also Muren's discourse in *Cinefex* 2 and 3 quoted in chapter 2.

34. *Top Gun*'s effects were by USFX, the San Francisco–based effects company led by Gary Gutierrez. Many of the pyrotechnics and miniature team worked previously at ILM. Ed Martinez, "Sky Wars," *Cinefex* 29 (February 1987): 57, 62.

35. Emphasis in original. Duncan, "The Man in the Iron Mask" [on *Iron Man*], 80–82. While *Top Gun* did in fact feature some aerial footage shot from fighter planes, the majority of the effects were achieved by USFX with miniature planes. See Martinez, "Sky Wars."

36. See Pierson, *Special Effects*, and Buckland, "Between Science Fact and Science Fiction," 177–192, for accounts of characters gaping at the digital effects onscreen as modeling audience reaction.

37. One might argue that, with the exception of perhaps *Doctor Strange*, the On-Earth MCU films tend to adhere more closely to the aesthetic established by *Iron Man*, while those primarily set Off-Earth, such as the *Thor* films and the *Guardians of the Galaxy* films, are allowed a looser, more fantastic aesthetic. I would argue that it is the art design that makes those films appear more fantastic than the On-Earth films, while the effects still largely adhere to an ILM/ISER aesthetic.

38. Curtin and Vanderhoef, "A Vanishing Piece of the Pi," 219–239.

39. This trend can be seen most prominently with the Russo brothers, who were best known for directing episodic television before directing *Captain America: The Winter Soldier*, *Captain America: Civil War*, *Avengers: Infinity War*, and *Avengers: Endgame*.

40. Don Witmer, "All Together Now," *American Cinematographer* (June 2012): 34.

41. Vincent Frei, "*The Avengers*: Jeff White—VFX Supervisor ILM," artofvfx .com, May 22. 2012, www.artofvfx.com/the-avengers-jeff-white-superviseur-vfx-ilm.

42. David Cohen, "How to Spot the VFX Pro's Signature," *Variety*, January 11, 2011.

43. The coverage of *The Avengers* in *Cinefex* lists all of these vendors, and IMDB .com adds another few, most likely shots farmed out by the first group for reasons of deadline: ILM (US), Weta Digital (NZ), Third Floor (US), Digital Domain (US), Hydralux (US), Lola (US), Evil Eye Pictures (US), Whiskey Tree (US), Cantina Creative (US), Fuel FX (Australia), Luma Pictures (US), Scanline (Germany), Trixter (Germany), Pixomondo (US/Germany), Modus FX (Montreal), Gentle Giant (US), The Base (Beijing), Method Studios (US), fx3x (Macedonia), and Lidar FX (US). If we include the physical effects houses Legacy Effects and New Deal studios (US), the total is twenty-two houses doing some sort of effects work on the show. Duncan Jesser, "The Avengers Initiative" [on *The Avengers*], 66; "*The Avengers*: Cast and Crew," IMDB.com.

44. According to artofvfx.com, about 700 were ILM shots and 400 were Weta shots. Frei, "*The Avengers*: Jeff White—VFX Supervisor ILM," www.artofvfx.com/the -avengers-jeff-white-superviseur-vfx-ilm.

45. Duncan Jesser, "The Avengers Initiative" [on *The Avengers*], 79, 85.

46. Even though location photography took place in Cleveland. Duncan Jesser, "The Avengers Initiative" [on *The Avengers*].

47. Emphasis in original. Duncan, "Q&A: Victoria Alonso," 19. The term "plussing" or "plus it" is usually attributed to Walt Disney, in relation to his desire to continually improve Disneyland according to guests' identified preferences. "In Walt's Own Words: Plussing Disneyland," Walt Disney Family Museum, last modified July 17, 2014, www.waltdisney.org/blog/walts-own-words-plussing-disneyland. Around the time of the Disney acquisition, Dennis Muren uses similar language of "plussing" effects shots: "Finding ways to give the shot even more than the audience expects." Glintenkamp, *Industrial Light & Magic: The Art of Innovation*, 194. The term has not just become media industry jargon, but also a management tactic as a way give criticism while indicating that all are working together in pursuit of excellence.

48. For a director's criticism of the Marvel collaborative atmosphere, see *Thor: The Dark World*'s director Alan Taylor's comments in Mike Ryan, "No, 'Terminator: Genisys' Director Alan Taylor Doesn't Like That Spoilerish Trailer, Either," uproxx .com, June 29, 2015, https://uproxx.com/movies/terminator-genisys-alan-taylor; Devin Farici, "The Marvel Creative Committee Is Over," birth.movies.death.com, September 2, 2015, https://birthmoviesdeath.com/2015/09/02/the-marvel-creative -committee-is-over.

49. Duncan, "Q&A: Victoria Alonso," 18; For VFX supervisors responding to this criticism, see Edwards, "The Marvel Effect," 86.

50. David S. Cohen, "Marvel Ups Victoria Alonso to Head of Physical Production," *Variety*, September 21, 2015.

51. Edwards, "The Marvel Effect," 86.

52. Edwards, "The Marvel Effect," 86.

53. Duncan, "Q&A: Victoria Alonso," 20.

54. Marvel, in fact, asked director Jon Watts to "channel" John Hughes films. Bill Desowitz, "'Spider-Man Homecoming': How Jon Watts Channeled John Hughes," indiewire.com, July 14, 2017, www.indiewire.com/2017/07/spider-man-homecoming-jon-watts-john-hughes-visual-effects-1201855275.

55. As director James Gunn put it, including the movement or mannerisms of real racoons compromised the credibility of the talking and acting character of Rocket, who by comparison seemed unnatural. The design of Groot required greater anthropomorphism than originally conceived. As MPC visual effects supervisor Nicolas Aithadi described: "The original versions [of Groot] were very tree-like, which made it difficult to relate to him. So we humanized him. . . . James [Gunn] wanted people to fall in love with Groot." Jody Duncan, "The Rocket Files" [on *Guardians of the Galaxy*], *Cinefex* 139 (October 2014): 20–23.

56. Shilo McClean advances this position. Shilo McClean, *Digital Storytelling: The Narrative Power of Visual Effects in Film* (Cambridge: MIT Press, 2007). For this discourse as it manifests in reviews, see Roger Ebert, "Iron Man," rogerebert.com, June 1, 2008, www.rogerebert.com/reviews/iron-man-2008; Owen Gleiberman, "Iron Man: EW Review," *Entertainment Weekly*, June 16, 2012, http://ew.com/article/2012/06/16/iron-man-2; Scott Foundas, "Heath Ledger Peers into the Abyss in The Dark Knight," *Village Voice*, July 16, 2008, www.villagevoice.com/2008/07/16/heath-ledger-peers-into-the-abyss-in-the-dark-knight; Roger Ebert, "No Joke, Batman," [on The Dark Knight], rogerebert.com, July 16, 2008, www.rogerebert.com/reviews/the-dark-knight-2008.

57. For example, see the Reddit thread "Is the MCUs CGI getting worse?," Reddit, www.reddit.com/r/marvelstudios/comments/8jck7i/is_the_mcus_cgi_getting_worse.

58. Darryn King, "*Star Wars* Sound Architect Ben Burtt Finds Himself in the Outer Rim," *Vanity Fair*, December 15, 2017, www.vanityfair.com/hollywood/2017/12/ben-burtt-star-wars-sound.

59. See, for example, Gowanlock, *Animating Unpredictable Effects*.

60. Pierson, *Special Effects: Still in Search of Wonder*; Albert La Valley, "Traditions of Trickery: The Role of Special Effects in the Science Fiction Film," *Shadows of the Magic Lamp: Fantasy and Science Fiction in Film* (1985): 141–158, and Richard Maltby and Ian Craven, *Hollywood Cinema: An Introduction* (Hoboken: Blackwell, 1995).

61. Rehak, *More Than Meets the Eye*.

62. David Cohen, "'Pacific Rim' Visual Effects Get Operatic Twist," *Variety*, May 29, 2013, https://variety.com/2013/film/news/pacific-rim-visual-effects-get-operatic-twist-1200488753.

63. Even if that image of the business does not always translate to good stable jobs and enriching careers, as discussed in chapter 1.

Conclusion

Epigraph: The Walt Disney Company, "Disney to Acquire Lucasfilm," October 30, 2012, www.youtube.com/watch?v=QIkqX5fG_tA&feature=emb_title.

1. Elsaesser, King, and Horvath, *The Last Great American Picture Show*.

2. Maya Montañez Smukler, *Liberating Hollywood: Women Directors and the Feminist Reform of 1970s American Cinema* (New Brunswick: Rutgers University Press, 2018). See also the "Women and New Hollywood" international conference at Maynooth University, Ireland, May 29–30, 2018, organized by Aaron Hunter and Martha Shearer, and Philis M. Barragán Goetz, "Breaking Away from Reverence and Rape: The AFI Directing Workshop for Women, Feminism, and the Politics of the Accidental Archive," *The Moving Image: The Journal of the Association of Moving Image Archivists*, vol. 15, no. 2 (Fall 2015), 50–371.

3. Peter Biskind, *Easy Riders, Raging Bulls: How the Sex-Drugs-and Rock'N Roll Generation Saved Hollywood* (New York: Simon and Schuster, 1999).

4. Elise Moore, "Elaine May's Male Gaze," issue 75, *BW/DR*.com, September 2019. Bérénice Reynauld, "For Wanda," in Elsaesser, King, and Horvath, *The Last Great American Picture Show*; Elena Gorfinkel, "Wanda's Slowness Enduring Insignificance," in *On Women's Films: Across Worlds and Generations* (London: Bloomsbury Academic, 2019), 27–48.

5. Marc Graser, "Disney Buys Lucasfilm, New 'Star Wars' Planned," *Variety*, October 30, 2012, https://variety.com/2012/film/news/disney-buys-lucasfilm-new -star-wars-planned-1118061434.

6. Christopher Palmeri and Emily Chang, "Star Wars Movies Will Take a Break After Episode IX, Disney Says," Bloomberg.com, April 11, 2019, www.bloomberg .com/news/articles/2019-04-12/star-wars-movies-will-take-a-break-after-episode-ix -disney-says.

7. Adam B. Vary, "How Disney and Lucasfilm Are Remaking Star Wars in the Image of Marvel Studios," *Variety*, December 19, 2020, https://variety.com/2020/tv /news/disney-star-wars-marvel-studios-1234866986.

8. Pete Hammond, "'The Mandalorian's' Jon Favreau & Dave Filoni on Bringing 'Star Wars' to TV and Scoring 15 Emmy Nominations," Deadline.com, August 14, 2020, https://deadline.com/video/the-mandalorian-jon-favreau-dave-filoni-emmys -disney.

9. Duncan, "Iron Clad," 61; Jody Duncan, "Zathura," *Cinefex* 105 (April 2006): 23.

10. Jody Duncan, "As Geeky as It Gets," *Cinefex* 169 (February 2020): 102; Kevin H. Martin, "Miniature Work Highlights Hybrid Approach to The Mandalorian Vfx," VFXVoice, April 14, 2020, www.vfxvoice.com/miniature-work-highlights-hybrid -approach-to-the-mandalorian-vfx.

11. Duncan, "As Geeky as It Gets," 101 and 105.

12. In rear-screen projection, prefilmed footage is projected onto large reflective screens behind the actors (or in front of the actors, in the case of front projection).

13. Duncan, "As Geeky as It Gets," 97.

14. It is also worth noting that although the Duncan *Cinefex* article "As Geeky as It Gets" strongly implies ILM invented this "virtual production" volume technology, it did not. Although not exactly the same technology, large-scale LED screens had been used in place of bluescreen backgrounds in such non-ILM productions as *Oblivion* (2013, largely Pixomondo and Digital Domain) and *Gravity* (2013, largely Framestore), and game engines had been used previously to a limited degree in *The*

Jungle Book (2016, largely MPC) and *Independence Day 2* (2017, fifteen-plus effects companies). It is generally held that Rob Legato, visual effects supervisor on *The Jungle Book* and *The Lion King*—who has never worked at ILM—deserves initial credit for his innovations with virtual production on his work at Digital Domain. He especially credits *Titanic* and *Avatar*, as well as *The Aviator* (2004) and *Hugo* (2011), with introducing him to game engines for more elaborate uses in *Jungle Book* and *Lion King*, where he introduced the technique to Favreau, who then took it to ILM.

Other companies worked on *The Mandalorian* besides ILM, but most are frequent outsource partners such as Hybride of Montreal and Base FX of Beijing. Pixomondo, Image Engine, Important Looking Pirates, MPC El Ranchito, and Ghost also delivered shots. Duncan, "As Geeky as It Gets," 100.

15. See Kirsten Howard, "Star Wars Fans React to The Mandalorian Season 2 Finale," DenofGeek.com, December 18, 2020; Andrea Towers, "'Mandalorian' Fans Are Losing Their Minds Because THIS 'Star Wars' Character Just Showed Up," The Wrap.com, December 4, 2020; Allie Hayes, "Chapter 13 Of 'The Mandalorian' Is Here And Fans Are Positively Losing Their Minds," BuzzFeed.com, November 27, 2020, www.buzzfeed.com/alliehayes/chapter-13-of-the-mandalorian-is-here-and-fans -are.

Bibliography

Abrams, Rachel. "Rhythm & Hues Seeks Coin for Int'l Expansion." *Variety*, October 11, 2012.

Acland, Charles. *American Blockbuster: Movies, Technology, and Wonder*. Durham: Duke University Press, 2020.

———. "An Empire of Pixels: Canadian Cultural Enterprise in the Digital Effects Industry." In *Reading between the Borderlines: Cultural Production and Consumption across the 49th Parallel*, edited by Gillian Roberts, 143–170. Montreal: McGill-Queens University Press, 2018.

Aftab, Kaleem. "Stephen Chow: Hong Kong Hustler." *The Independent*, July 9, 2013.

Allison, Tanine. "Blackface, *Happy Feet*: The Politics of Race in Motion Capture and Animation." In *Special Effects: New Histories/Theories/Contexts*, edited by Dan North, Bob Rehak, and Michael S. Duffy, 114–126. London: Bloomsbury Publishing, 2015.

Anderson, Soren. "'Warcraft': Orcs and Humans Battle in Cheesy-CG Land." *Seattle Times*, June 9, 2016.

Austen, Ian. "A Galaxy Far, Far Away Is Becoming Fully Digital." *New York Times*, May 25, 2000.

Bailo, Tino. *Grand Design: Hollywood as a Modern Business Enterprise, 1930–1939*. Vol. 5. Berkeley: University of California Press, 1995.

Banks, Miranda J. "The Picket Line Online: Creative Labor, Digital Activism, and the 2007–2008 Writers Guild of America Strike." *Popular Communication* 8, no. 1 (2010): 20–33.

Barraclough, Leo. "Industrial Light and Magic Opens R&D Division in London." *Variety*, October 15, 2014.

Bay, Michael. "Digital Domain." Michael Bay website. www.michaelbay.com.

Beck, Jay, and Vanessa Theme Ament. "The New Hollywood, 1981–1999." In *Sound: Dialogue, Music and Effects*, edited by Kathryn Kalinak, 107–132. New Brunswick: Rutgers University Press, 2015.

Beck, Jerry. "Weta Evolves into Global Giant." *Variety*, November 13, 2006.

Bell, David Christopher. "6 Reasons Modern Movie CGI Looks Surprisingly Crappy." cracked.com, May 12, 2015.

Belton, John. "Digital Cinema: A False Revolution." *October* 100 (2002): 98–114.

Bennett, James, and Niki Strange, eds. *Media Independence: Working with Freedom or Working for Free?* New York: Routledge, 2015.

Berlatsky, Noah. "Infinity War's Thanos Proves CGI Supervillains Are a Terrible Idea." The Verge, March 16, 2018.

Bhushan, Nyay. "DD, PentaMedia of India in Pic Pact." *Hollywood Reporter*, March 15, 2000.

———. "Frameflow in Sony's Imageworks Fold." *Hollywood Reporter*, February 22, 2007.

Bird, Katie. "Updated! Lens Flare, Indexicality, and J. J. Abrams." Special Affects. www.fsgso.pitt.edu.

Biskind, Peter. *Easy Riders, Raging Bulls: How the Sex-Drugs-and Rock'N Roll Generation Saved Hollywood*. New York: Simon and Schuster, 1999.

Bizony, Piers. *Digital Domain: The Leading Edge of Digital Effects*. New York: Watson-Guptill Publishing, 2001.

Block, Alex Ben. "WETA Physics." *Hollywood Reporter*, November 9, 2009.

Bode, Lisa. *Making Believe: Screen Performance and Special Effects in Popular Cinema*. New Brunswick: Rutgers University Press, 2017.

Bollinger, Kristen Elisabeth. "A New Hope for Copyright: The U.K. Supreme Court Ruling in *Lucasfilm Ltd. v. Ainsworth* and Why Congress Should Follow Suit." *Journal of Intellectual Property Law* 20, no. 1 (Fall 2012): 87–119.

Bordwell, David. *The Way Hollywood Tells It: Story and Style in Modern Movies*. Berkeley: University of California Press, 2006.

Bordwell, David, Janet Staiger, and Kristin Thompson. *The Classical Hollywood Cinema: Film Style & Mode of Production to 1960*. New York: Columbia University Press, 1985.

"Boss Man Edlund Shutters f/x House." *Wall Street Journal*, March 19, 1998.

Bredow, Rob, and Ron Howard. *Industrial Light & Magic Presents: Making Solo: A Star Wars Story*. New York: Abrams, 2019.

British Columbia. "Ministry of Finance." www.sbr.gov.bc.ca.

British Film Commission. "Film Tax Relief." britishfilmcommission.org.uk.

Brodie, Evelyn. "Innovation: Magic Goes to Market." *Independent* (London,), April 25, 1993.

Brodie, Patrick. "*Star Wars* and the Production and Circulation of Culture Along Ireland's Wild Atlantic Way." *Journal of Popular Culture* 53, no. 3 (June 2020): 667–695.

Brooker, Will. *Using the Force: Creativity, Community and Star Wars Fans*. London: Bloomsbury Publishing, 2002.

Brooks, Nancy Rivera. "Mouse of Babes." *Los Angeles Times*, July 10, 1996.

Brown, Colin. "New SW Pic May Follow JEDI Launch." *Screen International*, April 16, 1993.

Brown, Douglas. "To Disney Infinity and Beyond—Star Wars Videogames Before and After the Lucasarts Acquisition." In *Disney's Star Wars: Forces of Production and Promotion*, edited by William Procter and Richard McCulloch, 123–135. Iowa City: University of Iowa Press, 2019.

Brownstein, Bill. "The Making of Jurassic Park Offers Insights into Movie Magic." *Gazette* (Montreal, Quebec), September 20, 1993.

Bulbek, Pip. "The Jackson Effect." *Hollywood Reporter*, November 25, 2011.

Buckland, Warren. "Between Science Fact and Science Fiction: Spielberg's Digital Dinosaurs, Possible Worlds, and the New Aesthetic Realism." *Screen* 40, no. 2 (1999): 177–192.

Bulut, Ergin. "Glamor Above, Precarity Below: Immaterial Labor in the Video Game Industry." *Critical Studies in Media Communication* 32, no. 3 (June 2015): 193–207.

———. *A Precarious Game: The Illusion of Dream Jobs in the Video Game Industry.* Ithaca: Cornell University Press, 2020.

Burr, Ty. "Review: Launch of "'Star Wars: The Force Awakens' Takes the Faithful Full Circle." *Boston Globe*, December 15, 2015.

Byrge, Duane. "Kay, Jablov [sic] Lead ILM Unit." *Hollywood Reporter*, March 12, 1986.

Calder, Peter. "Workshop Taps Local Talents." *Variety*, December 16, 2002.

Caldwell, John Thornton. *Production Culture: Industrial Reflexivity and Critical Practice in Film and Television.* Durham: Duke University Press, 2008.

Carlson, Wayne. *History of Computer Graphics and Animation.* Columbus: Ohio State University Pressbooks, c. 2013.

Carpenter, Phil. "Commercial Spot: Cola Bears." *Cinefex* 60 (December 1994): 27–28.

Carver, Benedict. "Ralston to Helm Jumanji 2." *Variety*, June 3, 1999.

Casano, Ann. "Really Bad CGI That You Have to See to Believe." Ranker, September 3, 2020.

Catmull, Edwin. *Creativity, Inc.* New York: Random House, 2014.

Cavell, Stanley. *The World Viewed: Reflections on the Ontology of Film.* Cambridge: Harvard University Press, 1979.

Champlin, Charles. *George Lucas: The Creative Impulse: Lucasfilm's First Twenty-five Years.* New York: Harry N. Abrams, 1997.

Chapain, Caroline, and Krzysztof Stachowiak, "Innovation Dynamic in the Film Industry: The Example of the Soho Cluster in London." In *Creative Industries in Europe: Drivers of New Sectoral and Spatial Dynamics*, edited by Caroline Chapain and Tadeusz Stryjakiewicz, 65–94. New York: Springer, 2017.

Chase, Donald. "War of the Wizards." *American Film* 7, no. 8 (1982): 52–59.

Chow, Rey. *Entanglements, or Transmedial Thinking about Capture.* Durham: Duke University Press, 2012.

Chun, Wendy Hui Kyong. *Programmed Visions: Software and Memory.* Cambridge: MIT Press, 2011.

Chung, Hye Jean. *Media Heterotopias: Digital Effects and Material Labor in Global Film Production.* Durham: Duke University Press, 2018.

Cieply, Michael, and Brooks Barnes. "New Zealand Wants a Hollywood Put on Its Map." *New York Times*, November 24, 2012.

Clark, Charles. "The Moving Camera." *American Cinematographer* (June 1974): 688–689.

Clouzot, Claire. "The Morning of the Magician: George Lucas and *Star Wars* (1977)." In *George Lucas: Interviews*, edited by Sally Kline, 55–63. Jackson: University Press of Mississippi, 1999.

Cohen, David S. "Blockbusters Take Toll on F/X Shops." *Variety*, May 25, 2007.

———. "Building a Legacy." *Variety*, February 14, 2005.

———. "Can Ailing Fx House Fix Woes in Post?" *Variety*, September 12, 2012.

——. "DD Expands to Vancouver." *Variety*, October 6, 2009.

——. "Domain Expands to China." *Variety*, December 15, 2011.

——. "El Segundo-Based Company Sold as Layoffs Loom Around VFX Biz." *Variety*, March 29, 2013.

——. "F/X House in Taiwan Deals." *Variety*, January 2, 2012 [possibly 2010, smudged stamp].

——. "How to Spot the VFX Pro's Signature." *Variety*, January 11, 2011.

——. "Hues Hops to Canuck Shop." *Variety*, May 27, 2011.

——. "ILM at Center of VFX Storm." *Variety*, May 28, 2007.

——. "ILM Finds Beijing Base." *Variety*, May 24, 2012.

——. "Imageworks Looks to Rule F/x Field." *Variety*, June 17, 2009.

——. "Is the Force Still with Him?" *Variety*, February 13, 2005.

——. "It's Time to Fight the Fangs of Finance." *Variety*, October 11, 2012.

——. "Marvel Ups Victoria Alonso to Head of Physical Production." *Variety*, September 21, 2015.

——. "Offshore VFX: a Matter of Perspective." *Variety*, August 30, 2012.

——. "'Pacific Rim' Visual Effects Get Operatic Twist." *Variety*, May 29, 2013.

——. "Prana Wins Auction for Rhythm & Hues." *Variety*, March 28, 2013.

——. "R&H Hoping for Fast Exit from Bankruptcy." *Variety*, February 10, 2013.

——. "Rhythm & Hues Bankruptcy Reveals VFX Biz Crisis." *Variety*, February 12, 2013.

——. "'Spirit of Openness' ILM, Imageworks Tout Toon Software." *Variety*, August 10, 2011.

——. "'Star Wars,' 'Avengers' Spawn ILM London's Expansion." *Variety*, February 12, 2014.

——. "VFX Firm Is Now 'Well-Funded,' but Its Future in L.A. Is Clouded." *Variety*, July 29, 2013.

——. "'War' Is Hell for F/x Shops." *Variety*, May 22, 2006.

——. "'War of the Worlds': Blockbusters Take Toll on F/x Shops." *Variety*, May 25, 2007.

Cohen, David S., and Ben Fritz. "Digital Domain Docks with Bay." *Variety*, May 16, 2006.

Cohen, Patricia. "Perfecting Animation, Via Science." *New York Times*, December 30, 2010.

Cook, David A. *Lost Illusions: American Cinema in the Shadow of Watergate and Vietnam, 1970–1979*. Vol. 9. Berkeley: University of California Press, 2002.

Corliss, Richard. "They Put the ILM in Film." *Time*, April 13, 1992.

"Corrections." *Variety*, June 16, 2000.

Courtois, Charlotte. "Jouer Dans L'Espace Urbain Capitaliste De Disneyland Avec the Secret of Monkey Island: Monkey Island 1 & 2." *Géographie & Cultures*, no. 109 (March 2019): 99–118.

Cowles, Dan. "Startup Memories—The Beginning of Photoshop." Produced by Bob Donlon. 2011. Video, 17:49.

Crabtree, Sheigh. "Bay Master of Domain in VFX Stunner." *Hollywood Reporter*, May 16, 2006.

———. "DD Lays Off 17, Adds Motion Graphics Dept." *Hollywood Reporter*, April 3, 2001.

———. "DD Nukes Market." *Hollywood Reporter*, July 12, 2002.

———. "ILM Aims to Unify Digital Imaging." *Hollywood Reporter*, January 22, 2003.

Crafton, Donald. *The Talkies: American Cinema's Transition to Sound, 1926–1931*. Vol. 4. Berkeley: University of California Press, 1999.

Cubitt, Sean. *Digital Aesthetics*. London: Sage, 1998.

———. "Le Réel, c'est l'impossible: The Sublime Time of Special Effects." *Screen* 40, no. 2 (Summer 1999): 123–130.

Curtin, Michael, and John Vanderhoef. "A Vanishing Piece of the Pi: The Globalization of Visual Effects Labor." *Television & New Media* 16, no. 3 (2015): 219–239.

Curtis, Bryan. "The Turn Against Digital Effects." *New Yorker*, January 20, 2016.

Dawtrey, Adam. "London's CG Houses Share Digital Wealth." *Variety*, November 10, 2008.

———. "Soho VFX Biz Arises from Potter's Spell." *Variety*, February 28, 2011.

Dayton, Susan. "Backyard Odyssey" [on *Honey, I Shrunk the Kids*]. *Cinefex* 41 (February 1990): 34–67.

De Peuter, Greig. "Creative Economy and Labor Precarity: A Contested Convergence." *Journal of Communication Inquiry* 35.4 (2011): 417–425.

della Cava, Marco R. "Do You Believe in Magic? For 'Eragon,' Creating a Realistic Dragon Was a Tricky Task." *Washington Post*, December 13, 2006.

———. "Lucas: The Titan of Tech." *USA Today*, February 23, 2001.

Denson, Shane. "Crazy Cameras, Discorrelated Images, and the Post-Perceptual Mediation of Post-Cinematic Affect." In *Perspectives on Post-Cinema: An Introduction*, edited by Shane Denson and Julia Leyda, 193–233. Sussex, UK: Reframe Books, 2016.

———. *Discorrelated Images*. Durham: Duke University Press, 2020.

Derro, Marc. "Video Beat: Midair Morphing." *Cinefex* 58 (June 1994): 29.

Desowitz, Bill. "Alfonso Cuarón's Black-and-White 'Roma' Was a Cinematic Master Stroke." Indiewire, November 16, 2018.

———. "'Spider-Man Homecoming': How Jon Watts Channeled John Hughes." indiewire.com, July 14, 2017.

DiOrio, Carl. "DD, K-L get German Effects House." *Hollywood Reporter*, December 18, 1998.

———. "Ralston Re-ups, Claims 'Island.'" *Hollywood Reporter*, December 18, 1998.

———. "Rhythm & Hues Effect Layoffs." *Hollywood Reporter*, April 12, 1996.

———. "Sony Fx Gets Its Own Place." *Hollywood Reporter*, August 31, 1996.

———. "Tech Talk." *Hollywood Reporter*, June 4, 1998.

———. "THR E-mail." *Hollywood Reporter*, June 8, 1998.

———. "Titanic a Wash for DD Fxers." *Hollywood Reporter*, May 23, 1997.

———. "WB's Sarnoff Morphs to Sony." *Hollywood Reporter*, March 5, 1997.

DiOrio, Carl, and Josh Chetwynd. "Cameron Sinks Board Role at DD." *Hollywood Reporter*, August 20, 1998.

Donahue, Ann. "Digital Piracy: With 'Caribbean' and 4 Other Effects Noms, Could This Be ILM's Year?" *Variety*, January 8, 2004.

Dowd, A. A. "There's Nothing Immersive (or Fun) About This World of *Warcraft*." AVClub.com, June 8, 2016.

Dubner, Stephen J. "No Hollywood Ending for the Visual-Effects Industry." Produced by Greg Rosalsky. Freakonomics, February 22, 2017. Podcast, MP3 audio, 59:42.

Duncan, Jody. "As Geeky as it Gets." *Cinefex* 169 (February 2020): 101.

———. "Batman Grounded." *Cinefex* 115 (October 2008): 62–88.

———. "The Beauty in the Beasts." *Cinefex* 55 (August 1993): 42–95.

———. "Captain's Orders." *Cinefex* 138 (July 2014): 28–49.

———. "From Zero to Hero" [on *The Mask*]. *Cinefex* 60 (December 1994): 46–69.

———. "Iron Clad." *Cinefex* 122 (July 2010): 32–61.

———. "Joe Bauer on *Zathura*." *Cinefex* 105 (April 2006): 23–28.

———. "The Making of a Rockbuster" [on *The Flintstones*]. *Cinefex* 58 (June 1994): 34–65.

———. "The Man in the Iron Mask." *Cinefex* 114 (July 2008): 58–83.

———. "MCU: The Big Bang." *Cinefex* 158 (April 2018): 26–51.

———. "A Once and Future War." *Cinefex* 47 (August 1991): 4–59.

———. "Q&A: Victoria Alonso." *Cinefex* 158 (April 2018): 17–23.

———. "The Rocket Files" [on *Guardians of the Galaxy*]. *Cinefex* 139 (October 2014): 12–38.

———. "Star Wars II: Attack of the Clones: Love and War." *Cinefex* 90 (July 2002): 60–119.

———. "The Unusual Birth of Benjamin Button." *Cinefex* 116 (January 2009): 70–99, 188.

———. "Zathura." *Cinefex* 105 (April 2006): 23.

Duncan, Jody, Kevin H. Martin, and Mark Cotta Vaz. "Heroes' Journey." *Cinefex* 78 (July 1999): 74–145.

Duncan Shannon, Jody. "A Dark and Stormy Knight" [on *Batman*]. *Cinefex* 41 (February 1990): 4–33.

Ebert, Roger. "Iron Man." rogerebert.com, June 1, 2008.

———. "No Joke, Batman [on *The Dark Knight*]." rogerebert.com, July 16, 2008.

"Edlund Creates Species f/x." *Variety*, October 11, 1994.

Edlund, Richard. "Special Visual Effects for *Empire*." *American Cinematographer* (June 1980): 552.

Edwards, Graham. "Afrofuture: Black Panther." *Cinefex* 158 (April 2018): 54–82.

———. "The Marvel Effect." *Cinefex* 158 (April 2018): 84–98.

———. "Symphony of Colors: *Valerian and the City of a Thousand Planets*." *Cinefex* 154 (August 2017): 78–98.

Edwards, Phil. "We've Reached Peak Lens Flare. Here's How It Started." *Vox*, March 28, 2016. Video, 4:24.

Egan, Jack. "How Ross Came to Rule the Roost." *Variety*, July 28, 2003.

Eisenberg, Adam. "Ghostbusters Revisited" [on *Ghostbusters 2*]. *Cinefex* 40 (November 1989): 4–45.

Eisenstein, Sergei. *On Disney*. Edited by Jay Leyda. London: Methuen, 1986.

Ellenshaw, Harrison. "Creating Matte Paintings for EMPIRE." *American Cinematographer* (June 1980): 582–586.

Eller, Claudia. "Sony Pictures Seeks Buyer for Half of Digital Unit." *Los Angeles Times*, November 1, 2007.

Elliott, David. "Digitalize Me Hearties, Digitalize! It Took More Than 250 Wizards to Create the Effects for 'Pirates of the Caribbean: At World's End.'" *San Diego Union-Tribune*, May 27, 2007.

Elliott, Stuart. "The Media Business: Advertising; Coke Takes a Bearish Approach to Its New Winter Campaign." *New York Times*, July 7, 1993.

Elsaesser, Thomas. "The Blockbuster: Everything Connects, but not Anything Goes." In *The End of Cinema as We Know It: American Film in the Nineties*, edited by J. Lewis, 11–22. New York: New York University Press, 2002.

Elsaesser, Thomas, Noel King, and Alexander Horwath. *The Last Great American Picture Show: New Hollywood Cinema in the 1970s*. Amsterdam: Amsterdam University Press, 2004.

"Fade to Black." *Variety*, August 27, 1997.

Failes, Ian. "The Tech of 'Terminator 2'—An Oral History." vfxblog.com, August 23, 2017.

———. "Viewpaint: ILM's Secret Weapon on *Jurassic Park*." Vfxblog.com, 2018.

Faludi, Susan. *The Terror Dream: Fear and Fantasy in Post-9/11 America*. New York: Macmillan, 2007.

Farici, Devin. "The Marvel Creative Committee is Over." birth.movies.death.com, September 2, 2015.

Favreau, Jon. "Cool iPad App for Digital Version of *Cinefex* Magazine."

———. Foreword to *Industrial Light & Magic: The Art of Innovation*, by Pamela Glintenkamp. New York: Abrams, 2011.

Filmworks Staff. "Rhythm & Hues: Special Effects Powerhouse Offers Insight into VFX Industry." Filmworks, August 15, 2012.

Fisher, Lawrence M. "How to Manage Creative People: The Case of Industrial Light and Magic." strategy+business.com, April 1, 1997.

Flagen, Are. "Layers: Looking at Photography and Photoshop." *Afterimage* 30, no. 1 (2002): 10–12.

Flynn, Gillian. "Men and Myth." *Entertainment Weekly*, May 14, 2004.

Fordham, Joe. "God of Thunder." *Cinefex* 126 (July 2011): 14–38.

———. "*The Hulk*: Green Destiny." *Cinefex* 94 (July 2003): 74–126.

———. "A New Enterprise." *Cinefex* 118 (July 2009): 40–71.

———. "Starting Over: Batman Begins." *Cinefex* 103 (October 2005): 103–112, 118.

Foster, Frank. *The Story of Computer Graphics*. Frank Foster Films, 1999. Video, 1:32:17.

Foundas, Scott. "Heath Ledger Peers into the Abyss in The Dark Knight." *Village Voice*, July 16, 2008.

Frater, Patrick. "10 Reasons Why 'Warcraft' Opened Six Times Bigger in China Than in the U.S." *Variety*, June 13, 2016.

———. "China Is the New Hollywood, Says James Schamus." *Variety*, April 17, 2016.

———. "Digital Domain Holdings Reports $64 Million in Losses." *Variety*, March 30, 2017.

———. "Digital Domain Remains on the Sick List." *Variety*, September 1, 2014.

———. "Korea's Dexter Sets Up Beijing VFX Unit." *Variety*, November 28, 2013.

———. "Koreans Hope F/X Make a Monster Impression." *Variety*, November 17, 2005.

———. "'The Mermaid' Becomes Highest-Grossing Film Ever in China." *Variety*, February 22, 2016.

———. "Sony Flows into India F/X." *Variety*, February 21, 2007.

———. "'Wolf Warriors II' Takes All-Time China Box Office Record." *Variety*, August 7, 2017.

Frei, Vincent. "*The Avengers*: Jeff White—VFX Supervisor ILM." artofvfx.com, May 22, 2012.

———. "The Great Wall: Samir Hoon, VFX Supervisor—Industrial Light & Magic." artofVFX.com, March 8, 2017.

———. "Spider-Man—Homecoming: Theodore Bialek." artofvfx.com, July 26, 2017.

———. "Star Wars Episode VII—The Force Awakens: Roger Guyett." artofvfx.com, February 29. 2016.

Fritz, Ben. "Hollywood Visual-Effects Firms Fade to Black." *Wall Street Journal*, February 23, 2013.

Galloway, Alexander R. *The Interface Effect*. Cambridge: Polity, 2012.

Geagan-Breiner, Meredith, and Kyle Desiderio. "How Marvel Movies are Actually Created Years Before Production Begins." Insider.com. January 29, 2021.

"Ghostly Past: *Roma*." *British Cinematographer* 91 (January 2019).

Giardina, Carolyn. "California VFX Houses Fight to Stay Alive." *Hollywood Reporter*, February 4, 2011.

———. "How 'Roma's' Visual Effects Team Created That Intense Ocean Sequence." *Hollywood Reporter*, December 18, 2018.

———. "How 'The Revenant's' VFX Team Brought that Bear to Life." *Hollywood Reporter*, February 3, 2016.

———. "Revealing 'Rhythm & Hues: Life After Pi' Doc Exposes Grief, Anger and Troubled Business." *Hollywood Reporter*, February 26, 2014.

———. "Rhythm & Hues Sets Up Malaysian Shop." *Hollywood* Reporter, May 22, 2008.

Glieberman, Owen. "'Clash of the Titans': Are Special Effects Less Special in the CGI Era?" *Entertainment Weekly*, April 1, 2010.

———. "Iron Man: EW Review." *Entertainment Weekly*, June 16, 2012.

Goh, Gabey. "Rhythm & Hues Malaysia to Fly Solo Under New Identity." Digital News Asia, May 23, 2013.

Golby, Joel. "Worse than Cats? The Biggest CGI Disasters in Cinema." *Guardian*, July 19, 2019.

Goldberg, Michael. "Fire in the Valley." *Wired*, January 1, 1994.

Goldsmith, Ben, Susan Ward, and Tom O'Reagan. *Local Hollywood: Global Film Production and the Gold Coast*. Brisbane: University of Queensland Press, 2010.

Goodfellow, Kris. "Mayday! Mayday! We're Leaking Visuals! A Shakeout of the Special Effects Houses." *New York Times*, September 29, 1997.

Gorfinkel, Elena. "Wanda's Slowness Enduring Insignificance." In *On Women's*

Films: Across Worlds and Generations, 27–48. London: Bloomsbury Academic, 2019.

Gowanlock, Jordan. *Animating Unpredictable Effects: Nonlinearity in Hollywood's R&D Complex*. London: Palgrave Macmillan, 2021.

———. "A History of Simulation 'FX': How Dynamic Simulation Tools See and Manage the World." PhD diss., Concordia University, 2017.

———. "Simulation FX: Cinema and the R&D Complex." PhD diss., Concordia University, 2017.

Graser, Marc. "CG Shops Set to Tackle Toon Territory." *Variety*, February 28, 2002.

———. "Disney Buys LucasFilm, New 'Star Wars' Planned." *Variety*, October 30, 2012.

———. "F/x Heavy Tentpoles are Coming to Light." *Variety*, August 16, 2002.

———. "Fox to Sell Visual f/x Division to R&H." *Variety*, March 4, 1999.

———. "ILM Will Make Magic for Hulk, Next Potter." *Variety*, October 10, 2001.

———. "Meeper Intros Sony CG Toon Unit." *Variety*, February 28, 2002.

———. "Rhythm & Hues Drums up Own Slate." *Variety*, December 15, 1999.

———. "Sony Imageworks Taps F/xers Legato, Thomas." *Variety*, June 21, 1999.

———. "Title Graphics Enter Digital's Domain." *Variety*, August 12, 2002.

Groves, Martha. "Digital Yoda: George Lucas at Entertainment's High Tech Edge." *Los Angeles Times*, June 4, 1995.

Guenette, Robert. "The Making of Star Wars . . . as told by C-3PO and R2-D2." ABC, September 16, 1977. Video, 49:01.

Gurevitch, Leon. "Cinema Designed: Visual Effects Software and the Emergence of the Engineered Spectacle." In *Post-Cinema: Theorizing 21st-Century Film*, edited by Shane Denson and Julia Leyda, 270–296. Falmer: Reframe Books, 2016.

———. "The Straw That Broke the Tiger's Back? Skilled Labor, Social Networks and Protest in the Digital Workshops of the World." In *The Routledge Companion to Labor and Media*, edited by Richard Maxwell, 190–201. New York: Routledge, 2015.

Halbfinger, David M., and Andrew Ross Sorkin. "Sony Said to Be Pondering Partial Sale of Movie Units." *New York Times*, October 31, 2007.

Halberstam, Judith, and Ira Livingston, eds. *Posthuman Bodies*. Bloomington: Indiana University Press, 1995.

Halligan, Fionnuala. "Prepare for Battle." *Screen Intl*, July 15–28, 2005.

Hammond, Pete. "'The Mandalorian's' Jon Favreau & Dave Filoni on Bringing 'Star Wars' to TV and Scoring 15 Emmy Nominations." Deadline.com, August 14, 2020.

Hansen, Miriam Bratu. "The Mass Production of the Senses: Classical Cinema as Vernacular Modernism." In *Disciplining Modernism*, edited by Pamela L. Caughie, 242–258. London: Palgrave Macmillan, 2009.

Harrington, Clifford. "Filming with Filmorama." *American Cinematographer* (December 1955): 718–719.

Harris, Mark. "The Day the Movies Died." *GQ*, February 10, 2011.

Harrison, Rebecca. *The Empire Strikes Back*. London: British Film Institute, 2020.

Hayes, Allie. "Chapter 13 Of 'The Mandalorian' Is Here And Fans Are Positively Losing Their Minds." BuzzFeed.com, November 27, 2020.

Heather, Ben. "A Heavenly Trajectory: 20 Years of Weta." Stuff.co.nz, October 4, 2014.

Hodge, James J. *Sensations of History: Animation and New Media Art.* Vol. 57. Minneapolis: University of Minnesota Press, 2019.

Holben, Jay. "Conquering New Worlds." *American Cinematographer* (January 2010): 35–47.

———. "Robots Run Rampant." *American Cinematographer* (August 2009): 54–57.

Hollywood Reporter Staff. "Rushes." *Hollywood Reporter*, October 23, 1997.

Holmes, Nathan. *Welcome to Fear City: Crime Film, Crisis, and the Urban Imagination.* Albany: SUNY Press, 2019.

Holt, Jennifer, and Alisa Perren, eds. *Media Industries: History, Theory, and Method.* Hoboken: John Wiley & Sons, 2011.

Holt, Nathalia. "The Women Behind the Force." *New York Times*, February 12, 2017.

Howard, Kirsten. "Star Wars Fans React to The Mandalorian Season 2 Finale." DenofGeek.com, December 18, 2020.

Howie, Kahn, and Dan Winters, "Inside the Magic Factory." *Wired*, June 2015.

Hubbard, Janice. "Commercial Spot: Simian Simulation." *Cinefex* 52 (November 1992): 9–10.

Hutchinson, Corey. "The MCU Has a CGI Problem." Screenrant.com, February 19, 2018.

Idelson, Karen. "DD Pacts with Reliance: Post Partners Clock in with Global Plan." July 12, 2011.

Itzkoff, Dave. "How 'Rogue One' Brought Back Familiar Faces." *New York Times*, December 27, 2016.

———. "Jar Jar Binks, Coming at You in 3-D." *New York Times*, September 30, 2010.

———. "A Method Performance, All Right." *New York Times*, January 4, 2009.

Iwerks, Leslie. "Industrial Light & Magic: Creating the Impossible." Starz Encore, 2010. Video, 59:31.

Jacobs, Julia. "'Call of the Wild' Casts a Digital Star. Is He a Good Dog?" *New York Times*, February 23, 2020.

Jenkins, Henry. *Convergence Culture: Where Old and New Media Collide.* New York: New York University Press, 2006.

Jesser, Jody Duncan. "The Avengers Initiative." *Cinefex* 130 (July 2012): 64–91.

Johnson, Derek. "Cinematic Destiny: Marvel Studios and the Trade Stories of Industrial Convergence." *Cinema Journal* 52, no. 1 (2012): 1–24.

Johnson, Ted. "Visual-Effects Artists Urge Tariffs to Fight Runaway Production." *Variety*, August 6, 2014.

Johnston, Andrew. "The Rise of Computer-Generated Imagery, 1965–1989." In *Animation*, edited by Scott Curtis, 209–243. New Brunswick: Rutgers University Press, 2019.

Jones, Nick. "Seamless Composites? VFX Breakdowns and Digital Labour." YouTube, April 17, 2021. Video, 8:24.

———. *Spaces Mapped and Monstrous: Digital 3D Cinema and Visual Culture.* New York: Columbia University Press, 2020.

Kainz, Florian, Rod Bogart, Piotr Stanczyk, and Peter Hillman. *Technical Introduction to OpenEXR.* November 5, 2013.

Kaplan, David. "Believe in Magic." *Newsweek,* June 14, 1993.

———. "Secret Lair of the Jedi, Grain, and Green Slimers." *New York Times,* July 2, 1989.

Kaplan, David A. "Lights! Action! Disk Drives!" *Newsweek,* July 21, 1991.

Karon, Paul. "Domain Shrinking: F/X House Makes 54 Staffers Disappear." *Variety,* October 9, 1997.

———. "Sony Digital f/x Shop Gets a 'Hollow' Deal." *Variety,* July 20, 1998.

Kaufman, Debra. "Effects in the Vertical Realm" [on *Cliffhanger*]. *Cinefex* 54 (May 1993): 30–53.

Keating, Patrick. "What Does It Mean to Say That Cinematography Is Like Painting with Light?" In *Transnational Cinematography Studies,* edited by Lindsay Coleman, Daisuke Miyao, and Roberto Schaefer, 97–115. Lanham, MD: Lexington Books, 2017.

Keegan, Cáel M. *Lana and Lilly Wachowski.* Champaign: University of Illinois Press, 2018.

Keegan, Rebecca. "Hollywood's VFX Shops: Trouble in Boom Times." *Time,* May 21, 2010.

Keeling, Kara. *Queer Times, Black Futures.* New York: New York University Press, 2019.

Keil, Charles, and Kristen Whissel, eds. *Editings and Special/Visual Effects: Behind the Silver Screen.* New Brunswick: Rutgers University Press/Academy of Motion Picture Arts and Sciences, 2016.

Kenigsberg, Ben. "Tom Cruise's Most Dangerous Stunts in 'Mission: Impossible.'" *New York Times,* July 30, 2018.

Kimberlin, Bill. *Inside the Star Wars Empire: A Memoir.* Guilford, CT: Rowman & Littlefield, 2018.

King, Darryn. "*Star Wars* Sound Architect Ben Burtt Finds Himself in the Outer Rim." *Vanity Fair,* December 15, 2017.

King, Geoff. *Spectacular Narratives: Hollywood in the Age of the Blockbuster.* London: I. B. Tauris, 2000.

King, Thomas R. "The Hottest Movies Have the Coolest Effects." *Wall Street Journal,* November 14, 1994.

Klein, Norman. *The Vatican to Vegas: A History of Special Effects.* New York: The New Press, 2004.

Kline, Sally, ed. 1999. *George Lucas: Interviews.* Jackson: University of Mississippi Press.

Klinger, Barbara. *Beyond the Multiplex: Cinema, New Technologies, and the Home.* Berkeley: University of California Press, 2006.

Kokas, Aynne. *Hollywood Made in China.* Berkeley: University of California Press, 2017.

Kotkin, Joel. "Grass-Roots Business; Norma Desmond Had It Wrong: The Picture Makers Got Small." *New York Times*, May 23, 1999.

Krämer, Peter. *The New Hollywood: From Bonnie and Clyde to Star Wars*. New York: Columbia University Press, 2006.

Kroll, John. "From *Star Wars* to *Star Wars*—The Story of Industrial Light & Magic." Fox, June 15, 1999. Video.

La Valley, Albert. "Traditions of Trickery: The Role of Special Effects in the Science Fiction Film." *Shadows of the Magic Lamp: Fantasy and Science Fiction in Film* (1985): 141–158.

Lacey, Nick. *Introduction to Film*. London: Macmillan International Higher Education, 2016.

Lastra, James. *Sound Technology and the American Cinema: Perception, Representation, Modernity*. New York: Columbia University Press, 2000.

Lattanzio, Ryan. "Here Is the One Real Shot in 'The Lion King' Remake," Indiewire.com, July 28, 2019.

Lenerz, Gerhard. "Hollywood: Jurassic Park." sgistuff.net, November 12, 2019.

Lew, Julie. "Believe in Magic." *Newsweek*, June 14, 1993.

———. "FILM; Invisibility Is More Than Meets the Eye." *New York Times*, February 23, 1992.

———. "How to Make a Ghost." *Newsweek*, February 27, 1995.

Lightman, Herb. "Effects Photography for Empire: Interview with Dennis Muren." *American Cinematographer* (June 1980): 572–576.

———. "The Filming of Medium Cool." *American Cinematographer* (January 1970): 25–27.

Lodderhose, Diana. "Framestore Looks at Bigger Picture." *Variety*, January 17–23, 2011.

Lomax, Tara. "'Thank the Maker!': George Lucas, Lucasfilm, and the Legends of Transtextual Authorship across the Star Wars Franchise." In *Star Wars and the History of Transmedia Storytelling*, edited by Sean Guynes and Dan Hassler-Forest, 35–48. Amsterdam: Amsterdam University Press, 2017.

Loren, Christalene. "Video Beat: Deep Space Wormholes." *Cinefex* 55 (August 1993): 11–12.

Lydiate, Henry. "What Is Art? A Brief Review of International Judicial Interpretations of Art in the Light of the UK Supreme Court's 2011 Judgment in the *Star Wars* Case: *Lucasfilm Limited v. Ainsworth*." *Journal of International Entertainment & Media Law* 4, no. 2 (January 2012): 111–47.

Lyman, Rick. "Down to the Sea in Chips; Computers Open a Virtual World of Effects to Filmmakers." *New York Times*, June 20, 2000.

Mackenzie, Adrian. *Cutting Code: Software and Sociality*. Vol. 30. New York: Peter Lang, 2006.

Magid, Ron. "Cause and FX." *Hollywood Reporter*, December 3–9, 2002.

———. "Effects Team Brings Dinosaurs Back from Extinction." *American Cinematographer* (June 1993): 46–52.

———. "Imagining Middle Earth." *American Cinematographer*, December 2001, 60.

Magid, Ron, and David E. Williams. "New Zealand's New Digital Age." *American Cinematographer*, August 1996, 55–56.

Maison, Jordan. "Why People Can't Enjoy the VFX in the Star Wars Prequels." cinelinx.com, July 14, 2014.

Makinen, Julie. "With $150-million 'Great Wall,' Legendary Aims to Bridge U.S.-China Film Gap." *Los Angeles Times*, July 2, 2015.

Maltby, Richard. *Hollywood Cinema: An Introduction*. Hoboken: Blackwell Publishing, 2003.

Mandell, Paul. "Dennis Muren: First Effects Cameraman," *Cinéfantastique* 7, no. 1 (1978): 21–24.

———. "Tauntauns, Walkers, and Probots." *Cinefex* 3 (December 1980): 4–41.

Manovich, Lev. "Digital Cinema and the History of the Moving Image." In *Film Theory and Criticism: Introductory Readings 8th Edition*, edited by Leo Braudy and Marshall Cohen, 727–732. Oxford: Oxford University Press, 2016.

Manovich, Lev, Roger F. Malina, and Sean Cubitt. *The Language of New Media*. Cambridge: MIT Press, 2001.

Marchand, Francois. "Sony Pictures Imageworks Unveils New Vancouver Headquarters." *Vancouver Sun*, July 10, 2015.

Marriott, Michel. "Project Virtual Funk: The Digitizing of James Brown." *New York Times*, April 13, 2000.

Martin, Chase Bowen, and Mark Deuze. "The Independent Production of Culture: A Digital Games Case Study." *Games and Culture* 4, no. 3 (2009): 276–295.

Martin, Kevin H. "Life Neverlasting." *Cinefex* 52 (November 1992): 54–78.

———. "Miniature Work Highlights Hybrid Approach to the Mandalorian Vfx." VFXVoice, April 14, 2020.

Martinez, Ed. "Sky Wars." *Cinefex* 29 (February 1987): 52–67.

Marx, Andy. "ILM Plans More Light and Magic Tricks." *Variety*, December 16, 1993.

McCarthy, Michael. "Animated Cyber-Performers Take the Center Stage in Ads Special Effects Create Walking, Talking 'People.'" *USA TODAY*, June 2, 2000.

McClean, Shilo. *Digital Storytelling: The Narrative Power of Visual Effects in Film*. Cambridge: MIT Press, 2007.

McIntyre, Gina. "Hyperspace in Your Face; The 'Solo' Visual Effects Team Puts the Millennium Falcon Through Its Paces. It Proves to Be a Wild Ride." *Philadelphia Inquirer*, February 22, 2019.

McKercher, Catherine, and Vincent Mosco, eds. *Knowledge Workers in the Information Society*. Lanham, MD: Lexington Books, 2007.

McNary, Dave. "Animators Mull Union Offer." *Variety*, April 23, 2012.

Menne, Jeff. *Post-Fordist Cinema: Hollywood Auteurs and the Corporate Counterculture*. New York: Columbia University Press, 2019.

Michael, Charlie. *French Blockbusters: Cultural Politics of a Transnational Cinema*. Edinburgh: Edinburgh University Press, 2019.

Mihailova, Misha. "Virtually Unchanged: *The Lion King* (2019), Quantified Nostalgia, and Disney's Animated Denials." Unpublished paper presented at the Society of Cinema and Media Studies, 2021.

Miller, Toby, Nitin Govil, J. McMurrin, Richard Maxwell, and T. Wang, *Global Hollywood 2*. London: Bloomsbury Publishing, 2019.

Mitchell, Robert. "'Star Wars' Films 'A Gift for a VFX Company' as Industrial Light & Magic Opens London Studio." *Variety*, October 16, 2014.

———. "State of the Art Stays the Course in Soho." *Variety*, February 21, 2017.

Mittel, Jason. *Complex TV*. New York: New York University Press, 2015.

Moore, Elise. "Elaine May's Male Gaze." Issue 75, *BW/DR.com*, September 2019.

Mothersbaugh, Mark. "'Thor' [Ragnarok] Composer Knew Marvel Scores Sounded Similar, So He Decided to Change That." *Hollywood Reporter*, November 3, 2017.

Mulvey, Laura. *Death 24x a Second: Stillness and the Moving Image*. London: Reaktion Books, 2006.

Murphy, Mekado. "Fighting in Zero Gravity Just for Practice." *New York Times*, October 20, 2013.

———. "A First Mate Bares His Fangs." *New York Times*, November 18, 2012.

———. "'Mortal Engines': How the Filmmakers Created a Roaming London." *New York Times*, December 14, 2018.

———. "Questions About 'Gemini Man?' We Have Answers." *New York Times*, October 11, 2019.

Nair, Kartik. "Unfinished Bodies: The Sticky Materiality of Prosthetic Effects." *JCMS: Journal of Cinema and Media Studies* 60, no. 3 (2021): 104–128.

Nakamura, Lisa. *Digitizing Race: Visual Cultures of the Internet*. Vol. 23. Minneapolis: University of Minnesota Press, 2008.

Nama, Adilifu. *Black Space: Imagining Race in Science Fiction Film*. Austin: University of Texas Press, 2010.

Nashawaty, Chris. "'Warcraft': EW Review." *Entertainment Weekly*, June 8, 2016.

Natale, Richard. "Richard Edlund: Magician of the Silver Screen." *Los Angeles Herald-Examiner*, December 7, 1984.

Neale, Steve. "'The Last Good Time We Ever Had?': Revising the Hollywood Renaissance." *Contemporary American Cinema* (2005): 90–108.

Neonmarg, "Killer Schedules: Behind that Variety Story." FX Guide. Posted June 26, 2007.

Nesbet, Anne. *Savage Junctures: Sergei Eisenstein and the Shape of Thinking*. London: I. B. Tauris, 2003.

Neves, Joshua. "Southern Effects: *Kaiju*, Cultural Intimacy, and the Production of Distribution." *Cultural Critique*, no. 114 (Winter 2022, forthcoming).

Ngai, Sianne. *Our Aesthetic Categories: Zany, Cute, Interesting*. Cambridge, MA: Harvard University Press, 2012.

Nippert, Matt. "Inside Wellywood: How NZ Taxpayers Forked Out $575 Million for Hollywood to Film Here." *New Zealand Herald*, June 30, 2018.

Nishime, LeiLani. *Undercover Asian: Multiracial Asian Americans in Visual Culture*. Champaign: University of Illinois Press, 2014.

Noble, Safiya Umoja. *Algorithms of Oppression: How Search Engines Reinforce Racism*. New York: New York University Press, 2018.

North, Dan R. *Performing Illusions: Cinema, Special Effects and the Virtual Actor*. New York: Wallflower Press, 2008.

———. "The Spielberg Effects." In *A Companion to Steven Spielberg*, edited by Nigel Morris, 387–409. Malden, MA: Wiley, 2017.

———. "Super 8: Victory Through Lens Flare, Spectacular Attractions." September 3, 2011.

Norton, Bill. "Pandora's Paintbox." *Cinefex* 56 (November 1993): 54–69.

Odien, W. C. "The Rise and Fall of Norville Barnes" [on the *Hudsucker Proxy*]. *Cinefex* 58 (June 1994): 66–85.

Okun, Jeffrey, and Susan Zwerman, eds. *VES Industry Standard VFX Practices and Procedures*. New York: Focal Press 2010.

Olson, Eric. "Digital Domain Enters Germany." *Variety*, December 21, 1998.

Opam, Kwame. "Spider-Man: Homecoming's VFX Lead Unpacks the Secrets of the Staten Island Ferry Scene." theverge.com, July 14, 2017.

Oscars.org. "Animated Feature Film Award—Additional Resources." Rules & Eligibility. https://oscarsdev.oscars.org/oscars/rules-eligibility.

Overpeck, Deron. "The New Hollywood, 1981–1999: Editing." In *Editing and Special/Visual Effects*, edited by Charlie Keil and Kristen Whissel, 129–141. New Brunswick: Rutgers University Press, 2016.

Palmeri, Christopher, and Emily Chang. "Star Wars Movies Will Take a Break After Episode IX, Disney Says." Bloomberg.com, April 11, 2019.

Paquet, Darcy. "CG Shops Tout Their Chops: Korea Leads Asia in VFX, Starts Charge on H'wood." *Daily Variety*, February 8, 2008.

Parisi, Paula. "Digital Domain Taps Legato, Shimamoto." *Hollywood Reporter*, May 24, 1993.

———. "George Lucas' 'THR salutes ILM: George Lucas' Magic Lamp: Why the Famed Producer Director Pulled Together the Enormous Talent and Resources of ILM." *Hollywood Reporter*, April 9, 1991.

———. "Monster Job for Digital Domain." *Hollywood Reporter*, October 7, 1994.

———. "Tech Talk." *The Hollywood Reporter*, April 20, 2000.

———. "THR salutes ILM." *The Hollywood Reporter*, April 9, 1991.

Peishel, Bob. "Quick Cutes: Feline Fabrication." *Cinefex* 56 (November 1993): 17–18.

Pickett, Mallory. "Why Hollywood's Most Thrilling Scenes Are Now Orchestrated Thousands of Miles Away: The Money Issue." *New York Times*, May 4, 2017.

Pierson, Michele. "No Longer State-of-the-Art: Crafting a Future for CGI." *Wide Angle* 21, no. 1 (1999): 29–47.

———. *Special Effects: Still in Search of Wonder*. New York: Columbia University Press, 2002.

Phipps, Keith. "The Successful Failure of Ang Lee's *Hulk*." thedissolve.com, April 28, 2015.

Pollard, Tom. *Hollywood 9/11: Superheroes, Supervillains, and Super Disasters*. New York: Routledge, 2015.

Pollock, Dale. 1999. *Skywalking: The Life and Films of George Lucas*. New York: Da Capo Press.

Prince, Stephen. *Digital Visual Effects in Cinema: The Seduction of Reality*. New Brunswick: Rutgers University Press, 2011.

———. "True Lies: Perceptual Realism, Digital Images, and Film Theory." *Film Quarterly* 49, no. 3 (1996): 27–37.

Purse, Lisa. *Digital Imaging in Popular Cinema.* Edinburgh: Edinburgh University Press, 2013.

Pye, Michael, and Lynda Myles. 1979. *The Movie Brats.* New York: Holt, Rinehart & Winston.

"Raiders, Raptors and Rebels: Behind the Magic of ILM." Produced by Matthew Cullinan. ABC.com, July 19, 2015. Video, 42:12.

Rainer, Peter. "'Star Wars: The Force Awakens' Is the Best Movie in the Series Since 'Empire Strikes Back.'" *Christian Science Monitor,* December 16, 2015.

Ramos, Taylor, and Tony Zhou. "Every Frame a Painting." YouTube. Last modified December 2017.

Ratelle, Amy. "Chris Carter—Digital Beings: An Opportunity for Australian Visual Effects." *Animation Studies,* February 6, 2014.

Ravalli, Richard. "George Lucas Out of Love: Divorce, Darkness, and Reception in the Origin of PG-13." *Historian* 78, no. 4 (Winter 2016): 690–709.

Reddit. "Bad CGI in the Prequels." StarWars. April 22, 2017.

———. "In Your Opinion, What Has Been the Worst Moment of CGI or Green-screen in the MCU?" Marvel Studios. July 25, 2017.

———. "Is the MCUs CGI Getting Worse?" Marvel Studios. May 14, 2018.

———. "Why Did the First Two *Hulk* Movies Fail?" Movies [Reddit]. January 8, 2015.

Rehak, Bob. "The Migration of Forms: Bullet Time as Microgenre." *Film Criticism* 32, no. 1 (2007): 26–48.

———. *More Than Meets the Eye: Special Effects and the Fantastic Transmedia Franchise.* New York: New York University Press, 2018.

Rhythm & Hues. "Babe." Press release, 1995.

———. "Babe II." Press release, 1998.

———. "Rhythm and Hues." Press release, 1995.

Richard, Scott. *Cinema's Bodily Illusions: Flying, Floating, and Hallucinating,* Minneapolis: University of Minnesota Press, 2016.

Rinzler, J. W., Charles Lippincott, and Peter Jackson. *The Making of Star Wars: The Definitive Story Behind the Original Film: Based on the Lost Interview from the Official Lucasfilm Archives.* 1st trade paperback ed. New York: Ballantine Books, 2007.

Rittman, Alex. "Lucasfilm's ILM Opens London Studio." *Hollywood Reporter,* October 17, 2014.

Roberts, Paul. "Ego Trip" [on *Total Recall*]. *Cinefex* 43 (August 1990): 4–33.

Roberts, Gillian. "Cross-Border Film Adaptation and *Life of Pi*." In *Reading between the Borderlines: Cultural Production and Consumption across the 49th Parallel,* edited by Gillian Roberts, 225–242. Montreal: McGill-Queens University Press, 2018.

Rogerson, Pippa. "Conflict of Laws—Foreign Copyright Jurisdiction." *Cambridge Law Journal* 69, no. 2 (July 2010): 245–247.

Roddick, Nick. "Red River." *Sight and Sound* (December 2006): 32–34.

Rodowick, D. N. *The Virtual Life of Film.* Cambridge: Harvard University Press, 2009.

Rogers, Ariel. *Cinematic Appeals: The Experience of New Movie Technologies.* New York: Columbia University Press, 2013.

————. "Movie Magic: When It Comes to Special Effects, Dennis Muren Has Done It All." *Wall Street Journal*, September 15, 1995.

Rose, Frederick "Poof! They're Gone! It's a Boom Time for Special Effects Movies. And a Bust Time for the Companies that Create Them." *Los Angeles Times*, October 20, 1997.

Rosen, Phil. *Change Mummified: Cinema, Historicity, Theory*. Minneapolis: University of Minnesota Press, 2001.

————. "From *Change Mummified*." In *Film Theory and Criticism: Introductory Readings*, 8th ed., edited by Leo Braudy and Marshall Cohen, 734–743. Oxford: Oxford University Press, 2016.

Ross, Scott A. "VFX Business. Last modified January 22, 2014.

Rothkopf, Joshua, and David Ehrlich. "The 10 Worst CGI Special Effects in Movie History." Timeout, June 9, 2015.

Rothman, Matt. "Exec Shuffle." *Variety*, September 29, 1994.

————. "H'wood Enters Digital Domain." *Variety*, February 26, 1993.

————. "ILM, SGI Form Alliance Against Sky-high Sci-fi." *Variety*, April 8, 1993.

————. *On the Screen: Displaying the Moving Image, 1926*. New York: Columbia University Press, 2019.

Rottenberg, Josh. "'The Lion King': Is It Animated or Live-action? It's Complicated." *Los Angeles Times*, July 19, 2019.

————. "The New Way to Turn Back the Clock; De-aging Methods Used in 'The Irishman' Could Change the Face of Acting." *Toronto Star*, January 11, 2020.

Rubin, Michael. *Droidmaker: George Lucas and the Digital Revolution* 3. Gainesville: Triad, 2006.

Ryan, Mike. "No, 'Terminator: Genisys' Director Alan Taylor Doesn't Like That Spoilerish Trailer, Either." uproxx.com, June 29, 2015.

Ryzik, Melena. "Drawing Board for a Digital Age." *New York Times*, February 16, 2012.

Schatz, Thomas. "The New Hollywood." *Movie Blockbusters* (2003): 15–44.

————. "New Hollywood, New Millennium." In *Film Theory and Contemporary Hollywood Movies*, edited by Warren Buckland, 19–46. New York: Routledge, 2009.

————. "Seismic Shifts in the American Film Industry." In *American Film History: Selected Readings, 1960 to the Present*, edited by Cynthia Lucia, Roy Grundmann, and Art Simon. Hoboken, NJ: Wiley, 2015.

Schauer, Bradley. "The Auteur Renaissance 1968–1980." In *Cinematography*, edited by Patrick Keating, 84–105. New Brunswick: Rutgers University Press, 2014.

Schewe, Jeff. "Ten Years of Photoshop: The Birth of a Killer Application." *PEI: Photo Electronic Imaging Magazine* (February 2000): 16–25.

Schmit, Julie, and David Lieberman. "Silicon Valley Meets Hollywood Upstart Studios Cash in with Special Effects." *USA Today*, March 6, 1996.

Scoble, Robert. "A Look Back at 20 Years of Adobe Photoshop with One of the Founders." January 16, 2010. Video, YouTube, at 18:36.

Scott, Matthew. "Base FX @ 10: A Crazy Dream Became China's Leading VFX Studio." *Variety*, June 7, 2016.

Scrietta, Peter. "The Force Awakens Had More CG Visual Effects Shots Than the Phantom Menace." slashfilm.com, January 14, 2016.

Sharf, Zack. "Roger Deakins Refused to Shoot 'Blade Runner 2049' the 'Sloppy' Way Hollywood Studios Expect." Indiewire.com, April 8, 2020.

Shaviro, Steven. *Post Cinematic Affect*. Winchester: John Hunt Publishing, 2010.

Shay, Don. "30 Minutes with the Godfather of Digital Cinema." *Cinefex* 65 (March 1996): 58–67.

———. "Dancing on the Edge of the Abyss." *Cinefex* 39 (August 1989): 4–79.

———. "Dennis Muren—Playing it Unsafe." *Cinefex* 65 (March 1996): 98–111.

———. "Effects Scene: In the Digital Domain." *Cinefex* 55 (August 1993): 111–112.

———. "Mayhem Over Miami." *Cinefex* 59 (September 1994): 34–79.

———. "Of Ice Planets, Bog Planets, and Cities in the Sky: Interview with Richard Edlund." *Cinefex* 2 (August 1980): 4–23.

Shay, Don, and Jody Duncan, eds., "Twenty Questions." *Cinefex* 80 (January 2000): 24–27, 33–61, 135–136.

Shay, Estelle. "Quick Cuts: Sub Plots" [on *Crimson Tide*]. *Cinefex* 62 (June 1995): 11–16.

Sheikh, Aminah. "Indian Firm Behind Visual Effects in Avatar." *Business Standard* (Mumbai), December 20, 2009.

Sito, Tom. *Moving Innovation: a History of Computer Animation*. Cambridge: MIT Press, 2013.

Smith, Ethan. "Rapper's De-Light: Tupac 'Hologram' May Go on Tour." *Wall Street Journal*, April 17, 2012.

Smith, Thomas G. *Industrial Light & Magic: The Art of Special Effects*. New York: Ballentine, 1988.

———. "Reel Illusion." *OMNI* 9, no. 9 (June 1987): 70–79.

Smukler, Maya Montañez. *Liberating Hollywood: Women Directors and the Feminist Reform of 1970s American Cinema*. New Brunswick: Rutgers University Press, 2018.

Snider, Mike. "'Rings' Takes Special Effects to Another Level." *USA Today*, February 11, 2004.

Solomon, Charles. "How the 'Spider-Verse' Animators Created That Trippy Look." *New York Times*, December 25, 2018.

Sony Pictures Imageworks. "Anaconda." Press release, 1997.

———. "Stuart Little." Press release, 2002.

Sorensen, Peter. "Cyberworld" [on *Lawnmower Man*]. *Cinefex* 50 (May 1992): 4–74.

Spadoni, Robert. *Uncanny Bodies: The Coming of Sound Film and the Origins of the Horror Genre*. Berkeley: University of California Press, ca. 2007.

Squires, Scott. "Visual Effects Guilds." Effects Corner. April 18, 2013.

"Star Wars—The Force Awakens—Behind the Scenes—All Featurettes."

Strauss, Bob. "How Zhang Yimou Built 'Great Wall' with Matt Damon." *Los Angeles Daily News*, February 15, 2017.

Strauss, Neil. "'50's Sci-Fi Camp Goes High-Tech; Icky Giants That Hop, Fight and Think." *New York Times*, November 10, 1997.

Steinbock, Eliza. *Shimmering Images: Trans Cinema, Embodiment, and the Aesthetic of Change*. Durham: Duke University Press, 2019.

Stull, William. "Non-Glare Coating Makes Lens One Stop Faster." *American Cinematographer* (March 1940): 108.

Suellentrop, Chris. "Tantalizing Potential Outpaces Reality." *New York Times*, March 9, 2015.

Sulcas, Roslyn. "Andy Serkis, Caesar the Ape, Has a Message for the Academy." *New York Times*, July 6, 2017.

Szalai, George. "Digital Domain Files for Chapter 11 Bankruptcy." *Hollywood Reporter*, September 11, 2012.

Szostak, Phil, and Rick Carter. *The Art of Star Wars the Force Awakens*. New York: Abrams, 2015.

Tepper, Steven Jay. "Creative Assets and the Changing Economy." *Journal of Arts Management, Law, and Society* 32, no. 2 (2002): 159–168.

"The Host" (Bong Jun Ho). Magnolia Pictures. Press packet. Margaret Herrick Library. Open Collections, Weta Workshop Clipping Files. 2007.

Thapa, Anu. "Haunting Bollywood: Gender, Genre, and the Supernatural in Hindi Commercial Cinema." *Historical Journal of Film, Radio and Television* 38, no. 1 (2018): 219–220.

Thompson, Kristin. *The Frodo Franchise:* The Lord of the Rings *and Modern Hollywood*. Berkeley: University of California Press, 2007.

Tolette, J. P. *The Mouse Machine: Disney and Technology*. Champaign: University of Illinois Press, 2010.

Towers, Andrea. "'Mandalorian' Fans Are Losing Their Minds Because THIS 'Star Wars' Character Just Showed Up." The Wrap.com, December 4, 2020.

Tryon, Chuck. *Reinventing Cinema: Movies in the Age of Media Convergence*. New Brunswick: Rutgers University Press, 2009.

Turnock, Julie. "The Auteurist Special Effects Film: Kubrick's *2001: A Space Odyssey* and the 'Single Generation Look.'" In *The Hollywood Renaissance: Revisiting American Cinema's Most Celebrated Era*, edited by Peter Krämer and Yannis Tzioumakis, 71–90. New York: Bloomsbury Academic Press, 2018.

———. "Before Industrial Light and Magic: The Independent Hollywood Special Effects Business, 1968–1975." *New Review of Film and Television Studies* 7, no. 2 (2009): 133–156.

———. "The ILM Version: Recent Digital Effects and the Aesthetics of 1970s Cinematography." *Film History: An International Journal* 24, no. 2 (2012): 158–168.

———. "Patient Research on the Slapstick Lots: From Trick Men to Special Effects Artists in Silent Hollywood." *Early Popular Visual Culture* 13, no. 2 (May 2015): 152–173.

———. *Plastic Reality: Special Effects, Technology, and the Emergence of 1970s Blockbuster Aesthetics*. New York: Columbia University Press, 2015.

———. "Special Effects: Auteur Renaissance, 1968–1980." In *Editing and Special Visual Effects: Behind the Silver Screen*, edited by Charles Keil and Kristen Whissel, 116–128. New Brunswick: Rutgers University Press/Academy of Motion Picture Arts and Sciences, 2016.

———. "'The True Stars of *Star Wars*?': Experimental Filmmakers in the 1970s and 1980s Special Effects Industry." *Film History* 26, no. 4 (2014): 120–145.

———. "'Uninhibited, Thorough, and Wild Thinking': Reconsidering the Studio Era Through Special Effects." Presented at Society for Cinema and Media Studies, International Conference. Seattle, WA, March 2014.

Valdes, Marcela. "After 'Gravity,' Alfonso Cuarón Had His Pick of Directing Blockbusters. Instead, He Went Home to Make 'Roma.'" *New York Times*, December 12, 2018.

van Klingeren, Tom. "The EditDroid, Rise and Fall." 2014. Video, 37:16.

Variety Staff. "Disney Likely to Treat Lucasfilm Like Pixar." *Variety*, November 8, 2012.

———. "Ken Ralston Tops Fx Unit at Sony Pix." *Variety*, September 6, 1995.

———. "Rhythm & Hues Bankruptcy Reveals VFX Biz Crisis." *Variety*, February 12, 2013.

Vary, Adam B. "Disney Explodes Box Office Records with $11.1 Billion Worldwide for 2019." Variety.com, January 2, 2020.

———. "How Disney and Lucasfilm Are Remaking Star Wars in the Image of Marvel Studios." *Variety*, December 19, 2020.

Vaz, Mark Cotta. "Cruising the Digital Backlot" [on *Mission: Impossible*]. *Cinefex* 67 (September 1996): 90–105.

———. "A Knight at the Zoo" [on *Batman Returns*]. *Cinefex* 51 (August 1992): 22–74.

———. "Maximum Impact." *Cinefex* 45 (February 1991): 46–63.

Vaz, Mark Cotta, and Patricia Rose Duignan, *Industrial Light & Magic: Into the Digital Realm*. New York: Del Rey Books, 1996.

Vaz, Mark Cotta, and Shinji Hata. *From Star Wars to Indiana Jones: The Best of the Lucasfilm Archives*. San Francisco: Chronicle Books, 1994.

Venkatasawmy, Rama. *The Digitization of Cinematic Visual Effects: Hollywood's Coming of Age*. Lanham, MD: Lexington Books, 2012.

Verrier, Richard, and Ben Fritz. "Visualizing Disney's Deal." *Los Angeles Times*, November 1, 2012.

VFX-Montréal. "The Advantages of Montréal."

Vollans, Tim. "The Empire Strikes Back? Lessons from the Supreme Court's Judgment in *Lucasfilm Limited and Others (Appellants) v. Ainsworth and Another (Respondents)* [2011] UKSC 39, July 2011." *Journal of International Commercial Law & Technology* 7, no. 3 (July 2012): 276–81.

Walt Disney Company. "Disney to Acquire Lucasfilm." October 30, 2012. Video, 5:39.

———. "Disney to Acquire Lucasfilm Ltd." Press release, October 12, 2012.

———. *Fiscal Year 2019 Annual Financial Report*.

Walt Disney Family Museum. "In Walt's Own Words: Plussing Disneyland." Walt Disney Family Museum. July 17, 2014.

Waxman, Sharon. "Cyberface." *New York Times*, October 15, 2006.

———. "Wizards of Ah! More Than Ever, Hollywood's Special-Effects Experts Are Calling the Shots." *Washington Post*, July 5, 1996.

Weber, Jonathan. "The Force is Still with Him: Lucas Showcases Gadgets to Show He Remains King of Special Effects Hill." *Los Angeles Times*, April 8, 1993.

Weiner, Rex. "Cox, IBM Ready to Connect with Digital Domain." *Variety*, February 26, 1996.

———. "DD Inks Link with CSI Digital." *Variety*, October 21, 1996.

———. "Exec Sees No Windfall on 'Titanic.'" *Variety*, May 23, 1997.

Weta. *The Art of Film Magic: 20 Years of Weta*. New York: Harper, 2014.

Weta Workshop. "Weta Workshop." Press kit, 2004.

Whissel, Kristen. *Spectacular Digital Effects: CGI and Contemporary Cinema*. Durham: Duke University Press, 2014.

Whitten, Sarah. "Disney Bought Lucasfilm Six Years Ago Today and Has Already Recouped Its $4 Billion Investment." CNBC, October 30, 2018.

Williams, Trey. "Did Tom Cruise Really Do All the Stunts in 'Mission: Impossible— Fallout'?" *Wrap*, July 28, 2018.

Witmer, Don. "All Together Now." *American Cinematographer* (June 2012): 34–51.

Witty, Susan. "The Masters of Special Effects." *Geo Magazine* (June 1983): 42–48.

Wolff, Ellen. "Core California FX Companies Find Success Despite Exodus of Many Rivals." *Variety*, June 8, 2016.

———. "VFX Good Enough? Sez Who?" *Variety*, March 2, 2011.

Wolkomir, Richard. "High-Tech Hokum is Changing the Way Movies Are Made." *Smithsonian*, October 1990.

Wood, Aylish. *Digital Encounters*. London: Routledge, 2007.

———. *Software, Animation and the Moving Image: What's in the Box?* New York: Springer, 2014.

Wright, Benjamin. "The Auteur Renaissance, 1968–1980: Editing." In *Editing and Special Visual Effects: Behind the Silver Screen*, edited by Charles Keil and Kristen Whissel, 103–115. New Brunswick: Rutgers University Press/Academy of Motion Picture Arts and Sciences, 2016.

Wyatt, Justin. *High Concept: Movies and Marketing in Hollywood*. Austin: University of Texas Press, 1994.

Yip, George S., and Bruce McKern. *China's Next Strategic Advantage: From Imitation to Innovation*. Cambridge: MIT Press, 2016.

Yonover, Neal. "In a Talking Pig Eat Dog World, Can You Own f/x?" *Variety*, June 28, 1998.

Zoglin, Richard. "Lights! Camera! Special Effects." *Time*, June 16, 1986.

Index

Photos are indicated by italicized page numbers.

as Big Five effect house, 31, 32, 44; CGI and, 111–113; dominance of, 4, 23, 27, 33, 39–40, 44, 56, 230n6; fact-checking, 5, 113, 116, 122–123; on fire, 50–52; in media, 1, 20–21, 44, 48, 117, 127, 142, 253n24; Oscar win, 56; postproduction, 13, 51, 138; PR, 7–8, 25, 30, 36; previous scholarship, 8–13; publications, 27, 232n33; Silicon Graphics and, 137, 139, 140; The Walt Disney Company and, 6–7, 23, 56, 57–58, 187, 216–222; workers, 34, 37, 47. *See also* digital aesthetics, ILM; ISER in global marketplace, ILM and; rhetorical dominance, ILM FX history and

Industrial Light & Magic: Into the Digital Realm (Cotta Vaz and Duignan), 126, 136, 140–142, 252n19, 258n103; on *The Abyss*, 129; *Die Hard 2* and, 134; Favreau in, 118; Lucas in, 110; *Terminator 2* and, 133

Industrial Light & Magic: The Art of Innovation (Glintenkamp), 126, 252n19, 255n63, 258n103, 269n47

"Industrial Light & Magic" (TV documentary, 2010), 122

industry standard, 39, 119, 123, 139; ILM digital aesthetics, 6, 34, 59–60, 108, 145, 191–192

Intel, 251n8

intellectual property, 107–108, 147

international standard of effects realism in global marketplace, ILM and. *See* ISER in global marketplace, ILM and

Iron Man (2008), 57, 89, *89*, 95, 106, 108, 174, *185*, 187; analog feeling, 190–191, 194–198; effects style, 192–194; Favreau on realism and, 69, 197; lighting, *199*, 199–202, *201*, *202*, 208; Marvel Studios aesthetic and, 208–209; suit, *184*, *185*, 198–203, *201*, *202*, 208

Iron Man 2 (2010), 187, 191, 204, 205, 268n26

Iron Man film series, 61

ISER (international standard of effects realism) in global marketplace,

ILM and: alternatives, 172–183, *176*, *180*, *182*; ambitions, 154–158; with dominance, 144–151; in filmmaking, 158–172, *159–160*, *163–164*, *169*, *171*; industry, 151–153

"I Wasn't Born to Follow," 76

Jackson, Peter, 32, 36, 38, 45–48, 156

Jack the Giant Slayer (2013), 31, 54

James Bond franchise, 46, 268n29

Japan, *Godzilla* film series, 149

Jar Jar Binks (fictional character), 241n98

Jason Bourne films, 268n29

Jaws (1975), 32–33, 68, 72, 73, 91, 94, 95

Jazz Singer, The (1927), 114

Jenkins, Barry, 98, 104, 218

Jenkins, Patty, 206

Jing, Ting, 161

Jing, Wu 174

Joblove, George, 131, 132, 255n52, 255n61, 257n89, 257n90, 257n93; *The Abyss* and, 257n102; in yearbook, 255n62

Jobs, Steve, 124, 128, 129

John, Elton, 97, *97*

Johnson, Derek, 265n4

Johnston, Andrew, 112, 251n4

Jones, James Earl, 259n129

Journey to the West: The Demons Strike Back (2017), 262n22

joystick mechanism, 69–70

Jungle Book, The (2016), 232n28, 271n14

Jurassic Park (1993), 4, 7, 34, 85, 91, 117, 135, 187, 197, 214; Dern and Neill in, 67, *67*–68, 95; FX history and, 111, 113, 121, 135–141, 142; Spielberg and, 138, 259n124

Jurassic World (2018), 56

Justice League (2021), 110

Kacic-Alesic, Zoran, 260n130

Kaminski, Janusz, 99

Kay, Doug, 131, 132, 133, 255n61, 257n89, 257nn93–94; *The Abyss* and, 257n102; in yearbook, 255n62

Keaton, Buster, 177, 264n52

Keaton, Michael, 209–210

Keegan, Cáel, 9

Lucasfilm Ltd., 4, 6, 20, 47, 128, 187, 232n33, 251n2; industry standard, 119, 123; PR, 7–8, 118–120; Sprockets Systems division, 124, 125, 253n25, 254n44; The Walt Disney Company and, 59, 107, 213, 218–219, 244n1; yearbooks, 21–22, 118, 126–127, 132, 235n38, 253n27, 255n62, 256n64
Luma Pictures, 269n43
Luskin, John, 255n62, 257n89, 257n90, 257n99

Macintosh personal computer, 113, 123
MacKenzie, Michael, 258n109
Mac Squad, 132–133, 257n99
Mad Max: Fury Road (2015), 60
MAGI, 113, 130, 256n75
makeup prostheses, 28
Making of Jurassic Park (1995), 259n129
Malaysia, 151
Maleficent (2014), 46, 54
Malick, Terrence, 68
Maltby, Richard, 7, 9
Mandalorian, The (2019), 110, 214, 218–222, 271n14
Manex Visual Effects, 43
Maniac Mansion (video game, 1987), 119
Manovich, Lev, 7, 8, 10, 12, 14, 115, 194
Marino, Dan, 49
Marvel Cinematic Universe (MCU), 4, 23, 57, 191–192, *210*, 213, 221, 270n57; Marvel Studios aesthetic in, 208–212; Phase One, 187, 203, 204, 209, 265n3; superheros, 46, 172, 186–188, 194–195, 198–199, 204–205, 207, 209
Marvel Effect, 203–208, 213, 215
Marvel Entertainment, 56
Marvel Studios, 57, 108, 204, 206, 214, 220, 265n4, 267n18; aesthetic, 184–194, 208–212; photorealism and, 184, 195–197, 202, 267n15
Marvel Symphonic Universe, 266n5
M*A*S*H (1970), 85
Mask, The (1994), 140, 174, 260n132
Massive (software), 48, 165
Matby, Richard, 214

Matrix, The (1999), 40, 163, 173, 174, 214, 230n12
matte line position, 249n67
May, Elaine, 217
McMurray, George, 257n90, 257n99
MCU. *See* Marvel Cinematic Universe
Media Heterotopias (Chung), 148
Medium Cool (1969), *82*, 82–83, 84, 91, 107
Meg, The (2018), 17
Melancholia (2011), 262n22
Melford, George, 92, *92*
Memoirs of an Invisible Man (1992), 132
Men in Black (1997), 140
Menne, Jeff, 26, 217
Mermaid, The (2016), 150, 172, 174–179, *176*, 213
Method Studios, 269n43
Me Too movement, 217
Metropolis (1927), 249n64
Mézières, Jean-Claude, 171
MGM, 35
Midnight Cowboy (1969), 83
Midsommar (2019), 103, *104*
Mihailova, Misha, 229n3
Mill, The, 55
millennial blockbuster, golden age of the, 32, 44–50
Miller, Toby, 26, 145–146
miniature shot, *84*
Miramax, 56
Misbehaviour (2020), 153
Mission: Impossible—Fallout (2018), 80, 81
Mittel, Jason, 188
Modus FX, 269n43
Monkey King, The (2014), 172, 182, 265n57
monsters, 214; creature reveals, 90–98, *92–94*, *96–98*, 249n64; in *The Great Wall*, 149, 162–167, *164*; in *The Host*, 148, 149, 158–160, *159*, *170*, 179
Monsters, Inc. (2001), 49
Montreal, Quebec, 45, 151, 262n22
Morris, Jim, 122
Morrison, Jake, 184
Mothersbaugh, Mark, 266n5
Mouse Machine (Telotte), 9
movie credits, 28

117, 125, 156, 247n42; influence, 158, 190–191; *Jurassic Park* and, 138, 259n124

split screen, 71

Sprockets Systems, Lucasfilm Ltd., 124, 125, 253n25, 254n44

Squires, Scott, 29–30

Staiger, Janet, 9

Stained Glass Knight (computer-generated character), 111, 122, 123, 125–127, 130, 256n64

Stan Winston Studio, 156

Stargate (1994), 21

Star Is Born, A (1976), 73

Star Is Born, A (2018), 98, 103–104, *105*, 107, 250n78

Starlog (1976–2009), 21

Starman (1984), 79

Starship Troopers (1997), 44

Star Trek (2009), 61, 80, *81*

Star Trek: Generations (1994), 260n132

Star Trek II: The Wrath of Khan (1982), 79, 111, 122–123, 125

Star Trek: The Motion Picture (1979), 33

Star Wars: Episode IV—A New Hope (1977), 11, 27, 60, 74–75, 79, 91, 110, 167, 196, 249n65, 251n80; blockbusterization and, 32–33; creature reveal, 94, *94*, 97; Cuba and, 111–112; Griffin Lucas and, 251n2; ILM digital aesthetics, 64, 66, 67, 68, 69, 71, 72, 73; influence, 168, 194; with used future aesthetic, 72, 217

Star Wars: Episode II—Attack of the Clones (2002), 241n98

Star Wars: Episode I—The Phantom Menace (1999), 40, 127, 135, 141, 232n31, 241n98

Star Wars: Episode IX—The Rise of Skywalker (2019), 213, 218

Star Wars: Episode VIII—The Last Jedi (2017), 213, 219

Star Wars: Episode VII—The Force Awakens (2015), 60, 107, 189, 212, 218, 266n11

Star Wars: Episode VI—Return of the Jedi (1983), 94

Star Wars film series (1977–2019), 3–4,

6–7, 20, 44, 61, 107, 187, 219; aesthetic, 214; cuteness in, 232n31; DVD and Blu-ray releases, 117; prequels, 46, 47, 49

Steadicam, 82, 246n34

Stealth (2005), 197

Steinbock, Eliza, 9

Stokdyk, Scott, 171

Stork, Carl, 242n110

Story of Computer Graphics, The (1999), 112–113, 118

STX, 168

Sugarland Express, The (1974), 72, 247n42

suit, Iron Man, 184–185, *185*, 198–203, *201*, *202*, 208, 268n26

Super 8 (2011), 80

superheroes, 44–45, 46, 1729, 186–188. *See also Iron Man*

Surtees, Robert, 76

Sutherland, Ivan, 112

Swallow, John, 33, 152

T2 Trainspotting (2017), 153

Taking of Tiger Mountain, The (2014), 262n22

Talk to Her (2002), 155

Tang, Wilson, 65

Tarkovsky, Andrei, 247n39

Tau Films, 55

tax credits, 45, 46, 53, 56, 151, 153

Taylor, Richard, 47–48, 251n8

Teaford, Jonathan, 242n110

technological spectacle, 67, 197

Telotte, J. P., 9

Terminator 2: Judgment Day (1991), 4, 34, 35, 37, 129–136, 142, 260n132

Terminator 3: Rise of the Machines (2003), 47

Terminator Salvation (2009), 86

Textor, John C., 242n110

Thick of It, The (TV series, 2005–2012), 46

Thing from Another World, The (1951), 93

Third Floor, 269n43

Thompson, Kristen, 9

Thor (2011), 184, 187, 265n3, 268n37

Thor: Ragnarok (2017), 184, 208, 212

3D conversion, 28